WINDOWS NT

Windows NT
Microsoft
Cluster Server

WINDOWS NT

Windows NT Microsoft Cluster Server

Richard R. Lee

Osborne **McGraw-Hill**

Berkeley   New York   St. Louis   San Francisco
Auckland   Bogotá   Hamburg   London   Madrid
Mexico City   Milan   Montreal   New Delhi   Panama City
Paris   São Paulo   Singapore   Sydney
Tokyo   Toronto

Osborne/**McGraw-Hill**
2600 Tenth Street
Berkeley, California 94710
U.S.A.

For information on translations or book distributors outside the U.S.A., or to arrange bulk purchase discounts for sales promotions, premiums, or fund-raisers, please contact Osborne/**McGraw-Hill** at the above address.

Windows NT Microsoft Cluster Server

1234567890 AGM AGM 90198765432109

ISBN 0-07-882500-8

Publisher
   Brandon A. Nordin
Associate Publisher and
Editor-in-Chief
   Scott Rogers
Acquisitions Editor
   Wendy Rinaldi
Project Editor
   Heidi Poulin
Editorial Assistant
   Monika Faltiss
Technical Editors
   Jonathon Cragle
   Mark Smith
Copy Editor
   Nancy Crumpton

Proofreaders
   Sally Engelfried
   Rhonda Holmes
Indexer
   Valerie Robbins
Computer Designers
   Jani Beckwith
   Jean Butterfield
   Roberta Steele
Illustrators
   Robert Hansen
   Brian Wells
   Beth Young
Series Design
   Peter F. Hancik

This book is dedicated to my family, without whose support I would have never finished this book, and to the memories of my long-passed Grandfather who showed me how things work and inspired me to become an engineer.

AT A GLANCE

Part I	Planning Your MSCS Cluster

▼ 1   An Introduction to Clusters and Clustering
         Technology   3
▼ 2   Windows NT Server Enterprise Edition
         and MSCS   33
▼ 3   Planning for the Deployment of Your
         MSCS Cluster   55

Part II	Deploying Your MSCS Cluster

▼ 4   Installing and Configuring MSCS   77
▼ 5   MSCS Operation. 107
▼ 6   Other Windows NT Clustering/High-
         Availability Solutions 155
▼ 7   Creating Cluster-Aware Software Applications
         and Services 181

Part III	Maximizing the Capabilities of Your MSCS Cluster	

▼ 8   Windows 2000 and Microsoft Cluster Service
Phase 2   207

▼ 9   MSCS Cluster-Aware Applications
Reference Guide   229

▼ 10   Troubleshooting Procedures, Examples,
and Tools   255

▼ A   Storage Options for MSCS Systems   315

▼ B   Cluster-Aware Applications, Tools,
and Utilities Resource Guide   329

▼ C   MSCS Resource Guide   333

Glossary   343

CONTENTS

Acknowledgments   xvii
Introduction.   xix

Part I

Planning Your MSCS Cluster

▼ 1 An Introduction to Clusters and Clustering Technology   3

Early Pioneers of Clustering.   5
  Digital's VAX/VMS Clusters   5
  Tandem Knows Clusters, Too!   7
  IBM and Its Clustering Legacy   9
Other MSCS Early Adopter Partners.   11
  Hewlett-Packard   11
  NCR   12
  Data General   12
  Compaq Computer   13
  Intel   14
  Johnny-Come-Latelies.   15

Other Providers of Clustering Solutions and Products. 15
    Sun Microsystems 17
    Vinca Corporation 17
    Qualix/Octopus 18
Why Clustering? 18
    High Availability. 19
    Scalability 22
    Manageability 25
    Cluster Architectures 26
    Which Architecture Is Right for Me?. 30
Summary 32

▼ 2   Windows NT Server Enterprise Edition and MSCS 33
Pursuing the Enterprise 35
Enterprise Computing Defined 36
    Market Forces. 37
    Availability and Scalability Enhancements 38
    Bundled Cluster-ready Applications 41
    Other Applications Included with NTS/E 42
Information Resources for Supporting Windows NT
  Enterprise Edition. 42
Introducing Microsoft Cluster Server 44
    What It Can and Can't Do. 45
    Implementation Roadmap 47
    MSCS Main Activities 50
    Deployment Considerations 53
Summary 54

▼ 3   Planning for the Deployment of Your MSCS Cluster. 55
MSCS Concepts and Deployment Models. 56
    Two-Node High-Availability Clustering 57
    Cluster Models. 58
    Cluster Hardware Deployment Requirements 65
    Final Deployment Considerations 72
Summary 74

Part II

Deploying Your MSCS Cluster

▼ 4   Installing and Configuring MSCS. 77
Pursuing Nirvana 78
Preparing for Your Installation 80
    NTS/E Configuration Considerations. 80

Installing MSCS from Scratch   88
   Tools to Have on Hand   90
   Starting Your Installation   95
   Step-by-Step MSCS Installation   96
   Initial Tests and Setup Parameters   102
Wrapping It All Up   105

▼ 5 MSCS Operation   107

How to Successfully Operate Your Cluster   109
   Step 1—Getting Started   109
   Step 2—Mastering the Cluster Administrator   110
   Step 3—Getting to Know Your Groups and Resources   111
   Step 4—Setting up Your Failover Groups   112
   Step 5—Create a Dependency Tree for Each Group   118
   Steps 6 and 7—Learn All About Resources
      and Dependencies   119
   Step 8—The Resource Definition Process   121
   Step 9—Configuring Groups and Resources
      for Specific Applications   124
   Step 10—Configuring Generic Applications   143
   Step 11—Testing Failover/Failback on Your Cluster   144
Command Line Interface Control of Your Cluster   146
   Cluster   147
   Cluster Node   147
   Cluster Group   148
   Cluster Resource   149
   Cluster Resource Type   151
   Universal Abbreviations   152
Summary   153

▼ 6 Other Windows NT Clustering/High-Availability Solutions   155

Competitive and Collaborative Clustering Solutions   156
Alternative Clustering and High-Availability Solutions   156
   Middleware, Server-based Clustering   158
   Data Mirroring and Remote Copying Clusters
      (Server Based)   170
   Dynamic Load Balancing (Web and Thin-Client Servers)
      Clusters (IP Based)   171
   Storage Area Network (SAN) Clusters   177
   Switched SCSI Clusters   179
   Summary   179

▼ 7 Creating Cluster-Aware Software Applications and Services 181

The Wolfpack API 183
  The Cluster API 183
  Cluster Control Codes. 190
  The Resource API 190
  Cluster Administrator Extension API 196
Use of Enterprise Edition, Standard Edition, and Legacy-Type
  Applications with MSCS 199
  Making Existing Applications Wolfpack Compliant. 200

Part III

Maximizing the Capabilities of Your MSCS Cluster

▼ 8 Windows 2000 and Microsoft Cluster Service Phase 2 207

Windows 2000 Server—Product Overview 208
  Scalability and Availability Enhancements 212
Windows 2000 Cluster Service—General Overview 214
  Microsoft Cluster Service Phase 2 217
  System Area Networks, Virtual Interface Architecture,
    and the WinSock/SAN API 218
Planning for the Deployment of Windows 2000
  Cluster Service. 223
  Deployment Checklist. 224
Can't Wait for Windows 2000 and Cluster Service Phase 2?. 225
  Interim Scalability and Availability Solutions 225
  IBM/Lotus Domino/MSCS Cluster Solution. 226
  IBM-Microsoft "Cornhusker" Switched MSCS Clusters. . . . 226
Summary 227

▼ 9 MSCS Cluster-Aware Applications Reference Guide 229

Cluster-Aware Applications, Utilities, and Tools. 230
  Internet Collaboration Applications
    (Mail and Messaging) 231
  Relational Databases. 235
  Enterprise Resource Planning 243
  Enterprise Systems and Storage Management
    Applications. 246
  Other MSCS Applications, Tools, and Utilities 250
Summary 253

▼ **10** Troubleshooting Procedures, Examples, and Tools 255

Tips, Examples, and Tools for Troubleshooting MSCS. 256
    Problem: Both the public and private networks
      are unavailable 257
    Problem: Node 2 cannot join the cluster due to
      a logon error. 257
    Problem: Physical disk resources unavailable 258
    Problem: Installation of cluster-aware application
      is successful, but it won't come online 258
    Problem: RPC server errors originating from
      second node 258
    Problem: NT Backup cannot access all shared SCSI
      storage devices 259
    Problem: How do I increase paging file size on my nodes
      when I have one boot drive and my other storage
      is on the shared bus? 259
    Problem: How do I Implement availability and better
      management to my Oracle database using my
      MSCS cluster? 260
    Problem: I recently made changes to my cluster and
      want to verify its health and functionality 260
Frequently Asked Questions (FAQs). 261
Troubleshooting Methodologies and Resources 263
    Shutting Down and Restarting Your Cluster
      under Varying Scenarios. 263
    Test Utilities 266
Typical Registry Entries 269
    Why Do I Need to Know these Registry Settings? 270
HKEY_LOCAL_MACHINE Registry Entries 272
    Cluster Group Registry Settings 273
    Cluster Network Registry Settings. 274
    Cluster Node Registry Settings. 275
    Cluster Resource Registry Settings. 275
HKEY_CURRENT_USERS Registry Entries (HKCU) 296
    Cluster Administrator Registry Settings. 297
MSCS Files, File Types, and Installation Locations 303
    MSCS Identification 304
    Destination Directories for Installation and
      Operational Files 304
    Files and Services to be Uninstalled 304
    Files and Services to be Installed 304

Source Disk Files 305
Cluster Driver Files 305
Cluster Files. 305
Cluster Administrator Files 306
Other Cluster Files 306
Resource Type Names 306
Service Names (Descriptions). 307
Service Pack 4 for Windows NT 4.0 (All Editions) 307
Service Bulletins from Microsoft Technical Support 308
Summary 314

▼ **A**   Storage Options for MSCS Systems 315

Storage Interconnects, Devices, and Subsystem Options 316
Storage Interconnection Standards. 316
General Storage Considerations 318
Storage Device Options 319
Storage Solution Options 321
Automated Tape Libraries. 324
Optical Jukeboxes 326
Storage Management (SM) Options 326
Summary 328

▼ **B**   Cluster-Aware Applications, Tools, and Utilities Resource Guide 329

Cluster-Aware Applications 330
Product Suites 330
Mail and Messaging Solutions 330
Relational Databases. 330
Enterprise Resource Planning 331
Enterprise Systems Management. 331
MSCS Management 331
Storage Management 331
Microsoft Windows Load balancing Server. 332
Other Applications, Tools, and Utilities 332
Summary 332

▼ **C**   MSCS Resource Guide 333

Resources for Your Cluster 334
Overview 334
Microsoft Resources 335
Early Adopter Hardware Partners 336

Other MSCS Solution Providers   338
Vendors with MSCS Cluster-Aware Applications   339
Magazines Focused on Windows NT   340
Information Technology Consulting Firms   340
For More Information   341
Additional Reading on Clusters   341

▼   Glossary   343

Index   359

ACKNOWLEDGMENTS

especially want to thank the following folks without whose help this book would have never been possible:

Wendy Rinaldi and Heidi Poulin at Osborne/McGraw-Hill (my taskmasters).

Mark Smith and Jonathan Cragle of *Windows NT Magazine* (my technical editors).

Russell Ashworth, Dave Johnson, and Tim Keefauver at Tandem Computer (cluster support and sanity checks).

David Floyer of IDC for his perspectives and market analysis data on "Clustering and Windows NT."

Microsoft and all the other vendors who put up with my strange requests and provided me with evaluation copies of their clustering products.

This book was researched and prepared on a Tandem CS-150 MSCS Cluster with a ServerNet SAN interconnect.

INTRODUCTION

This book on Microsoft's Cluster Server (MSCS) is more than a hands-on reference for solutions designers, systems administrators, and support personnel—it is a guidebook into the treacherous world of enterprise computing and Windows NT. It covers more than Microsoft's current forays into clustering, it encompasses the vast majority of high-availability/scalability solutions available for Windows NT today, as well as into the future.

I wrote this book for every member of the IT staff who must contend with daily availability and reliability issues, scalability challenges at every turn, and growing emphasis by management "to do more with less" in terms of systems administration. Every IT staffer who has had to drag themselves out of bed in the middle of the night to find a solution to get the "killer app" back up and running due to a failed application/service on Windows NT will find this book of value.

Clustering is one of the few tools in any IT designers toolbox that can fix a number of major systems problems without having to abandon the business model (low-cost, high-volume) that Windows NT has been built on—not to mention making significant contributions to anyone's TCO reduction efforts.

Section Overview

This book is divided into three sections:

▼   Part I   Planning Your MSCS Cluster

■   Part II   Deploying Your MSCS cluster

▲   Part III   Maximizing the Capabilities of Your MSCS cluster

There are also three appendices and a glossary that cover the following areas:

▼   Appendix A   Storage Options

■   Appendix B   Cluster-Aware Applications Resource Guide

■   Appendix C   Microsoft Cluster Server Resource Guide

▲   Glossary

Part I: Planning Your MSCS Cluster

Part I covers the concepts behind clustering and MSCS. In this section, I provide extensive details explaining why clustering is such a critical technology for solving problems regarding availability, scalability, and manageability. Within this section is a comprehensive overview of Windows NT Enterprise Edition and Microsoft Cluster Server and how, when combined together, you can improve availability, scalability, and manageability of your NT environment. In addition, I give an overview on how to plan for the use of MSCS with your business-critical applications and services.

CHAPTER 1   Chapter 1 focuses on the history of clusters and clustering dating back to its commercialization on the 1970s by Digital and Tandem. It follows the ongoing development of this technology and its maturation as a solution for availability, scalability, and manageability challenges in most IT environments. Chapter 1 also traces the history of how MSCS was conceived in terms of being the cornerstone of Microsoft's endeavors to move from the desktop into the data center (i.e., enterprise computing). This background information details the partnership between Microsoft and the industry's leaders in clustering that brought about MSCS in its first Phase (as part of NTS/E) as well as how this joint effort continues today as the entire team works on Phase 2 (Windows 2000 Datacenter Server).

CHAPTER 2   Chapter 2 provides both a general overview of NTS/E as well as specific information on how this enterprise-oriented version of Windows NT provides major enhancements to scalability, availability, and manageability on an overall basis. Chapter 2 also provides a complete technical overview of MSCS and its functional components. You'll also find an explanation of its strengths and weaknesses in respect to how MSCS is most applicable as a problem solving tool in IT environments.

CHAPTER 3   Chapter 3 charts the process of designing and deploying your cluster. Both designing and deploying are key areas to accomplishing measurable benefits from MSCS—all major and minor areas of detail are explored in full. This includes deployment models, system requirements, and network integration.

Part II: Deploying Your MSCS Cluster

Part II covers the actual deployment of your MSCS Cluster environment, with an eye on how to operate and configure your cluster and its applications/services for maximum benefits. It also provides detailed information on other Windows NT clustering solutions and how they relate to MSCS (collaboratively or competitively). Finally, there is a major section on making your new and legacy applications and services cluster-aware by using the Wolfpack API to varying degrees.

CHAPTER 4   Chapter 4 is focused on the process of installing (and reinstalling) and configuring MSCS to provide high-availability, enhanced scalability, and improved manageability in a variety of application environments (cluster-aware and non-cluster-aware). Included in this chapter are test scenarios to insure the health and correct functionality of your cluster and its applications once installed and configured. Throughout the chapter you are guided on a step-by-step basis as to the proper way to install, configure, and test your MSCS cluster regardless of the deployment model used. This includes storage, networking, and basic cluster operations.

CHAPTER 5   This Chapter focuses on the day-to-day operation of your MSCS cluster environment. It includes basic steps for use in operating MSCS from start-up, to installing and configuring applications and services, to testing the entire cluster. You must master this detailed process if you are going to get your MSCS cluster environment to work properly, so I have spared no details.

You will learn how to set up failover groups and their resources for use with cluster-aware applications and services, as well as how to configure those that are non-cluster-aware to become more highly available via the use of the Generic Application and Services resources. You will also learn how to create "dependency trees" for determining how an application or service should failover and failback in respect to the order and types of resources required by each type of application and Windows NT service.

CHAPTER 6   Chapter 6 gives you an overview on the leading clustering and high-availability options for Windows NT and how these enhance MSCS's overall performance and capabilities. This chapter provides a good snapshot of the broad range of high-availability options for Windows NT and gives you some food for thought on how to push the envelope with add-ons for MSCS.

CHAPTER 7   I wrote this chapter with the programmer (or hacker) in mind. It is a comprehensive overview of the Wolfpack API specification for cluster-aware applications and resources. I provide numerous examples of how to write cluster-aware

DLLs for new applications and how to modify legacy applications to become partially cluster-aware to take better advantage of MSCS than running as a generic application or service via MSCS's built-in DLL Wrapper. Chapter 7 covers the entire gamut of programming for MSCS and is a must-read for programmers who support MSCS environments.

Part III: Maximizing the Capabilities of Your MSCS Cluster

Part III focuses on MSCS as a core technology in your IT environment and how you can maximize its benefits today and long into the future. It covers future versions and releases supported by Windows 2000 as well as the growing list of cluster-aware applications available now and how they maximize the capabilities of MSCS. Finally, there is a comprehensive tome on supporting your MSCS clusters through thick and thin.

CHAPTER 8   Chapter 8 is written with the future in mind. It is a glimpse of what MSCS will evolve into as Windows 2000 is rolled out and Microsoft Cluster Service Phase 2 becomes available. It also provides detailed instructions to migrate your existing MSCS environment from its Windows NT 4.0 baseline to Windows 2000 Advance Server, including the addition of the Active Directory infrastructure.

Chapter 8 is also a comprehensive overview of Microsoft and its clustering partners roadmap toward fault tolerant and scalability clustering. It is a useful tool for planning deployments today with future upgrades in mind as well as to easily make the jump from the world of NT today to the word of Windows 2000 tomorrow.

CHAPTER 9   Chapter 9 is an overview of all the major applications available today that are MSCS cluster-aware and can take full (or partial) advantage of MSCS's high-availability and scalability enhancements.

Within this chapter are detailed descriptions of all the "killer apps" that drive the enterprise today such as OLTP, ERP, Mail and Messaging, and Decision Support. Each is covered in detail, not only in respect to its basic characteristics, but as to how MSCS provides major enhancements and improvements.

CHAPTER 10   Chapter 10, alone, justifies purchasing this book. I offer a comprehensive guide to riding the MSCS rapids and surviving. It runs the gamut from bug fixes and work-arounds, to test procedures, to FAQs, to detailed MSCS Registry Entries and options. This chapter is a necessary tool to use in keeping MSCS and its applications/services up and running under a variety of conditions.

Appendices

Storage is a critical component of MSCS and **Appendix A** covers all the options available for MSCS and the capabilities that these options provide to a clustered environment. All types of storage solutions and storage management products are covered and discussed with a clustered environment in mind.

Appendix B is a detailed source of information on how to obtain demonstration and evaluation copies of all the varied types of cluster-aware applications discussed in Chapter 9. In lieu of a CD-ROM containing obsolete versions of these applications, I have assembled a list of sites to download or request a self-expiring copy of the latest release from.

Appendix C is a comprehensive guide for gathering all types of information and other resources required to plan, deploy, operate, administrate, and support your MSCS cluster. It ranges from soup to nuts in terms of the types of informational resources available.

Clustering has its own peculiar vernacular and in order to traverse this rocky terrain, you must learn terms and their definitions. Contained within this **Glossary** are a very broad listing of clustering terms and acronyms defined with clear-cut language and ideas.

PART I

Planning Your MSCS Cluster

CHAPTER 1

An Introduction to Clusters and Clustering Technology

Clustering is defined by most IT professionals as combining one or more servers together with the appropriate middleware and interconnects to achieve all, or at least one, of the following attributes:

▼ Higher levels of system reliability (i.e., availability)

■ Increased processing power (i.e., scalability)

▲ Improved manageability

There are secondary benefits that can be derived as well. They include:

▼ Improved interoperability with other computing platforms

■ Reduced Total Cost of Ownership (TCO) based on Server Consolidation and the use of Virtual Servers (as opposed to dedicated physical servers)

▲ Higher Return on Investment (ROI) and Economic Value Added (EVA) than stand-alone application servers

Others in the computer industry, such as Gregory Pfister, author of *In Search of Clusters*, regard clusters as "a type of parallel or distributed system that consists of a collection of interconnected whole computers that behave like a 'savage multi-headed pooch!'"

Microsoft defines a cluster in respect to Phase 1 of their Microsoft Cluster Server (MSCS) as "a two-node high-availability solution" based upon the well known Windows NT Server 4.0 Enterprise Edition network operating system. In regard to Phase 2 of MSCS, Microsoft refers to it as "nirvana," where such computing ills as the lack of scalability, availability, and manageability are nonexistent.

Clusters and clustering can be regarded as a very effective tool applicable to only those scenarios where appropriate. Clustering is not a panacea, nor does it provide any type of free lunch in the process. Clusters are similar to high-performance race cars—they require specialized care and attention, but when they are at their peak and are driven by a seasoned veteran, *look out*! They can do things that no other architecture can, much less at anything close to the same cost.

Regardless of whatever definition you prefer, a cluster's major strength is that it appears to the end user as a single system image (and IP address), with little hint whatsoever of what computing, storage, networking, and administrative resources are behind it.

Clustering of computing assets into a single system image is not a new technique at all. Commercialized in the late '70s/early '80s by Digital Equipment Corporation and Tandem Computer Corporation, clustering has become the de rigueur method for achieving high levels of linear scalability, enhancing system availability, and providing varying degrees of fault-tolerance, along with significantly improving management of critical data and computing assets. Clustering is a long accepted practice in the mainframe and UNIX worlds of computing and is available in many shapes and sizes from manufacturers such as Digital Equipment Corporation, Compaq/Tandem, Data General, IBM, Sun Microsystems, Sequent Computer, NCR, Status Computer, and many others.

Many of these same platform manufacturers have also announced clustering solutions for Windows NT (both proprietary and based on MSCS), which are the focus of this book. I will explore all of the details and capabilities associated with MSCS Phase 1, along with projecting what the future holds for Phase 2. I will also review in detail other NT clustering solutions available in the market today. This review will endeavor to provide an objective analysis of all NT clustering solutions and the unique advantages that each solution offers.

EARLY PIONEERS OF CLUSTERING

Clustering was originally conceived as a method to meet rapidly expanding end-user demands placed upon IT systems when the idea of having low-cost, standard, high-volume servers (e.g., UniProcessor, SMP, NUMA, and MPP) was merely a dream. In both the mainframe and minicomputer markets of the '70s and '80s, there were growing requirements by end users for high-availability, scalable, fault-tolerant systems that could not be met by stand-alone systems. These end users also wanted to better utilize existing computing assets, peripherals, and networking schemes that they had so heavily invested in. The majority of these end users were in the scientific/engineering and financial services market segments where the demand for each of these attributes was always well beyond what any manufacturer could deliver in a single chassis.

Digital's VAX/VMS Clusters

Digital Equipment Corporation developed as their first clustering solution the VAX Cluster for their VAX VMS platform, long the worldwide standard in the scientific and engineering communities. Digital has been a leader in clustering ever since. With more than 85,000 clustered systems in the field, including some 5,000+ for Windows NT (non-MSCS), they have both the longest track record and most know-how of any platform provider when it comes to clustered computing systems. Digital's clustering endeavors have spanned a number of generations of computing technology, and today's offerings include versions for both OpenVMS (Galaxy) and Digital UNIX (TruClusters) (see the time line in Figure 1-1). Over time, Digital pioneered such major technological innovations as the Cluster Interconnect (CI), a high-speed, fault-tolerant switched interconnect for cluster resources; the Memory Channel (MC), a wide-bandwidth very large memory (VLM) system for parallel database applications; the Distributed Lock Manager (DLM), a key data management scheme used in shared-everything clusters with distributed relational databases (Digital/Oracle Rdb); and others such as the Quorum Resource. In addition to increasing performance (i.e., scalability), Digital's clusters were also designed to eliminate any single point of failure across the computing

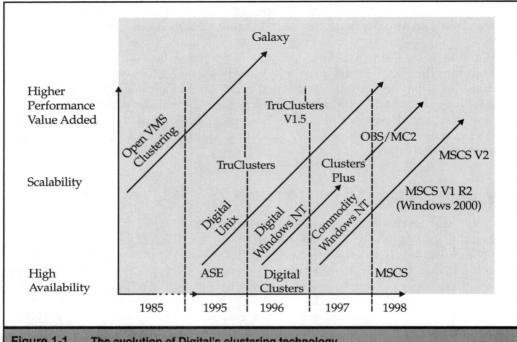

Figure 1-1.   The evolution of Digital's clustering technology

enterprise (i.e., availability), as well as to provide an easy mechanism for disaster recovery (see Figure 1-2).

Digital's Galaxy clustering system for OpenVMS is their latest offering of this highly developed architecture and can support more than 256 Alpha-type CPUs with an MC/VLM capacity of 1TB and multiple PBs of wide-bandwidth-attached storage. Their UNIX TruClusters product features similar capabilities, albeit slightly scaled back to fit in the UNIX/Alpha platforms' performance envelope. Even today, Digital continues to hold the highest TPC benchmark for a distributed parallel database (Oracle Parallel Server) based on the use of an Alpha-driven OpenVMS cluster with memory channel.

Digital was also the first platform provider to establish a strategic alliance partnership with Microsoft regarding the Windows NT OS and MSCS for use in Enterprise Computing environments. As an "early adopter" partner, Digital contributed significant intellectual property, development, and testing resources to MSCS. Currently, Digital offers its own proprietary clustering solution for NT, Digital's Clusters Plus, along with MSCS, and plans to merge these two efforts at some future date (after the release of MSCS Phase 2). These cluster offerings are supported on both the Alpha and X86 SMP platforms and, in the future, will include the IA-32 Deschutes and IA-64 Merced CPUs.

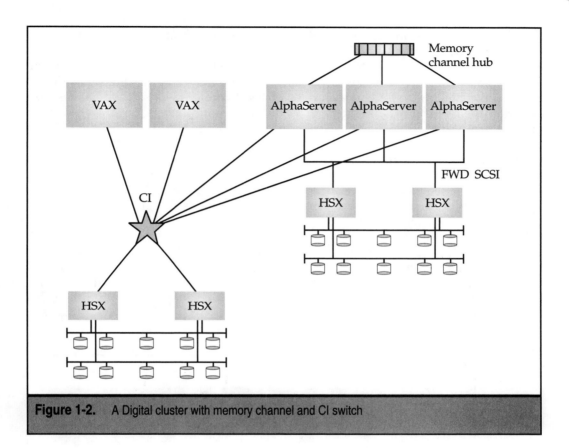

Figure 1-2. A Digital cluster with memory channel and CI switch

Tandem Knows Clusters, Too!

Tandem commercialized their first clustered systems around the same time as Digital. Today, Tandem boasts that they have provided clustered solutions for their financial services and transaction-driven customers for two decades. All of their NonStop Himalaya system offerings are essentially "clusters in a box" and provide linear scalability and continuous availability (at a rather healthy price). Using both a shared-nothing approach and a specialized architecture to support true fault-tolerance, the Tandem NonStop Himalaya line of clustered servers are, for the most part, totally fault resistant—if not completely fault proof—providing 99.99 percent availability year in and year out. Tandem achieves this by using redundant components and signal paths, along with a specialized operating system and middleware that manages all resources within the server and "take over" applications that have stopped due to either a hardware or software fault. (ServerWare middleware technology is used here also, along with Tandem's proprietary NonStop Kernel.) Tandem has shipped more than ten thousand

Himalaya-type servers to date and has the undisputed lions' share of the market for such true mission-critical applications as stock exchanges, brokerage houses, 911 telephone exchanges, and bank ATM networks. Their line of UNIX (Integrity) and Windows NT clusters (based on their own Cluster Availability Solution—CAS) provide similar levels of high availability, housed in a variety of SMP configurations. Tandem has also extended their NonStop technology to Windows NT through SQL/MX, a database product that utilizes NSK-lite as a cluster layer residing on top of MSCS. This solution presently supports up to 16 nodes for high-scalability requirements and will be incorporated into MSCS Phase 2. Now a wholly owned subsidiary of Compaq, Tandem is responsible for the high end of Compaq's overall enterprise computing offerings and has recently proclaimed their new slogan: "The Cluster is the Computer." This slogan (coined by Roel Piper, former Senior Vice President of Worldwide Sales) is now part of an entertaining commercial aired on select TV cable channels. (See the accompanying CD-ROM for a peek.)

All of Tandems' clusters feature the use of a high-speed, low-latency, scalable, and fault-tolerant interconnect technology developed for attaching nodes within the cluster. This interconnect provides a path for the cluster heartbeat, shared data, and node-to-node communications (such as DLM) without creating CPU drag or network bottleneck syndrome (see Figure 1-3). Given the name *ServerNet*, this technology is used

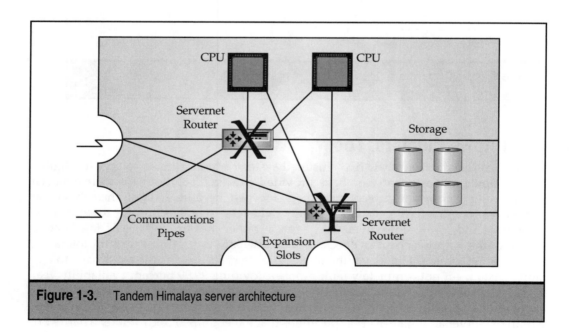

Figure 1-3.   Tandem Himalaya server architecture

in all of their Himalaya, UNIX, and NT clusters and has been licensed to and adopted by many SMP platform providers who offer MSCS. ServerNet is based on the concept of a system area network (SAN) and is one of the cornerstones of the Virtual Interface Architecture (VIA) specification recently announced by Intel, Compaq, and Microsoft for interconnecting clusters of standard high-volume servers.

NOTE: The *VIA Specification* is in addition to another recently published specification: the *Windows NT Server 5.0 Hardware Developers Specification.* Both of these will have significant impact upon clustering supported by MSCS Phase 2 and beyond. Additional information on these two specifications can be found in the "Additional Reading" on Clusters section in Appendix D.

Like Digital, Tandem formed a strategic alliance for the enterprise with Microsoft early on regarding the development of MSCS. As one of the original seven "early adopter partners," they contributed significant intellectual property and development resources to this effort (i.e., the "Cluster Regroup" algorithm, ServerNet SAN interconnect, shared-nothing clustering topologies, etc.).

Since their merger, Tandem and Compaq have focused their Windows NT clustering strategies exclusively on MSCS, along with continuing to support existing clustering solutions on their other platforms (Himalaya and Integrity). Tandem's early Windows NT clustering product, CAS, along with the more recently announced NSK-lite will eventually merge with MSCS (after Phase 2), and via the use of the well documented MSCS API, Tandem will migrate their ServerWare cluster-aware applications to MSCS as well (SQL/MX and others).

IBM and Its Clustering Legacy

Not to be forgotten or left out, IBM has a rich legacy of providing clustering solutions. These range from systems based on the workhorse mainframe S/390 (formerly known as MVS) Parallel Sysplex (see Figure 1-4) to the CAS based on their RS/6000 SP AIX family of servers. Each of these systems features an architecture able to support full data sharing, along with scalable parallel processing in a clustered computing environment. Both platforms are highly scalable, with the ability to support tens of nodes providing simultaneous access by up to some 64,000 active users on the Parallel Sysplex (32 nodes of 10-way processors) and up to several thousand on the HACMP.

There are approximately 1,500 Parallel Sysplex clusters in use worldwide and 10,000+ of the HACMP. IBM was also one of the seven early adopter partners that provided expertise along with test and support resources to Microsoft during the development of MSCS Phase 1. IBM has announced a line of MSCS cluster solutions that have been validated by Microsoft, along with options from Vinca for higher levels of fault-tolerance and data availability. In addition, IBM has begun porting many of the features and

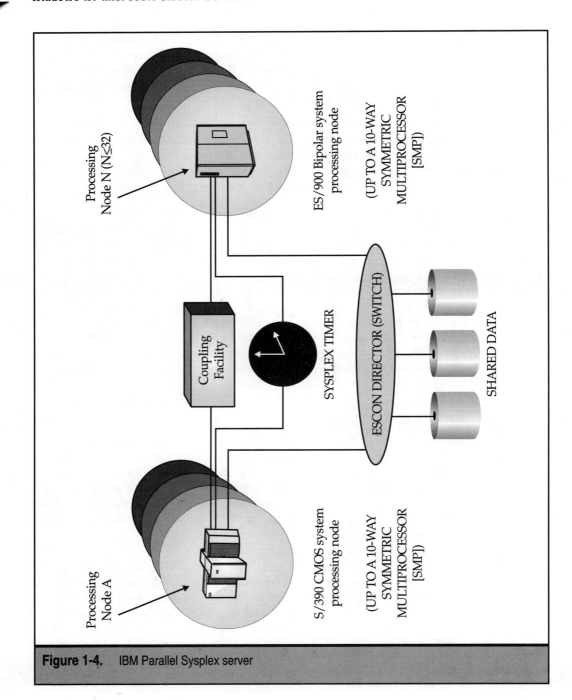

Figure 1-4. IBM Parallel Sysplex server

capabilities of their HACMP system over to Windows NT. It is believed that this product will co-exist with both MSCS as well as Oracle's Parallel Server, which utilizes a shared-disk model. This effort is intended to provide higher levels of scalability for parallel database applications and to interoperate with AIX environments, neither of which are currently provided by MSCS.

OTHER MSCS EARLY ADOPTER PARTNERS

In the early, early days of MSCS (just after Dave Cutler came over from Digital to Microsoft) there were only three of the so-called "strategic alliances for enterprise computing" in place (IBM, Digital, and Tandem) at Microsoft. As Wolfpack developed beyond conceptualization, it became important for Microsoft to open up its development effort to a wider community of clustering experts (and platform partners). These companies (HP, NCR, DG, Compaq, and Intel) joined forces with IBM, Digital, and Tandem to become known as the early adopter partners for Wolfpack. This collaborative effort has been a critical component of making MSCS not only a well rounded solution, but one with wide industry endorsement out of the gate.

Hewlett-Packard

Hewlett-Packard also has a strong track record in providing what they call "availability solutions," to the high-end computing community in regard to their HP9000 UNIX line with their MC/ServiceGuard clustering option. They recently announced a comprehensive set of solutions for their NetServer Windows NT server series based on the use of MSCS, along with the support of other hardware and software options (such as HP OpenView Network Node Manager) to help round out these solutions. HP is focusing its clustering strategy on those enterprise computing end users who want to interoperate both UNIX and Windows NT from the desktop to the data center with similar levels of availability, scalability, and management. HP is strongly pursuing a leadership position in the MSCS NT clustered server segment of the market similar to one that they enjoy in the UNIX space of the market. They, too, made significant contributions and investments in MSCS during its development, with strong emphasis on those issues involving UNIX and NT interoperability.

NCR

For some time now, NCR has been providing a unique and innovative clustering solution that they developed called LifeKeeper. LifeKeeper is available in both UNIX and Windows NT versions and currently supports more than 16 nodes in a shared-disk configuration. They were also one of the original seven early adopter partners in the development of MSCS Phase 1 and have announced a range of Microsoft-validated MSCS solutions, along with options to improve reliability and availability overall. Both MSCS and LifeKeeper are key components of NCR's "high-availability transaction processing" product strategy. LifeKeeper is positioned by NCR as a premium high-availability enterprise offering, while MSCS Phase 1 is an entry-level high-availability offering. They perceive that in today's market both solutions can exist until such time as MSCS Phase 2 is available and directly competes with LifeKeeper.

Data General

Data General has been providing high-availability solutions for their AViiON line of UNIX and Windows NT servers via their relationship with Veritas and the use of their FirstWatch product for several years now. They also offer their own products, Application Transparent Failover (ATF) and NT Alert (NTA), to enhance the availability and reliability of all these Veritas-based systems. DG currently offers MSCS Phase 1 validated systems, with optional packages such as ATF and NTA to augment their capabilities overall.

In a departure from the other early adopter partners, DG is strongly focused on the emerging NUMA-type architecture for use in the Windows NT server environment, including clustering. They have been providing these type of systems in UNIX versions and want to leverage their leadership in this alternative architecture to provide highly scalable NUMA-type servers using four-way (and eight in the future) standard high-volume servers (Pentium Pro) boards from Intel for the NT space of the market. They believe that the NUMA architecture can extend well beyond the limits of current (and future) SMP architectures while utilizing the low-cost SHV server component base that SMP systems are built upon. This same philosophy has recently been extended to include solutions based on the Deschutes IA-32 (Xeon) and Merced IA-64 processor families.

In spite of this focus, DG has announced several versions of their "NT cluster in a box" featuring the use of MSCS, Veritas, or Oracle Fail-Safe as a cluster engine. All of these cluster in a box systems are based on SHV servers in four-way SMP configurations, along with Clariion storage solutions, housed in a common enclosure.

Compaq Computer

Compaq, currently the undisputed leader in providing both Windows NT servers and workstations, has had a high-availability option available for their NT server product line (Recovery Server), along with being firmly committed to MSCS. As the market leader, their participation as an early adopter partner with Microsoft was critical to MSCS reaching critical mass in both the platform vendor and end-user communities. Now that they have expanded their enterprise computing business by acquiring Tandem, Compaq is uniquely positioned to provide MSCS clustering solutions from the department to the data center, all across the enterprise.

Compaq has announced several products based on MSCS, and as Microsoft's in-house server provider, they enjoy the unique advantage of seeing these products in actual use prior to being beta tested or being released to the general public. (Microsoft uses its own internal IT environment to test all of its products in advance of outside beta testing and general release to the public.)

Compaq will be announcing many new MSCS systems as they ramp up in terms of "self-certification." It is expected that these systems will range from two-way to eight-way SMP in configuration, while supporting such advanced options as fiber-channel and ServerNet for peripheral and private network interconnection. Compaq will have significant competition for these products from many of the other MSCS providers who have significantly longer track records in fielding and supporting clustered solutions.

NOTE: With Compaq's acquisition of Digital Equipment Corporation, it is clear that Compaq will remain the undisputed leader in providing NT from the desktop to the data center, with many of these solutions based on MSCS and ancillary offerings from both Digital and Tandem to round them out.

Intel

As the seventh early adopter partner in the MSCS consortium, Intel has played an interesting, if not extremely influential, role. Not only does the company provide the lions' share of all the CPUs that NT Server will be hosted on (see Figure 1-5), but they also provide a similar majority of all the SMP motherboards and specialty chipsets (PCI, I2O, etc.) to these same platform vendors. Intel is much more than a CPU provider; they determine and dictate present and future architectures and specifications for the lions' share of all the server and desktop platforms that will be built by anyone. Their involvement in MSCS has fostered both the Virtual Interface Architecture and NT Server Hardware Design specifications discussed earlier. They are also driving other major NT Server initiatives such as Hot Swappable PCI & PCI 64, I2O (intelligent I/O), and IEEE

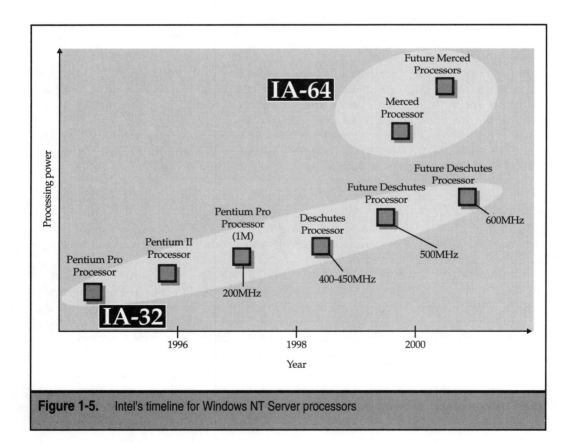

Figure 1-5. Intel's timeline for Windows NT Server processors

1394 storage interface. Intel's role is not just acting as an interested party, but plotting the future of computing, much in the way that Microsoft does from the software side.

Johnny-Come-Latelies

Subsequent to the formation of the MSCS development consortium (i.e., the early adopter partners), a number of other interested parties expressed their willingness and desire to help out or at least join the crowd in terms of being MSCS advocates. Those companies include platform providers, such as Dell Computer, Micron Computer, Stratus Computer, Fujitsu/Amdahl Corporation, and Siemens-Nixdorf, along with software developers such as CA, Oracle, SAP, and Vinca Corporation. All of these organizations have devoted tremendous amounts of engineering and test resources to help the cause including MSCS in the enterprise.

OTHER PROVIDERS OF CLUSTERING SOLUTIONS AND PRODUCTS

Although the Wolfpack early adopter partners do represent a great deal of clustering know-how and all are market leaders, they have by no means a monopoly over the concept of clustering. There are a number of other vendors (hardware and ISVs) who have influenced the development of clustering technology over time. Many of these same vendors have either competing or complementary products to MSCS.

To put this all into perspective, Table 1-1 provides a summary of all vendors' current offerings of clustering products.

Manufacturer	Cluster Name	Architecture	OS Platform	Number of Nodes	CPU Type	Total Number of CPUs
DG	AV 20000 (Veritas)	SD	UNIX	2-4+	X86 NUMA	128
DG	Cluster-in-a-box (Veritas)	SD	NT	2	X86 SMP	16
Digital	OpenVMS Galaxy	SD	VMS	2-8+	Alpha SMP	256
Digital	Tru-Clusters	SD	UNIX	2-4+	Alpha SMP	128

Table 1-1. A Comparison of Various Types of Clustering Systems Available Today

Manufacturer	Cluster Name	Architecture	OS Platform	Number of Nodes	CPU Type	Total Number of CPUs
Digital	Digital Clusters Plus	SN	NT	2	X86/Alpha SMP	16+
IBM	S/390 Parallel Sysplex	SN and SD	S/390	2-32	Proprietary	320
IBM	HACMP	SD	UNIX	2-16	RISC 6000	128
NCR	Life-Keeper	SD	UNIX	2-16+	SPARC	64+
NCR	Life-Keeper	SD	NT	2-16	X86 SMP	64
Octopus	SASO	SN	NT	2	X86/Alpha	16
Oracle	OPS	SD	NT	2-4	X86/Alpha SMP	32
Oracle	FailSafe	SN	NT	2	X86/Alpha SMP	16
Sun	Enterprise	SD	Solaris UNIX	2-4	Ultra-SPARC	256
Tandem	Himalaya	SN	N.S.K.	2-64	MIPS	100s
Tandem	Integrity	SN	UNIX	2-16	MIPS	128+
Tandem	CAS	SD and SN	NT	2+	X86 SMP	16+
Tandem	NSK-Lite	SN	NT	2-16	X86 SMP	128+
Veritas	First-Watch	SD	UNIX/NT	2-4	RISC/X86 SMP	32+
Veritas	Clock Server	SN	NT	2-32	SMP	256+
Vinca	Co-Standby Server	SN	NT	2	X86 SMP	16
Microsoft	MSCS Phase 1	SN	NT 4.0 EE	2	X86/Alpha SMP	16

Table 1-1.   A Comparison of Various Types of Clustering Systems Available Today (*continued*)

Manufacturer	Cluster Name	Architecture	OS Platform	Number of Nodes	CPU Type	Total Number of CPUs
Microsoft	MSCS Phase 1 for Windows 2000	SN	Windows 2000 EE	2+	IA-32/ Alpha SMP	32+
Microsoft	MSCS Phase 2	SN and SD	Windows 2000 EE	2-16	IA-64/ Alpha SMP	128+

*SD = Shared-disk architecture, SN = Shared-nothing architecture

Table 1-1. A Comparison of Various Types of Clustering Systems Available Today (*continued*)

Sun Microsystems

Sun, firmly entrenched in the world of UNIX, has recently entered into the field of providing clustered servers. For the past few years Sun has offered products for use as highly available NFS servers, along with supporting high-end parallel database environments (such as Oracle, SyBase, and Informix). Based on their Solaris operating system and using predominantly a shared-disk model, the Sun Enterprise Cluster Series is available in a number of various configurations ranging from two to four nodes in total. These solutions are based on a merger of the earlier Ultra Enterprise Cluster PDB and Ultra Enterprise Cluster HA solutions sets and the use of Veritas' Volume Manager to provide availability, scalability, and management of these clusters. Sun's focus is on supporting their installed base of enterprise computing customers, with little or no interest in how Windows NT interoperates in these environments or what threat it represents to this installed base.

Vinca Corporation

Vinca has two products for the NT high-availability marketplace. One is Standby Server, a server-mirroring solution that connects a secondary NT server to a main server. Data is mirrored between the two servers via an industry-standard dedicated data link. When the main server has a failure, users are automatically switched to the secondary server.

Vinca's other product is Co-Standby Server. This product is a server-mirroring solution that supports workloads on both servers simultaneously, with failover to the surviving server if one fails. Co-Standby Server is similar in concept to MSCS and supports some aspects of its API for application commonality. IBM offers Standby Server as part of their NT high-availability server line, as well as MSCS. The Vinca products are favored for environments where interoperability with OS/2 is required, as they are the only ones in the industry that support OS/2 as an integrated client.

Qualix/Octopus

Qualix recently acquired Octopus, a provider of "real-time server and data protection for Windows NT." The Octopus product family includes HA+ for real-time data protection and high availability and DataStar and HP real-time data protection for NT servers and workstations. The company reports to have shipped some 15,000 licenses to date for this product (on NT and UNIX platforms). Octopus has versions for both the Intel X86 and Digital/Intel Alpha CPU, along with a UNIX version for OEM customers.

Octopus HA+ is touted as an "n-node" cluster-type high-availability solution and sold primarily on a direct basis (via resellers), with some OEM support.

WHY CLUSTERING?

In today's business-critical computing world, MIS executives, systems administrators, and IS planners are being challenged on many fronts simultaneously. Business-critical computing now encompasses the entire enterprise. What was previously considered as a "nice to have" service or application is now critical to the day-to-day operation of the business (see Table 1-2). These business-critical applications span from the desktop to the data center, as well as being external to the enterprise, and all require computing solutions that are available (reliable), scalable, and manageable on a 24×7×52 basis.

Application Class	Business-critical Y/N	Number of Users
Mail and messaging	Yes	Tens of thousands
Internet/intranet/ extranet	Yes	Tens of thousands
Online transaction processing	Yes	Thousands
Online analytical processing/DSS	Yes	Hundreds
File/print services	Yes	Thousands
Branch office activities	Yes	Hundreds to thousands

Table 1-2. The Growing List of Business-critical Applications

NOTE: Some 35+ percent of these applications run 24 hours/day and must be constantly available (99.9+ percent) and supported during that time.

Clustering has proven itself to be highly capable as a tool for use in meeting these challenges. Clusters have three primary attributes: availability, scalability, and manageability.

High Availability

When a business/mission-critical system fails and data becomes unavailable, it is no longer a matter of the "network being down," but of the "business being down!"(as quoted from the Microsoft/Tandem Wolfpack briefings). Some people, such as Linda Sanford of IBM, regard this type of high-pressure IT environment as "bet-the-business computing." This is hardly a situation that anyone in management treats lightly, and these days it is getting a great deal of attention, especially with virtually every business today being wholly dependent upon its IT systems.

Availability is defined as the time that a system is capable of providing service to its users (i.e., uptime). It is expressed as a percentage that represents the ratio of the time in which the system provides acceptable service versus the total time during which the system is expected to be operational. (For reference, some potential 525,600 minutes of uptime are in each year.)

A more germane measurement that hits closer to home for most administrators is downtime. Downtime is the ratio between the time to repair a system outage versus the MTBF of such outages. Table 1-3 gives an overview of the time to repair or recover from many of the sources of downtime.

According to *Fortune 1000 Company Surveys*, conducted by the Strategic Research Division of FIND/SAP & Contingency Planning Research Group, downtime costs

Downtime Source	Recovery Method	Average Outage Time
Scheduled maintenance	Restart	60-180 minutes (typically)
Application failure	Reboot/Reload	15-60+ minutes
Operator error	Reboot	15-60 minutes
OS failure	Reload	30-90 minutes
Blue Screen of Death	Restart/Reload	30-120 minutes
Hardware failure	Diagnose/repair	1-3 hours
Power/environmental	Third party repair	1-5 days
Natural disaster	Relocate/Restart	1-30 days

Table 1-3. Sources and Methods Required to Remedy Downtime

U.S.-based businesses in excess of $4 billion per year, with an average outage ranging in cost from tens of thousands to millions of dollars depending upon the type of business. It is not only costly in terms of lost revenue but decreases worker productivity, increases customer dissatisfaction, and pushes up technical support costs. The following table provides a sampling of these costs by the type of business being operated.

Industry	System Outage Duration	Average Cost in Dollars
Manufacturing operation	1 hour	$28,000
Retail store	1 hour	$140,000
Brokerage operation	1 hour	$6,500,000
Banking data center	1 hour	$2,500,000+
Industry average	4 hours	$330,000

NOTE: Strategic Research Corporation says that the average Fortune 1000 company experiences 1.6 hours of downtime per week at an average cost of $29,000.

In addition, the sources of these outages vary as much as the cost, with the majority being hardware oriented. Availability has become the single most critical factor in terms of not only choosing which computing architecture to use for a particular application (in terms of its importance to the enterprise), but where the most significant IT investments and administrative attention needs to be focused on. The following table shows the relationship between the cause of the outage versus the frequency with which it happens overall.

Failure Type	Cause	Frequency
Storage	Hardware	25 percent
CPU	Hardware	25 percent
Application or OS	Software	25 percent
Network	Hardware	20 percent
Operator	Human	5 percent

High-Availability Server Architectures

The best way to increase availability on an overall basis is to prevent faults from occurring in the first place. In an effort to improve availability, manufacturers have developed various types of high-availability computer architectures. These range from standalone systems to standby/replicated servers and to fully fault-tolerant systems. At the sweet spot in this range of choices is clustering, not only in terms of price but in terms of system complexity and manageability.

Figure 1-6 shows the relative cost versus availability of common computer architectures, and Figure 1-7 refers to the relative cost of each architecture versus

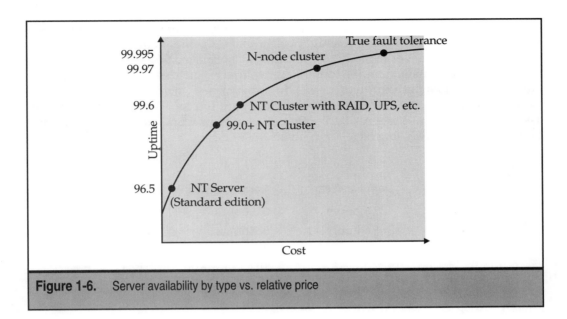

Figure 1-6. Server availability by type vs. relative price

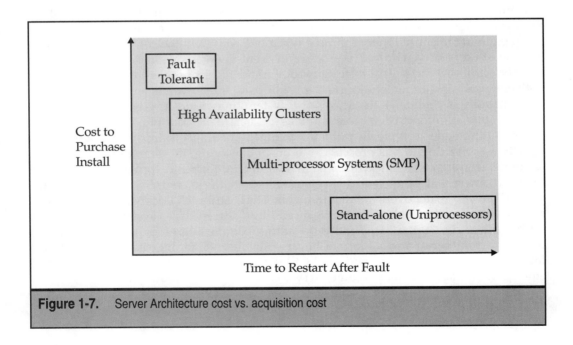

Figure 1-7. Server Architecture cost vs. acquisition cost

downtime. As one can see, there is a wide difference between the uniprocessor architecture and the fully fault-tolerant one. In today's genre, fault-tolerance refers to system availability in the range of 99.9X percent and is achieved through the use of highly refined design and manufacturing techniques required by such levels of availability (e.g., outages of minutes per year, worst case). In terms of most high-availability clustered systems, outages of 30 to 90 seconds per incident are typical. These outage durations assume that when one system fails, another takes over its workload and clients a short time later. See the following table for more information.

Server Availability (percent)	Downtime/Year	Downtime/Week	Downtime/Day
95.1	429.3 hours	8.3 hours	71 minutes
96.5	306.6 hours	5.9 hours	50.5 minutes
99.6	35.04 hours	40.4 minutes	5.8 minutes
99.9	8.76 hours	10.1 minutes	1.44 minutes
99.995	7 minutes	Less than 1 minute	Unmeasureable

Scalability

The number two (sometimes number one if you're a high-performance database professional) criteria for choosing clustering as an architecture is scalability. Scalability is a key issue in the entire IT environment when one considers the constantly fluctuating number of users, driven by both seasonal and event-oriented demand requirements that must be serviced effectively. System slow-downs are no less problematic than outages to both end users and administrators and must be contended with on an ongoing basis.

Scalability is defined as the ability of a system to increase its computing power by adding either additional processors or nodes (clusters). The addition of these processors or computing nodes is typically not a linear function because extra system overhead is usually associated with this process. In terms of clustering, the shared-nothing (MSCS supports this architecture exclusively in Phase 1) architecture provides the highest degree of linear scalability available versus its cousin, the shared-disk architecture, due primarily to its greater overhead requirements. The Distributed Lock Manager (DLM), or concurrency control algorithm, required by shared-disk systems to control multiple-accesses to the same file does add a certain degree of additional system overhead resulting in a small loss of linear scalability. High degrees of scalability are found in today's mainframe and UNIX SMP/NUMA servers, but is just starting to emerge in the standard high-volume (SHV) server world of Windows NT.

Scalability is an issue that affects not only the choice of whether or not to use clustering, but what types of processor configurations to use as cluster nodes.

SMP vs. Other Architectures

The SMP is considered by some to be a very basic shared-everything cluster architecture with multiple processors sharing the same memory, operating system, and other common components (such as networking and power), all in a common package (see Figure 1-8). In terms of the server architecture food chain, SMPs lie between the uniprocessor (at the bottom) and the parallel processor (at the top). In fact, it features many of the advantages found in both of these other architectures. In terms of the uniprocessor, the SMP presents a singular, global view of memory to applications, and in respect to the parallel processor, the SMP puts multiple processors to work in parallel.

A major reason that Windows NT Server 4.0 (which shipped more than 1.6 million copies in its first 12 months) has been so successful is its support of Intel's Standard High-Volume Server (SHV) strategy. Since the late '80s, platform providers have been manufacturing functionally identical servers with components from multiple vendors. This competition has created an environment where costs are held low while functionality and performance remain high. During this time, Intel developed a four-way Pentium Pro motherboard that allowed platform providers to configure it as an SMP and to then deliver even higher levels of server performance at very low prices (which, especially in respect to their UNIX equivalents, can cost twice as much). The commoditization of this four-way configuration and its sweet spot on the price versus performance curve was a major reason why Microsoft chose to cluster for scalability on Windows NT, rather than to pursue higher CPU counts in the form of SMPs (see Table 1-4). This sweet spot exploitation by both the platform and the OS provider has put the UNIX SMP manufacturers at an extreme cost disadvantage. It is further envisioned that

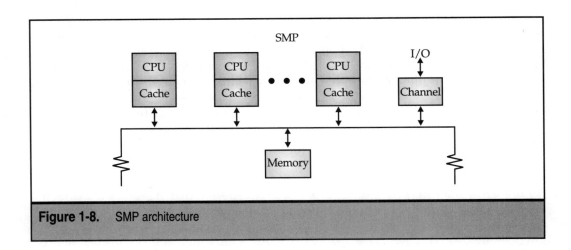

Figure 1-8.   SMP architecture

Number of Processors	Scaling Factor (x)	Reference Number Processors
1	1	–
2	1.9	1
4	1.5	2
6	1.2	4
8	1.7	4

Table 1-4.   Intel Pentium Pro (P6) SMP Scalability (Measured and Projected)

in the next few years Intel will commoditize both eight-way (and higher) IA-32 and IA-64 SMPs in the same fashion as the four-way Pentium Pro. This will provide even more capabilities to both standalone and clustered Windows NT servers and further differentiate NT-based servers from those in the UNIX community, regardless of configuration (standalone or clustered). As one can see, economics, rather than just simple raw performance, is of much more significance when making strategy decisions of this nature.

Somewhat in competition with this strategy is an extension of the SMP architecture called ccNUMA (cache coherent Non-Uniform Memory Access) (see Figure 1-9). Currently offered by Data General, Sequent, Convex/HP, and others, it is an adaptation of the SMP architecture that eliminates many of the bottlenecks and bus limitations that threaten the scalability of SMP beyond the four to eight processors found today. However, on an implementation level, ccNUMA utilizes the same Intel four-way (and higher) Standard High-Volume Processor server boards as its SMP cousin. Wide-scale adoption of this architecture will require Microsoft to re-port Windows NT for this architecture, along with many applications being rewritten to take full advantage of its overall attributes. It is uncertain as to whether this will ever happen, but you should definitely stay tuned to see how this progresses.

Concurrent User Support

A number of enterprise computing analysts have reported that Windows NT does not meet the Concurrent User Support requirements of many customers and that this will have to be remedied prior to its being adopted widely for enterprise computing. Current forecasts are that Windows NT will have to support a minimum of 1,500 concurrent users in the next two years to even be in the ball game. Currently, based on four-way SMP

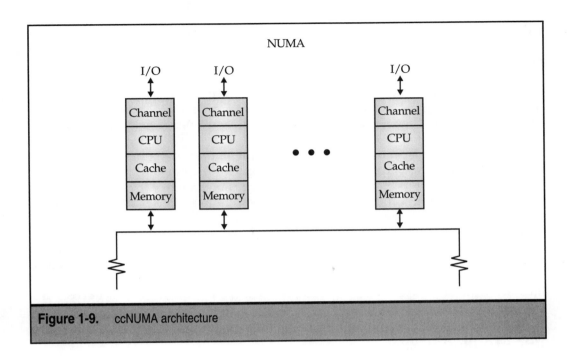

Figure 1-9.   ccNUMA architecture

standalone performance, the maximum number is around 500. UNIX can currently support around 3,000, and large mainframes handle 10,000 plus (S/390 Parallel Sysplex).

Two methods are available, along with a hybrid of the two, to meet this challenge. One is to continue to scale standalone SMPs for Windows NT to eight-way and beyond, and the other is to implement n-node clustering, adding as many four-way or eight-way nodes as necessary to meet demand. It is envisioned that eight-way+ MSCS Phase 1 clusters will be used to meet growing demand requirements until such time as Phase 2 is released at the end of this decade.

Manageability

Managing a wide variety of disparate servers is a nightmare for administrators today, along with being a major cost center. The third major attribute that clustering brings to the party is its ability to ease this management burden.

In terms of the "do more with less" mantra that management is chanting these days, an implied requirement is to reel in and consolidate the large number of servers across the enterprise. The number of these servers has grown dramatically during the past five years as most IT organizations have bandaged their scalability and new requirements needs by adding yet another server. In a comprehensive server consolidation plan found today, these servers are re-architected or upgraded to be so-called "symmetric virtual servers" (MSCS Phase 1 clusters). These assets now appear to the end users as single images of dedicated "islands of computing," but are in actuality a portion of a larger server configuration, such as a cluster. This idea has become so popular with enterprise computing customers that Digital (now Compaq) has coined its own slogan regarding this phenomena. The company believes that, according to John Swan, European Programs Manager, Compaq StorageWorks, "If you own a server today, there will be a cluster in your life tomorrow."

In respect to management, clusters typically present themselves as a single-system image to end users, applications, and the network, while providing a single point of control to administrators. This single-system image is presented to the administrator as either the physical server itself or as virtual servers (e.g., cluster failover groups), allowing the administrator to centrally manage the cluster as a group of symmetric virtual application servers or a group of physical resources, as appropriate.

Clusters are also supported by popular enterprise management schemes such as UniCenter TNG (CA), OpenView (HP), and TME10 (Tivoli) along with others. These products are available in cluster-aware versions that support enhanced control and interface with clusters and their applications, further reducing management costs and network administrators' labor.

Cluster Architectures

Two principle architectures are in use today for clustering. They differ primarily in the way that the nodes access the clusters' disks. One architecture is called shared-disk, or the shared data model, (see Figure 1-10), and the other is called shared-nothing, or the data-partitioning model (see Figure 1-11). Each has its own strengths and weaknesses in terms of scalability, parallel database support, and so on. Both of these principle architectures are in wide use across the marketplace and supported by the Windows NT platform. Microsoft has chosen the shared-nothing architecture for MSCS, while Oracle has chosen the shared-disk architecture for its Parallel Server clustering system.

Shared-Disk Architecture

As shown in Figure 1-10, the shared-disk architecture allows all nodes of the cluster to have direct access to (some or all of) the disks, or disk subsystems, where shared data is resident in the cluster. Shared-disk works very well for those applications where there are a relatively few number of writes to disk and most system activity is read driven. Databases, such as Oracle Parallel Server, conform well to this model. The only other items that are needed are a local database buffer cache, to maintain synchronization and coherency with other nodes, and a DLM to control and synchronize disk access. These two items do add overhead, which is a major reason why shared-disk is not as linearly scalable as its counterpart shared-nothing, but do not have the serious limiting factor that some pundits report.

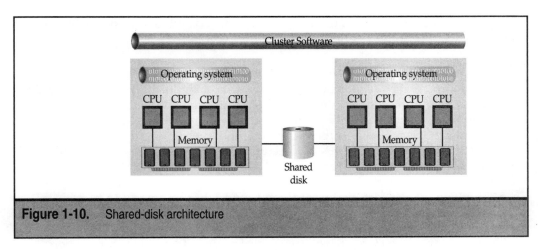

Figure 1-10.   Shared-disk architecture

One of the greatest strengths of the shared-disk architecture is its ability to dynamically balance workloads (as in a parallel database) across all nodes of the cluster. This greatly improves availability and prevents "phantom outages" due to system slow-down. It also allows much more graceful failovers during outages—the remaining nodes simply take on a larger workload for an application already running, rather than

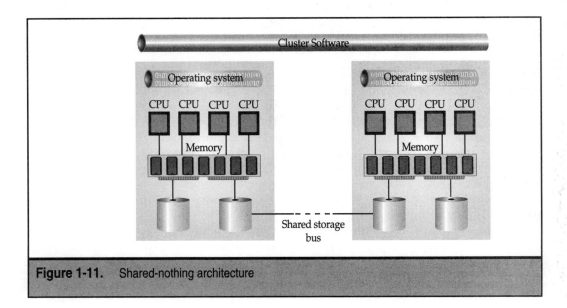

Figure 1-11.   Shared-nothing architecture

having to wait for the transfer of resources from the failed node and reconnecting to users on the network.

Shared-Nothing Architecture

Figure 1-11 depicts the architecture of the shared-nothing, or partitioned data cluster, architecture. Shared-nothing architectures imply that each node has its own memory and storage resources. During a failure, these resources are dynamically redistributed to the surviving members of the cluster for use or work until such time as the faulted node "fails back" and rejoins the cluster. In this architecture, there are no problems with either cache coherency or distributed concurrency control (DLM) as found in NUMA and shared-disk architectures; consequently, system overhead is lower and scalability is more linear. Shared-nothing allows each node's processor (and other resources) to provide all the performance that it can. It is for these reasons (and probably some others) that Microsoft and its early adopter partners chose this architecture exclusively for MSCS.

Shared-nothing clusters have two weaknesses that both developers and administrators must contend with. First, in parallel application environments, a great deal of attention must be paid to tuning the overall system to match the processing capacity and projected workload for each node. Real-time fluctuations in demand can result in over- or under-utilization of processor resources. Second, each active node has exclusive access to its data and resources; however, another node requiring this same data must request to have it sent over the network (public or private) to perform its processing. When it has finished, it must then (in most cases) send the new data back over the network to the node that owns it. This can create large amounts of internetwork traffic and drag on CPU resources. One means to help overcome this is via a wide-bandwidth, low-latency private interconnect like Tandem's ServerNet, which can operate at hundreds of MBs per second.

Shared-Everything and Hybrids

Shared-everything is the model that SMP (and its cousin ccNUMA) conform to. So, if you are using SMP servers in your cluster (and who isn't?), then you really have a number of smaller clusters within your overall cluster. The only problem with this analogy is that unlike clusters, SMP servers do have single points of failure.

As discussed earlier, SMP systems suffer from other shortcomings as well. Their scalability is limited by the fact that as more CPUs are added, the incremental effective capacity diminishes due to overhead increases associated with interprocessor communication, memory contention, and storage access problems. Figure 1-12 shows these scalability limitations.

However, when you combine small-scale SMPs with a shared-nothing architecture (creating a hybrid, so to speak), you get very close to true linear scalability. This is in effect

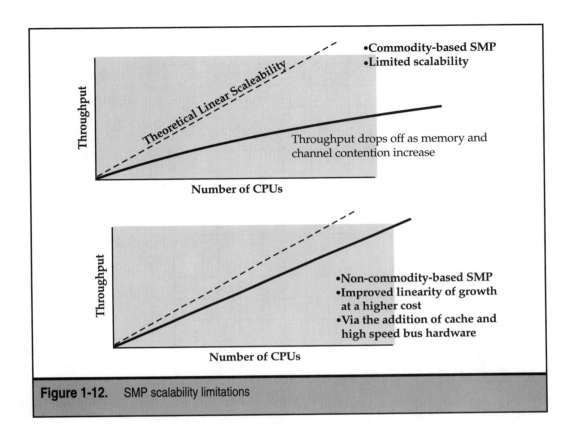

Figure 1-12. SMP scalability limitations

what MSCS is banking on in terms of meeting ever-growing scalability requirements and is critical to the Phase 2 plan (see Figure 1-13).

TRUE HYBRIDS For its S/390 Parallel Sysplex cluster, IBM uses a virtual shared-disk architecture (see Figure 1-14). This best-of-both-worlds approach features the use of data partitioning (shared-nothing) among the nodes while appearing to parallel databases (such as DB2 parallel edition and Oracle Parallel Server) as a shared-disk machine. This hybrid is achieved by creating both logical processing and storage nodes in the cluster. This architecture has much higher scalability than traditional shared-disk, while eliminating much of the node-to-node communication of shared-nothing systems. This architecture's great shortcoming is its price. It can only be found on IBM's most expensive

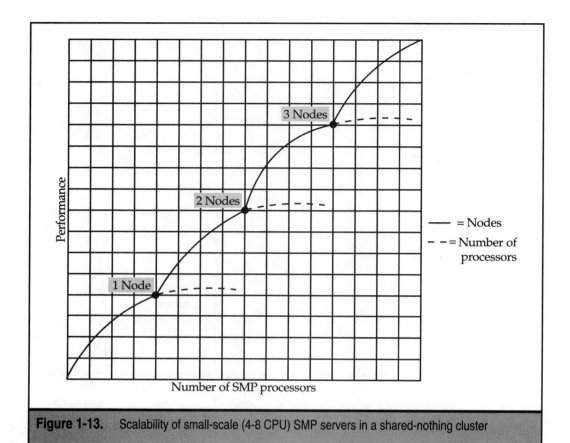

Figure 1-13. Scalability of small-scale (4-8 CPU) SMP servers in a shared-nothing cluster

platform, the S/390 Parallel Sysplex, and flies in the face of the Windows NT business model that utilizes high-volume, low-cost components on a standardized, high-performance OS with the lowest TCO of any in the enterprise.

Which Architecture Is Right for Me?

In order to choose the right clustering architecture, you must first make fast and hard decisions regarding which applications you are going to cluster. In many cases, by choosing the application, you have by default chosen the cluster architecture at the same time (e.g., Microsoft SQL Server = shared-nothing, Oracle Parallel Server = shared-disk). Obviously, you will not be able to have both of these applications/architectures existing on the same cluster, so make your initial choices wisely.

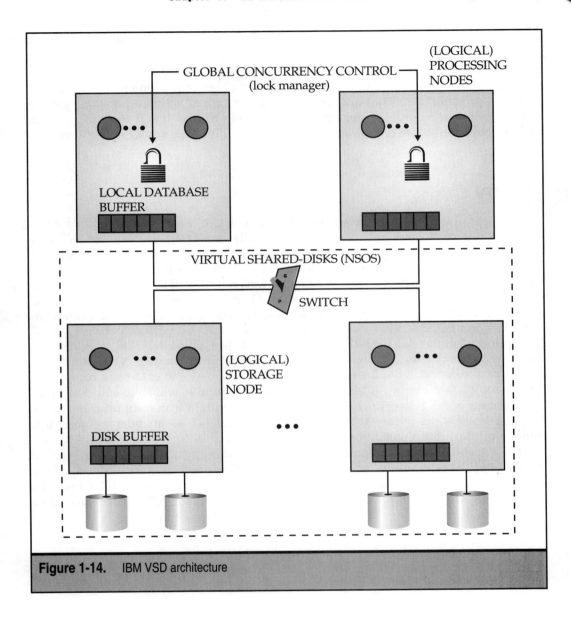

Figure 1-14.   IBM VSD architecture

If your requirements are more mundane, such as file and print or mail and messaging, your safest choice is going to be shared-nothing because this is where most of the market momentum is headed. Your other choice then becomes one of operating mode.

This subject will be covered in great detail in later chapters, but you should also consider what operating mode you want the cluster to operate in. Current modes are

Active/Active, where both nodes have independent workloads and applications running at the same time, and Active/Inactive, where only one server is running applications and serving requests, while the other is "standing by" to take over this work if the first should fail. Both of these have a place in the hierarchy of enterprise computing and fill a particular need. The most common choice is Active/Active, especially if you are running symmetric virtual server applications such as Microsoft SQL Server EE, which can run multiple copies of the application and then divide its workload between two nodes.

SUMMARY

The purpose of this first chapter was to introduce you to clusters, or at least update you on the status of clusters and clustering, especially in respect to Windows NT as a platform. For those of you who are new to clustering, I hope I managed to dispel some of the myths and rumors regarding this technology. By now, hopefully you believe that clustering is not some black art, but yet another well-refined tool that you can use in your day-to-day adventures in enterprise computing. I hope that I also quashed the notion that Microsoft invented clustering or has the market cornered in terms of know-how (revenues from UNIX clusters are growing at more than 30 percent per year CAGR [Compound Annualized Growth Rate] in spite of declining UNIX OS sales overall). MSCS will become the de facto clustering solution for Windows NT, not because Microsoft developed it, but because of the current economics in enterprise computing. Also, over 2,000 Windows NT Server applications are now available, and more than 150,000 units of NT Server are being licensed each month (30+ percent utilize NTS/E). Nothing besides the sheer critical mass of Windows NT as an interoperable, true multi-vendor platform will drive the success of MSCS.

The rest of this book is devoted to the specifics of Microsofts' Cluster Server as found in the Enterprise Edition of Windows NT 4.0 (and beyond), as well as the business-critical applications being developed or ported to it. I will also discuss other NT Clustering solutions available in the marketplace. When you think of NT clusters and their cluster-aware applications, this should be your single reference to turn to.

CHAPTER 2

Windows NT Server Enterprise Edition and MSCS

Everyone should be familiar by now with the dearth of documentation, other information resources, and lack of straightforwardness found in version 1 releases of products from Microsoft. Windows NT Server Enterprise Edition is no exception to this long-standing trend.

The following are the main objectives of this chapter:

▼ Provide a detailed overview of Microsoft Cluster Server 1.0 with emphasis on its capabilities today, tomorrow, and in the future, along with defining why this product is so critical to Windows NT for Enterprise Computing.

■ Develop a roadmap for the user or administrator to use in accessing all the available documentation and informational resources available on this product.

▲ Identify those applications that are cluster-aware and can be utilized today with MSCS 1.0.

Windows NT Server Enterprise Edition is comprised of two disks. Disk 1 has an autorun mode in which a window is displayed to help you through the installation process. (This window is shown in Figure 2-1.) Disk 2 however, has no such autorun mode and you must know in advance which directory and application you are looking for when attempting to install MSCS and other applications included with Windows NT Server Enterprise Edition. (You may, however, be prompted to insert disk 2 when installing such items as SP3, etc.) A view of these directories is shown in Figure 2-2.

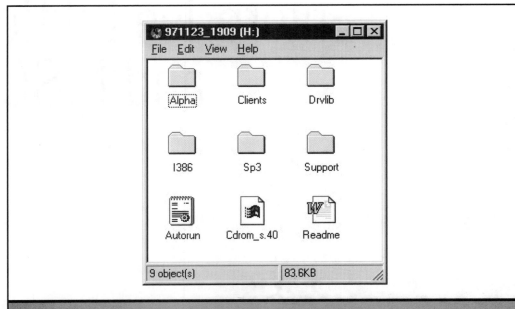

Figure 2-1.   Contents of disk 1, Windows NT Server Enterprise Edition

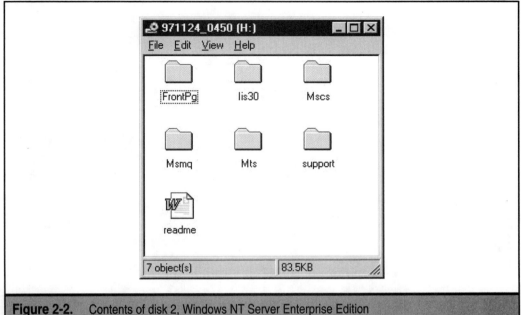

Figure 2-2.   Contents of disk 2, Windows NT Server Enterprise Edition

PURSUING THE ENTERPRISE

After three years of effort and hundreds of millions of dollars invested in R&D (by both Microsoft and its early adopter partners) and testing, Microsoft announced and began delivering Windows NT Server Enterprise Edition in the fall of 1997. NT Server/E (or NTSE or NTS/E), as it is commonly referred to, is a new release of Windows NT Server 4.0 that combines all of the integrated and easy-to-use capabilities of the Standard Edition of NT Server. It also adds high-availability (via MSCS), enhanced performance (scalability via expanded memory and CPU support), and a comprehensive set of new and upgraded applications (such as Internet Information Server, Microsoft Transaction Server, and Microsoft Message Queue Server). This two-disk CD-ROM was released for manufacturing in late September 1997 and is designed to coexist with other editions of NT Server (Standard, Small Business, and Terminal Server).

The entire design and marketing impetus of this product family is to position Microsoft to move up the computing food chain (see Figure 2-3) from file and print services to the enterprise computing segment of the market. To accomplish this, Microsoft has had to begin to address the three main shortcomings of previous versions of Windows NT Server, which were: insufficient levels of scalability, availability, and manageability. This migration to the top of the computing solutions pyramid is intended

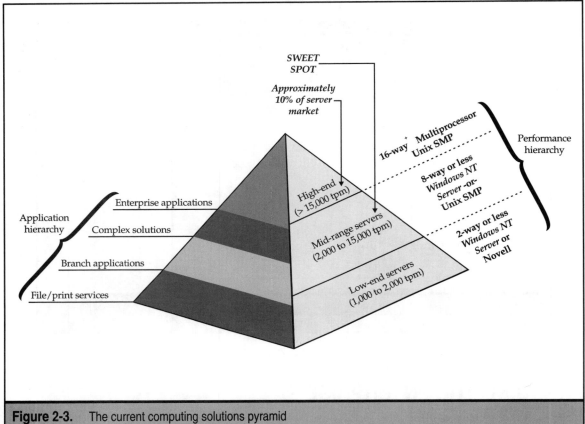

Figure 2-3. The current computing solutions pyramid

to take place in well-defined phases, and as you can see in Figure 2-4, with each new release of both Windows NT Server and Cluster Server, additional levels of scalability, availability, and manageability will become available.

ENTERPRISE COMPUTING DEFINED

Enterprise computing is one of those nebulous terms being bandied around by almost everyone in the computer industry, with few actually able to put their finger on a definition. Microsoft defines it as any customer with 1,000 seats or more. Others define it in terms of the class of customer (Fortune 1000) or the types of business-critical applications that are utilized by customers across their business enterprises, or even perhaps in respect to the large number of overall requirements that any system must meet.

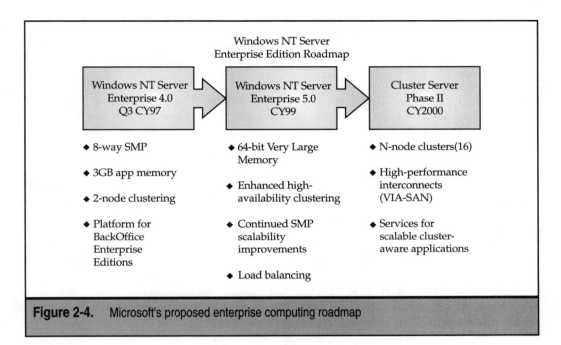

Figure 2-4. Microsoft's proposed enterprise computing roadmap

A good way to think of enterprise computing is as "availability from every dimension." This means that no matter the circumstances in terms of user demand, geographic disbursement of resources, or environmental conditions, access to both data and computing resources is always available (or at worst case, with slight delays). Meeting these requirements is a challenge for any computing system today, not just Windows NT. To meet it head on, you must undertake tremendous efforts to improve reliability and increase uptime. Meeting all of these criteria is critical to any enterprise computing customer today, and it will only grow in the future.

Market Forces

David Floyer, a leading analyst at IDC, in his report *Clustering and High-Performance System Interconnect on Intel Architecture 1995-2001* (February 1998), has compiled a comprehensive list of enterprise computing market forces influencing clustering for use in many application areas.

These forces are as follows:

▼   The increasing number of applications and servers that must be managed within and between business units

■   The increasing challenges of managing service levels, data integrity and consistency, and interoperability within and between the applications of business units

- The demand for lower systems management costs and better control and utilization of computing resources

- The demand for high availability and continuous access to systems and data, particularly as the number of users external to an organization increases

- The requirements for larger "single view of data" systems to support the "virtualization" of organizations and the increasing externalization of business processes

- The availability of fibre channel, fibre channel-arbitrated loop (FC-AL) and SSA technologies that enable access to disk by all nodes in a cluster

▲ The availability of high-speed/low-latency systems interconnect technology at reasonable costs, which from 1998 onward will be increasingly based on the Intel Virtual Interface Architecture (VI)

Being fully cognizant of these market forces, Microsoft and its hardware partners (Compaq, HP, Intel, IBM, DG, NCR, etc.) have embarked on a path to capitalize on this opportunity via the first release of Windows NT for the Enterprise—NTS/E 4.0 This journey will not be without its bumps, bruises, and sidetracks. However, if all the parties remain committed to the process, it is an investment that will have significant rewards when completed. The enterprise computing market today is equal in dollar value to the entire desktop market overall and is much less fraught with competition and price erosion, a forgotten concept in the desktop marketplace. In fact, in David Floyer's IDC report, he predicts that the market opportunity for NT Clusters of all types will be in excess of $4 billion by the year 2000, with a growth rate of 96 percent CAGR. These details have not escaped the attention of the server hardware community by any means, and they are driving not only the actions of the hardware solution providers, but the ISVs who provide the "killer apps" that run the enterprise.

Critical to making this journey a success will be major improvements in the key enterprise computing requirements of scalability, availability, and manageability. In the following sections, I will discuss the improvements and enhancements found in this first release of Windows NTS/E to meet these requirements.

Availability and Scalability Enhancements

In a number of surveys and analyst reports such as *Debunking the NT/SMP Scalability Myth* (the Aberdeen Group, Inc., Volume 9/Number 20, November 1996) and *Countdown to Scalability* by Karen D. Schwartz (from the now defunct *Datamation Magazine*, September 1997), the two big deficiencies or barriers-to-entry for Windows NT into the enterprise are scalability (i.e., CPU counts and cluster nodes) and availability (of which reliability is the major component). To address these shortcomings, Microsoft has made major enhancements to the existing capabilities of NT Server 4.0, along with adding higher availability and scalability via MSCS.

The Microsoft Cluster Server (Phase 1) component of NTS/E relates directly to the need for improvements in availability and scalability (i.e., high-availability via two-node failover, with scalability enhancements). See Figure 2-5 for a basic block diagram of an MSCS cluster.

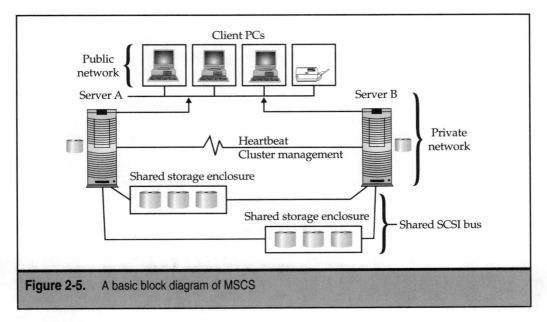

Figure 2-5. A basic block diagram of MSCS

Availability

Fundamentally, Enterprise Computing customers demand much higher levels of availability than is found in most operating systems, in spite of NT 4.0's built-in reliability enhancement features:

- ▼ Application fault isolation
- ■ Preemptive multitasking and protected memory
- ■ Software RAID (striping and mirroring)
- ■ File system journaling (NTFS)
- ■ UPS support (the UPS vendor APS has a cluster-aware version of their product line for use with NTS/E)
- ■ Replicated directory and backup logon support
- ▲ Instrumented monitoring, logging, and alerting

These built-in availability enhancements produce an average of 96.5 percent of system uptime (in most common server configurations), well below the needs of most enterprise computing customers.

MSCS, through its two-node failover model, provides enhanced availability via the following:

- ▼ Early detection of failures and warning to administrators
- ■ Automatically restarting failed applications on surviving cluster nodes (typically within 30 to 90 seconds)
- ▲ Permitting scheduled and unplanned server maintenance without affecting users' access to applications and data

These enhancements provide availability on the order of 99.5 percent (again hardware dependent to some degree, as well as the type of application being run during the testing). For most enterprise-computing customers this level of uptime is well within the acceptable range today.

Scalability

In terms of scalability enhancements, MSCS Phase 1 provides specific applications the ability to use both nodes for additional processing power, along with each node having its own storage and networking resources (devices and interconnection) to limit contention and increase effective bandwidth. For example, you could use SQL Server 6.5 EE (two copies running simultaneously and using the same database in the Symmetric Virtual Server mode) in a 16-processor mode by combining two eight-way SMP nodes. This additional computing power would be available to all users until such time that a failure occurs on one node and failover takes place. At that time performance would be reduced based on only eight processors being available.

NOTE: Phase 2 of MSCS will support 16+ nodes. This will allow for both higher levels of availability as well as linear scalability. This will enable administrators to add "horsepower on demand" to meet the needs of business-critical applications.

4GB RAM TUNING The overall architecture of Windows NT Server 4.0 supports up to 4GB of RAM. In the Standard, Small Business, and Terminal Server editions, 2GB of this capability are relegated to the OS kernel, with the remaining 2GB for applications. In the Enterprise Edition, up to 3GB of memory can be allocated to applications, effectively increasing the capacity by 50 percent. This allows more demanding applications (those that are memory-intensive by nature) to run more in memory, reducing the amount of disk and network accesses and improving cache "hit rates" overall. This also reduces "thrashing," which occurs when databases must constantly access disk for data as opposed to memory.

NOTE: With the release of NT Server 5.0, both MSCS Phase 1 and Phase 2 will have VLM support. This will allow 64-bit processors from Intel, Digital/Intel, and others to address up to 32GB of RAM, a potential eight-fold improvement in performance for demanding applications. This capability will also allow for the use of devices such as Digital's Memory Channel to support parallel database applications (such as Oracle OPS, IBM DB2, Informix XPS, and Microsoft SQL Server 7.x). In addition, large applications such as mail and messaging will be able to support a larger number of users.

EIGHT-PROCESSOR SMP LICENSE (WITH UP TO 32-PROCESSOR SUPPORT FROM SELECT OEMS)
As the industry overall continues its movement toward SHV servers, both the cost and configurations for SMP systems will improve dramatically. Most server vendors have announced eight-way SMP servers (either Pentium Pro or Deschutes) for 1998 delivery, with some (such as Data General and NCR) beginning to deliver higher level configurations for even better performance. There are a number of competing

architectures for these eight-way and higher systems, but at this point it appears that the Intel/Corollary approach will become the de facto standard in the industry. With the release of the Deschutes family of IA-32 processors, many of the issues associated with commodity-type eight-way SMP's will fall by the wayside. These systems overall allow for greater scalability in terms of application requirements, as well as supporting the general "server consolidation" taking place across the enterprise. Server consolidation is as large a requirement for these eight-way-plus systems as supporting processing-intensive applications. Server Consolidation will utilize these eight-way SMP's to replace the growing number of disparate servers scattered across the enterprise via the virtual server mode and will quickly become a major component of every IT organizations' plans and efforts to reduce total-cost-of-ownership (TCO).

NOTE: When Phase 2 of MSCS is released sometime around the year 2000, it is expected that the IA-32 Deschutes class processors will have long replaced the Pentium Pro series, with the IA-64 Merced class processors just becoming available. There will, however, continue to be 64-bit Alpha processors available for use in SMP configurations up to 32-way and higher. It is anticipated that both the Alpha and Merced CPUs will compete for 64-bit Windows NT opportunities, with both also able to support UNIX requirements. All of these technology improvements will greatly increase the power of any eight-way or higher SMP, especially when combined with Phase 2's n-node clustering for true linear scalability.

Bundled Cluster-ready Applications

Windows NT Enterprise Edition also includes "cluster-aware" versions of three back office-type applications. They are the following:

▼ *Microsoft Transaction Server 1.1*   Microsoft Transaction Server is defined as an environment, which makes it easier to develop and deploy high-performance, scalable Internet, intranet, and extranet applications. In essence, it is a transaction monitor. Version 1.0 was included in the Standard Edition of NT Server, and with the addition of MTS Service Pack 2A, it becomes version 1.1 with support for clustering. Cedar-type library support and an updated client config utility are included as well.

■ *Microsoft Message Queue Server 1.0*   Microsoft Message Queue Server is a store-and-forward messaging service that allows applications running at different times to communicate across various networks and systems that may be offline. MSMQ provides guaranteed message delivery, security, routing, and prioritization of messages in the queue. It is supplied in a standard version in other releases of NT Server 4.0. In NTS/E it is enhanced to support clustering and more concurrent users, along with advanced routing and gateways.

▲ *Microsoft Internet Information Server 3.02 (via SP3)*   Microsoft Internet Information Server is a network file and application server supplied in a standard version in other releases of NT Server 4.0 (along with Service Pack 3, which upgrades it from version 2.0 to 3.02).(Version 4.0 of IIS is also cluster-aware. An upgrade to this version can be found in the NT Option Pack.) In NTS/E it is clusterable to support higher availability. IIS supports HTTP, FTP, and Gopher protocols.

Other Applications Included with NTS/E

Other components and applications that are included are the following:

▼ *Windows NT Service Pack 3*   Windows NT Service Pack 3 contains updated versions of the software products listed below, as well as new components that add functionality to Microsoft Internet Information Server.

NOTE: Windows NT Service Pack 3 must be installed prior to attempting to install MSCS. This is done automatically after the successful installation of NTS/E (a pop-up dialog box asks if you wish to install it).

■ *Microsoft Index Server 1.1*   Index Server is a built-in search engine that provides full-text indexing, searching, and "hit highlighting" of many types of information in a variety of formats, including HTML, Microsoft Office, or text documents. Index Server provides a way to quickly locate specific information on intranet or Internet sites.

■ *Microsoft FrontPage 97*   FrontPage 97 Server Extensions allow one-button publishing and graphical site-management tools to keep information organized. FrontPage 97 Server Extensions enable users to develop their corporate intranet, Internet, and extranet sites.

▲ *Seagate Crystal Reports*   Crystal Reports is a client/server report writer that is used to create presentation-quality reports and integrate them into database applications. Crystal Reports is used to create reports from Web server log files and includes pre-formatted Web log reports.

INFORMATION RESOURCES FOR SUPPORTING WINDOWS NT ENTERPRISE EDITION

You can find valuable and timely information on each component of Windows NT Enterprise Edition on the two CD-ROM disks and on the Web. The following is a list of these places along with Web site locations for other materials pertinent to NTS/E and MSCS:

▼ *NT Enterprise Edition Administrator's Guide and Release Notes*   Located in two spots: as the readme.doc file in the root directory of both disk 1 and disk 2 and as a help book file in the Support/Books directory on disk 1 under the name of Ntseadm.hlp (or, to get all help books in one box, use either Book_cp.hlp or Book_net.hlp).

- *Evaluation Guide—A Guide to Evaluating Microsoft Windows NT Server, Enterprise Edition*   Located at **www.microsoft.com/NTServerEnterprise**.

- *Microsoft Cluster Server Release Notes*   This is the readme.doc file in the Mscs root directory on disk 2.

- *Microsoft Cluster Server Administrators Guide*   This is a help book file in the Support/Books directory on disk 1 under Mscsadm.hlp. Also included in this location is a series of Word files beginning with Mscsadm00.doc, going to Mscsadm0 through Mscsadm5, then to Mscsadma.doc and Mscsadmg.doc.

- *Supporting Microsoft Cluster Server: Course 958*   A course dedicated to MSCS offered by Microsoft Training. You can access information about this course at **www.microsoft.com/train_cert**. See Figure 2-6 for a look at its home Web page.

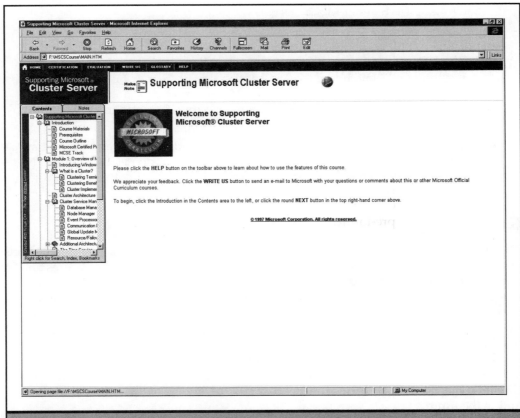

Figure 2-6.   Introduction page for Course 958

- *Frequently Asked Questions*   Microsoft has a list of questions associated with MSCS. You can access this list at **www.microsoft.com/ntserverenterprise/ support/clusterfaq.asp**.

- *Microsoft Windows NT Service Pack 3*   Under the SP3 directory on disk 1 is a readme.doc file with all the information on this service pack's contents and setup, along with an Adobe Acrobat PDF file, Nt4sp3.pdf, containing the same information.

- *Microsoft Internet Information Server*   Under the Iis30 directory on disk 2 is a directory called asp. Within this directory is an HTML type file readme that contains information on IIS3.0 and its modules. Also, in the last section in the Mscsadm.hlp book file is a section on setting up IIS under MSCS.

- *Microsoft Transaction Server*   Under the Mts directory on disk 2 is a readme.doc file containing a document entitled *Microsoft Transaction Server Version 1.1 Release Notes*. In the last section of the Mscsadm.hlp book file is a section on setting up MTS under MSCS.

- *Microsoft Message Queue Server*   Under the Msmq directory on disk 2 is a readme.txt file containing a document entitled *Microsoft Message Queue Server Release Notes*. Also, in the last section of the Mscsadm.hlp book file is a section on setting up Msmq under MSCS. Another useful source of information is an autorun HTML file used for setting up MSMQ and for getting information from the MSMQ Web site at **www.microsoft.com**; it's found in the Msmq directory on disk 2.

- ▲ Information on the latest problems, fixes, and workarounds can be found at **www.microsoft.com/support**. In the online search mode, select Windows NT Server as the platform, and enter **Enterprise**, **Cluster**, or another relevant term as your keyword for searching.

INTRODUCING MICROSOFT CLUSTER SERVER

Microsoft Cluster Server is intended to provide maximum availability of applications and other resources to clients on a network. It is designed to overcome failures and to support routine maintenance via failover to another server in the cluster. Failover is designed to be either automatic or manual, with management of the entire cluster from a central administration console, i.e., the GUI driven Cluster Administrator located on one node of the cluster or a designated administration worskstation. You can also use the CLI to control the cluster and to run scripts from

MSCS provides major improvements in availability, scalability, and manageability, but it is neither a panacea nor without its shortcomings. In the next few sections we will discuss its capabilities and how you can best take advantage of them (today, tomorrow, and in the future).

What It Can and Can't Do

Microsoft Cluster Server is not a cure-all. It cannot remedy all that ails Windows NT or computers in general, but it will increase the availability, scalability, and manageability of the majority of the applications residing on it (in comparison to any single server running the same applications). The following paragraphs explain some benefits (and shortcomings) of MSCS.

MSCS provides the ability to perform failover of applications (and their resources) and users to the surviving node when one node in a Phase 1 cluster becomes unavailable. This lack of server availability can take many forms. They include the following (in order of frequency of occurrence):

▼ CPU, memory, storage, or other hardware fault/failure

■ Software application failure or "hang"

■ Network or NIC card failure

■ Operator error

■ Routine and scheduled maintenance (i.e., software and hardware repair and/or upgrades or setup)

■ Localized power outage

■ Localized catastrophic failure

▲ System slow-down due to server resource overload

In any of these scenarios, the active node has its user workload and resources failover to the surviving node via the cluster manager when it detects an outage (i.e., loss of heartbeat). This failover typically takes from 30 to 90 seconds, with most users not knowing anything has changed. Obviously, in order for this to work, both nodes must have the same applications residing on them. Not all applications or resources need to failover. Only those that are critical or cluster-aware need to be enabled for failover and failback. Those that are not critical to supporting key business functions should not be set up for failover in order to keep server workloads within reason.

Failback of resources is also provided by MSCS. Failback occurs when the node that was previously unavailable is brought back online and is ready to resume its workload (in response to a reestablished heartbeat). User workloads and resources are then transferred back to their original node with virtually no interruption or loss of service. Once again, this transition takes 30 to 90 seconds in most cases and can be done either automatically or manually depending upon policies defined by the administrator.

Another benefit of MSCS is the scaling of applications when an application has the ability to divide its workload among nodes (cluster-aware databases only), while sharing a common data set. Databases are typically one type of application with such capabilities. Microsoft SQL Server 6.5EE and Oracle Parallel Server are examples of such applications (SQL Server 6.5EE uses symmetric virtual servers to achieve scalability, as opposed to the parallelization used by OPS).

Improved manageability is another benefit provided by MSCS. This occurs when multiple servers running disparate applications are consolidated onto an MSCS cluster. In this scenario, increased SMP CPU counts are utilized, along with improved availability provided by the cluster itself. Supporting these larger capacity servers is the use of so-called virtual servers, which appear to users as dedicated systems but actually only exist within the framework of the cluster itself. These consolidated and better protected applications can now be controlled via one GUI administrator while appearing as a single system image to end users.

MSCS Phase 1 Benefits and Shortcomings

MSCS Phase 1 provides a well-defined cluster-aware Win32 API. This API currently supports application types that utilize the shared-nothing architecture of MSCS. Shared-disk architectures, along with their Distributed Lock Managers (DLMs—from Oracle and others) will be supported in future releases of MSCS and its cluster-aware API. This API provides system status, cluster communications, and recovery feature access. MSCS Phase 1, however, cannot do everything that is needed to meet the requirements of enterprise computing.

The following are a few of these shortcomings (many of which are addressed in future versions of the software):

▼ Only two nodes are available for failover/failback. N-node clustering is required to achieve true linear scalability, a must in meeting growing uptime and end user demand requirements. N-node clustering also supports true "takeover" of failed applications without loss of data in transit (i.e., fault-tolerance).

■ MSCS is not lock-step fault tolerant. It does not support the movement of running applications to the level of 99.9X percent availability. However, much higher levels of availability than any standalone server are achieved, through the use of NT Server's inherent fault-management capabilities as well as through MSCS clustering.

■ MSCS Phase 1 is unable to recover a shared state, i.e., transactions on the fly can be lost. When transaction-type data is in transit between a client and the server and the server fails before it has confirmed/recorded the transaction, the process must be re-created using rollback and restart from the log files. MSCS's philosophy is that all client/server transactions should be atomic, following the Atomic Consistent Isolated Durable rule.

■ MSCS Phase 1 cannot recover from a failure of the quorum resource drive/volume. If the quorum resource is permanently corrupted (i.e., hardware RAID unrecoverable failure), then the cluster cannot be formed, and all unprotected (non-backed up) resource data will be lost. Microsoft has provided several utilities to repair a damaged QR as well as to start up the cluster without one, but both require prior knowledge of the clusters configuration and database in order to rebuild it. If this information is unavailable due to a catastrophic failure, then recovery is limited or unavailable in most cases and you must rebuild the cluster from scratch. Chapters 3 and 4 provide more information on the quorum resource and its requirements, while Appendix A discusses a number of the options available to better protect it.

- MSCS Phase 1 does not support very-large-memory (VLM) configurations (more than 2^{32} bytes of addressable memory) for use with distributed database systems. This will be increased in steps, first when the NT 5.0 release of MSCS Phase 1 is made available and then in the Phase 2 release of MSCS.

▲ MSCS Phase 1 is available only for use on specific platforms and configurations. A list of specific Microsoft-validated configurations is available as a hardware compatibility list (HCL) from Microsoft at **www.microsoft.com/ ntserverenterprise**. In the near future, each of the early adopter partners will have the option of "self-certifying" other configurations of their products in respect to MSCS.

NOTE: This means that you cannot, for the most part, cobble together a cluster from servers that you have lying around your shop. You must use validated configurations, with all components being identical (down to the firmware and software revision level). MSCS Phase 1 does not support the use of dissimilar servers or those from different vendors to form a cluster. Interim releases of Phase 1 or those from specific vendors (Digital) may support mixed configurations in the near future.

Despite these shortcomings, MSCS Phase 1 brings substantial increases in availability, scalability, and manageability to the world of Windows NT Server. Over time, MSCS will evolve into a much more robust product, with greater capabilities and true fault-tolerance. This evolution is expected to occur over the next two to three years as NT 5.0 is released, along with MSCS Phase 2.

Implementation Roadmap

Chapter 1 outlined the history of clusters and much of the rationale as to why Microsoft chose their overall approach to clustering. This section discusses the specifics of MSCS Phase 1 and the approach that Microsoft chose in terms of the architecture and development path for this iteration of MSCS.

Figure 2-7 details the overall MSCS Object Element architecture. This architecture features a number of basic object elements (six in total). Each of these elements has a well-defined roll and provides specific functionality to MSCS. These basic elements are the following:

Element	Function
The Resource/Failover Manager	Resource management
The Event Processor	Event passing and Cluster Service initialization
The Database Manager	Configuration database management
The Global Update Manager	Atomic updates to all cluster members
The Node Manager	Cluster membership management
The Communications Manager	Inter-node communications

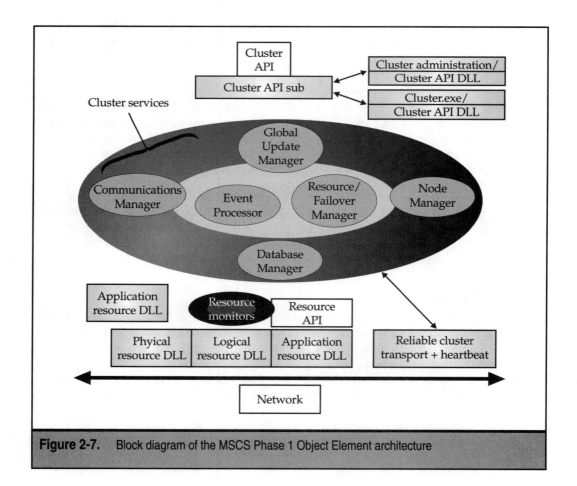

Figure 2-7.   Block diagram of the MSCS Phase 1 Object Element architecture

The following sections describe these six main object elements.

The Resource/Failover Manager

The Resource/Failover Manager is responsible for the following

▼ Managing resource dependencies

■ Starting and stopping resources by directing the Resource Monitors to bring resources online and offline

▲ Initiating failover and failback

In supporting these tasks the Resource/Failover Manager receives resource and cluster state information from the Node Manager and Resource monitors. When a resource becomes unavailable due to a fault or outage, the Resource/Failover Manager attempts to restart the resource on its primary node and, failing that, initiates a failover of the resource to the surviving node. This activity is referred to as "pushing a group" to another node.

The Event Processor

The Event Processor is responsible for all communications within the cluster. It is also responsible for connecting events to applications and other components of the Cluster Service. These activities include the following:

▼ Maintenance of cluster objects

■ Response to application requests to open, close, or enumerate cluster objects

■ Communicating signal events to cluster-aware applications and services, as well as other components of the Cluster Service

▲ Starting the Cluster Service and bringing the node to an offline state for processing by the Node Manager to make it a part of a cluster

The Database Manager

The Database Manager is responsible for creating and managing the cluster database, a key component of the Cluster Service. The database contains data about the cluster, the resource types, and failover groups. A copy of this database is stored in the registry of each node (see Chapter 10).

Each node has a database manager, which is synched up using the Quorum Resource. The DM, via the Cluster Service, provides access to the cluster's configuration database, as well as coordinating updates to the registry and facilitating atomic updates across the cluster.

The Global Update Manager

The Global Update Manager provides update services to all other components in the Cluster Service. It allows for changes in the online/offline state of resources and updates all parts of the cluster when these changes are made.

The Node Manager

The Node Manager provides the heartbeat of the cluster. This heartbeat consists of messages sent once per second (this is a default value) between the nodes in the cluster to determine the health and status of each node and its communications paths. When the Node Manager encounters a heartbeat fault it signals the Resource/Failover Manager to provide failover services. The Node Manager also initiates failover if all components of the Cluster Service are not functional on any node. The Node Manager utilizes the Quorum Resource to arbitrate which node has survived and designated resources fail over to it.

The Communication Manager

All components of the Cluster Service communicate with counterparts on other nodes via the Communication Manager. The Communication Manager is responsible for the following types of inter-node communications:

Component	Type of Communication
KeepAlive protocol	Cluster Service Failure Check
Resource group push	Failover initiation
Resource ownership negotiation	Failover resource ownership
Resource state transitions	Resource status tracking—all nodes in the cluster
Enlist and join a cluster	Initial communications and start-up of new cluster members
Database updates	Two-phase commit control for Cluster Service database updates

MSCS Main Activities

In conjunction with the six object elements composing MSCS are a number of processes and activities critical to the cluster's operation. In order to better understand how MSCS functions, I have included detailed descriptions of these activities.

Name Abstraction

Name abstraction is a central concept to all clustering implementations. In clusters you remove the physical links and dependencies to where the actual name existed (this name can either be the server itself or the applications that reside on it). The original name no longer exists within the context of a specific node/server, but "floats" as necessary around the cluster. This same logic is true for other types of services and resources. This process allows you to take an application or a service and move it to anywhere it can run on a cluster without users ever knowing.

NOTE: MSCS relies on the use of virtual servers that have defined network names, IP addresses, services, storage devices, and other resources, but are in essence a subset of the cluster overall. Users address these virtual servers without ever interfacing directly with the cluster or its nodes by name or IP address.

Quorum Resource

Another central concept to all clusters, the quorum resource, is a disk and/or volume that arbitrates for a resource (during cluster startup and after failure detection) using the challenge/defense protocol (see Figure 2-8). The quorum resource determines cluster ownership by allowing only one server (node) to know the clusters' configuration and to act as the decision-maker for cluster services. The quorum resource also stores the cluster registry and logs. It also tracks changes to the configuration database in MSCS when any member is missing or inactive to prevent temporal partitions, or "split-brain" phenomena, that can occur when changed configuration data is not updated (see the Node Manager description for more information). The quorum resource was one of the intellectual property items contributed by Digital Equipment in its 1995 Strategic Alliance with Microsoft.

Cluster Heartbeat

The cluster heartbeat is central to clustering as it depends upon the namespace as well as the quorum device. It provides the means for the quorum resource to determine which node owns it, as well as to determine the status of the regroup function. In practice it is the

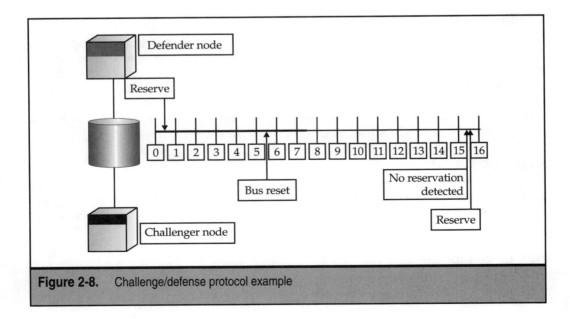

Figure 2-8. Challenge/defense protocol example

private (or public) network connection between the nodes in the cluster. (See the Node Manager description for more information.)

Cluster Log

The cluster log provides details of what's happening in the cluster service. It is also used to provide abstractions for cluster-aware applications to use. Information for use by applications includes cluster registry, failover manager, and namespace impersonation.

Membership

Membership is used to add and remove active nodes from the cluster on an orderly basis. A defined cluster is all the nodes in that particular cluster (by name and IP address), with an active cluster being a subset of that cluster comprised of the active nodes and the quorum resource. (See the Communication Manager description for more information.)

Regroup

Regroup functions by recomputing the members of the cluster. Each node in the cluster sends a heartbeat message to its peers at a rate of once per second (default setting). If two or more messages are lost, regroup occurs based on the suspicion that the sending node is inactive. Based upon the results of the use of a five-round protocol, the cluster agrees (or does not agree) to regroup after checking communications amongst the nodes. The cluster manager informs the upper levels of the cluster hierarchy of the event (via the global update); see the Node Manager section for further information. Tandem contributed the algorithm for this function to MSCS.

Global Update

Global update propagates global updates to all nodes in the cluster. It is also responsible for maintaining the replicated cluster registry. Updates are propagated based on an algorithm that uses a "locker node," typically the oldest node in the cluster (or the first one added) that receives update messages from the cluster, updates itself, and then sends the message on to the next oldest node on the cluster for the same type of processing. The global update was one of the intellectual property contributions made by Tandem to MSCS in its 1996 Strategic Alliance agreement with Microsoft.

Cluster Registry

A separate registry from the local Windows NT registry, the cluster registry maintains updates on members, resources, restart parameters, and other configuration-oriented information. The local Windows NT Registry contains a copy of this registry data as well. (See the Database Manager section for more information.)

Resource Monitor

The resource monitorr object provides polling functions to check to see which nodes are alive or not. It detects failures via polling or from failure events (log interface). The resource monitor receives messages from the failover manager in terms of when to restart the cluster. (See the Resource/Failover Manager section for more information.)

Failover Manager

The failover manager assigns groups to nodes based on failover parameters such as resource availability and what services are available on the node in particular. Resources in a node that can be moved in a failover include the following:

- ▼ Windows NT services
- ■ Applications
- ■ SCSI-attached disks
- ■ TCP/IP addresses
- ■ Network names
- ■ File shares
- ■ Print spoolers
- ■ IIS virtual roots for WWW, FTP, and Gopher
- ■ Time services
- ▲ Others based upon custom DLLs developed with the Microsoft Cluster Server Software Developers Kit (SDK)

This movement during a failover is based on the understanding that these resources can run on only one node at a time. (See the Resource/Failover Manager section for more information.)

Time Service

The time service within a cluster is critical and must increase monotonically; otherwise, applications can become confused, disoriented, or even psychotic. Time is maintained within failover resolution, which is not hard because it may take up to 90 seconds. Time also exists as a resource in the cluster so one node may own it with the others periodically correcting their drift from it (as a reference). Time also becomes even more relative in a cluster when you accept the fact that for some applications it may take up to ten minutes before it will failover manually due to DLL (dynamic link library) and timeout delays.

Deployment Considerations

In regard to deploying MSCS, it is absolutely necessary to know up-front the capabilities and shortcomings of this product. Having this knowledge will then allow you to capitalize on its strengths completely while developing a plan to minimize risk based upon its weaknesses.

A key area to focus on in planning this deployment is to identify early on those specific applications that are both critical to the enterprise and cluster-ready (much less those that are cluster-aware). This will allow planners to set expectation and performance levels accordingly without false starts and mid-course corrections. It will also allow you to examine how to bootstrap those legacy applications that need to be either migrated and replaced with newer versions or made cluster-aware via one of the many methods currently available.

SUMMARY

In this chapter I have discussed in detail Windows NT Server Enterprise Edition, a major upgrade to the standard edition of NT Server. Windows NT Server/E is intended to attract the attention of a specific audience: enterprise computing users. At four times the cost of the standard edition of NT Server, this edition provides much of what this community has been looking for in terms of improvements in availability, scalability, and manageability. Not the last word from Microsoft by any means, this edition is the first phase of many in respect to continuous improvements in these key areas.

In Chapter 3, I will deal with the specifics of planning for the deployment of MSCS (and NT Server/E's other features), while in Chapter 4, I will go through an installation and set up these products based on specific application scenarios.

CHAPTER 3

Planning for the Deployment of Your MSCS Cluster

lanning for the orderly integration of clusters into your computing environment should not be considered an onerous exercise by any means. It's more of a thought-provoking process that is required in order to maximize the potential for successful utilization of this technology. This planning effort eliminates, for the most part, those fits and starts found in situations where one is generally flying by the seat of one's pants in terms of deploying new technology. Cluster planning requires a good knowledge of the challenges, in terms of what you are trying to achieve with your cluster, as well as the capabilities and nuances of the clustering solution being planned. I will endeavor to bring to the forefront the types of challenges that can be overcome by using clusters as well as the pragmatics needed to get there.

This chapter will provide a detailed perspective on what MSCS can and cannot do and what deployment model is most synergistic in terms of meeting your particular requirements. I will also discuss those few cases where it is inappropriate to use MSCS (or any other NT clustering solution available in the market) to try and solve a more global problem.

MSCS CONCEPTS AND DEPLOYMENT MODELS

Microsoft Cluster Server (MSCS) Phase 1 is in essence a two-node failover/failback clustering environment. It is generally described as a high-availability solution for use in those situations where a standalone server (such as uniprocessor or SMP) is simply not reliable or powerful enough to meet the $24 \times 7 \times 52$ (many computing shops today run three non-stop production shifts on a 24 hours/day, 7 days/week, 52 weeks/year basis) requirements of the organization. Even with the most robust components and the design and manufacturing technologies used today, the majority of commercially available SHV servers and OSs only provide 9 percent (or slightly greater) availability out of the box on an annual basis. This lack of availability can be improved by adding redundant components and data paths, along with using a nonstop type operating system. However, this approach generally adds significant costs and complexities to the solution and flies in the face of the Windows NT cost model, which promotes low-cost and high-functionality. The Windows NT operating system provides some availability enhancement support (via RAID, UPS, preemptive multitasking, protected memory, file system journaling, NTFS, etc.), but stops short of meeting the 98 to 99.XX percent availability that many end-user organizations now demand.

NOTE: Using the most common configurations and methods of measurement show that Windows NT performs at about the 96.5 percent availability level out of the box, so to speak.

To achieve even higher levels of resource uptime, one needs to employ a well-known high-availability method, such as clustering. MSCS in theory provides some 99.9X percent of system and resource uptime, which can be enhanced further by the use of remote disk mirroring and other single-point-of-failure reduction methods from providers such as Vinca and Octopus. In this chapter, I will focus solely on MSCS, and I will discuss these ancillary products in Chapter 6.

NOTE: Marathon Technologies provides NT server solutions that not only eliminate potential single points of failure through redundant component path architectures, but add MSCS to their servers for increased availability and improved manageability. For more information, go to **www.marathontechnologies.com**.

Two-Node High-Availability Clustering

Two-node clusters are the most prevalent configuration in the world of clustering; they make up 88 percent of clusters. (More than 250,000 clusters of all types are in use today worldwide.) The majority of end users of two-node clusters are looking for high-availability as the primary benefit from this type of solution. Scalability is next in importance, for the most part, although it is sometimes tied with manageability as the number two benefit of clustering (most scalability clusters are four nodes or larger in configuration). In a two-node cluster solution, most end users find that scalability improvements are icing on the cake by having a more reliable computing environment that, "oh, by the way," performs better and is managed as a single entity without increased complexity. (Manageability improvements exist with any cluster type due to the ability to consolidate servers under the control of one management interface, as well as through the use of virtual servers to replace dedicated single-function solutions.) These benefits are often under-appreciated when one speaks about why clustering should be used to meet a particular computing challenge, but they exist nonetheless.

High-availability in a two-node configuration is realized via running instances of critical applications on both nodes of the cluster. When one node becomes unavailable or its responsiveness slows (usually due to an outage), the surviving node starts up its copy of that particular application and prepares to take over the workload and user connections from the failed node (these resources are transferred from the failed node to the surviving node by the cluster manager). This process can take tens of seconds to several minutes, depending upon the type of application and its network resources (e.g., hard connection versus connectionless), as well as the operational mode of the cluster (e.g., Active/Active versus Active/Standby). These availability enhancements mean dramatically reduced levels of downtime; sometimes hours per week or month can be reduced to minutes per month, worst case (99.XX percent availability). This equates into significant increases in operational efficiency, as well as reductions in loss of business opportunity and worker productivity.

In a two-node clustering environment (regardless of which architectural/operational model is utilized), one node is usually considered "primary" with the other considered "secondary." This nomenclature has nothing to do with who is higher on the food chain or more muscular, but refers to the roles that the two nodes have in terms of owning the quorum resource and other cluster resources. With few exceptions, the node that comes online first takes ownership of this resource (the QR for short) and becomes the cluster resource manager and database administrator. (One clear exception is when the primary node fails to start its cluster server or has public or private network failures on startup.) Owning the quorum resource makes it the primary node by default. In so-called "clusters in a box," the node that comes online first is usually processor number one in terms of power-up sequencing, and in those situations where two standalone processors are used, either node could come up first, depending upon the power distribution scheme.

Cluster Models

Clusters can be implemented in more than one fashion. There are two basic models, the Active/Active and the Active/Standby (or Inactive if you prefer), along with five or more variants of these two. These models provide the systems designer and other IT architects with a wide range of choices of how to deploy MSCS for the particular type of application(s) that will reside on it, as well as the types of benefits that the planner is looking for. I will explore these in more detail in the coming pages with particular emphasis on choosing the right model for the particular benefits you are looking to achieve in your IT environment.

The Basics

In clustering there are two fundamental (although not necessarily mutually exclusive) methods for implementing a two-node (or even N-node) cluster. With Active/Active, both nodes can support independent workloads during normal operation and then assume additional workloads during failover (the surviving node assumes this new but temporary workload). Or, as found with Active/Standby, one node (the Standby node) can completely back up the other (the Active node) should it fail while assuming a standby mode during normal operations. In this mode the standby server is not supporting an independent workload but is up and running, waiting for failover of the Active node and its workload. I will further explore the distinctions between these operating modes in the following chapters.

ACTIVE/ACTIVE CLUSTERS In Active/Active mode, both nodes are allowed to have varying workloads and applications residing on them. They each perform work independent of the other, with instances of those applications set up for failover/failback residing on both nodes (note that two licenses are required for each cluster for these cluster-aware applications). These active applications should not conflict with each other if at all possible (the exception is file and print services or those applications being operated in the symmetrical virtual server mode—SQL Server 6.5 EE). For example, if node 1 is running MS IIS with node 2 as its designated failover, node 2 should not be running MS IIS (with its own resources and clients) simultaneously (and vice versa). Otherwise, when either node fails over, the surviving node will be required to close out its own IIS activities and then restart IIS with the failed node's resources. This definitely does not improve availability by any measurement method. In addition, both nodes need to be sized appropriately in terms of their CPU horsepower, memory, and storage capacity. For example, if node 1's workload (those applications marked for failover/failback) is approximately 50 percent of the server's capabilities, then node 2 needs to have at least that amount in excess capacity (and vice versa) to be able to successfully take over the failed workload. This requirement can be abated temporarily by manually closing out low priority applications on the surviving node when a failover occurs. This should be considered a short-term bandage and not an appropriate fix to an inadequate resource problem.

ACTIVE/STANDBY CLUSTERS In Active/Standby mode, the active node is online and doing work while the inactive node sits in a "hot standby" mode waiting for any type of failure to occur on the primary node. Both nodes are active in respect to having formed a cluster, with essentially one being a duplicate of the other in terms of having instances of all those applications that will failover/failback residing on it (again two separate licenses are required for each of these applications on the cluster). In this mode, the standby server may be smaller in memory and storage capacities because it is sized only for the workload that it must support during failover. This mode of operation is the most inefficient in many respects because the standby node is utilized only in the event of a failure, but it does allow for the smoothest failover and failback because its only purpose is to support the primary node. To achieve this quick transfer, the standby node has the failover-designated applications up and running, just waiting for the other resources (physical disk, network name, IP address, etc.) to transfer over during a failover. Oracle uses this mode for its Fail Safe product, which resides on top of MSCS and provides for the highest levels of availability for users of their standard Oracle 8 database (non-OPS).

Figure 3-1 is a typical two-node MSCS cluster.

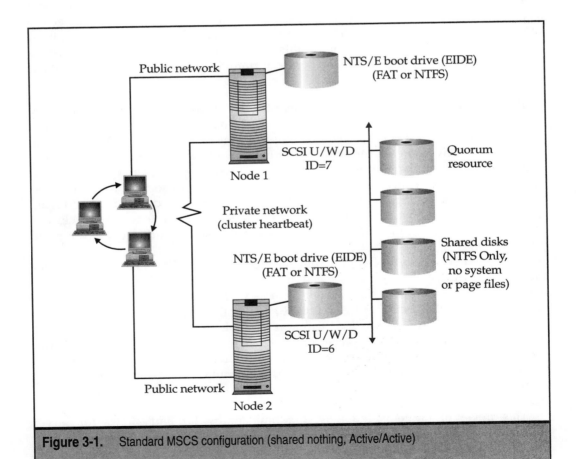

Figure 3-1.   Standard MSCS configuration (shared nothing, Active/Active)

COMMON REQUIREMENTS   No matter which mode you choose for your two-node cluster, both nodes must have instances of those applications, which are designated for failover/failback, installed on them. Because the licensing fees can be costly, you should set up your two-node cluster only for those applications that are critical and can actually benefit from a two-node configuration. These include File Servers, Print Spoolers, Internet and Messaging, as well as specific cluster-aware applications from Microsoft and other companies.

NOTE: Cluster-aware File and Print services are included with NTS/E, along with IIS and other applications.

Cluster Deployment Models

When utilizing MSCS Phase 1 in your production environment, there are a number of ways to configure your cluster to best achieve desired results. In each of the five models, there are varying benefits, most of which are specific to the mode of operation being advocated. When choosing one of these particular modes for deployment, you need to recognize that the mode chosen defines how the cluster can operate on an overall basis and that there are few options to change this once you have it up and running. There is also little flexibility in these models in terms of running more than one on a particular cluster.

HIGH-AVAILABILITY WITH STATIC LOAD BALANCING   This model provides high-availability with basic performance with one node online and maximum performance when both nodes are online. This is a classic Active/Active implementation where both nodes make their resources available in the form of virtual servers, which can be detected and accessed by clients. Capacities on each node are structured such that they can run at optimum performance during normal operation, with somewhat diminished performance when having to assume the workload of a failed node during failover. Figure 3-2 depicts this type of two-node cluster. This is the trade-off that all Active/Active clusters have to make—high-availability versus reduced performance during failures, a small price to pay given the results.

Static load balancing in shared nothing clusters is achieved by sizing the nodes for their normal workloads (e.g., CPU speed, memory, and storage), with some degree of over-capacity to handle the failover workload as well. This requires prior knowledge about failover applications that are configured during the setup of your cluster.

Recommended applications for this mode of deployment run the gamut, ranging from file and print services where each node has a share set up on it (file sharing and print spooling), to symmetric virtual servers type applications such as SQL Server 6.5 EE. Cluster policies are structured such that each group defaults to a preferred server during normal operation, with both nodes being enabled for failback of these groups once the resources on the preferred server are re-established.

This mode of usage is the most predominant by far and allows for server consolidation efforts across the enterprise, as well as supporting much higher availability of related applications (which are typically run on separate servers). Both of these

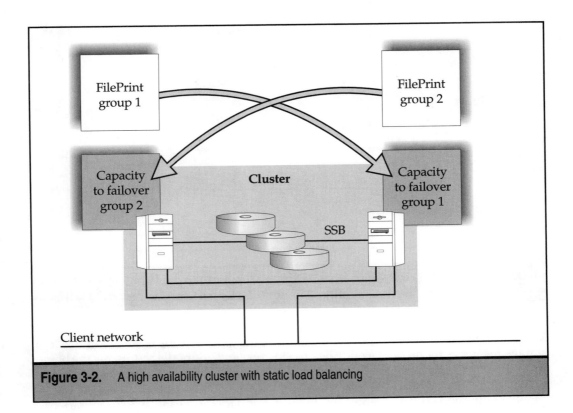

Figure 3-2.   A high availability cluster with static load balancing

attributes dramatically improve the total cost of ownership of these servers/applications and provide major improvements in system uptime (especially for critical services and applications).

HOT-SPARE WITH MAXIMUM AVAILABILITY   This model utilizes the Active/Standby cluster mode. It provides maximum availability and no performance degradation during failover for business-critical type applications but does require an investment in hardware and software that sits idle most of the time. This model is implemented by Oracle for their Fail-Safe solution, as well as by Vinca with their Standby-Server (which is not based on MSCS). As you might expect, this is the second most used model for clusters and has very straightforward benefits for those that choose it. Figure 3-3 is a block diagram of this type of deployment model.

To review a more detailed explanation on this model, see the previous section, "Active/Standby Clusters."

PARTIAL CLUSTER SOLUTION   This model, for all practical purposes, is really how most users will employ MSCS. In it are a mixture of applications/resources that can failover/failback (i.e., are cluster-aware), along with those that cannot (are non-cluster-aware). The cluster-aware applications are set up in a normal manner under

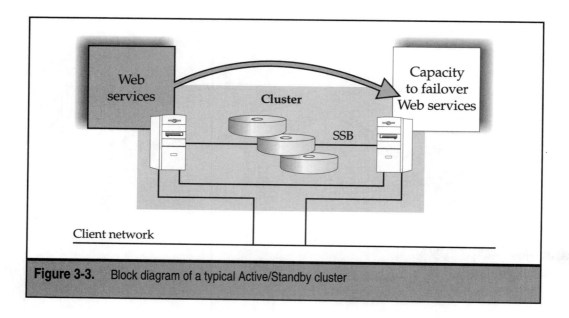

Figure 3-3.   Block diagram of a typical Active/Standby cluster

MSCS using shared storage resources, and those that are non-cluster-aware utilize local storage resources found on the node where they reside. This model represents the best of both worlds in terms of maximum server utilization, while gaining the benefits of clustering where possible. Figure 3-4 illustrates this type of cluster model. The main benefit of this mode is that it represents the real world for most users who run a variety of applications and services on their servers. As the applications and services become truly business-critical, the customers can elect to purchase cluster-aware versions to be added to the cluster.

VIRTUAL SERVER ONLY (NO FAILOVER)   This model utilizes the MSCS virtual server concepts without having formed a cluster; that is, it can be supported on any node that has a MSCS cluster server running. Figure 3-5 is a diagram of this type of model. In principal, you can install MSCS on one node only, use the Cluster Administrator to define failover groups, and then define and add resources to create virtual servers on any desired type. These servers appear to end users as dedicated servers, but are a virtual subset of your single-node cluster. This can be especially handy when servers are down and you need a quick fix to keep your end users happy. It is not necessarily recommended as a permanent mode of operation, but it is one that can prove to be quite useful in many circumstances (assuming that you are willing to spend the money for licenses of NTS/E for stand-alone servers).

Microsoft describes it as "a method of organizing resources for the convenience of administrators and clients." Given the challenges of getting MSCS up and running, much less optimized, this method can be regarded as a way of "walking before you run" in terms of deploying MSCS in a production environment.

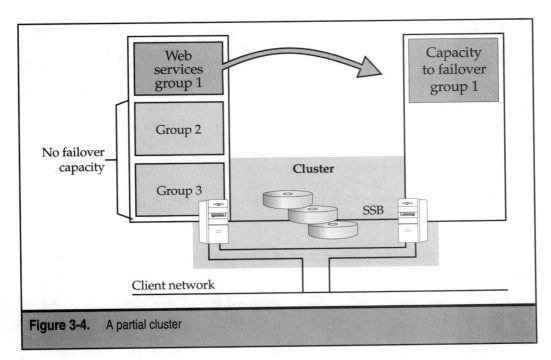

Figure 3-4.   A partial cluster

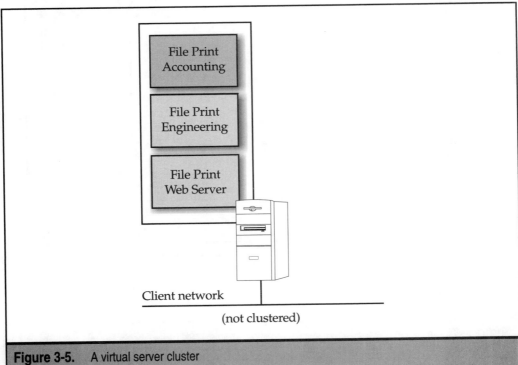

Figure 3-5.   A virtual server cluster

HYBRID SOLUTION   The hybrid model is a combination of all the others previously described. A growing number of actual deployments of MSCS will employ this model based on the pragmatics that each IS organization must contend with today. In some situations each node, with its own specific applications, provides failover and failback to the other node with its own specific applications. The applications on each of these nodes will not be related, and some will not be cluster-aware at all. But in a properly configured cluster, they can all coexist and take advantage to varying degrees of the myriad of benefits that a MSCS Phase 1 cluster supplies. Figure 3-6 shows a hybrid cluster model.

Regardless of which of these five models (or others that you run across) that you use for your particular environment, all of them provide some tangible benefits when using MSCS Phase 1. Higher availability and improved manageability are the primary benefits to be derived from these models, with some scalability enhancements in modes that utilize virtual symmetric servers.

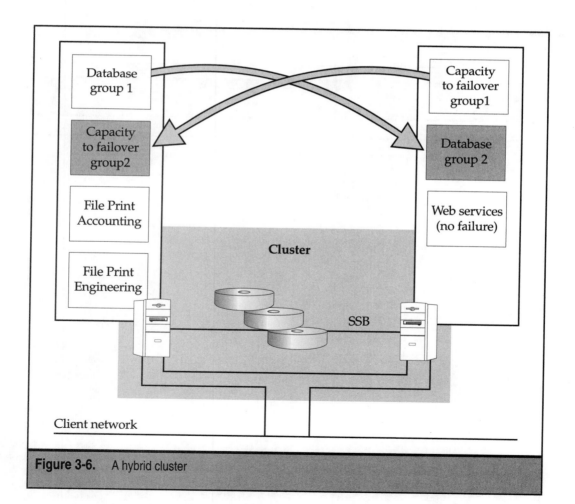

Figure 3-6.   A hybrid cluster

The Limitations of MSCS

As mentioned before, MSCS is not a universal remedy for all that ails your computing environment (neither is any cluster, for that matter). In MSCS Phase 1, the main benefits derived are high availability, manageability, and to some limited extent, scalability. MSCS and most other clustering solutions in spite of their overall abilities cannot overcome the following scenarios:

▼ Overall network outages

■ RAID set failure (more than two parity drives lost or two stripe sets lost on logical volumes)

■ Sustained power outages (beyond what local and distributed UPS systems can support)

■ Database file failures (except in those cases where a replication server is available)

■ Loss of data due to operator error

■ Failure of more than one node (Phase 1)

▲ Complete loss of the quorum resource (MSCS's single point of failure)

These types of problems are beyond the fault-tolerant capabilities of most Windows NT computing systems (other than Marathon's Endurance series), so they should not be necessarily regarded as fundamental limitations of MSCS or clustering in general, but they should be considered when planning and deploying your cluster solution.

Cluster Hardware Deployment Requirements

When planning to deploy an MSCS cluster, you need to choose a minimum hardware configuration to support your requirements. For the most part, both nodes will be part of the same configuration, but in some cases the secondary node only plays a backup or standby role and therefore does not need to be as large or robust as the primary node. This does not mean, however, that the second node should not meet the minimum overall requirements.

Minimum Hardware Requirements

Microsoft and its hardware partners have certified a growing number of basic configurations for use with MSCS. These configurations are found on a Hardware Compatibility List that Microsoft maintains on its Web site at **www.microsoft. com/hwtest/hcl**. At this site you will find complete system configurations (called *clusters*), with separate lists for SCSI adapters, fibre channel adapters, and RAID systems.

The minimum hardware configurations to be used by anyone planning for and deploying MSCS are as follows.

NOTE: All of these components appear on Microsoft's Hardware Compatibility List for MSCS, as well as conforming to the recently-announced joint MS/Intel Windows NT Server 5.0 Hardware Developers Specification.

CPU:

▼ IA-32 Pentium Pro 200MHz with 512KB L2 cache (minimum 1MB recommended). See Figure 3-7 for a photograph of an Intel IA-32 (Pentium Pro 200) processor

▲ IA-32 Deschutes 400MHz or higher

Memory:

▼ Up to 4GB in total if you are running large, cluster-aware applications

■ 64MB minimum, 128MB recommended (Windows NTS/E and MSCS support only)

■ 300MB recommended (file and print services support only)

▲ Up to 4GB in total capacity for supporting OS and applications per node

Figure 3-7.   Intel IA-32 processor (Pentium Pro 200)

Disk Storage:

▼ EIDE or SCSI boot disk: 4.0GB (minimum) (Windows NT Enterprise Edition and utilities)

■ Quorum resource: 1GB+ shared SCSI (hardware RAID 0+1 configuration recommended)

▲ Shared SCSI: Multiple 4–9GB+ drives with 2GB partitions

NOTE: A second disk in the 4–6GB capacity range can be added to support non-cluster-aware applications.

Storage Interconnection:

▼ SCSI-2 fast/wide/differential

■ Ultra-SCSI wide/differential

■ IBM SSA

■ Fibre channel—Arbitrated Loop (FC-AL)

▲ Fibre channel—Switched fabric

Internetworking:

▼ Public network

   ■ 100Mb Ethernet

   ■ FDDI

   ■ ATM

   ■ Gbit Ethernet

▲ Private network

   ■ Tandem ServerNet

   ■ 100Mb Ethernet

   ■ Fibre channel—switched fabric

   ■ SCI (Scalable Coherent Interface)

   ■ Gbit Ethernet

Table 3-1 provides rule-of-thumb recommendations for CPU configurations (uniprocessor vs. SMP).

CPUS   The CPU recommendations in Table 3-1 are based on what most IT environments are experiencing as minimum configurations. As you can see, the high-end R-db's require

Cluster Application	Server Configuration	Initial Number of CPUs	Total CPU Capacity
File and print services (virtual server)	Uniprocessor	1	2
High-availability file and print services	SMP	2	4
IIS 3.0/4.0	SMP	2	4
MMQS	SMP	1	2
MTS	SMP	1	4
Exchange 5.5 EE	SMP	2	8^+
SQL Server 6.5 EE	SMP	4	8^+
Oracle 8.0	SMP	4	8
Lotus Domino	SMP	4	8

Table 3-1. Recommended Server Configurations for Particular Application Areas

the most capabilities in terms of the number of processors (not to mention memory and storage), with the mail and messaging solutions close behind. As of this writing, a number of eight-way SMPs have been announced, along with the introduction of the IA-32 Deschutes processor family. This family is expected to grow in speed to 700MHz or more prior to the introduction of the IA-64 Merced family. The Deschutes and Merced lines will coexist for some time well into the new millenium and offer upgrade paths in terms of processor speeds and word sizes. The Digital/Intel Alpha processor currently has speeds in excess of 1GHz and is available in a number of SMP sizes. It is anticipated that the eight-way SMP will be the commodity SHV configuration beginning in 1999. Twelve and 16-way SMPs in SHV configurations should begin to be available in the year 2000.

NOTE: No matter which CPU configuration you choose, you must plan additional capacity (for the CPU and memory) to support failover loads. Depending upon the deployment model you choose, this can be up to 100 percent (if the loads that are failing over are basically equivalent). The minimum requirement is at least 50 percent for most models.

STORAGE INTERCONNECTIONS AND NETWORKING   SCSI-2 and Ultra-SCSI are currently the standard topologies that most SHV servers are using. Both utilize multi-conductor copper cabling for interconnections and have finite overall lengths that can be supported without problems. They require active termination schemes at both ends of the cables and are available in differential and non-differential models for noise immunity improvement. For all MSCS deployments, the use of wide and differential modes is recommended (i.e., HBAs, bus cabling, and drives/controllers). Using this mode provides the best combination of noise immunity and speed, at a very attractive price.

Options for these hardwired SCSI interconnections (as opposed to using optical connections like fibre channel) include hubs and switches. These eliminate the issues and problems associated with using tri-link and "Y" cables as well as power up sequencing in terms of which node powers the SCSI bus first. They also provide well behaved terminations and high-impedance paths for failed HBAs (eliminating the potential to bring down the entire shared-storage bus in the cluster). The following series of figures represents a range of shared-storage interconnect options: Figure 3-8 shows MSCS with a

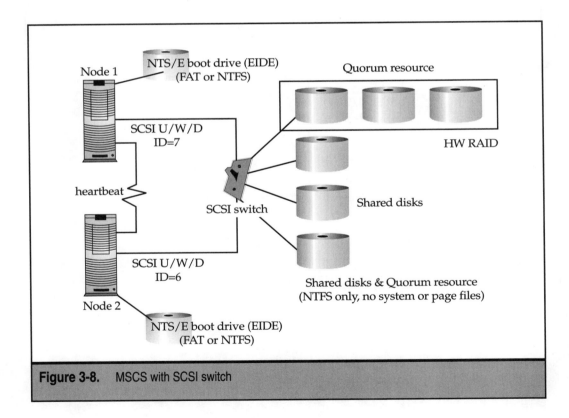

Figure 3-8.   MSCS with SCSI switch

SCSI switch, Figure 3-9 depicts MSCS with an SCSI hub configuration, and Figure 3-10 shows a standard shared SCSI MSCS configuration.

Networking device options for MSCS are wide and varied. When choosing the appropriate technology, you need to consider whether the technology is for public or private networks.

Public networks require a standard format that can be supported by the enterprise's infrastructure of hubs, routers, and switches, not to mention installed cabling. This does not necessarily limit your options; it just requires coordination with the networking side of the IT organization to determine which topology and technology are best.

The MSCS private network can be based on using the same public network connections (excluding NICs). This reduces overall network speed somewhat and decreases the clusters overall failure tolerance but is the least expensive. In light of these

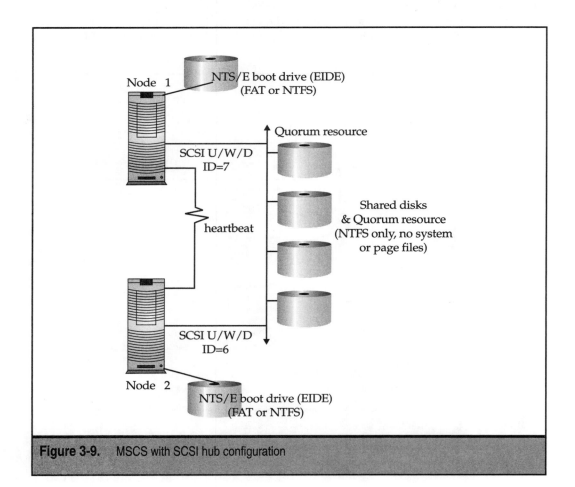

Figure 3-9. MSCS with SCSI hub configuration

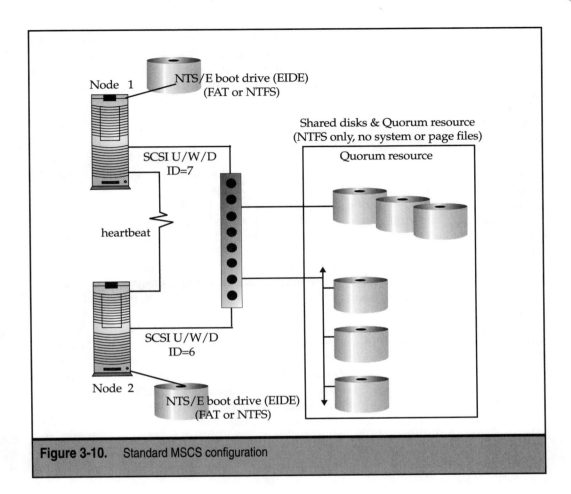

Figure 3-10.   Standard MSCS configuration

limitations, it is strongly recommended that a dedicated "cluster communications only" network be utilized. This network can utilize 10MB/s Ethernet (or IBM's Token Ring networking topology) all the way up to Tandem's ServerNet (ServerNet is part of the joint Intel/Microsoft/Compaq *VI Architecture Standard*) or fibre channel. These high-end technologies do not offer any performance improvement in MSCS Phase 1 for the most part, but will with Phase 2. They all feature a high-speed, low-latency performance envelope that is critical to transferring cluster and application data between nodes. The bottom line is that a dedicated private network is the best choice.

For both storage interconnections and networking, it is anticipated that system speeds of 1GB/s or higher will become the norm in the market within a short time (fibre channel [switched fabrics], SSA-2, ServerNet, Gb-Ethernet are all examples of multigigabit networking topologies in use today). All technology options in this area are quickly becoming commodities, and as MSCS matures to Phase 2, a high-speed private interconnect network will become paramount for moving cluster data within the nodes. These future options all have their own relative merits and should be well supported by MSCS.

STORAGE   Storage decisions for MSCS clusters need to be made for both local servers and shared-storage (which are usually SCSI devices).

The local node-based storage supports two functions. One is for booting NTSE/E, along with storing the tools, utilities, and applications that are required to support it. The other is for storing those non-cluster-aware applications that may be accessed through the cluster's virtual server IP addressing scheme but will not be shared with the other node or nodes (single node cluster in virtual server mode). Both of these requirements can be supported on either EIDE or SCSI drives resident within the server or via a second SCSI channel not shared with the rest of the cluster. EIDE controllers are built into most server motherboards today, so using an EIDE controller as the boot disk is very much the norm, although the use of SCSI is growing. In some cases, users prefer to use SCSI throughout, so the EIDE controller can be bypassed as the boot device in favor of a second SCSI HBA.

The second SCSI HBA not only supports the use of non-shared SCSI drives (boot and local storage) within the server/node and cluster but also allows for other peripheral devices such as tape backup and optical disk drives to be attached to this server. This can add great flexibility to any server/node and cluster without much cost or complexity. The use of both an EIDE boot drive for NTS/E and a second SCSI HBA to support these other peripherals is strongly recommended (if you do not already have two SCSI HBAs).

A number of choices is available for shared SCSI devices/solutions. Hardware RAID solutions definitely should be used for both the quorum resource (RAID 0+1 configuration), along with supporting those storage requirements for cluster-aware applications and data sets on each node of the cluster. Appendix A is devoted to discussing these storage solution options in detail and should be consulted for further information.

Finally, storage capacities (ironically enough, and storage appetites) will continue to double every 12 to 18 months for the foreseeable future, with costs-per-GB continuing to decrease equally as fast. Hardware RAID solutions will also continue to decline in price, with shared SCSI and RAID functionality projected to be built into most IA-32 and IA-64 motherboards in the very near future. This all bodes well for keeping overall storage costs low while maintaining high functionality, which is in concert with the overall Windows NT cost model.

Final Deployment Considerations

As I get down to the finish line here in terms of planning your MSCS deployment, you need to consider a couple of additional items before wrapping up this phase of the overall activity set. In this section, I will discuss how to organize your failover/failback application groupings, as well as how to design your MSCS cluster(s) domain model to fit easily into your organization's overall domain structure.

Defining Failover Groups

Prior to finally deploying your MSCS solution, you should take the time required to organize your applications and their associated resources into failover groups. These groups (and their associated resources) become the actual elements that are failed over and failed back. In essence each cluster-aware application will have a group consisting of many of the following:

▼   The cluster-aware application or service itself

■   The shared disk that it resides on (Physical Disk)

■   The network name and IP address

■   The spool folder (Print spoolers)

■   The share's name (SMB file share)

▲   Other dependent resources as required, such as Virtual Root

MSCS has built into it some very basic administration wizards that can be used to set up these groups and assign their resource; I will discuss them in Chapter 5 once MSCS is installed (the subject of Chapter 4) and running.

Domain Planning

MSCS supports three basic domain configurations:

▼   Independent servers configured as a cluster in the same domain

■   Two backup domain controllers in the same domain

▲   A primary and backup domain controller pair on the same domain

For many applications the preferred configuration is that of a PDC and BDC with the primary node being the PDC (for others the simplest is stand-alone servers). This keeps domain security manageable and, regardless of the status of the cluster, the domain is kept up and available. In addition, you must also re-establish domain trusts with other domains that this pair will need to communicate with. You should be aware that this mode does add additional overhead, which needs to be accounted for when planning capacity. The best approach is to locate all of your MSCS clusters under one domain, with one cluster configured as a PDC-BDC and all others as stand-alone servers. This produces the highest functionality with the lowest overhead.

Other applications such as MS SQL Server EE and MS MQS recommend that you set up each server as independent and use another server on the network as the domain controller.

As stated earlier, the simplest overall setup is to have all MSCS clusters on one domain that is controlled by a separate and independent PDC-BDC pair. This provides the following features:

▼ It eliminates access control problems among local groups and users.

■ Minimal resources are required to support logon and replication.

▲ The overall domain structure is more easy to manage and establish trust relationships within.

This overall domain configurations model can then be easily integrated into existing domains across the enterprise.

SUMMARY

Executing for the deployment of your MSCS solution requires doing some initial research and planning effort, which pays for itself in spades at a later date. A thorough checklist of areas to cover and specific items to look at in-depth is a real time saver and eliminates the need to start over from scratch at some point in the deployment if you missed setting an important criterion.

In the next chapter, I will install MSCS on our Tandem CS-150 "cluster in a box." This system is a two-node Pentium Pro SMP Server with ServerNet for private networking and Ethernet 100 for public networking and SCSI shared disks. It is a good representation of all the types of MSCS Phase 1 clusters available in the market today.

PART II

Deploying Your MSCS Cluster

CHAPTER 4

Installing and Configuring MSCS

One of the few sections in Microsoft's Cluster Administrator's Guide that is fairly concise is the one on how to install MSCS. However, you will find that many of the accepted practices they advocate and the simplicity of the installation that they infer can be far from the norm that you experience with your cluster. The purpose of this chapter is to provide the reader with an alternate view of how to install and configure MSCS for basic operation. Regardless of which treatise you choose to use in meeting your needs, it is critical that you have all your up-front cluster planning completed prior to installing MSCS. Having completed this activity in advance of your actual installation, you should then fully understand the implications of every parameter that you choose or configure during the process.

Much of this information will be moot if you have purchased a pre-configured cluster from one of the many vendors of such solutions. This section will become germane if you need to re-install MSCS at any later time or wish to upgrade existing server and storage assets to create a MSCS cluster.

PURSUING NIRVANA

Success in installing Microsoft Cluster Server can be measured in several ways.

▼ The ending dialog box pops up and tells you that you have "successfully installed MSCS" (which is the normal convention for Microsoft's install utilities). Figure 4-1 shows both the message pop-up as well as a service message in the Event Log. It is good practice to always look for both during all phases of using MSCS.

■ The ending dialog box tells you that you have successfully installed MSCS, and after you restart both nodes, MSCS actually forms a cluster with both nodes joining it.

▲ You can get both successful install messages and still have the system hang up and die on you even though the dreaded "blue screen of death" never reared its ugly head during the entire installation process. The blue screen of death is a type of "hang trap condition" which occurs when a software failure halts operation of the CPU. This type of failure requires a power-down restart, something that is a complete anathema to high- availability computing and is frequently encountered when installing Windows NT on unstable systems.

You will quickly learn when you do a full installation of NTS/E that if you make any type of configuration error, you will have to start over (many times on both nodes) with a fresh installation (the next illustration depicts one of those start-from-square one situations). Experiencing this frustrating scenario several times will teach you to make sure that you not only have all your information about your cluster plan ready before you start, but that you never divert from the standard set of procedures for installing either NTS/E or MSCS. Thankfully, in most cases NTS/E and MSCS will be pre-installed on your cluster prior to your receiving it, and you'll avoid the frustration of having to start all over again. However, if you should ever lose your boot disk or suffer a catastrophe involving the quorum resource (QR), you'll probably encounter it.

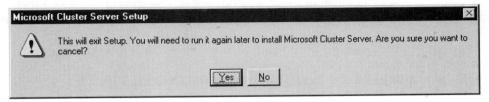

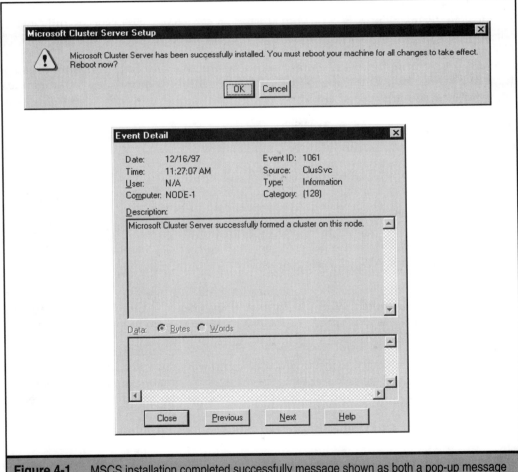

Figure 4-1. MSCS installation completed successfully message shown as both a pop-up message and as indicated in the Event Viewer Log

PREPARING FOR YOUR INSTALLATION

Prior to your actual installation of MSCS on both nodes, you should pull all your cluster configuration information together. The installation process can be painless or disastrous depending upon how well prepared you are. If not done correctly the first time you will probably have to uninstall MSCS and start all over, so it is best to have your ducks in a row before going down this path. Achieving this requires you to develop a methodology, or cluster plan, that gathers all the appropriate information on all aspects of your cluster and the networks that it must interface with.

NTS/E Configuration Considerations

Prior to actually installing MSCS on your cluster, you will have had to successfully install Windows NT Server Enterprise Edition 4.0 on each node. During the setup of NTS/E, you will configure a number of items, which specifically relate to how MSCS will operate once it is up and running. These items need to be well thought out in advance because they have far-reaching implications for your cluster and how it operates and integrates into your computing environment.

Domains and Domain Controllers

MSCS can be configured in one of three ways in terms of how domain controllers are set up on each node:

▼ *Primary domain controller (PDC/BDC)* Backup domain controller (pair, same domain)

■ *Backup domain controller (BDC/BAC)* Backup domain controller (same domain)

▲ *Independent server / independent server* Each server is a member of overall domain that MSCS will reside in

Each of these domain controller configuration choices has different implications for your existing domain model, as well as for system overhead (i.e., for capacity planning). The following considerations should be factored into your overall deployment plan.

▼ *BDC/BDC* In this mode you preserve your existing domain model without making any changes to it. You do add some system overhead to each of these servers due to their requirements to backup the primary domain controller. However, if that PDC should fail, any of these servers could be re-configured to take over as PDC (in this respect, you should assign a pecking order to which BDCs are in the queue to take over PDC responsibilities if called upon).

■ *PDC/BDC*   In this mode you have created a new domain for MSCS to reside on and therefore must establish "trusts" with the existing domains in your enterprise so that the users can access your MSCS domain. These trusts will be either one-way or two-way, depending upon how you have implemented your overall domain model. If you operate a "farm of clusters" in your particular environment, it is recommended that you designate one cluster as the PDC/BDC for the entire farm. This will give you the best of both worlds— all of your clusters will operate under one common domain while reducing system overhead.

■ *PDC/BDC*   In this mode you should establish the PDC as your primary node and the BDC as the secondary. This will make security issues easier to contend with.

■ *PDC/BDC*   In spite of the BDC "taking over" if the PDC fails, this is not a function of MSCS, and therefore the domain roles cannot be set up as resources for failover. Again, you should have some predetermined pecking order to which BDCs are designated to take over in the event of a PDC failure. This is a process controlled under NTS/E, not MSCS.

▲ *PDC/BDC*   Domain controllers require substantial computing and memory resources for performing directory replication and server authentication services to clients, assuming there are a large number of them (e.g., more than 5,000 per domain is a standard rule of thumb). This can use up a lot of each server's capacity and therefore limit its usefulness in supporting the cluster-aware (and non-cluster-aware) applications that reside on it. Many applications such as Microsoft SQL Server and Exchange Enterprise Editions specifically require that you not use either domain controller model (PDC/BDC or BDC/BDC) and that you establish each node as an independent server.

As recommended in Chapter 3, the simplest model is to use a single domain for all of your MSCS clusters and their nodes. All nodes are setup as BDCs (other than one that is the PDC for the entire domain). This mode keeps security and replication issues at a minimum, while eliminating access-control problems and reducing logon requests. Figure 4-2 is a block diagram of such a domain model.

Names and IP Addresses

When setting up your public and private network interface cards (NICs) and protocols, you must provide a unique name and IP address for each cluster node. You will have to set up your private network cards (if using a separate public and private network

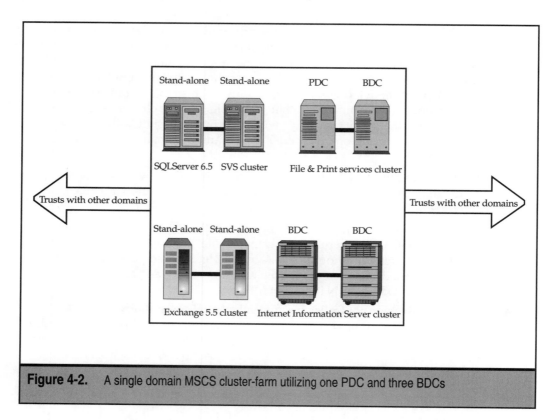

Figure 4-2.   A single domain MSCS cluster-farm utilizing one PDC and three BDCs

scheme) and protocols as well. In setting up these you should be prepared to input the following information:

- ▼ Public network name
- ■ Node name
- ■ Node "public network" NIC type (with driver disk, if required)
- ■ Node "public network" IP address and subnet information
- ■ Public networking protocols (TCP/IP only)
- ■ Private network name
- ■ Private network NIC type
- ■ Private network IP address a subnet information
- ▲ Private network protocols/drivers (if using Tandem ServerNet, fibre-channel or some other high-speed, low-latency interconnect, such as VIA, SCI, ATM, Gb Ethernet)

Figure 4-3 shows these parameters for ServerNet.

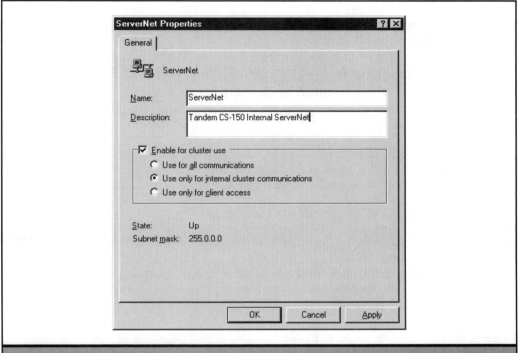

Figure 4-3.   ServerNet parameters shown on the MSCS network properties window

NETWORKING NOTES   When configuring both your private and public networks, you should be cognizant of the following:

▼   MSCS does not currently support the use of IP addresses that are assigned from Dynamic Host Configuration Protocol (DHCP) servers. You should make sure that this functionality is not enabled on either server during the setup of NTS/E.

■   You can use IP addresses that are static (from a list) or are leased on a permanent basis from a DCHP server in your computing environment. You will need to obtain addresses for the following items:

　　■   Node 1 public network connection

　　■   Node 2 public network connection

　　■   The cluster itself

　　■   The administrator's console

- If you are using a private network for cluster communication and heartbeat monitoring and assuming that these network interfaces do not support any other client interaction, then you can use IP addresses for the PN that come from the Internet Assigned Numbers Authority (IANA). These addresses are set aside specifically for such purposes. Those numbers are in three classes:
  - *Class A* 10.0.0.0 through 10.255.255.255 (use this group first if you can)
  - *Class B* 172.16.0.0 through 173.31.255.255
  - *Class C* 192.168.0.0 through 192.168.255.255
- ▲ These reserved IP addresses can be used in sequence with a default subnet mask of 255.0.0.0. They should **never** be routed outside the cluster, and finally, no default gateway or WINS servers should be referenced for this network.

This information, when configured properly during NTS/E installation, gets replicated to MSCS during its installation by default. At that time you do need to select which NIC (and IP address, etc.) gets used for the public and private networking, but this information is already in place.

If you have followed the flow of this book, this type of information should be readily available from your cluster design and deployment planning which you did in Chapter 3.

Storage

When setting up NTS/E you will have to configure your shared storage bus drives (and the non-shared storage bus for non-cluster-aware applications) for each node as well. During this time, the nodes' shared buses should be disconnected at the receiving shared nodes end. This will eliminate the potential for any bus arbitration or lockout problems (unless you are using hubs or switches).

In configuring these drives you will need to perform the following tasks (in order based on our experience):

1. Format all MSCS data and application drives for NTFS. You can use FAT on your boot drive, but I do not recommend this for a variety of reasons. You should also enter some detailed information about each drive/volume when you format them. This information is typically in the form of the vendor, model number, serial number, overall capacity versus number of partitions, location, and usage. I find that this reduces confusion when troubleshooting these storage devices.

2. Disable the use of disk data compression.

3. Assign unique drive letter (a letter that's different from those on the other nodes) identities for each drive and/or partition. These IDs should be different from those automatically assigned by NTS/E. You can assign alphanumeric labels to these drives at this time as well. The following illustration shows the dialog box for setting drive letters, and Figure 4-4 shows what two properly

configured nodes look like in the Disk Administrator window after completing the tasks described previously.

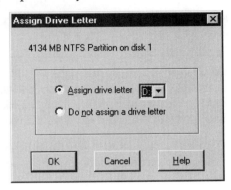

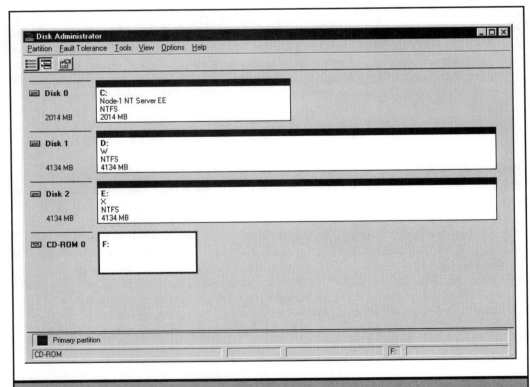

Figure 4-4. Properly configured boot and shared drives (Node 1)

MSCS NOTE: You will need to assign these same drive letters from both nodes. The first time, the shared bus will be disconnected at the receiving end. The second time, the bus will be connected, but with the node that originally assigned the drive letters turned off. Although somewhat unorthodox in concept, this is the procedure that I've had the best luck with.

MSCS NOTE: NTS/E will establishes a unique disk signature number for each drive at this time. MSCS relies on NTS/E to keep track of these signatures to track disk resources. If any of these drives fail after installing MSCS and you replace it, you will have to run Disk Admin on that node again to establish a new disk signature that MSCS can then recognize and use.

4. Establish and configure hardware RAID sets for the designated quorum resource drive (on the primary node), along with those for the application areas on the shared storage bus. Although the use of hardware RAID for the shared storage bus is considered optional by some people, it is strongly advised for the QR. The use of RAID will eliminate single points of failure in your cluster, along with making your application storage more robust and available.

MSCS NOTE: It is anticipated that in the NT 5.0 release of MSCS and MSCS Phase 2 that software RAID will be supported (levels 0 and 1). It is still my opinion that only hardware RAID should be used, specifically those systems that write RAID set signatures on the disks themselves and do not store the information in either a local HBA cache or on a systems disk. This is the only practical way to insure the bulletproof integrity of the QR as well as your application and user data on the shared storage bus.

Administration

When setting up control over your servers (i.e., designating administrators) during NTS/E, you should give careful consideration as to whether the same people (account names) you designate as administrators for the servers themselves will also have unencumbered access to MSCS (i.e., for installation and administration) as well. MSCS will ask you for the name of this person during its setup, and it is important to have this information readily available. Many organizations may want to designate a specific class of "cluster admins" for these tasks as they do require a somewhat premium skill-set to manage. Figure 4-5 shows how it is used by MSCS later in the installation. When inputting this information, remember that it has to be identical for both nodes, and obviously, that person or persons should have existing accounts on both nodes as well as the domain that they reside upon.

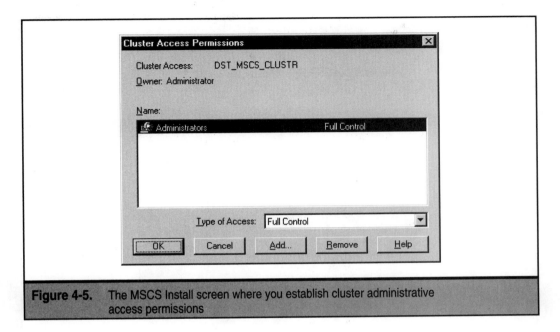

Figure 4-5.   The MSCS Install screen where you establish cluster administrative access permissions

Node Performance Optimization

Prior to setting up MSCS and as a final step after your successful installation of NTS/E, it is recommended that you complete the following tasks:

1. Optimize the paging file size and location.
2. Optimize server performance.

OPTIMIZE THE PAGING FILE SIZE AND LOCATION   You should size the paging file to be at least two and a half (five is better yet!) times the total memory available on the server, and you should ensure that its location is set up for the EIDE boot drive, not one of the shared (or non-shared) drives. An optimal situation is one where a second (or third) EIDE drive is used strictly for the paging disk. These setup parameters can be found in the Server Control Panel under the Performance tab, which leads to the Virtual Memory dialog box (see Figure 4-6).

MSCS NOTE: In conventional NT Server installations, it is common to optimize the paging file by spreading it over several drives rather than putting it on just one. This eliminates some of the actuator thrashing that happens in disk drives and improves bandwidth through the use of multiple data paths. However, in NTS/E this can be counter-productive unless you have more than one drive on your EIDE (or SCSI) boot drive adapter. In that case, you could spread the data over multiple drives, especially when you have nodes that utilize the full 4GBs of memory supported by NTS/E.

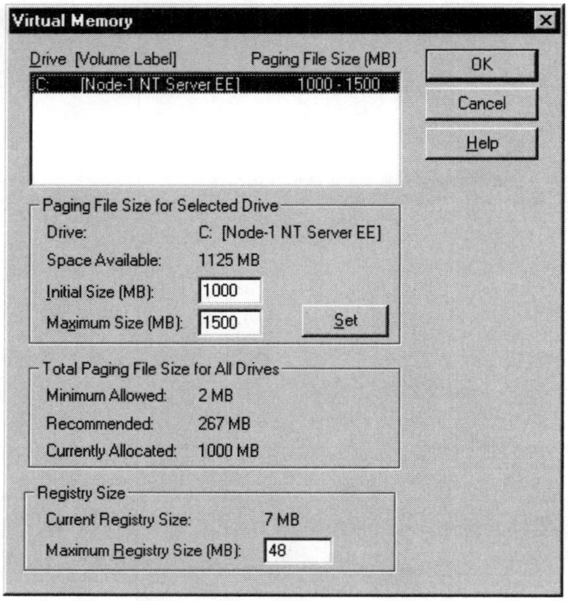

Figure 4-6.   Setting up the paging file in the Virtual Memory window

OPTIMIZE SERVER PERFORMANCE   If you are planning on using MSCS for high availability file and print services, you should optimize the configuration of both the preferred server, as well as its failover counterpart, for this type of use. To do so, open the Network Control Panel, and under Services, double-click on the Server icon (see Figure 4-7).

INSTALLING MSCS FROM SCRATCH

Installing MSCS should not prove to be too difficult, especially after the successful installation of NTS/E on both nodes. However, if NTS/E was not successfully installed, you may very well have to start over if you find that you can't install MSCS or it won't come up on restart.

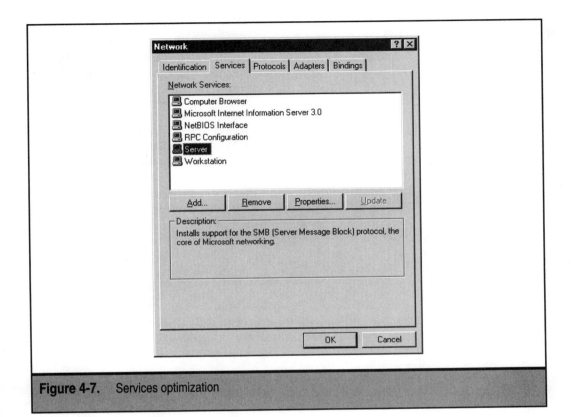

Figure 4-7. Services optimization

NOTE: To verify this, please consult the Event Viewer under the Administration Tools program grouping. The following illustration shows how this information is presented. The Event Viewer is one of the most important monitoring and logging tools included with NTS/E and will be discussed later in this section.

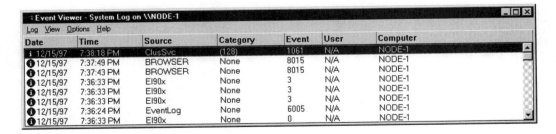

Tools to Have on Hand

Included in NT 4.0 are a number of tools and utilities that observe and alter the status of many elements crucial to MSCS (such as networking, storage, and CPU and memory utilization). The following list provides those tools used most often:

▼ *Event Viewer*   To observe and manage the log files of each node. There are three types of log files that can be viewed easily with Event Viewer: System, Security, and Application. The System and Application logs will be the most important to monitor in respect to MSCS. When using Event Viewer you will see varying colors of flags associated with the events (red being a failure or problem). You can scroll down the list to see the sequence of events that happen when NTS/E and MSCS start up as well as during operation. To find out further information regarding an event, just double-click on it and a dialog box will appear with an explanation as to the nature of this particular event and its impact on the system. MSCS has numerous messages that can appear under the event viewer. Hopefully, most of you will never encounter them in your day-to-day activities, as most of them are not good news at all.

■ *Services Applet in Control Panel*   To observe and alter the status of the cluster server during startup and operation (see Figure 4-8). Under the services applet, you will be able to observe which services load at startup and their status, along with being able to double-click them individually to confirm or change their mode of operation.

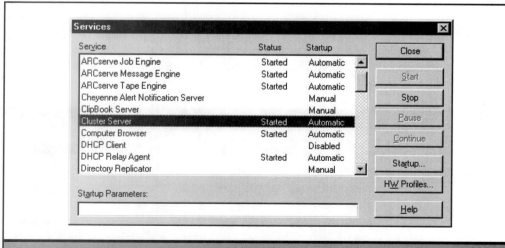

Figure 4-8.   The Services window showing server status

MSCS NOTE: When you double-click Cluster Server under the services control panel, you will see at the bottom the password that you entered for the cluster administrator. Sometimes when starting up MSCS after a change has been made, you will find an error message in the Event Log that says that the node could not join the cluster due to a logon error. By double-clicking the Cluster Server services setting you can manually reenter the systems administrators password and then re-start your cluster.

- *Task Manager*   To observe and monitor the status of the cluster server and cluster proxy during operation (see Figure 4-9). This will allow you to measure memory usage of MSCS with all of its cluster-aware applications and processes, along with other elements of NTS/E.

- *Disk Administrator*   To observe and configure the local, shared, and non-shared disk drives (see Figure 4-10). Disk Administrator is a critical tool for managing, configuring, and troubleshooting disk problems (boot, shared, and non-shared). It can determine whether a disk is online to a particular node—if the disk is not grayed out and is selectable under the disk administrator then it is online and available to the node that owns it.

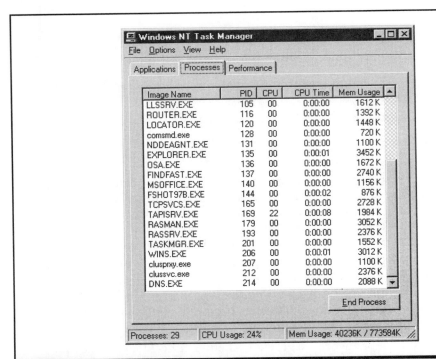

Figure 4-9.   Task Manager view of the cluster executables

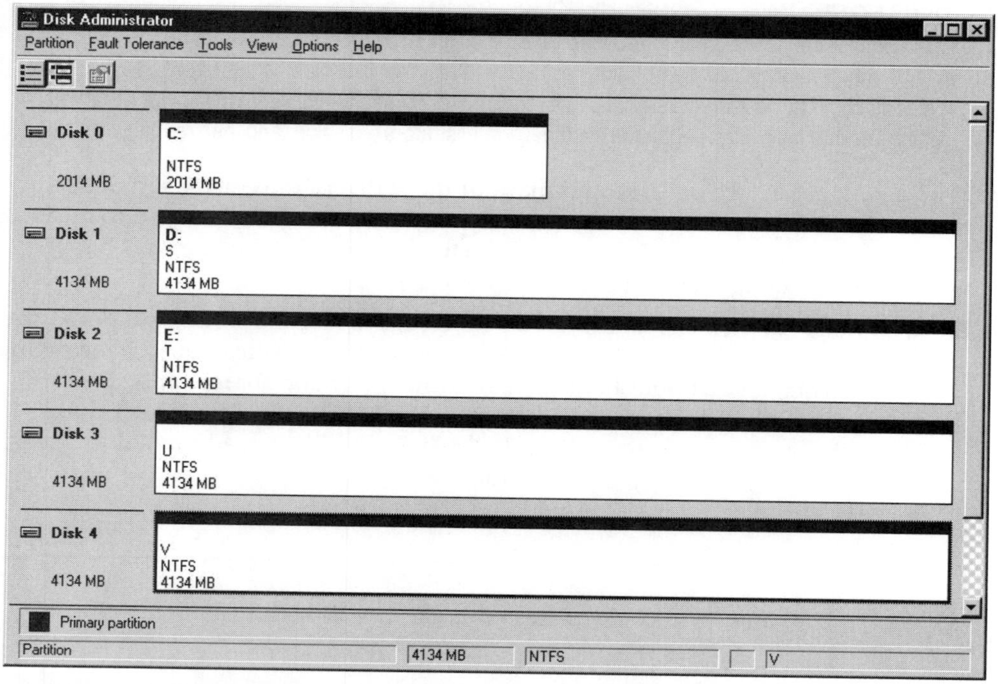

Figure 4-10. Disk Administrator view of the local and shared disks on the cluster

- *My Computer view, NT Explorer, and Net View* All of these can be used to varying degrees to observe the status and contents of all storage devices available to each node (see Figure 4-11 and Figure 4-12). Depending upon your personal preference, you can use either NT Explorer or Net View to observe the status of file shares being exported from virtual servers in the cluster.

- *Performance Monitor* To observe details of application and system behavior, including performance. Performance Monitor is critical to load balancing of cluster-aware applications across the nodes, as well as monitoring the impact of system messaging and other detractors of overall performance.

- *Windows NT diagnostics (Winmsd.exe)* To examine your entire NT system (drivers, resources, network usage, etc.). Another critical tool for use in ferreting out problems during your installation and under normal (and abnormal) operating conditions.

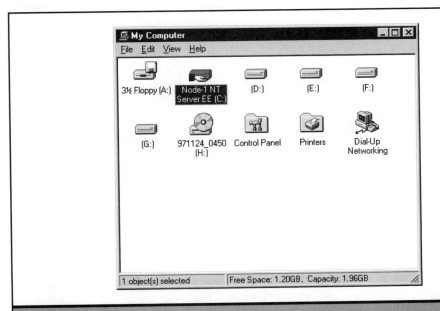

Figure 4-11. My Computer view of the drives and their status (Node 1)

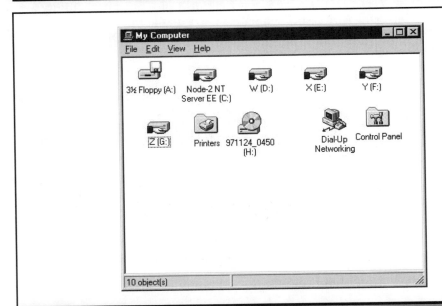

Figure 4-12. My Computer view of the drives and their status (Node 2)

- *Ping Utility* To check, at a low level, communications between nodes (for public and private networks). Ping can also be utilized to verify the operation of virtual server setup under MSCS.

▲ *Regedt32* This utility is used to examine and modify the contents of the Registry, especially in respect to those items particular to MSCS and its networking. Appendix B contains sample Registry information for a typical MSCS installation.

In addition to those already available from the NT desktop, you should add the following items to assist you in the verification and troubleshooting of an MSCS installation. You have the following utilities and tools loaded on each node prior to MSCS installation:

▼ *Ipconfig Utility* To display and index all NIC information. This is important in respect to keeping track of multiple NICs that may be identical in specifications but assigned to different tasks and roles in your cluster (for both Public and Private networks).

- *Cluster Sanity Test* Located in the MSCS Support folder, this utility is used to test your cluster after installation. It requires loading several support files into a dedicated directory and then running the program from the DOS command line (see Figure 4-13).

▲ *Dll-agator or some other DLL monitor/status reporting tool* Third party utility for analyzing which DLLs are associated with a particular application and their status. MSCS and its cluster-aware applications utilize many DLLs. Understanding their location and status is critical during troubleshooting, especially during failover/failback events.

The following tools and utilities are all available on the most recent version of the Windows NT Server Resource Kit (as well as that of Exchange):

▼ *SCSI Probe* To display the status of SCSI buses and diagnose problems with them. This is an especially handy tool when troubleshooting shared SCSI buses and storage devices.

- *Netcons* To display the status of current network connections. This is very handy when examining and diagnosing problems associated with public and private networks, as well as virtual servers.

▲ *Filever* To examine and display the version information of .exe and .dll files. A very handy tool for upgraders (whether it be applications, versions of NTS/E and MSCS, or Service Packs).

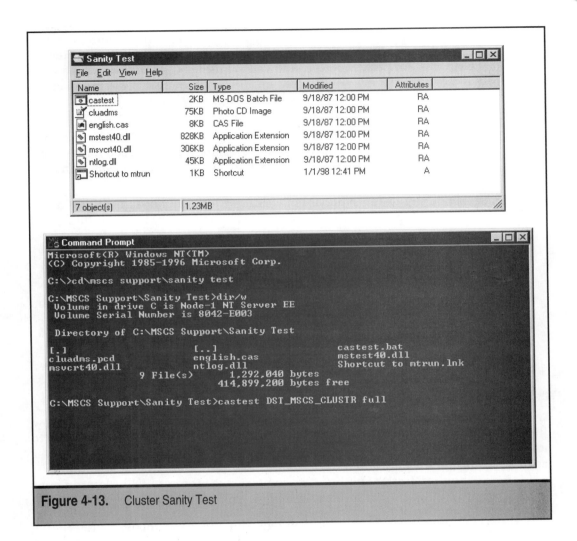

Figure 4-13. Cluster Sanity Test

Starting Your Installation

Prior to running MSCS setup on Node 1, perform the following tasks:

NOTE: Verify that Windows NT Service Pack 3 (SP3) has been applied to both nodes. In early production releases of NTS/E, the installation of SP3 after successfully installing NTS/E was not automatic. As of build 1381 it is automatically installed after NTS/E SP3 is located on disk 1 of the NTS/E two CD-ROM set. You should not make any further changes to your hardware configuration after installing SP3; otherwise, you will have to reinstall it. Install SP3 prior to starting your MSCS installation. SP3 is easy to install, and you should be able to do so in a few minutes on most systems. You must restart each node after successfully completing your installation.

1. Connect the shared storage bus to both nodes. Make sure that all terminations are correctly set and, if you are using Y cables or tri-link connectors, that they are connected properly at each end. If you are using SCSI hubs or switches, make sure these devices are powered up and configured for the appropriate SCSI mode. If you are using SCSI SSA or fibre-channel external storage systems, make sure these are powered up and properly configured as well.

2. Connect the private network to each node. If you are using ServerNet or some other high-speed interconnect, ping test communications back and forth prior to proceeding to the next step. Ping will show the IP address and subnet mask of the device being communicated with. Verify these for correctness.

3. Connect each node to the public network. Ping test communications to and from each node prior to proceeding to the next step. Verify for correctness as in step 2.

4. Verify that the system you are using for running the Cluster Administrator is connected to the public network. If you are going to administrate the cluster from one of the nodes (which is not the preferred choice because of the potential for that node to fail), then you can skip this step. You can set up both local and remote administration of the cluster if you so choose. This solution provides the best of both worlds. Use Ping to test and verify the specifics of the Cluster Administrator's IP address and subnet, as well as that it is alive and well. You will need to use it soon after MSCS is installed for a variety of tasks.

Step-by-Step MSCS Installation

In order to make the installation of MSCS as successful as possible, you must follow directions carefully and in the order they are given. Otherwise, you open yourself up to encountering the "dreaded blue screen of death" or at a minimum having to start all over again until you get it right.

The following are the steps necessary to complete the process with the least amount of difficulty:

1. Having completed all the prepatory steps, shut down both nodes.

2. Power up Node 1 first. Allow it to go through its self-test routines, and when it gets to the point where NT Loader asks you which version of the OS to load, press the SPACEBAR to suspend the load. Leave the node in this mode for now.

3. Power up Node 2. Allow it to proceed to NT Loader and suspend its further loading of the OS as well.

4. Return to Node 1, and press the SPACEBAR. Allow NTS/E to finish loading, and log on with your administrative ID and password. Leave Node 2 in its suspended mode until after Node 1 has had MSCS successfully installed and restart.

5. Place disk 2 of NTS/E in your drive, and run *Drive Letter*\Mscs\cluster\ *Platform*\setup.exe. (The next illustration shows how to run the MSCS installation from the Windows Start menu.)

6. Follow the prompts until MSCS asks "Form a New Cluster?" MSCS will then ask a series of questions. Some require accepting the default value, while others require specific information to be provided or choices to be made. Whatever you choose you are stuck with once MSCS completes its installation, and many of the items (such as shared drive choices, administrator configuration, etc.) that you choose during the installation of Node 1 apply to the entire cluster. Click Next.

7. Enter the name of your cluster. Click Next.

8. Enter the path that you want MSCS to install your cluster files in. Choose the default because doing so places these files on the same drive as NTS/E and not on the shared (or non-shared) drives. (This selection will not choose the boot drive for storing the Quorum Resource.) Click Next.

9. Enter the name and password (and domain, if different) for the account that will manage the cluster. Click Next

10. In the next step you will add and remove logical and physical storage devices from the storage bus(es) that you want to set up in MSCS as shared cluster disks. MSCS scans for all HBAs (host bus adapters) other than EIDE and adds, by default, those drives to its overall list of shared drives. It will also indicate which RAID sets are available for use at this time as well. It is up to you to add and remove them from this list as needed.

11. Next, having identified the drives on the shared bus, you will now pick the all-important Quorum Resource. By default MSCS chooses the first available drive from Node 1 (usually drive letter D). You can accept this choice or not accept it. Because it has been strongly recommended that you use hardware RAID for protecting this resource, you must select the particular RAID set you designated for that purpose at this time. Figure 4-14 shows how MSCS displays information on your choice of Quorum Resource.

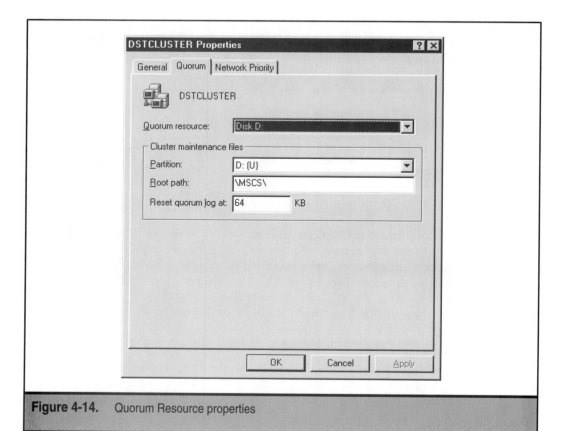

Figure 4-14. Quorum Resource properties

12. Setup will look at all your networking resources and ask you to choose your private network and its settings, along with determining a name for the public network. Figure 4-15 shows the Network Priority tab for setting up your private network, and also the Properties window for the private network. Figure 4-16 shows setting up your public network. Click OK until finished.

13. MSCS will ask you for the IP address and subnet pertaining to the Windows NT workstation that you want to use by default to administer the cluster from. Click Next when you have entered this information.

14. At this point installation on Node 1 is completed. Click Finish, and wait for MSCS to tell you the installation was successful (shown earlier in Figure 4-1). At this point you will be asked to restart Node 1 prior to installing MSCS on Node 2. I will depart a bit from the instructions provided by Microsoft at this point.

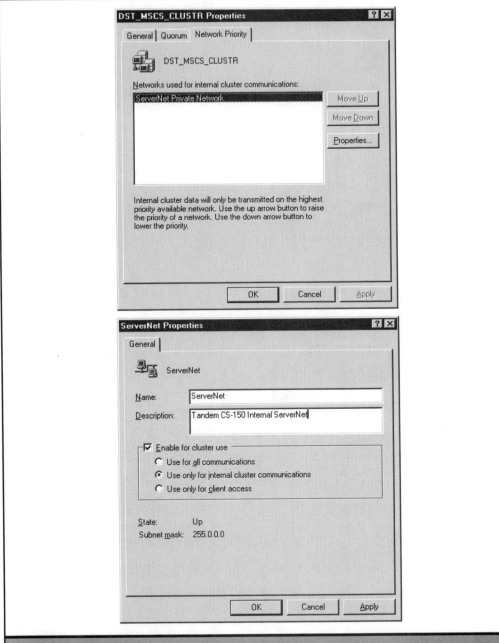

Figure 4-15.   Setting up the private network

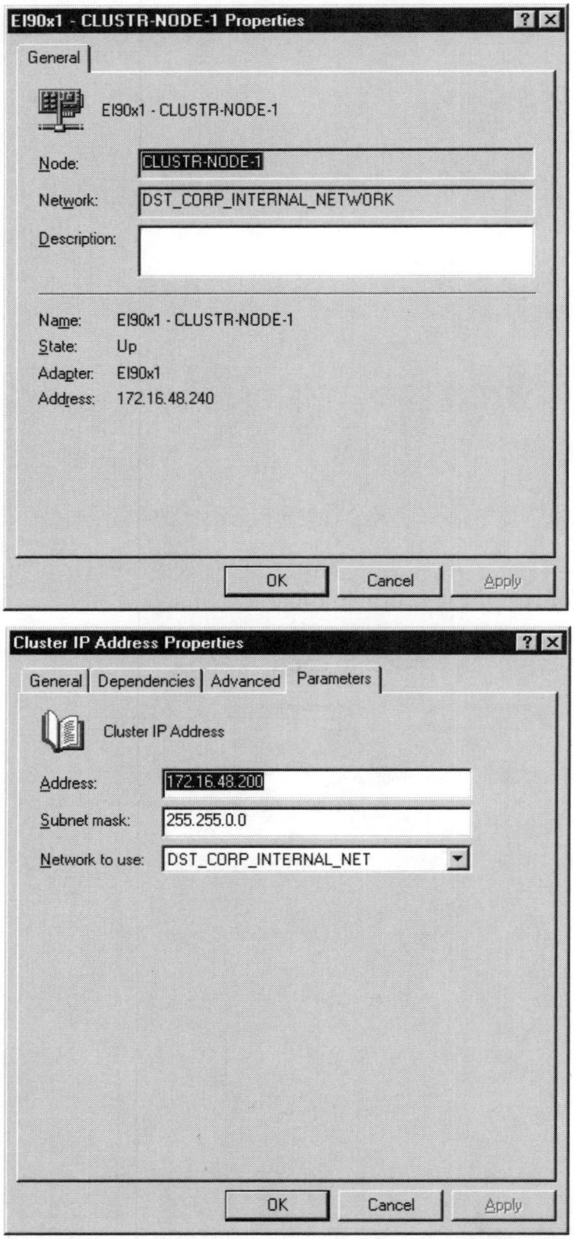

Figure 4-16. Setting up the public network

15. Select No in regard to restarting Node 1, and shut it down completely. Once you have completed shut down for Node 1, shut down Node 2 by turning off the power to it. This is okay to do at this point because the OS never really loaded on Node 2, and no files will be corrupted.

16. Repeat steps 2 through 4. After logon of Node 1 is complete, run Event Viewer to determine if there were startup problems with MSCS. Red symbols to the left of the descriptor will indicate it if this is the case. If you encounter the red symbols on the left, drill down by double-clicking on them to determine where the problem or problems are. If such problems exist, jump to the troubleshooting section (Chapter 5) of the *Microsoft Cluster Server Administrator's Guide* or see Appendix B for further assistance. As with all Windows NT licenses from Microsoft, you are entitled to several incident calls. If you cannot determine the source of your problem at this time it might be advisable to use one of those event chits to help you sort through whatever problem you are experiencing at this point.

17. If you had no problems with startup, run Cluster Administrator from the Administrative Tools Application pull-down menu. You will be asked to enter a cluster name (as shown in the following illustration). Enter the name and watch to see how Cluster Administrator comes up. Prior to installing the second node, Cluster Administrator should look like the window shown in Figure 4-17. If no red indicators are displayed, it is safe to proceed with the installation of Node 2. Press the SPACEBAR on Node 2 to continue boot up and then log on.

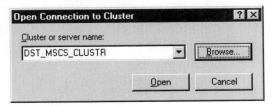

18. Repeat steps 5 through 8, choosing the cluster name already entered instead of a new one (select Join, not New). You will then be asked for the logon ID and password entered for the administrator when you installed Node 1. Enter this information again without any changes. Click Next.

19. Click Finish. You can go get a cup of coffee now while you wait for the installation to finish. When it does, select No in response to the restart prompt. Instead, shut down both nodes, and power them back up with Node 1 first and Node 2 a couple of minutes behind (especially if they are a PDC-BDC pair). This will hopefully eliminate system messages about the primary domain server not being available.

20. Log on to both nodes and check their startup logs in Event Viewer. Assuming that there are no problems on either node, start Cluster Administrator on Node 1 and watch your cluster form (or not) before your very eyes. Figure 4-18 shows what a properly working cluster should look like on startup.

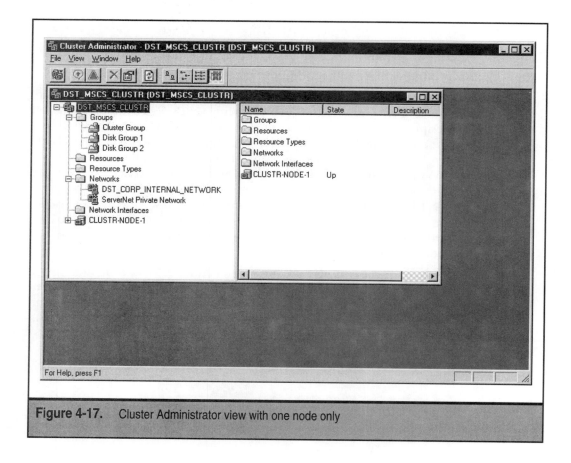

Figure 4-17. Cluster Administrator view with one node only

At this point you should have successfully installed MSCS on both nodes and formed a working cluster. It is now time to do initial testing and set up the cluster prior to installing cluster-aware applications and setting up failover/failback groups.

Initial Tests and Setup Parameters

Despite appearances, it is prudent to test your cluster at this time. This will determine if it is working properly independent of the behavior of any applications that you may desire to place on it. I will also set up basic parameters for the cluster to operate within.

Testing

The tests that you should run are simple and will quickly determine the health of your cluster. I will focus on networking, storage, and cluster operations.

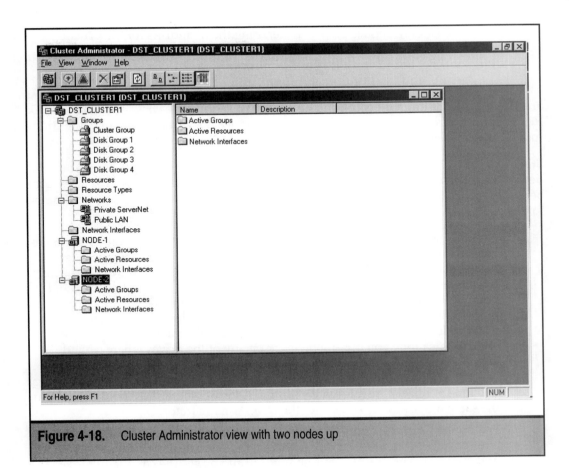

Figure 4-18.   Cluster Administrator view with two nodes up

NETWORKING   A few basic tests will determine if your networks are configured correctly and are up and running:

1. Ping testing (back and forth) of the cluster's IP address, along with those of the nodes themselves from the administrator workstation where the Cluster Administrator is setup. You should be able to ping all three with no problem (and in turn ping from the nodes back to the workstation), along with seeing them under Network Neighborhood (by name and address) as well as with NT Explorer.

2. Set up a shared file folder on each node. Then, from Network Neighborhood on any of the nodes or the Cluster Administrator workstation, you should be able to open these shared folders and see their contents. This will also determine if the public network is properly configured.

3. From either of the nodes on the cluster, ping the IP address for the private network on the other node. Do this in reverse as well. This will determine if this subset of the network is operating properly.

These tests assume that you know which network and IP address is which. All you are doing is verifying basic communications. You can also click on the Network Resources icons from the Cluster Administrator and see the status of all four connections (public and private).

SHARED STORAGE BUS   The tests that you are going to run on the shared storage bus will determine if all drives are up and running and whether they can be moved as a resource between the two nodes without any problems. To test your storage, perform the following tasks:

1. Go into Disk Administrator on both nodes and view all drives connected to the system. You should observe that each node continues to own its particular drives, but you should be able to see the other nodes as well. If during startup one node or the other captured all the shared storage due to initiator lockout, you will see all drives on one node and none on the other (seeing the drive means it is highlighted, not grayed out). You can further verify the status of the disks by looking at them with My Computer or NT Explorer on each node as well. In this mode you can double-click on any of the drives where a hand appears (the hand indicates that the drive is shared but local to that node) and see the data on that drive. You should check the quorum resource drive during this time to make sure it is not corrupted. All in all, the drives should appear in the same mode as they did under the Disk Administrator.

2. Within the Cluster Administrator the disk groups are displayed under the Groups folder (as Disk Group 1, Disk Group 2, etc.). You should click on each of these groups once and then right-click until you see the command Move Group. This test will move the physical disk's ownership from one node to another and then back again. Click on this command, and from the view on the right side of the Cluster Admin, you should be able to see the disk group move from one node to the other (and then back again when you repeat the process). Figure 4-19 shows the disk groups under the Cluster Administrator. If you can move the disks successfully back and forth then they are properly configured in the cluster and working.

CLUSTER OPERATIONS   To quickly test the operation of your cluster, you can use a couple of methods and tools.

The easiest way is to set up a test scenario in advance based on using either Clock or Notepad. You can then introduce a failure manually by the CA or physically in the public or private networks and watch the failover of this application and its resources (Physical disk and Generic Application). You can then re-establish the failed network connection and observe failback of the application (this assumes that you have set the scenario for both of these modes).

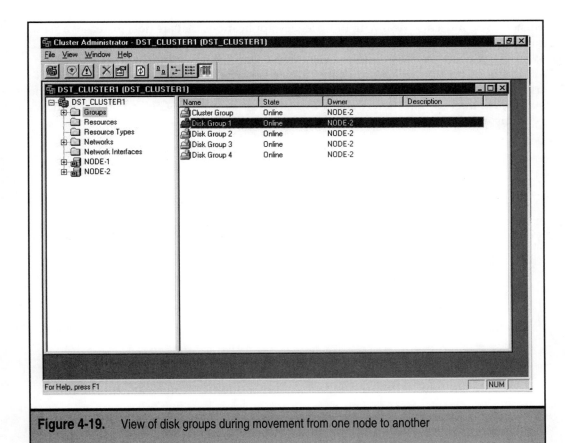

Figure 4-19.   View of disk groups during movement from one node to another

Set up the Cluster Sanity Test (according to the directions in the .txt file "casread") referred to earlier in this chapter and run it. This test will determine the general health and proper configuration of your cluster with messages prompting you otherwise.

Finally, you can move resources around from the Cluster Administrator just to see that they are working properly. This fiddling around is fairly rudimentary but does give you a flavor of how the cluster behaves without cluster-aware applications running on it. In Chapter 5, you will learn to fully familiarize yourself with all the operations of the CA, as well as how to configure failover groups and resources for a variety of applications and services.

WRAPPING IT ALL UP

Now that you have successfully installed NTS/E and MSCS and set up your basic cluster, it's time to start tackling all the issues and challenges associated with installing and operating those cluster-aware applications that you are planning on using with your clusters. You must also deal with those legacy applications that are not cluster-aware but can nonetheless benefit from some of MSCS' capabilities as provided for with the DLL Wrapper (Generic Applications and Generic Services) that is supplied with MSCS.

In Chapter 5, you will become familiarized with the operation of the CA and how to use it in setting up cluster-aware applications and services. In Chapter 7, I will cover the specifics of many applications that are available for use with MSCS (and other Windows NT Cluster solutions as well).

CHAPTER 5

MSCS Operation

Now that you have either installed NTS/E and MSCS on your servers or purchased a pre-configured MSCS system off the shelf, it is time to start operating your cluster. Integral to operating MSCS is mastering the use of the Cluster Administrator (CA)—the key interface to all aspects of your cluster—as well as setting up all of your applications and services for failover.

NOTE: You can also use the NT command line to administer the cluster, especially if you want to use scripts.

For the most part, the Cluster Administrator is responsible for creating and managing all failover groups and resources (see Figure 5-1 for a depiction of how these are related). Many groups and resources must be created manually before the cluster-aware application is installed with the Cluster Administrator having final control over most

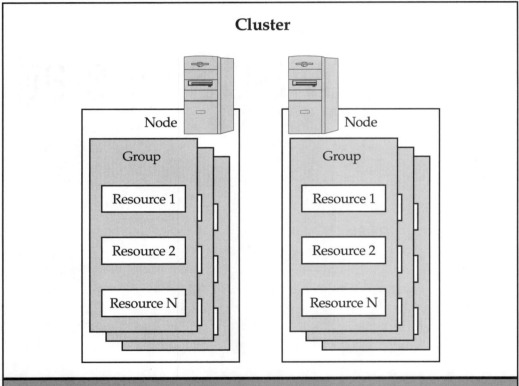

Figure 5-1. Diagram of cluster that shows relationship between groups and resources

details. The cluster administrator is also used to add and evict nodes, to determine which networks are used for private and cluster communications, and to determine ownership of the quorum resource and other resources, as well as to display the status of all nodes and groups in the cluster.

HOW TO SUCCESSFULLY OPERATE YOUR CLUSTER

In the first section of this chapter, I will review the Cluster Administrator and all of the functionality it provides; in the second section I will go through, on a step-by-step basis, how to configure a number of common applications and services using the Cluster Administrator. Having completed these steps you will then be able to operate your cluster-aware applications and services in a high-availability environment under the deployment model(s) you have chosen.

Step 1—Getting Started

The first step in moving forward is to start up your cluster (if it has not already done so automatically after the first node came online). MSCS forms a cluster on startup (unless you change this feature from the Services control panel to either manual or disable mode). Although the cluster is up and running after login on both nodes, you don't have any real control over it until you start the Cluster Administrator (or elect to use the command line interface).

You can operate the Cluster Administrator from either node or remotely from the NT administrative workstation that you previously configured during your installation. To start up CA, click on Cluster Administrator under the Administrative Tools (Common) program grouping. This will start the Administrator and check the initial status of the cluster. Any connections that were left open at the end of the most recent CA session are automatically restarted. Any problems will appear on the GUI screen as flags and icons. Figure 5-2 shows the CA controls and the functionality available from them. The following table provides a listing of the warnings and status messages that you may encounter with CA:

Icon	Warning Message
Yield Sign	Resource/Group/Node Problem/Error
Circle with X	Resource/Group/Node Failure
Circle with clock	Operation Pending
Circle with Diagonal Line	Resource/Group/Node Offline

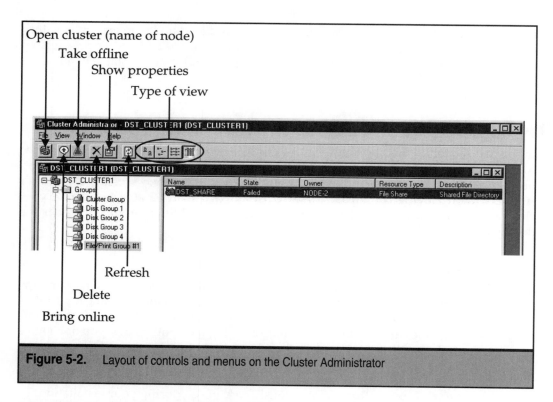

Open cluster (name of node)
Take offline
Show properties
Type of view

Refresh
Delete
Bring online

Figure 5-2. Layout of controls and menus on the Cluster Administrator

Step 2—Mastering the Cluster Administrator

Mastering the Cluster Administrator is paramount to properly creating failover groups and to configuring your cluster for day-to-day operation. To accomplish this, you need to spend time navigating around its control buttons and pull-down menus. You should also take a look at the default resources contained in both the Cluster Group and the Disk Group(s) when you first start up your cluster. Finally, you should look at the properties of each of these resources in the default groups to better understand their interdependent relationships. This process should help you to quickly become very familiar with the CA.

The main administrative tasks that the Cluster Administrator performs are the following:

▼ Add, delete, and rename failover/failback groups and resources

■ Change the state of these groups and resources (take them offline or bring them online)

■ Initiate manual failure(s) of groups and their resources (including failover and failback)

■ Transfer ownership of groups from one node to another

- Transfer ownership of resources from one group to another
- Facilitate connection to the cluster
- Add and evict nodes from the cluster
- ▲ Configure the public and cluster interconnect networks

Step 3—Getting to Know Your Groups and Resources

The two most significant concepts that you must contend with in setting up your cluster are groups and their resources.

Groups are a collection of related (or dependent) resources that are managed as a single unit. Each group contains those resources required to run the specific application or service that the group is configured for. The group (or failover group in some vernaculars) is the unit that actually fails over and fails back in a high-availability cluster. All of the resources in the group fail over and fail back together, although based on dependency settings some resources may start up prior to others; i.e., the Physical Disk starts up prior to the IP Address, etc. Groups that contain both a Network Name and IP Address Resource are considered virtual servers and can be accessed directly by clients on the public network attached to the cluster.

Resources are entities (physical or logical) that provide a specific service to a client. The resources provided with MSCS are supported by specific DLLs that communicate with the Resource Monitor and the cluster service. See Figure 5-3 for a listing of these DLLs.

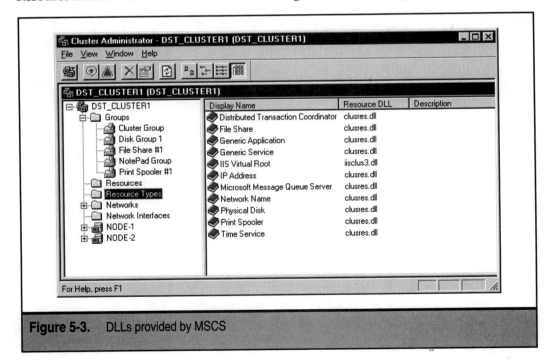

Figure 5-3. DLLs provided by MSCS

Resources may have dependencies, which are the relationships between two or more resources in the same group on the same node. For example:

▼ A resource may depend upon any number of other resources.

■ A specific resource can be brought online only after all the other resources that it depends on (if any) are brought online first. This works in reverse when taking resources offline.

▲ A resource and all of its dependencies must failover and failback together—i.e., as a group.

To visualize the process of creating groups and resources (with and without dependencies), it is useful to create dependency trees. Figure 5-4 shows a dependency tree for IIS (Internet Information Server).

Step 4—Setting up Your Failover Groups

Once you have the cluster successfully up and running, it is then time to create groups using the wizard supplied with MSCS, or you can choose to modify an existing group. This process is completed well in advance of installing any cluster-aware applications, which may have their own setup wizards. The process of creating groups is based on the initial planning that you did in earlier chapters and should go fairly smoothly.

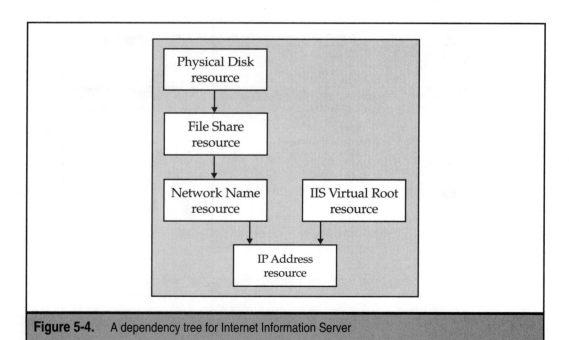

Figure 5-4.   A dependency tree for Internet Information Server

Each cluster has two default groups that appear under the Administrator: the Cluster Group and the Disk Group(s). Figure 5-5 is a view of these two default groups. The default Cluster Group has very specific resources, including the Time Service, which only it can utilize. The default Disk Group(s) contain only Physical Disk Resources; there is one group for each drive or volume that was selected as being a shared storage bus storage device during MSCS setup. This can be changed after setup to accommodate the addition or subtraction of drives/volumes from the shared storage bus.

The Cluster Group contains an IP Address Resource (the previously defined IP address for the cluster), a Cluster Name Resource (the previously defined name for the cluster), and a Time Service Resource (critical to keeping all elements of the cluster in sync regardless of status). These are fixed from the time of the initial installation and should not change.

The Disk Group (one for each drive or volume on the shared-disk storage bus) contains a Physical Disk Resource.

When setting up or administering your cluster, it is important that you never delete or rename the Cluster Group. You can use it as a model for creating new groups, but under no circumstances should you make changes without first thinking long and hard about the consequences, which usually include the inability to get the cluster to form after the next time you reboot.

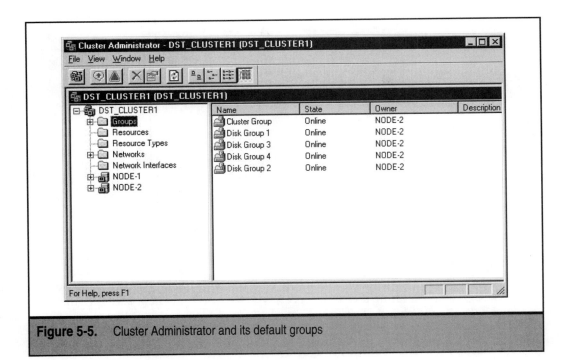

Figure 5-5. Cluster Administrator and its default groups

Group Configuration Requirements

Each group has three modules that must be configured that set the basic failover/failback properties for each Failover Group. The properties determine how quickly and under what conditions the cluster executive responds to a failure, as well as determine which Groups will fail back automatically or manually. Failure to configure these properties correctly will cause your cluster to perform below your expectations.

▼   General Properties

■   Failover Properties

▲   Failback Properties

GENERAL PROPERTIES   Within the General Properties module are two fields that must be completed and one that is optional, as shown here:

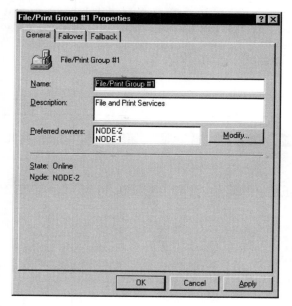

The fields are as follows:

▼   *Name*   This is the field in which you enter the unique name for this particular group. It is used for administrative purposes only and does not necessarily need to be the same name as the Network Name (a name resource that you assign when creating a virtual server, which is used for client access to the application within that group).

■   *Description*   This is an optional field and is used by the administrator to describe the nature of the group.

▲   *Preferred Owners*   This field is for entering the node(s) that can own the group. Preferred owner(s) must be entered in order for failover to occur and for static load balancing purposes where the workload from this group will reside during normal operations.

These settings can be edited any time during and after the time you set up your groups and resources by using the Properties function from the CA. To do this, you must highlight the group and then select properties to begin your editing.

FAILOVER PROPERTIES   Located under the Failover tab in the Cluster Group Properties Wizard, this configuration determines the group's failover properties. The dialog box is shown here:

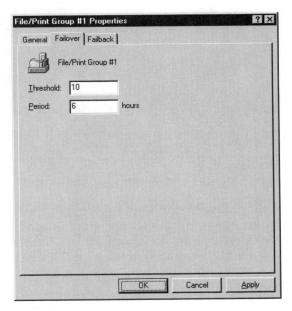

To properly configure this module, enter data in the following fields (or you can choose the defaults that are provided):

▼   *Threshold*   This field determines the maximum number of times that the group is allowed to failover during the failover period. If this number is exceeded by a particular recurring fault, then the group is taken offline until an administrator corrects the problem. The default value is ten times.

▲   *Period*   This field determines the maximum time period in hours over which the failover threshold cannot be exceeded. If this time threshold is exceeded during the period set, then the group will be taken offline. The default value is six hours.

FAILBACK PROPERTIES   Located under the Failback tab, this module is used to configure the failback characteristics of the group, as shown here:

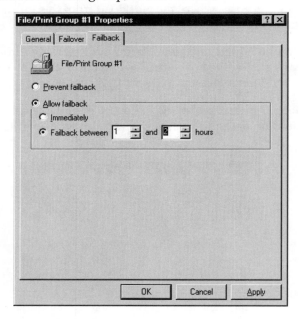

Four buttons can be completed:

▼ *Prevent failback*   If you enable this function, the group will not automatically failback to its preferred node that it resided on prior to failover. This allows the administrator to manually bring the group online after checking the status of the node and what initially caused it to failover. This function is enabled by default.

■ *Allow failback*   This field has one switch and two configuration fields that affect how the group fails back. You choose one or the other of the following:

■ *Immediately*   This setting allows the group to failback immediately after its original node is back online and the heartbeat has been reestablished.

■ *Failback between*   This allows failback to occur only during specified hours after the original node is back online and the heartbeat has been reestablished. This setting is useful because it allows for a "timeout," during which the administrator can monitor the status of the node and observe the failback while it is in process. It also allows the administrator to schedule failback during off hours when any potential application of service disruptions can be better managed.

Creating New Groups or Modifying Existing Ones

Two methodologies can be used when setting up your groups. You can either create a new group using the Administrative Wizard, or you can modify an existing Disk group by adding resources and changing its name (as a final step in the process). Either method works fine; however, modifying an existing group is a much simpler approach for most administrators. This is due to the fact that the group already has a key resource dedicated to it—the Physical Disk.

CREATING A NEW GROUP   By clicking on File | New | Group, you create a new group using the built-in wizard, as shown here:

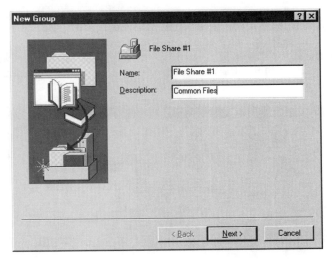

To complete this process, follow these steps:

1. Enter the required information in all three modules (general, failover, and failback properties).
2. Click Finish when done.
3. Click the group name once to select it.
4. Click the Bring Online icon (the second icon from the left) at the top of the CA, or choose File | Bring Online.

You are now ready to add the appropriate resources to your group.

MODIFYING AN EXISTING DISK GROUP   New groups can also be created by modifying an existing Disk Group. This method is the simplest as each of the default Disk Groups has a Physical Disk Resource pre-assigned to it. The only limiting factor is that when MSCS comes up for the first time after install, it will have only as many Disk Groups as there are

Physical Disks available, including one that allows access to the disk that the Quorum Resource is located on. (As stated earlier, I strongly recommend against putting applications or data on the Quorum Resource disk.) You can create additional Disk Groups by adding more physical or logical disk drives.

To do this you must complete the following steps:

1. Right-click an existing Disk Group.
2. Choose File | New Resources under CA. Add additional resources as required.
3. Rename the entire group.
4. Bring the group online.

This allows you to make changes to an existing group and its resources that are already online, while getting feedback from the cluster at every turn to make sure that you are going in the right direction. (Getting this feedback is a major benefit given how quirky this process can be.) See the following illustration for a view of how to modify an existing Disk Group.

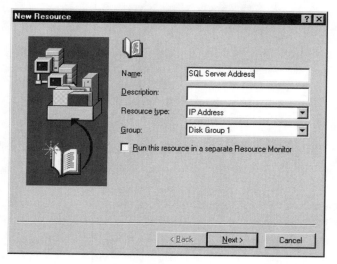

Step 5—Create a Dependency Tree for Each Group

The easiest way to master the process of determining which resources are required by your group is to make a dependency tree similar to the one shown previously in Figure 5-4. This was mentioned earlier in this chapter and it is up to the Administrator to determine whether they want to create their tree at this stage of the setup or as part of developing their overall deployment plan, which is usually done well in advance of this step.

This tree maps the relationships between all resources in a group and shows how they interact. A dependency tree also shows the effects on dependent resources of taking any resources offline. It also indicates the effects (if any) on other groups that share resources (e.g., IP Address and Network Name). Creating this tree should be completed up front in your cluster preparation phase to eliminate last minute hiccups.

To create your dependency tree, follow these steps:

1. Write down all of the resources that will be used in each group
2. Draw lines with arrows between resources that have direct dependencies upon each other.

Direct dependencies exist when two resources are directly connected on the tree. Indirect dependencies exist when an intermediate resource is found between two other resources such that they are not directly dependent upon each other. An example of this is that in most virtual server type groups the IP Address always has a direct dependency on the Physical Address, while the Network Name has an indirect one.

Steps 6 and 7—Learn All About Resources and Dependencies

Once you have created your failover group, provided its description, and brought it online, you are ready to add resources to it. I discussed the concept of resources earlier in the chapter in substantial detail, but at this point you will be adding the real heart of the failover group in terms of the required physical and virtual resources.

Resources

Regardless of the type of resource you are using, three configuration settings are common to all of them. These settings are similar to those for configuring groups. The three modules are the following:

▼ General Properties
■ Dependencies Properties
▲ Advanced Properties

GENERAL PROPERTIES   Located under the General tab in the Resource Properties dialog box are four fields that must be completed and one optional field. They are the following:

▼ *Name*   The unique name of the resource. Once set, it cannot be changed.

■ *Description*   An optional description of the resource from the viewpoint of the administrator.

■ *Possible Owner*   The nodes that run this particular resource. This list was defined when the resource was created. Both nodes must be possible owners of this resource. This is required for future compatibility with MSCS Phase 2.

■ *Resource Monitor*   You choose to have a separate Resource Monitor or not in this information box. By default this setting is not enabled but should be used for those resources that may not be functioning correctly. This will isolate the behavior of such a resource from the multiple sources feeding the overall Resource Monitor.

▲ *Status*   A fixed display of the current status of this particular resource. It shows the type, the group to which it belongs, and the node that it is running on. These settings cannot be changed.

DEPENDENCIES   This dialog box has a number of items shown in a box on the left (or it has none if it is the first level of dependency). You can add the items as dependencies by selecting them and then moving them to the box on the right. For a listing of the required dependencies by resource type, see Table 5-1.

ADVANCED   The properties in this dialog box affect how a resource behaves during a failure. The default values are based on the unique characteristics of each resource type (all resources have these settings). These settings are optimized and should be used first unless specified otherwise by an application or technical note.

The key data fields are the following:

▼ *Restart – Don't Restart*   If you elect not to restart the resource after a failure, it will failover. If you choose to have MSCS restart the resource, then you must specify if you want it to affect the rest of the group that the resource is part of, and you must then tell MSCS how many times it should attempt to restart the resource before failover. You provide the time frame that these restarts should take place in as well.

■ *Looks Alive*   This setting determines how often MSCS checks a resource on a basic level to see if it "looks alive."

■ *Is Alive*   In this mode MSCS takes a detailed look at the resource to verify that it "is alive."

▲ *Pending Timeout*   This setting determines how long a resource is in a pending state (online/offline) before it must resolve its status or fail.

PARAMETERS   This dialog box is specifically tailored to the needs of each particular resource. The information contained in this box is sometimes fixed and unchangeable or does not exist at all (e.g., time service). It has very specific control over generic applications and services, as well as over other applications. The specific parameters that can be controlled for each resource are the following:

Resource Type	Parameters
DHCP	Specify path to DHCP database
DTC	None
SMB File Share	Specify which users and how many in total may access the share
	Specify the name of the share and the path to its folder

Resource Type	Parameters
Print Spooler	Specify the path to the print spooler folder
	Configure the job completion timeout
IIS	Specify which service the virtual root will be for
	Specify the path to the directory disk resource
	Configure the alias for the virtual root
	Configure the types of permissions for users who access the virtual root
MSMQ	None
Generic App	Specify the application command line and current directory
	Specify the use of the network name for the computer name, if applicable
Generic Service	Specify the service name and its startup parameters
	Specify the use of the network name for the computer name, if applicable
IP Address	Specify the IP address, subnet mask, and network parameters
	Specify the cluster network to use
Network Name	Configure the computer name
Physical Disk	Specify which drive to use

Step 8—The Resource Definition Process

To add resources, follow these steps:

1. Highlight the group that you want to add resources to.
2. Left-click to choose New, then Resources.
3. Begin adding resources.

To add a resource, follow these steps:

1. Select the type of resource you want to add from the pull-down menu.
2. Begin adding the information that each resource type requires including a unique name and description

You will be asked to enter many types of information as well as to select dependencies based on the type of failover group that you are configuring. (See Figure 5-5 for a list of these groups.) Repeat this process until you have properly configured all resources and dependencies. See Table 5-1 for a listing of resources and dependencies based on the types of failover groups.

Failover Group Type	Resources and Dependencies
Windows NT SMB File Share	Share Name
	Path to share location
	Comment regarding share
	Maximum number of users at one time
	Access permissions
	Physical Disk (dependency)
	IP Address (dependency)
	Network Name (dependency)
Windows NT Print Spooler	Spool folder name
	Identify possible owners
	Path to spool folder location
	Network Name (dependency)
	IP Address (dependency)
	Physical Disk (dependency)
Windows NT DHCP Server	DHCP database path
	IP Address (dependency)
	Physical Disk (dependency)
Microsoft Distributed Transaction Coordinator (DTC)	Network Name (dependency)
	IP Address (dependency)
	Physical Disk (dependency)
Microsoft Internet Information Server (IIS) (3.02 or later):	Web service type (FTP, WWW, or Gopher, if supported)
	Root directory path
	Directory alias
	Possible owners
	Access types (FTP and WWW only)
	Physical Disk (dependency)
	IP Address (dependency)

Table 5-1.   Resource and Dependencies by Type of Failover Group

Microsoft Message Queue Server
(MMQS)

Distributed Transaction Coordinator
(dependency)

Network Name (dependency)

IP Address (dependency)

Physical Disk (dependency)

SQL Server (dependency)

Microsoft SQL Server 6.5 Enterprise
Edition (or 7.0)

Network Name (dependency)

IP Address (dependency)

Physical Disk(s) (dependency)

Generic Service (optional)

Microsoft Exchange 5.5 Enterprise
Edition

IP Address (dependency)

Network Name (dependency)

Physical Disk (dependency)

Other Applications/Resources	
Generic Service	No dependencies
Generic Application	No dependencies
Network Name	IP Address
Time Service	No dependencies
IP Address	No dependencies

Table 5-1. Resource and Dependencies by Type of Failover Group (*continued*)

Although creating new groups is straightforward in principle, it is actually much easier to use the alternate method in which you modify an existing disk group to create your new group and its resources/dependencies.

Step 9—Configuring Groups and Resources for Specific Applications

In this section you will apply all the knowledge gained regarding failover groups and their resources and interdependencies to help set up the following types of application failover groups:

▼ SMB File Share

■ Print Spooler

■ Internet Information Server (3.02 or 4.0X)

■ Exchange 5.5 Enterprise Edition

▲ SQL Server 6.5 Enterprise Edition (or 7.0)

In each case I will describe all the steps necessary to set up a group and assign resources and dependencies. You must repeat this process for the second node prior to installing the applications.

SMB File Share

A file share is used to provide access to a group of shared files or folders by authorized users. It is a fundamental service provided by all OSs and although mundane in stature, it is business critical for most enterprises; making it highly available will reduce many outages experienced by users when trying to access their data.

Creating a high-availability file share under MSCS requires most of the same procedures used for setting up a standard Windows NT file share, along with adding File Share, Physical Disk, and Network Name (optional) resources.

CONFIGURING YOUR FILE SHARE   In the following steps you will create and configure a file share called File Share #1.

To create a File Share Group, follow these steps:

1. From the Cluster Administrator, choose File | New | Group.

2. In the New Group window, enter the name **File Share #1** along with a description **common files**.

3. Specify the Preferred Owners (both, with Node-2 as first in order).

4. The CA will inform you that the group has been created successfully.

5. Click once on the new file share to select it. Bring it online by clicking the Online button or by choosing File | Bring Online.

6. From the My Computer window choose the shared drive your file share will be located on. Create a folder with the share name that you are planning on using. Return to the CA window.

After you've completed the previous steps, you're ready to add resources to the file server/share. To do so, complete the following steps:

1. Click once on the new file share to select it.

2. From the CA GUI window, choose File | New | Resource.

3. You will see the New Resource Wizard. Enter the name **Corp_Data**, the description **corporate data share**, and resource type **File Share**. The group name will be filled in already, as shown here:

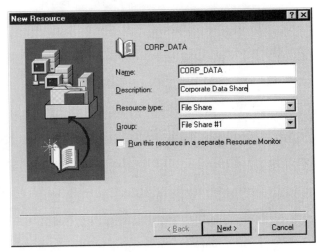

4. Fill in the Possible Owners of this resource (for both nodes).

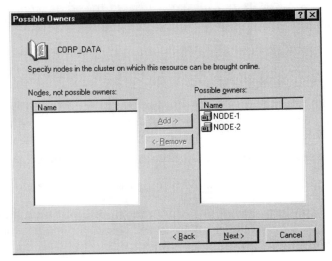

5. Skip the Dependencies dialog box for now, and go to the File Share Parameters dialog box.

6. Provide a share name **Shared Corporate Data**, full network path to the share on the shared-disk bus **V:/Shared**, and any comment that you would like, such as **Office files**...

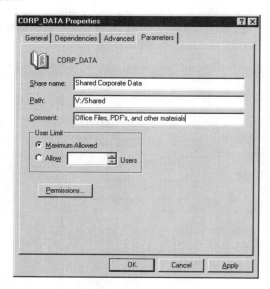

7. Specify the User Limit (specify the maximum or a fixed number).

8. Click Permissions. Specify those users who may access the share. Specify what type of access those users will have. Click OK to end data entry.

9. Click Finish.

10. Choose File I New I Resource again.

11. Choose Physical Disk as the resource type. Enter a name **Drive T** and description (if desired). Click Next.

12. Skip the Possible Owners and Dependencies dialog boxes. The Disk Parameters dialog box will display the drives available. Choose the appropriate drive resource V:(ntdsk3), and click Finish.

13. Check to see that the group and its resources come online.

In addition to these steps, you should be cognizant of the following settings.

▼ Both nodes of the cluster must be members of the same domain for the permissions that are set to be available when either node has the resource (File Share) online.

- The user account that the cluster service used to log on must have at a minimum read access to the directory. If not, the cluster service will not be able to bring the file share online.

▲ To make the file share more robust overall, it is recommended that it contain a Network Name Resource as well. This will allow users to access the share by a name and not by a hard connection to the cluster name. This is done to prevent lack of access to the share if the cluster name group does not failover, but the disk and file share resources do during a failure.

When finished setting up your group, you may add or modify specific parameters to obtain additional capabilities or flexibility via the use of the Properties command.

Print Spooler

A print spooler is a printer that has been configured on a local server and is then available to other clients and servers on a shared basis. In a clustered environment, this print spooler can be made highly available by setting up a virtual server and adding resources to the print group, such that in the event of a failure or network outage the printer and its queue remain up and running. When the Print Spool resource fails over, any documents currently being printed will be restarted on the other node.

After modifying the existing group and adding resources, you must perform the following operation on each node:

1. Install the printer ports and printer drivers. Use the local print folder, and make sure that the print ports have the same name on both nodes.

2. Add printers to the clustered spooler

CONFIGURING YOUR PRINT SPOOLER   A print spooler is a networked application that provides a dedicated printing function, allowing users to offload print queues from their desktop system and to share high-volume or special printers. In enterprise environments, printing has become a business-critical requirement and is key to productivity. A high-availability print spooler is a major benefit to those organizations that want both maximum productivity and print-job throughput.

In the following steps you will modify an existing Disk Group and create a print spooler named Print Spool #1.

To modify the existing Disk Group, follow these steps:

1. Click on a Disk Group (3).

2. From the CA, choose File | New | Resource.

3. In the New Resource window, choose IP Address as the resource type. Enter the name you want for this resource.

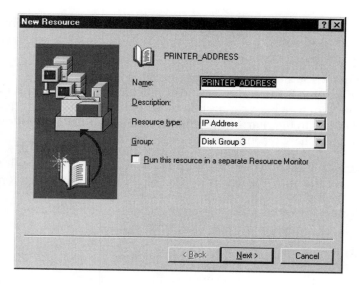

4. Click Next.

5. Skip over ownership (unless changes are required), and move to Dependencies.

6. Choose the disk resource (Disk U), and add it as a dependency. Click Next.

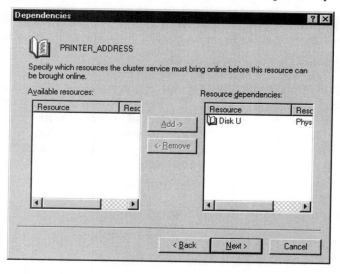

7. Enter the IP address and subnet mask that you wish to use (172.16.240.210, 255.255.240.0, respectively). Choose the network on which this should reside (Public LAN). Click Finish.

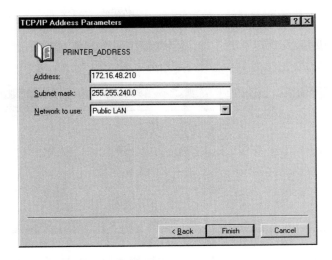

8. From the CA, choose File | New | Resource.

9. In the New Resource window, choose Network Name as the resource type. Enter the name you want for this resource (**PRINTER_QUEUE**), and add any description that you want. Click Next.

10. Skip over Ownership, and move to Dependencies. Click on both Physical Disk and IP Address, and add them to the dependencies on the right. Click Next.

11. In the Parameters dialog box, enter the unique network name that you wish (**PRINTER_QUEUE**). Click Finish.

12. From the CA, choose File | New | Resource. Choose Print Spooler as the resource type, and enter a name and description (for administrative purposes). Click Next.

13. Skip Ownership, and move to Dependencies. Click all three resources on the left, and add them to the Dependencies list for this resource. Click Next.

14. In the Parameters section you will see the folder that you initially set up as the default folder. Change this, if required, along with the job completion timeout. This parameter will depend upon the printer as well as the characteristics of file sizes and network used, so it may need to be tweaked later. This tweaking will be based on analyzing the average daily number of print jobs in the queue, as well as their characteristics; this is done to optimize performance and quality.

15. From the CA, click Online, or choose File | Bring Online to see if your print spooler comes up.

16. From the CA, choose File | Rename. You can now rename your Disk Group with its new name (Print_Spooler #1). See the three screens in Figure 5-6 for a view of this process.

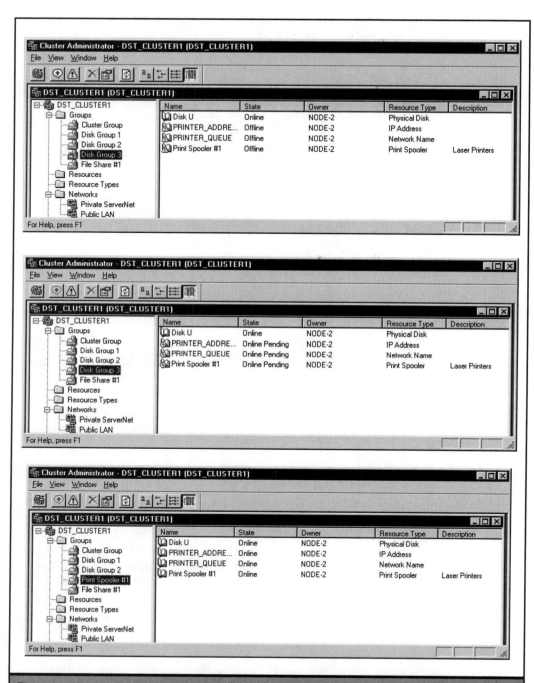

Figure 5-6.   Bringing your new print spooler online

Once the spooler is configured and running, it will behave like any other cluster-aware application:

▼ Any documents that are in transit from an application to the spooler will be discarded during a failover and must be re-spooled.

▲ MSCS will not take a Print Spooler Resource offline or move it until all jobs in the queue are completed.

Microsoft Internet Information Server

Because V3.02 comes included in Windows NT Service Pack 3 (V2.0 is installed when NTS/E is set up), I will focus on it as the baseline. Prior to setting up our IIS virtual root and performing a simple test, it is necessary that you install IIS 3.02 or later on both nodes in the same manner (using the same directory names, etc.). You will then use the IIS virtual root resource (among others) to provide failover capabilities for IIS virtual directories. These virtual directories are those that are located outside the home directory but appear to browsers as subdirectories of the home directory. They are created automatically by MSCS during the setup process for IIS.

INSTALLING INTERNET INFORMATION SERVER   To set up the IIS virtual root, follow these steps:

1. From the CA, choose File | New | Group. Provide a name and description for your IIS group. Specify the preferred owners, and click Finish. Bring it online.

2. From the CA, choose File | New | Resource. Choose Physical Disk as the resource, and provide a name and a description. Fill in the appropriate owners and dependencies.

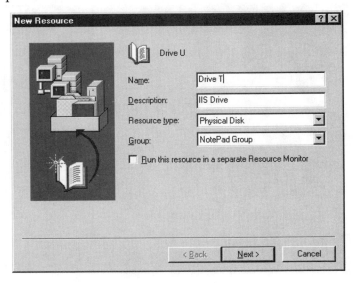

Complete the fields in the Disk Parameters dialog box, and click Finish.

3. From the CA, choose File | New | Resource. Choose IP Address as the resource, and provide a name and a description.

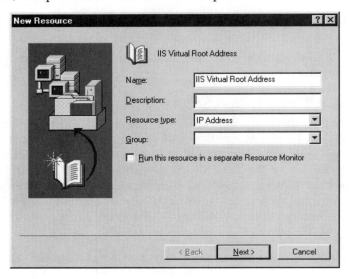

Skip over the Preferred Owners, and assign the physical disk as a dependency. Enter an IP address and subnet mask, along with accepting or modifying the client network that the cluster is connected to by default. Click Finish.

4. From the CA, choose File | New | Resource. Choose Network Name as the resource, and provide a name and description (for administrative use only at this point).

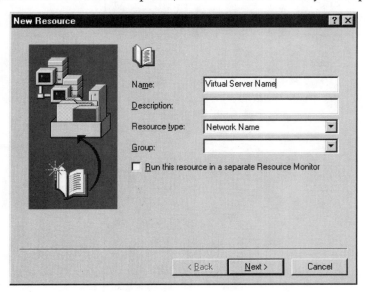

Click past Preferred Owners, and assign the IP address and physical disk as dependencies. In the Network Name Parameters dialog box, enter the unique name for this virtual server. Click Finish.

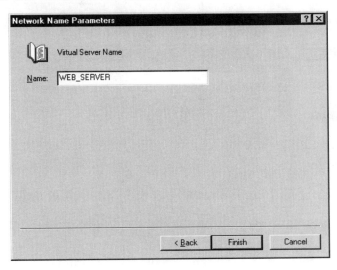

5. From the CA, choose File | New | Resource. Choose IIS Virtual Root as the resource. Provide a name and description for this resource. Click past the Preferred Owners, and add the physical disk, IP address, and network name as dependencies. Click to the Parameters dialog box.

6. In the Parameters dialog box, choose WWW. Enter a path to the directory for the IIS Root (c:\website\Share) and the alias that you want to use (Node-1). Click Finish.

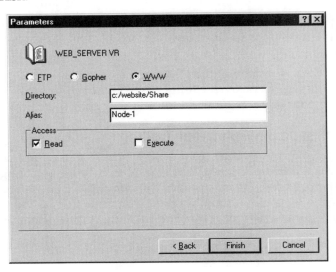

7. Select the name of your IIS group (if it's not already selected). From the CA, choose File | Bring Online, and observe MSCS bring your IIS group online.

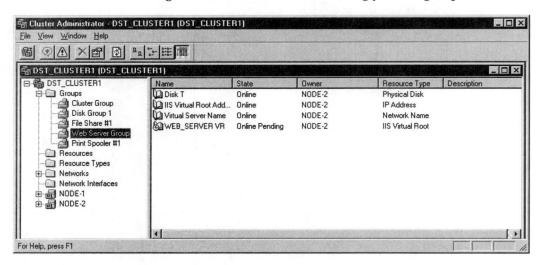

Your IIS virtual root is now online and ready for some simple tests. These tests can be performed via a Web browser from the Administrative client, as described in the following steps:

1. Enter the name of the virtual root in your browser. Verify the connection by viewing sample material that you previously loaded into the Web site (or online information already loaded if IIS has previously been in service).

2. From the CA, right-click on the IIS group name, and select Move Group. Observe the status icons on the CA to see if the group fails over to the other node.

3. Click on Refresh on your client browser, and observe if the connection is maintained.

4. From the CA, right-click on the IIS group name, and select Move Group again. Observe the status icons to see if the group fails back correctly. Confirm this by refreshing your browser again.

Microsoft Exchange 5.5 Enterprise Edition

Exchange requires many resources from MSCS. Many of these are configured when running the Exchange Setup Wizard, but a number may be preconfigured for easier installation. When Exchange is installed under MSCS, it is configured in a high-availability model (Active/Standby) rather than one that provides load balancing (Active/Active). Figure 5-7 is a diagram of an Exchange virtual server.

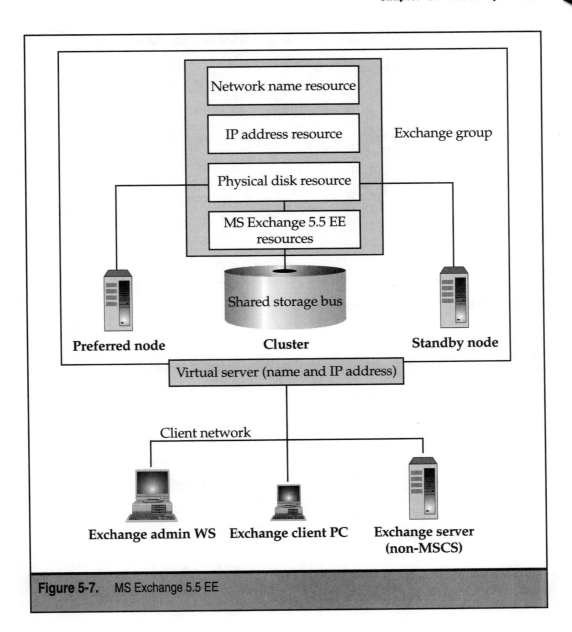

Figure 5-7. MS Exchange 5.5 EE

INSTALLING EXCHANGE 5.5 To preconfigure the group and resources, follow these steps:

1. From the CA, choose File | New | Group. Enter a name and description for the Exchange group.

Click Finish. Bring the group online.

2. From the CA, choose File | New | Resource. Choose Physical Disk as the resource. Enter a name and description for the resource. Click next.

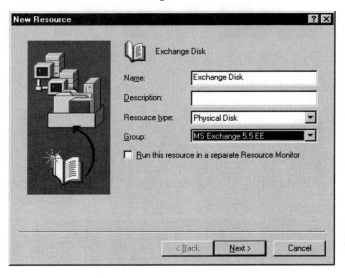

Verify the preferred owners of the resource, and click past Dependencies to Parameters. Select the physical drive, and click Finish.

3. From the CA, choose File | New | Resource. Choose IP Address as the resource. Provide a name and a description for the resource.

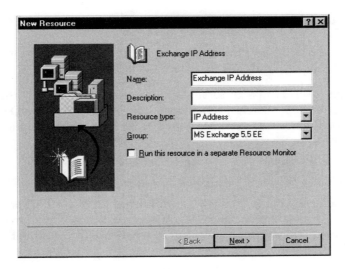

Click past Preferred Owners to Dependencies. Choose the physical disk as the dependency to add, and click Next. Within Parameters enter the IP address and subnet for the resource, along with choosing the network that it will reside on. Click Finish.

4. From the CA, choose File | New | Resource. Choose Network Name as the resource. Provide a name and a description for the resource.

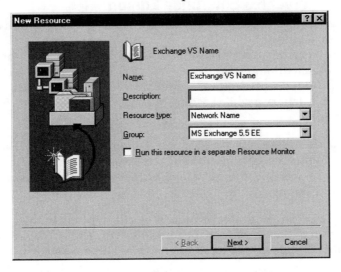

Click past Preferred Owners to Dependencies. Add the IP address and physical disk as dependencies, and then click Next. In the Preferences dialog box, enter the name that you have chosen for your virtual server. Click Finish.

5. Click on the Exchange group to select it. From the CA, choose File | Bring Online. Verify that all resources in the group come online without problem.

6. Repeat this process for Node-2.

After you've preconfigured the group and resources, you'll need to install and test Exchange Server. To do this, follow these next steps:

1. On Node-1, run Exchange Server Setup. Select the Exchange group that you set up earlier in step 1. Exchange will install files on the Physical Disk Resource as well as on the non-shared drive where NTS/E resides. Some files may be installed on non-shared drives.

2. Follow the Installation Wizard, and complete the installation.

3. Run Exchange Server Performance Optimizer on Node-1.

4. Install Exchange using the Installation Wizard on Node-2. Choose Update Node as the installation choice. Many files will not be copied to the second node because they were installed on the shared disk(s) during the installation of Node-1.

5. Do not run Performance Optimizer on Node-2.

Test failover and failback of the Exchange group and resources via the Cluster Administrator. This can be accomplished by moving the Group and its Resources from Node-1 to Node-2 and back again. During this process you observe the Resources coming offline, moving to the other node and then coming back online again.

Microsoft SQL Server 6.5 Enterprise Edition

SQL Server can operate in Symmetric Virtual Server mode for maximum availability and some increased scalability.

In this mode each node runs two instances of SQL Server. One is for primary purposes supporting its own clients and workload, while the other is for failover support (for the other node). In this mode queries can be split between the two nodes, which can share some portions of the database while keeping others separate. See Figure 5-8 for a diagram of SVS on SQL Server.

NOTES ABOUT ADMINISTERING SQL 6.5 EE   SQL Server is a complex relational database on its own. When you configure it for both high-availability and use it in its Symmetric Virtual Server mode, it is even more challenging to manage. To minimize the difficulty, I have included considerations to be aware of.

▼ A virtual SQL Server is always remote, even when running SQL Enterprise Manager on the same node as the virtual server. The virtual server is not bound to the underlying node so it can be run from either node.

■ Your virtual SQL Server must be started and stopped via the Cluster Administrator. If you use SQL Server Enterprise Manager or SQL Service Manager to stop your virtual SQL Server, MSCS will perceive this as a failure and attempt to restart the virtual server on the other node.

▲   When your virtual SQL Server is running on the backup node, client utilities
    must be run from either that node or a separate client system (the latter is the
    preferred method).

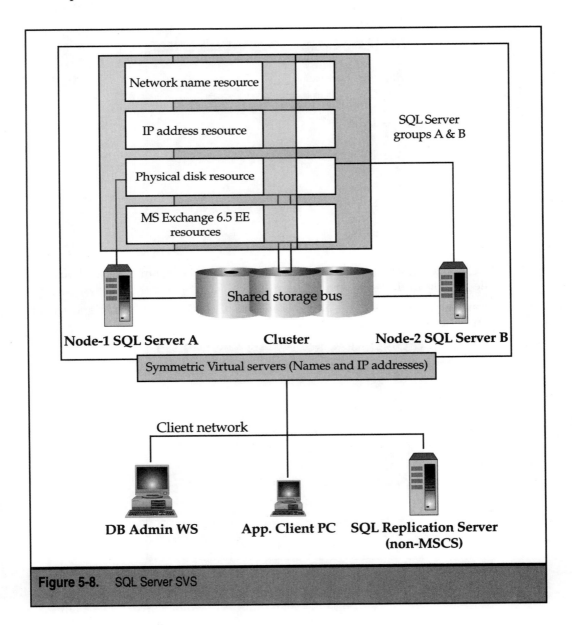

Figure 5-8.   SQL Server SVS

INSTALLING SQL SERVER   To configure the SQL Server group and resources, complete the following steps:

1. From the CA, choose File | New | Group. Enter a name and description for your SQL Server group.

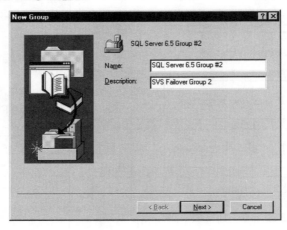

   Click Finish. Click on the group name once to select it. From the CA, choose File | Bring Online.

2. From the CA, choose File | New | Resource. Choose Physical Disk, and enter a name and description for this resource.

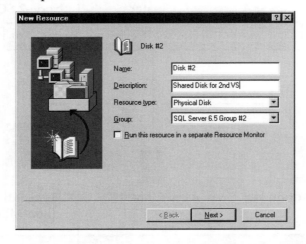

   Click to Preferred Owners, and verify the choices. Click past Dependencies to Parameters, and enter/choose the physical disk. Click Finish.

3. From the CA, choose File | New | Resource. Choose IP Address, and enter a name and description for the resource.

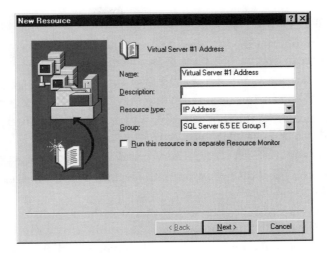

Click past Preferred Owners to Dependencies. Click on the physical disk in the box on the left, and transfer it as a dependency. Click Next to Parameters. Enter the IP address and subnet mask for your virtual SQL Server. Choose the network that it will reside on, and click Finish.

4. From the CA, choose File | New | Resource. Choose Network Name, and enter a name and description for this resource.

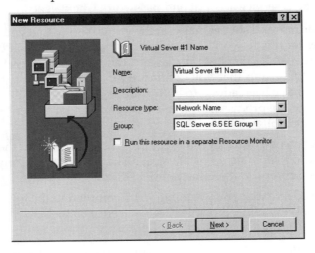

Click past Preferred Owners to Dependencies. Choose both the physical disk and IP address, and transfer them over as dependencies. Click Next to go to Parameters. Enter the unique name for your virtual SQL Server, and click Finish.

5. Select the name of your SQL group. From the CA, choose File | Bring Online. Verify that all resources in your SQL group come online.

6. Repeat the previous steps for Node-2.

After you've configured the SQL Server group and resources, you'll need to install SQL Server. In order to do this, complete these steps:

1. From the CA, choose File | Take Offline, and click on all resources for the IIS, MTS, and DTC services (assuming that they had previously been online)

2. Run Setup.exe from the root directory on the SQL Server Enterprise Edition CD-ROM. Begin your installation on Node-1.

3. Disable Automatic Start for SQL Server and SQL Executive services.

4. Specify the physical disk resource path for both the SQL Server Install and the Master Database Install.

5. Choose the Named Pipes network protocol as the default. You may also choose IP and RPC as additional choices.

6. Complete the installation, and start SQL Server. Check the installation, and stop the server.

7. Double-click on the SQL Cluster Setup icon on the SQL Server 6.5 Enterprise Edition CD-ROM.

8. Select Install Virtual Server. Click Next.

9. Enter the system administrator password for SQL Server. Click Next.

10. Enter the SQL service account and password. Click Next.

Enter the IP address and subnet mask for the virtual server that you set up previously. Click Next, and enter the network name for the virtual server. Click Finish. The virtual SQL Server is now installed on both nodes and can be moved between the two nodes. Since it joined a SQL group that you configured in advance, the registry keys for the virtual SQL Server have been added to both nodes.

The next stage of the process is to create a second virtual server (Symmetric Virtual Server). Complete the following step:

- Repeat steps 1 and 2 of the previous procedure. Assign the second virtual server to a separate set of physical disks. Do not install any files from both virtual servers on the same physical disk.

Next, you'll need to check your installation by completing the following steps: Bring your virtual SQL Server online. From the CA, click once on the server group. Choose File | Bring Online.

1. Run SQL Enterprise Manager on the primary node for that virtual server.

2. From the Register Server dialog box, enter the virtual SQL Server's name in the Server box. Click Register.

3. Register the other server using the same process.

4. If both servers register successfully, your installation is complete and operational.

Step 10—Configuring Generic Applications

Having configured all of your cluster-aware applications, you probably want to create a virtual server for one (or more) of your other non-cluster-aware applications. This will give you the ability to manually failover this application or service in the event that the primary node becomes unavailable.

Setting up Your Non-Cluster Aware Application or Service

In spite of the desire to use cluster-aware applications to get the maximum benefits from your MSCS cluster, there are many requirements for making non-cluster-aware applications more available or to simply utilize the Virtual Service mode in MSCS to consolidate applications within a clustered environment.

1. From the CA, choose File | New | Group. Provide a name and description for your group. Enter the order or the preferred owners. Click Finish.

2. Click on your group name once to highlight it. From the CA, choose File | Bring Online. Verify that your group comes online.

3. From the CA, choose File | New | Resource. Choose Physical Disk. Enter a name and description for this resource. Click Next, and select the preferred owners. Click Next, and enter the drive that you want for this resource.

4. From the CA, choose File | New | Resource. Choose IP Address. Enter a name and description for this resource. Click Next past Preferred Owners to Dependencies, and choose the physical disk as a dependency. Click Next, and enter the IP address and subnet mask as parameters as well as specifying which network you want to use. Click Finish.

5. From the CA, choose File | New | Resource. Choose Network Name. Enter a name and description for this resource. Click next past Preferred Owners to Dependencies, and choose the physical disk and IP address as dependencies. Click Next, and enter the unique name for this virtual server. Click Finish.

6. From the CA, choose File | New | Resource. Choose Generic Application, and enter a name and description for this resource. Click Next twice to arrive at Dependencies. Choose all three resources on the left, and transfer them over as dependencies. Click Next to Parameters, and enter the command line information for the generic application along with its directory. Click Next again to Registry Replication. Enter any registry keys that must be replicated to both servers. Click Finish.

7. Click the generic application group. From the CA, choose File | Bring Online. Verify that your group comes online successfully.

Step 11—Testing Failover/Failback on Your Cluster

After mastering the process of creating and modifying groups and resources, you may want to set up a simple application that can be used by administrators to test the cluster and its behavioral characteristics. These tests should be conducted immediately after installing a new application or service to verify its proper operation. It is also good practice to routinely test each application or service for proper failover and failback behavior. You should note the time required for each process to fully execute and the impact this has in respect to connected users (obviously during off hours or with non-production data and applications).

To accomplish this you can use a simple application such as Notepad, which is located in the root directory for NTS/E on the boot drive. To set up this test application, complete the following steps:

1. From the CA, click on Cluster Group to select it.

2. From the CA, choose New | File | Resource. Choose Generic Application. Enter a name and description for this resource. Click Next (accepting the defaults) until you get to Parameters. Enter the application's name and location. Click OK to allow it to interact with the desktop.

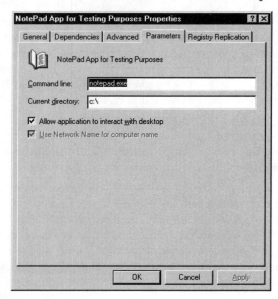

3. Click Next to Registry Keys, and then click Finish.

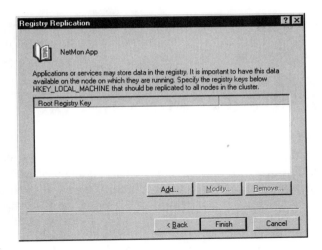

4. From the CA, choose File | Bring Online. Verify that the entire Cluster Group comes online.

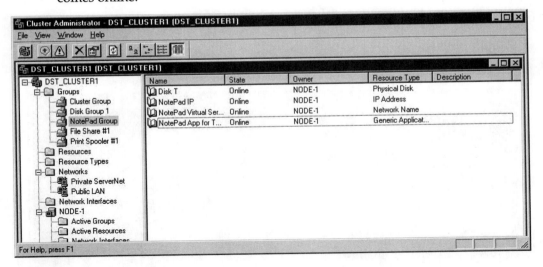

To test the generic application, follow these steps:

1. Select the Cluster Group by clicking on it once.

2. From the CA, choose File | Move Group. Notepad should stop on the primary node and restart on the secondary node. Verify these operations, and then manually failback the Cluster Group to the primary node.

3. If these movements occurred without failure, your cluster is working properly. If not, monitor each resource during the operation to determine which is failing and adjust its parameters accordingly.

COMMAND LINE INTERFACE CONTROL OF YOUR CLUSTER

For those administrators who like to write and use their own scripts for unattended control or use the CLI for control purposes on an occasional basis, MSCS has a duplicate set on functionality separate from the Cluster Administrator for use from the command line. By evoking cluster.exe from the Windows NT command prompt, you will see a display similar to the one shown in Figure 5-9. You can use cluster.exe to administer MSCS clusters from either node of the cluster, or from any other computer running SP3 with version 4.0 of either Windows NT Server or Workstation. Cluster.exe is installed on both nodes of the cluster when you install the Cluster Administrator GUI. By entering the appropriate command syntax and variables, you can essentially duplicate the major control functions found under the Cluster Administrator.

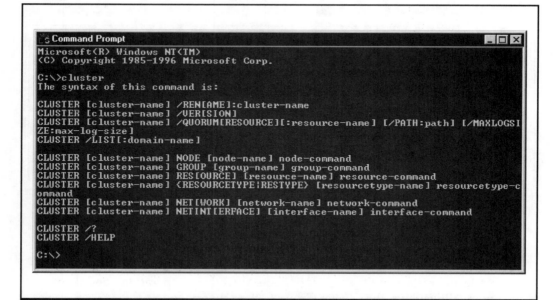

Figure 5-9. The CLI for cluster.exe from the DOS shell

The following are general scripting notes:

▼ You must use quotation marks around all names that contain spaces when setting properties to True or False—use 1 for true and 0 for false.

■ Many of the commonly available scripting tools for Windows NT administration have added extensions to their libraries to support MSCS operation.

▲ There are five basic cluster command groupings: Cluster, Cluster Node, Cluster Group, Cluster Resource, and Cluster Resource Type. Each has its own area of control and options to support it.

Cluster

The following is the basic Cluster syntax:

CLUSTER [cluster-name] /Option

A listing of all options and what they are used for is provided here:

Command	Description	Variables
/REN[AME]: cluster name	Renames Cluster	New Cluster Name
/VER[SION]:	Lists Version of MSCS	n/a
/QUORUM[RESOURCE]:	Changes QR Values	Resource Name and Path and Max Log Size Settings, QR Name, QR location, Size of Quorum log
/LIST:[domain name]	Lists all clusters in domain	n/a
/HELP	Cluster command Help	n/a

Cluster Node

The basic Cluster Node syntax is:

CLUSTER [cluster name] NODE [node name] /option

The following table lists these options and their descriptions:

Command	Description	Variables
/Status	Displays the node's status	n/a
/Pause	Pauses the node	n/a

Command	Description	Variables
/Resume	Resumes a paused node	n/a
/Evict	Evicts the node from the cluster	n/a
/Properties [propname=propvalue]	Displays the node properties	Set the value of the specific node properties
/HELP	Cluster Node command Help	n/a

NOTE: By default there is only one cluster node property supported by the cluster software, and there are no private properties on cluster nodes unless a software vendor wishes to add them for extended functionality.

Cluster Group

The basic Cluster Group syntax is:

CLUSTER [cluster name] GROUP [group name] /option

Table 5-2 lists these options and their descriptions.

Command	Description	Variables
[group name}/Status	Displays the status of the group	n\a
/Status [/node:node name]	Displays all online groups on a node	n\a
/Create	Creates a new group	n\a
/Delete	Deletes a group	n\a
/Rename: new group name	Renames a group	New Group name
/Move to	Moves group to another node	Node name and Waiting time
/Online	Brings a group online	Node Name and Waiting Time
/Offline	Takes a group offline	Node Name and Waiting Time

Table 5-2. Cluster Group Commands

/Properties[propname-propvalue]	Displays a group's properties	(See following Note)
/PrivProperties[propname=propvalue]	Sets Private Group Properties	(See following Note)
/List Owners	Displays preferred owners	n\a
/SetOwners:node list	Specifies Preferred owner	Preferred Owner
/Rename:new group name	Renames a Group	New Group Name
/Help	Cluster Group Help	n\a

Table 5-2. Cluster Group Commands (*continued*)

NOTE: With commands that require a waiting time to be input, this value is entered to tell the cluster how long to wait before canceling the command if it does not complete successfully. Also, there are no private group properties available.

There are a number of Cluster Group Common Property names, along with varying ways to use them. The following table provides a summary:

CG Common Property Name	Usage
PersistentState	Describes the last known persistent state
FailoverThreshold	Number of times the CS attempts a failover
FailoverPeriod	The time in hours over which the CS attempts to failover a group
AutoFailbackType	True to allow failback, False to prevent it
FailbackWindowStart	24-hour timing for failback to initiate
FailbackWindowEnd	24-hour timing for failback to end

Cluster Resource

The basic Cluster Resource syntax is

CLUSTER [cluster name] RESOURCE [resource name]/option

Table 5-3 is a list of these options and their descriptions.

Command	Description
/Status	Displays the status of a resource
/Create /Group:group name /Type:res-type	Creates a new resource in a specified group
/Delete	Deletes a resource
/Rename:new resource name	Renames a resource
/AddOwner:node name	Adds a node name to the list of possible owners
/RemoveOwner: node name	Removes a node name
/ListOwners	Lists all possible owners
/MoveTo:group	Moves the resource to a different group
/Properties [propname=propvalue]	Displays and sets specific resource properties
/PrivProperties [propname=propvalue]	Sets the value of private resource properties
/Fail	Fails the resource
/Online	Brings the resource online
/Offline	Takes the resource offline
/ListDependencies	Lists all dependencies for a particular resource
/AddDependency:resource	Adds a dependency for a particular resource
/RemoveDependency:resource	Removes a dependency for a particular resource
/Help	Provides Cluster Resource help

Table 5-3. Cluster Resource Options and Descriptions

There are a number of Resource Properties Names as well. The following table outlines them based on their functionality:

Property Name	Usage
Description	Changes the textual description
DebugPrefix	Specifies the debugger
SeparateMonitor	Sets the Monitor Sharing mode
PersistentState	Defines the last known state of the resource
LooksAlivePollInterval	Polls interval in seconds
IsAlivePollInterval	Sets poll interval in seconds
RestartAction	Mode where Failed Resource is handled
RestartThreshold	Determines number of restart attempts
RestartPeriod	Determines amount of time for restart
PendingTimeout	Status Resolution Timeout Period

Cluster Resource Type

The basic Cluster Resource Type syntax is:

CLUSTER [cluster name] RESOURCETYPE [resource type display name] /option

See the following table for a listing and detailed description of these options:

Command	Description
/List	Lists resource types available
/Create /DLLName:dllname /Type:Type name	Creates a resource type
/Isalive:interval /LooksAlive:interval	Sets interval lengths
/Delete [/Type]	Deletes a resource type
/Properties [propname=propvalue]	Displays resource type properties
/PrivProperties [propname=propvalue]	Sets private resource properties
/Help	Cluster Resource Type Help

As with the other properties listings, the Cluster Resource Type has a number of common settings as well. The following table describes them.

Name	Usage
Name	Changes display name
Description	Changes resource description text
DLLName	Specifies the DLL for a particular resource type
DebugPrefix	Specifies the debugger for the Resource type
AdminExtensions	Describes the class identifiers for the CA
LooksAlivePollInterval	Specifies the interval
IsAlivePollInterval	Specifies the interval

Universal Abbreviations

Cluster.exe supports a number of abbreviations for day-to-day use by administrators. The following table lists common abbreviations:

Name	Abbreviation
AddDependency	AddDep
DLLName	Dll
ListDependencies	ListDep
MoveTo	Move
Online	On
Offline	Off
PrivProperties	Priv
Properties	Prop or Props
QuorumResource	Quorum
RemoveDependency	RemoveDep
Rename	Ren
Resource	Res
ResourceType	ResType
Status	Stat
Version	Ver

SUMMARY

Having survived all of these steps and mastered the Cluster Administrator in the process, you are now ready to go forward and cluster your computing empire. There are other considerations to take into account when doing so, such as the following:

▼ What applications are cluster-aware under MSCS?

■ How can I make my non-cluster-aware legacy applications take better advantage of the high availability that MSCS provides?

■ How does MSCS integrate into my enterprise management scheme?

■ What storage management planning do I need to support?

▲ Can I improve the overall availability of MSCS further?

These and other fundamental questions will be answered in subsequent chapters of this book that focus on applications, competitive and collaborative solutions, MSCS Phase 2, and storage. Chapter 10 is devoted to troubleshooting to help solve many of the problems and quirks that arise with MSCS.

CHAPTER 6

Other Windows NT Clustering/High-Availability Solutions

COMPETITIVE AND COLLABORATIVE CLUSTERING SOLUTIONS

To reiterate what I said earlier in this book, MSCS is neither the first nor the only clustering/high-availability solution for Windows NT. A number of product offerings utilize similar architectural approaches (failover via middleware), with differences in the details of their implementation, as well as many others that use completely different technical approaches. Several vendors offer products that can coexist with MSCS and take advantage of its tight integration with the Windows NT operating system kernel and industry-standard API to provide improvements in performance. These products collaborate with MSCS to provide even higher levels of availability and manageability than found in the core release of MSCS or from competing solutions.

These solutions all meet the loosely defined requirements of a cluster (such as single system image, high-availability, scalability, and so on). Some (load balancing IP type clusters) provide this capability on the front-end of a system, while others (for example, server clusters, SCSI clusters, mirroring-type clusters, and so on) provide it on the back-end. It is possible to combine the front-end back-end clusters for specific types of application or services environments such as Web services and thin-client networks. Microsoft's recent acquisition of Valence Research has produced such a solution. The Convoy load-balancing cluster (now called MS WLBS) can be used with MSCS to provide a highly available and scalable IIS (Gopher, FTP, and HTTP) environment, which is depicted in Figure 6-1. (This functionality will be provided in a later release of NTS/E for both Windows 4.0 and Windows 2000.) This solution is a good strategy for those folks who operate growing Web server farms that need not only higher levels of availability (user requests and resource level), but scalability on demand as well (up to 32 nodes can be supported by WLBS today). This combination of solutions is unique to particular application areas.

A similar opportunity exists when one considers using a mirroring-type clustering solution (available from Legato FullTime or Vinca) on the back-end, in conjunction with a load-balancing type such as Cubix's LBS for Windows NT Server Terminal Server Edition on the front-end. This combination creates a high-availability/scalability cluster for thin-client terminals. Figure 6-2 illustrates this type of cluster.

This chapter will discuss a wide range of clustering/high-availability solutions for Windows NT, including solutions such as Convoy (MS WLBS), Legato FullTime's Octopus, and Vinca's Standby Server.

ALTERNATIVE CLUSTERING AND HIGH-AVAILABILITY SOLUTIONS

A growing number of vendors provides clustering/high-availability solutions for Windows NT. These solutions run the gamut in terms of technology, performance, and cost. Each offers some type of benefit that is unique in respect to other offerings, as well as each fitting into an overall hierarchy of the clustering solutions for NT as a whole . This hierarchy is based on performance versus price and complexity.

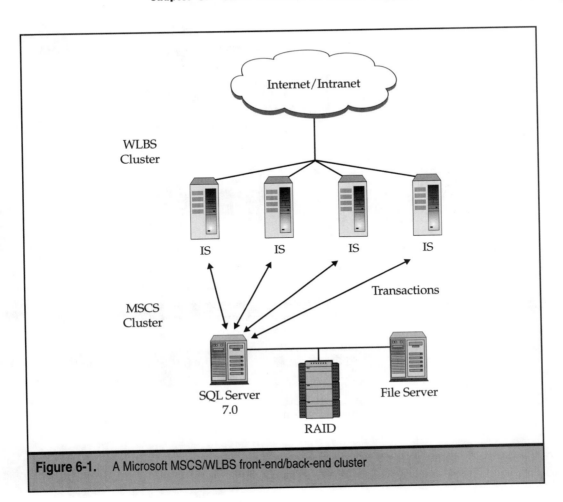

Figure 6-1. A Microsoft MSCS/WLBS front-end/back-end cluster

The range of solutions that are included in this chapter are based upon the following technical approaches:

▼ High-availability middleware with failover and failback capabilities (MSCS; server based)

■ Extended or remote data mirroring (server based)

■ Dynamic load balancing (Web and thin-client servers; IP based)

■ Storage area network clustering (SAN based)

■ Switched SCSI clustering (SCSI based)

▲ Hybrids (hardware, software, middleware, and so on)

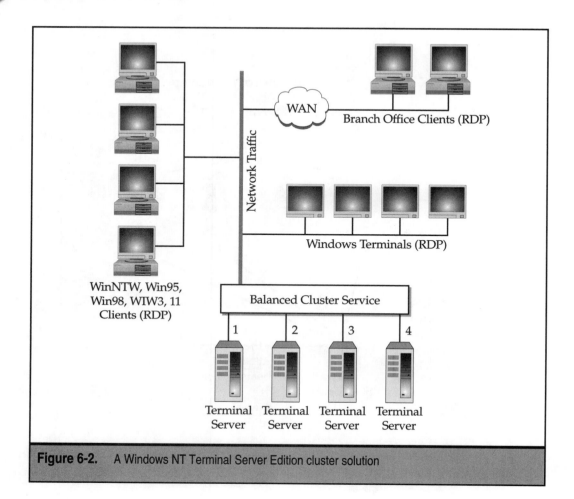

Figure 6-2. A Windows NT Terminal Server Edition cluster solution

All of these solutions compete with MSCS to some extent, with several offering MSCS extensibility options. We will discuss each one in respect to their advantages and disadvantages. We will also discuss how they can be added to your MSCS solution to provide additional functionality, system availability, or other benefits.

Middleware, Server-based Clustering

These server-based, middleware-driven solutions are the most directly competitive with MSCS. Many of these solutions are offered by Microsoft's MSCS vendor partners and are used primarily as platforms for their own early adopter customers who need enhanced capabilities and cannot wait for a "generalized" solution from Microsoft. These product efforts are also a test bed for MSCS concepts and capabilities, such as N-node scalability and Memory Channel, which will become available in the near future.

Others are for the most part directly competitive with MSCS and use similar architectural constructs and management methodologies. Each of these is aimed at the same target markets—that is, high-availability, increased scalability, and enhanced manageability of NT applications and services. All of these competitive solutions feature the use of standard versions of NT Server (although NTS/E can be used to support expanded application memory and SMP CPU count) and are not as particular about matching the hardware and peripherals on the two (or more) nodes in the cluster. However, none of them fully support the use of the Wolfpack API; they must use their own "personality modules" for key applications or other sensing methods to control failover and failback.

High-availability middleware solutions are based on code, which resides between the OS and the applications and services supported by it. This middleware (with some assistance from hardware, such as the cluster heartbeat private network, shared-storage bus, and its devices) monitors the behavior and availability of key resources and services (such as storage devices, network names, and IP addresses). In the event that any of these fail or become unavailable for an extended period of time (which can be defined by an administrator), then the clustering middleware transfers ownership either automatically or manually, of these resources to another designated node in the cluster for restart and reconnection to clients. The failover node then processes client requests and runs these applications and services until such time as the middleware tells the node to stop. Then the middleware transfers these resources back to the primary node. The majority of these competitive solutions monitor a single heartbeat per server, while MSCS monitors the server heartbeat, along with two separate heartbeats for each application ("LooksAlive" and "IsAlive"). These additional heartbeats, part of the Wolfpack API specification, are used to determine if a failure is on the server or within the application or service itself. This level of monitoring is one of the key differentiating features of MSCS in respect to its granularity (that is, down to the application resource level rather than simply failing the server overall). It accounts for the significance of the Wolfpack API for use with cluster-aware applications and services residing on high-availability solutions such as MSCS.

Clustering middleware has been the most popular methodology for creating high-availability clusters for some time now and continues to be extended in capabilities and performance with each new generation. Most clusters using this approach are currently two to eight nodes maximum, which creates limited opportunities for scalability provided by N-node clusters. Some scalability can be realized by using shared-nothing, parallel-type databases (such as IBM DB2 UDB and SQL Server 7.0) that can logically break a single query into multiple subqueries that are processed on separate nodes of the cluster for improved performance.

An industry endorsed, cluster-aware API to support these middleware-driven clusters has been a missing ingredient for some time now. With the recent release of the Wolfpack API (in 1995) from Microsoft and its early adopter partners, an opportunity currently exists for many of these solutions to be more tightly integrated with both the OS and its cluster-aware applications. This can improve overall performance while reducing the costs associated with custom DLL and personality module development.

These solutions come primarily from two camps. Those that are direct competitors of MSCS and those that are from vendors who are part of the MSCS family. We will discuss the two camps separately.

Competitive Solutions

These middleware-based clustering solutions come from vendors who have developed their own end-to-end clustering solution for Windows NT along with other platforms. For the most part, all of these directly compete with MSCS, although several take advantage to some degree of the Wolfpack API, therefore enabling the use of MSCS cluster-aware applications with their clustering solution, for example Veritas and NCR.

The key competitors of MSCS on the basis of features, functions, and price are:

▼   Veritas First Watch

■   NCR LifeKeeper

■   Oracle Parallel Server

▲   Legato FullTime Cluster

In terms of basic features and functionality, most of these offerings are on a par with MSCS, and several have increased functionality. All feature a two-node configuration as a minimum, with additional nodes supported for increased scalability (typically four) by LifeKeeper and Parallel Server. Table 6-1 compares the features available from these solutions.

VERITAS FIRST WATCH   Introduced in 1997 for Windows NT, First Watch has been available from Veritas for UNIX platforms (SunOS, Solaris, HP/UX, and IBM AIX) since 1993. First Watch is a two-node, system-level software failover solution. It is targeted at application areas such as databases, Web, and Internet servers. First Watch for Windows NT is a port of their versions for UNIX and utilizes some aspects of the Wolfpack API (for example, IsAlive) to enable the use of MSCS applications.

Solution	Maximum Number of Nodes	Percent Availability (typical)	Scalability	Middleware	Mirroring	Wolfpack API	Core Platform
MSCS	2	99.5+	Limited	Yes	No	Yes	NT
LifeKeeper	32	99.99	Yes	Yes	Yes	Yes	UNIX
FirstWatch	2	99.98	No	Yes	No	Partially	UNIX
OPS	4	99.9X	Yes	Yes	No	No	UNIX
FullTime	100	99.9X	Yes	Yes	No	No	NT

Table 6-1.   Comparison of Middleware Clustering Solutions for Windows NT

Veritas is well known for both its volume management and file system products in the OEM marketplace. The product will supply a version of Volume Manager in the core release of Windows 2000, which replaces the existing Windows NT fault-tolerant disk administrator, ftdisk, which does not work with MSCS today. Also, Veritas will collaborate with Microsoft on the development of a cluster file system (CFS) for use with Phase 2 of MSCS.

Very similar in features and structure to MSCS (for example, its use of Virtual Servers), First Watch uses multiple heartbeats (via multiple network connections and through the SCSI disk drives) and a Web browser–based interface to manage local and remote clusters. It also uses the following agents to monitor applications and their resources for failures, outages, and hangs:

- File agent
- FTP agent
- Gopher agent
- IIS Web Server agent
- MS SQL agent

- NetBackup agent
- File Share agent
- Netscape Web Server agent
- Oracle agent
- Services agent

First Watch can support Windows NT versions 3.51 and later and uses standard versions of these applications, with specific types of agents available to monitor the health and status of these applications and NT services. Given its limited level of adherence to the Wolfpack API, it can support the use of cluster-aware applications as well. In the event of a failure, it is not necessary for any node to be "rebooted" to either failover its applications and resources or to have them failback at a later time. First Watch can support applications that are either state-full or state-less in terms of client interaction. Availability of 99.98 percent is typical of a fully configured First Watch system on Windows NT.

First Watch agents are responsive to the following types of failures and outages:

▼ Heartbeat losses
■ Process halt or hang
■ Reboot
■ Power failure (AC or DC)
■ User-defined events
■ Application failure
▲ Manually induced failures or failover requests

As part of its initiative in the growing marketplace for Storage Area Networks (SANs), Veritas recently announced a new clustering solution, Veritas Cluster Server, which will ultimately replace First Watch. This product is based on SAN clustering and can support up to 32 nodes today, with 128 or more in the near future. We will discuss Cluster Server in the section "Storage Area Network (SAN) Clusters," later in this chapter.

NCR LIFEKEEPER   LifeKeeper is another high-availability software product with its roots in the UNIX world that has been ported over to Windows NT. It has been available since 1992 and is positioned by NCR as their premium solution for NT and UNIX users. LifeKeeper supports up to 32 nodes and is purported to provide high-availability (99.99 percent and higher), scalability, and enhanced manageability in transaction-oriented environments. The most recent version of LifeKeeper for Windows NT is 2.02.

LifeKeeper is based on the use of middleware and remote mirroring. The availability components can be used separately (middleware versus mirroring), and their mirroring can be used with MSCS. NCR has delivered thousands of systems utilizing LifeKeeper for such industries as retail, medical, and telecommunications.

LifeKeeper 2.0 and later supports the use of the Wolfpack API and can interface with all of the current and future MSCS cluster-aware applications, giving this product a definite edge over other non-MSCS offerings. In addition, because LifeKeeper is currently a multi-node solution, it can support the following functionality:

▼ *Multi-directional failover*   In high-demand environments, a node that has multiple applications running on it may parse out these applications to other nodes during periods of high usage. This is a form of load-balancing on the fly.

■ *N-way failover*   Applications and resources can be configured to failover to any other node in the cluster, with these other nodes having a priority assigned to them in respect to each particular application and its resources in the failover mode. This eliminates the hard pairing associated with two-node clusters and eliminates outages due to multiple failures.

▲ *Cascading Failover*   This mode supports a domino effect in terms of a failover sequence for key applications and their resources. It is another method to overcome multiple failures.

LifeKeeper has many features that are sorely lacking in MSCS today. The majority of these features have been developed based on years of experience and customer feedback that has enjoyed in their position at the top of the transaction-processing market. MSCS Phase 2 will have to employ many of these types of features and capabilities if it is going to supplant a product such as LifeKeeper.

ORACLE PARALLEL SERVER (OPS)   OPS (v7.3 and later), a parallel database in concept, has been the premier cluster-aware application environment for many years. The fastest TPC and TPD numbers for any parallel-type database are still held by Oracle on a clustered platform (usually on a Digital Alpha server-based UNIX cluster). It is ported to every major version of UNIX, along with VMS, MVS, and Windows NT. Thousands of sites worldwide run this application in a scalability-mode, with high-availability and improved manageability to boot.

NOTE: TPC and TPD are transaction performance ratings performed by vendors using standard tests developed by the Transaction Performance Council, an independent benchmarking organization. See *www.tpc.org* *for more information on these benchmark type tests.*

Oracle Parallel Server provides both higher availability and scalability in a parallel server environment. Availability is derived by using multiple instances of the Oracle database application spread across the nodes of the cluster. In the event of a failure on any node, the surviving instances can take over the workload of the failed node, while rebalancing their new workload on the fly. These failures can include failure of a node or a disk or a network outage. Scalability is achieved by allowing all nodes to simultaneously access the same database via its shared-disk architecture, with disk access arbitration being provided by a Distributed Lock Manager (DLM). This is the key difference between Oracle's shared-disk cluster architecture and Microsoft's shared-nothing architecture.

OPS for Windows NT is provided by "certified" vendors who, working closely with Oracle, have created a shared-disk clustering environment that OPS can layer on top of. These vendors include IBM, NEC, Dell, DG, HP, and Compaq. These vendors have created an operating systems dependent (OSD) interface layer. This layer consists of a cluster manager (CM), inter-process communications (IPC), I/O, and other components. All of these components act as a single DLL in the OPS runtime environment. This layer is implemented as a set of separate and coordinated hardware and software modules that are supplied by the hardware vendor.

NOTE: Oracle, in November of 1998, announced a new initiative called Big Iron that will capitalize on their experience with OPS to build an Internet-based database infrastructure that uses large servers with no operating system. Instead, the initiative will use an Oracle OS specifically designed to maximize performance, reduce complexity, and increase interoperability.

▼ The cluster manager (CM) provides a common view of cluster membership across your OPS cluster and manages the nodes and their participation in the cluster. It is responsible for monitoring the health of all members of the cluster and making changes to its topology in response to outages and other events. The CM communicates and controls the DLM in respect to node membership and isolating failed nodes.

■ The inter-process communication (IPC) module defines the protocols and interfaces required for OPS to transfer messages between instances. It utilizes an asynchronous queued message model to send and receive messages between the nodes as fast as the interconnect hardware allows.

▲ The input/output (I/O) module provides the cluster with access to the shared storage devices by all the nodes in the cluster. Its key component is the DLM, which coordinates the access to shared databases and maintains both consistency and data integrity. All shared disk accesses are mediated by the DLM, whether they are Win32 or NT I/O calls using the Windows NT raw file system.

Oracle has a unique API for managing the OSD, which is referred to as the Oracle Call Interface (OCI). OCI is used to access OPS from a C-based program. Calls are made directly to OCI functions from C-based programs to direct the execution of SQL statements. This API is not currently compatible with the Wolfpack API but may be in some limited manner in the future.

LEGATO/QUALIX FULLTIME CLUSTER Qualix, now a division of Legato, has had an NT-based clustering solution for some time under the name of Octopus. Octopus is a mirroring-type cluster, as opposed to FullTime Cluster, which is middleware based. FullTime Cluster was introduced in 1998 and is purported to support up to 100 nodes in a failover/failback clustering environment.

FullTime Cluster installs agents on each node of the cluster and then uses a centralized management console to administer and monitor the status of the entire cluster. All applications and services are called "resource groups," and each is configured to optimize their failover and failback performance. FullTime Cluster also features the use of a Rules engine, which is used to configure how resource groups and nodes behave during a variety of events. Rules can be established to monitor the workload across the cluster and then to dynamically balance this load among the nodes for optimum performance. FullTime's cluster engine monitors heartbeats from each node, and Qualix has developed their own SDK for use with this product to make applications and services cluster aware.

FullTime Cluster is one component of a suite of FullTime products available to enhance overall NT performance and manageability.

Collaborative Solutions

These middleware solutions come from the MSCS early adopter vendor partners and offer "advanced development platforms" to those customers who need increased functionality (availability, scalability, and manageability) and other benefits today, while being fully MSCS compatible at some time in the future. They are all designed with total MSCS interoperability in mind, regardless of whenever it was that they were first introduced to the market.

COMPAQ/DIGITAL CLUSTERS PLUS FOR WINDOWS NT Clusters Plus is similar to MSCS, with expanded capabilities in some key areas (for example, number of nodes, protocols supported, and NT Version support). It has been an early adopter test bed for most of the concepts that are fundamental to MSCS.

Clusters Plus achieves high-availability through failover techniques that redirect interrupted services and resources to clients using a backup path. It is managed and addressed as a single server. Failover of named pipes, Server Messaging Block (SMB) file shares, and applications that utilize NetBEUI, NetBIOS, and IP sockets are supported. Over the course of the past three or more years, Digital delivered more than 10,000 copies of this product to the market.

Since Compaq acquired Digital, much of their focus has been to closeout Clusters Plus development activities and to completely transition customers and direction to solutions based on MSCS Phase 1 and Phase 2, especially those customers who need early enhancements. This has been made possible by the pooling of capabilities between the Digital, Tandem, and Compaq HA groups, along with a much tighter relationship (a Frontline Partnership between Compaq and Microsoft) with the MSCS developers at Microsoft.

Table 6-2 compares the middleware-based clustering solutions with MSCS.

COMPAQ/TANDEM NSK-LITE   Tandem has had an early adopter, proof-of-concept Windows NT clustering program for many years. Its first incarnation was a two-node middleware-type failover solution called Cluster Availability Solution (CAS). Several thousand of these systems were delivered over the course of several years. Subsequent to Tandem's acquisition by Compaq, this product effort was closed out, and customers were migrated to MSCS when it became generally available in the fall of 1997.

In parallel with the CAS effort was the porting of Tandem's well-known Non-Stop Kernel (NSK) middleware (with transaction monitoring, mirroring, and so on) to Windows NT. NSK has been the benchmark of high-availability and scalability in transaction-oriented environments for many decades. With Windows NT poised to be the next widely supported platform for the enterprise, it was logical that the inherent capabilities that NSK possessed would be required as well. At the much-heralded Scalability Day hosted by Microsoft in May 1997, Tandem demonstrated a prototype of NSK-Lite when they showed a 2 TB database spread over a 16-node NT cluster.

NSK-Lite is not currently available as a standalone product, but is a component of Tandem's Non-Stop SQL/MX relational database application. This tightly integrated cluster and database is the cornerstone of Tandem's contribution to Phase 2 of MSCS.

Solution	Max Nodes	Percent Availability	Scalability	Middleware	Mirroring	Wolfpack API	Core OS
ClustersPlus	4	99.6+	Yes	Yes	No	No	NT
NSK-Lite	16+	99.9	Yes	Yes	Yes	Yes	Himalaya
Co-Standby Server	2	99.9	Limited	Yes	Yes	No	NetWare
Fail Safe	2	99.5+	No	Yes	No	Yes	NT
MSCS	2	99.5+	Limited	Yes	No	Yes	NT

Table 6-2.   Comparison of Competing Middleware-based Clustering Solutions with MSCS

Many of the advancements found in NSK-Lite will be implemented directly in MSCS Phase 2, including the following:

▼ *Transaction Monitoring and Management*   These tools are used to monitor and manage all transactions to ensure that changes to the database are either completed successfully (committed) or backed out, so that data always remains consistent (in either a post-transaction state or a pre-transaction state). These tools also keep track of all database changes via a log, which can then be used to recover any transactions that were interrupted due to an outage.

■ *Process Pairs*   This feature is a primary and backup process running on separate processors. The primary process sends checkpoints to the backup process. If the primary process fails, the backup takes over. This methodology is referred to as "fail fast" (as opposed to the slower process of failover) and is based upon the backup process anticipating the failure of the primary and then "taking over" without affecting the work in process or user connections.

▲ *Encapsulated Disks*   Disk encapsulation creates a very efficient usage of system resources because less data is passed through a shorter stack of layers in the system in regards to moving data between the physical file system (NTFS) and the database engine itself. A tool called the Data Access Manager (DAM) is used to access the physical files within the database and under NTFS. It performs SQL selection, projection, and aggregation on the data before sending it to the database engine. The DAM is considered a process and therefore a process pair can be associated with it.

Much of what is included in the underlying clustering solution for NSK-Lite will be found in MSCS Phase 2, based on a licensing agreement signed in 1998 between Microsoft and Compaq. It will also be included in advanced solutions from Compaq and its subsidiaries (Tandem and Digital), along with other vendors who have licensed this technology for their solutions. See Figure 6-3 for a block diagram of NSK-Lite and SQL/MX. (We will discuss SQL/MX in more detail in Chapter 9.)

NSK-Lite is a major technological achievement when one considers how lightweight many users believe that Windows NT is in respect to UNIX and other platforms. Not only has this development platform been used to support the terrabyte-sized database at Scalability Day 1997, but it is also the core of a 72-node cluster that Compaq/Tandem recently delivered to Sandia National Labs in Albuquerque, New Mexico. This scalability cluster has shattered the world record for sorting a terrabyte-sized database, a key measure of systems performance.

VINCA CO-STANDBY SERVER   Vinca is a startup company founded by Novell's former CEO, Ray Noorda. Still closely aligned with Novell, Vinca has developed two high-availability solutions for Windows NT, both based on the use of mirroring, with

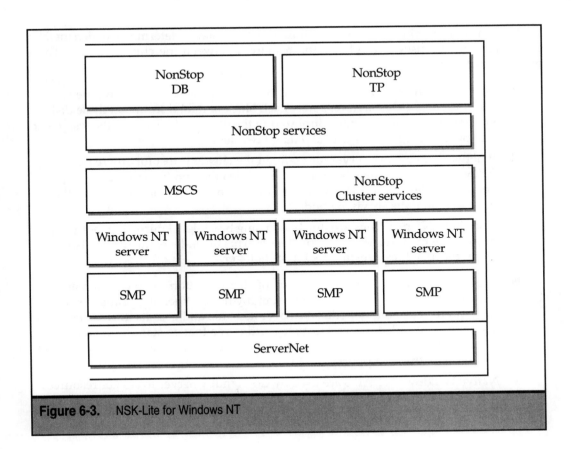

Figure 6-3.   NSK-Lite for Windows NT

Co-Standby Server's middleware added into the stew. In addition, Vinca was one of Microsoft's partners who signed on board with the MSCS initiative after the early adopter partners.

Vinca has developed a robust core technology based on server mirroring. Both of their products utilize mirroring as the primary method to insure high-availability. Given this approach, Vinca's solutions are not as sensitive about the size and characteristics (such as OS version, memory matching, and firmware levels) of the two servers as they are about the type of cluster interconnect and the capacity of the mirrored storage devices. This mirroring technology (and the engine that supports it) is much more comprehensive than other available solutions. Co-Standby Server mirrors files, directories, IDs, Registries, IP addresses, applications, and all other aspects of each server. At the core of Vinca's mirroring technology is the use of resource mirroring.

In resource mirroring, the type of resource being clustered determines which method Co-Standby Server uses to duplicate the resources between the clusters nodes. These methods include:

▼ Disk Mirroring of clustered disk partitions is used when an NT volume is configured as a clustered resource. Each block of data residing on these disk volumes is mirrored and/or duplexed to the other disk device in its designated mirror set. This protects critical data on two-levels:

1. If network access to a server (or node) in the cluster is lost for any reason, a failover occurs that switches the name for the failed node to the surviving node. This allows users to access their data from the mirror set, without the need to reboot the surviving node.

2. Since both NT partitions are duplexed using block-level mirroring, both devices are then treated as one by the OS. This block-level mirroring also supports open files, creating foolproof failover.

■ Registry staging tracks the installation of all applications on the cluster and mirrors all Registry entries to the co-standby node. When the primary node fails and the co-standby node takes over its name and uses its mirrored data, it also stages the failed server's Registry settings so that co-standby server assumes the failed server's behavior characteristics in terms of the applications and services that it supports.

▲ Native Windows NT APIs are used by Co-Standby Server to cluster resources such as IP addresses, print spoolers, SMB shares, and NetBIOS server names. Co-Standby Server also supports the use of the Wolfpack API on a limited basis.

To achieve all of this, Co-Standby Server requires three drives per server:

▼ System boot drive
■ A drive for primary storage for applications and their data
▲ Mirrored data drive

Added into this mix is Co-Standby Server's middleware, which controls failover and failback based on the determination of whether a resource becomes unavailable or an outright outage occurs.

From an overall perspective, Co-Standby Server looks and behaves a lot like MSCS (in its use of virtual servers, cluster admin GUI, and so on) but is based on different core technology. It has different failover characteristics but, for the most part, does the same job. In some respects, it is more of a competitive solution, but in others, it is collaborative. My opinion is that it is more of the latter than the former.

Vinca's other high-availability solution, Standby Server, uses the active/standby mode among the cluster nodes, with mirroring as its primary availability mechanism. This solution can be layered on top of MSCS to increase overall availability, although it substantially increases management complexity in the process. This type of solution is not recommended for the weak of heart, but it does provide enhanced availability and is fully compatible with MSCS.

ORACLE FAIL SAFE   In spite of the fact that Oracle's OPS is a very competitive product for clustering, Oracle regards it as very market-specific in terms of meeting the needs of a well-defined customer set (that is, high-end, transaction, and OLAP oriented). Oracle has been working very closely with Microsoft since the early days of Wolfpack to make its core database compatible and tightly coupled to the capabilities of MSCS. As a result of this effort, they have developed a companion product to MSCS for Oracle databases, called Fail Safe.

Fail Safe is a high-availability option for "Oracle on NT" solutions that are used in conjunction with MSCS. It features both a client- and server-side set of applications.

On the client side it includes:

▼   *Oracle Fail Safe Manager*   Responsible for Fail Safe (FS) configuration and management via a GUI. Functionality supported includes creating and configuring FS groups, adding and removing resources, setting failover and failback conditions, workload balancing, bringing resources online and taking then offline, and job event scheduling for databases.

■   *Oracle Enterprise Manager*   Responsible for comprehensive performance tuning and other management operations. On the server side it includes:

   ■   *Oracle Database Server (7.3 or later)*   A single instance of this standard database for Windows NT is utilized in a active/standby configuration.

   ■   *Oracle Fail Safe Server*   A multithreaded, distributed RPC server that works closely with MSCS to monitor and configure cluster resources and Oracle databases on the cluster. Functions include failover response time optimization, dependency structures, SQL Net configuration, database monitoring, and database import/export.

No changes are required to existing database applications in order to access Fail Safe databases, and it effectively works with partitioned data and workloads. Fail Safe is bundled with the Oracle for Windows NT database application and requires a fully configured MSCS cluster to operate.

Fail Safe is similar to Tandem's SQL/MX in that it appears as any Oracle database administration interface, regardless of platform; it appears as the familiar Tandem SQL database. Oracle Fail Safe is a key add-on for those users who want high-availability from their familiar Oracle database. This product bridges the gap between the world of NT and that of Oracle.

Data Mirroring and Remote Copying Clusters (Server Based)

Long a bastion of data protection, data mirroring—or remote data copying—has become a widely applied technique for use in clustering. Many vendors today offer middleware clusters (such as Vinca Co-Standby Server and NCR LifeKeeper), with data mirroring as a fundamental component (or option) to extend availability to even higher levels. Several vendors offer mirroring-based cluster solutions, with basic control software that controls the mirroring process. The two most prominent of these are Legato/Qualix's Octopus HA+ and NSI Software's Double-Take for Windows NT. Both of these solutions use data mirroring or remote copying to protect data and make system resources highly available.

The most significant benefit of mirroring-type clusters is that they can support both Windows NT servers and workstations, as well as mixed versions of NT 4.0 server. This is a strong motivation for upgraders to improve the high-availability of their network machines without having to incur significant cost and complexity. Another important aspect of what mirroring-type solutions offer is that they protect disk-based data, much of which can be lost if a catastrophic event occurs within a disk drive or subsystem. Non-mirroring-type clustering solutions all suffer from single points of failure in this regard, and mirroring is a fundamental component of any fault-tolerant scheme.

Legato Octopus HA+

Octopus HA+ has been in the market for some time, with literally thousands of installations around the world. It utilizes data mirroring to protect application and shared data resources. When it is initially installed on both the source and target nodes, it initializes the cluster by copying all designated files from the source to the target node over the network using standard protocols. The systems administrator chooses specific files and folders for mirroring rather than entire drives. Octopus uses a set of processes called "mirroring then forwarding" to manage data after this initialization process.

Octopus HA employs two basic techniques to achieve high-availability. They include the following:

▼ Mirroring is a process where changes in data on the source node are recorded in a Octopus log file.

▲ Forwarding is a process where the source node sends change data to the target machine based on the information contained in the log file.

These processes can affect open files and work to provide continuous backup, helping systems administrators to overcome undesired file deletions and other calamities. Octopus enables systems administrators to select multiple location options for mirrored data and to update target nodes in real time.

In the event of a failure or outage, Octopus allows the target node to automatically assume multiple machine names and IP addresses for any of the nodes that are designated to switch over to it. This switchover is typically automatic and transparent to users connected to the cluster.

Octopus can support 16+ nodes and utilizes standard NIC cards and protocols over both LAN and WAN connections. It can run on any version of Windows NT 4.0 and can work in conjunction with MSCS to provide higher levels of overall availability and fault-resilience to an NTS/E environment.

NSI Software Double-Take

Double-Take (D-T) is a remote copying cluster-like solution that provides continuous data backup. D-T monitors file changes occurring on one or more source node and replicates the changes on a real-time basis to a target server over the network. When a failure or outage occurs, the target server is available to support access to all replicated files and can assume the name and IP address of the failed server as well.

During installation, a software module is set up on each source and target server. Using a client application, the system administrator designates which data will be replicated and where the copies will be stored. The initial data-copying operation is performed, and then the cluster is ready for automatic copying of change data.

A failover module is installed on the target server and continuously monitors the source servers. During a failure the target server can assume the network name and IP address of the failed server, as well as its own. Scripts are then used to restart applications, and clients may then be reconnected to them.

The primary difference between D-T and remote mirroring solutions is that D-T works at the NOS level, not the physical disk driver level. It intercepts changes from the source's file system and replicates these to the backup target node. This is a simple, yet elegant, means to achieve higher availability and fault-resilience. NSI's Double-Take is a popular solution in the NT marketplace. Refer to Table 6-3 for a product comparison.

Dynamic Load Balancing (Web and Thin-Client Servers) Clusters (IP Based)

This segment of high-availability solutions for Windows NT is growing in significance, especially in light of the successful launch of Windows NT Terminal Server for thin-client environments and the acquisition of Valence Research's Convoy Clustering software for IP environments to meet the growing demands in the Web-based application environments.

Solution	Number of Nodes	Mirroring/Copying	Mode
Octopus	16+	Mirroring	Active/active
Double-Take	Many	Copying	Active/standby

Table 6-3.   A Comparison of Mirroring/Copying-type Clustering Solutions

Cubix Balanced Cluster Service (BCS)

In mid-1998 Cubix announced a product—Balanced Cluster Service (BCS)—for clustering and load-balancing Windows NT Terminal Server Edition (TSE). BCS creates a cluster by linking multiple TSE servers to form a cluster that appears as a single server (to provide scalability), as well as incorporating a load-balancing scheme that spreads user connections evenly among the nodes in the cluster (providing availability). This scheme helps to insure that server utilization is maximized (and evenly distributed, based on the characteristics of each node running TSE), as well as increasing availability should any node experience failures or outages. BCS has been endorsed by Microsoft for use with Windows NT Terminal Server Edition, which cannot use the capabilities found in MSCS (part of NTS/E). As of today, it is the only availability and scalability solution for use with TSE. See Figure 6-4 for a block diagram of this solution.

Balanced Cluster Service can support a minimum of eight nodes per cluster, with as many as 25 client connections per processor/per node depending upon the task levels being experienced. Cubix's focus for BCS is to use the product to provide high levels of scalability and availability for TSE (and its Remote Data Protocol, RDP, clients), using highly commoditized, SHV SMP servers in two-way configurations. Cubix asserts that a combination of low-cost SHV SMPs and their BCS clustering solution provides much higher payback and performance than using smaller numbers of standalone four- and eight-way SMPs for Windows NT TSE environments (referred to as using both horizontal and vertical scaling and is depicted in Figure 6-5).

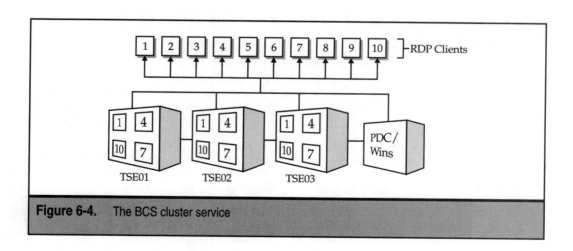

Figure 6-4.   The BCS cluster service

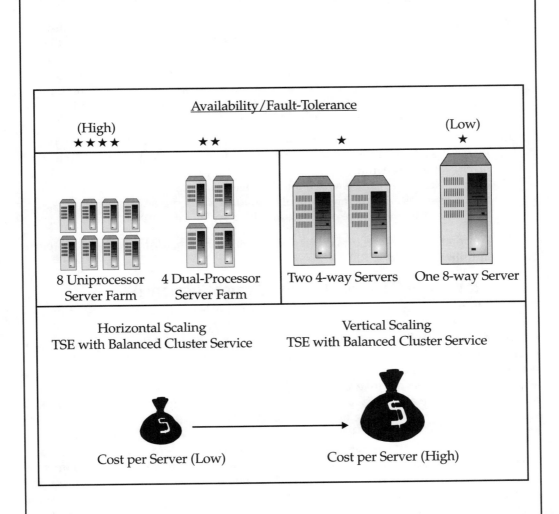

Availability/Fault-Tolerance

(High)
★★★★   ★★   ★   (Low)
★

8 Uniprocessor   4 Dual-Processor   Two 4-way Servers   One 8-way Server
Server Farm   Server Farm

Horizontal Scaling   Vertical Scaling
TSE with Balanced Cluster Service   TSE with Balanced Cluster Service

Cost per Server (Low)   Cost per Server (High)

Figure 6-5.   Horizontal and vertical scaling as provided by Cubix's BCS

In terms of operation, there are two components to consider:

▼ *Availability* During normal operations each RDP (which is part of Windows NT TSE) client is connected to a particular server (or node). In the event that this node fails or becomes unavailable to the network, the sessions assigned to the failed server are distributed to other servers (based on predetermined administrative settings). Users see this transfer as a request to re-log on if they were involved in a session when the failover occurred, or the transfer is transparent to users the next time they log on.

▲ *Scalability* As operational workloads (more RDP clients and TSE sessions) increase, system administrators can simply add more nodes to their BCS cluster (each having a separate license for TSE), and they dynamically resize the cluster overall. Resources can be added and removed without users ever having to know. Systems adminstrators can also do load-balancing on the fly in the event that the resources that are available are finite and yet not fully utilized.

BCS supports any Microsoft-certified TSE configuration, along with all the client types that utilize embedded RDP.

Microsoft/Valence Research Convoy Cluster Software (WLBS)*

Key to Microsoft winning a dominant share of the Web services and e-commerce solutions markets was solving scalability and availability deficiencies found in NT-based solutions. Most of these deficiencies were due to single SMP servers becoming overloaded well in advance of any projections that were based on "hits per day" estimates made when the system was deployed. In many cases, the actual traffic on these servers was orders of magnitude higher than any peak projections. Systems administrators were always scrambling to free up resources and add more capabilities, while load-balancing was done on the fly via Performance Monitor observations made from their consoles.

Convoy Cluster Software takes multiple Web-based servers (up to 32 currently) and creates a high-availability and scalability environment around them. This environment is characterized as a front-end cluster because these nodes are working to service incoming IP traffic requests that are being routed to static, back-end database servers. These back-end servers can operate under MSCS and can be co-located on one of the front-end Web servers if capacity is sufficient. MSCS can also be used hand-in-hand with Convoy to create a very high-availability environment for Web-based services such as FTP, HTTP, and Gopher. In this methodology, MSCS handles the back-end database (or other application) and data service layer, while Convoy handles the front-end client layer (UI). Convoy supports up to 32 nodes, with all appearing as one IP address to the outside world. Refer back to Figure 6-1 for a block diagram of this type of front-end/back-end cluster.

Convoy installs a standard NT networking driver (see Figure 6-6 for a diagram of the network interface and refer to Figure 6-7 for a look at Convoy's configuration module) and runs on existing networks. It is fully transparent to applications and IP clients. Under normal operations, Convoy automatically balances networking traffic among the nodes in the cluster. Performance can be scaled upward by the addition of nodes (up to 32). During a failure or outage of any particular node, Convoy automatically reconfigures the cluster and directs client connections to the surviving members. Once the failed node is available for work again, it can rejoin the cluster, and Convoy will once again dynamically reconfigure the cluster to distribute connections across this node as well.

Each Convoy cluster node requires two NIC cards; one for cluster traffic only and the other to handle network traffic not under the control of Convoy. Each node runs a separate instance of the clustered application (for example, IIS or mail). Each node runs its own instance of IIS and other Web applications with Convoy routing requests among the available nodes. Only one instance of the mail service is run within the cluster, and Convoy then controls the flow of Web traffic to enable only one particular node at a time to handle traffic, with the others being available in the case of a failure or outage.

Although Convoy is capable of acting as a front-end high-availability solution (for communications/connection services, for example) to support a static back-end database server (data, printing, and transactional services), this is not the only mode that can be supported. To gain increases in speed, while increasing fault-tolerance (the back-end database server is a SPF), you can replicate all of the contents of the back-end database across multiple servers. These distributed copies of the database must be resynchronized periodically as pages are updated.

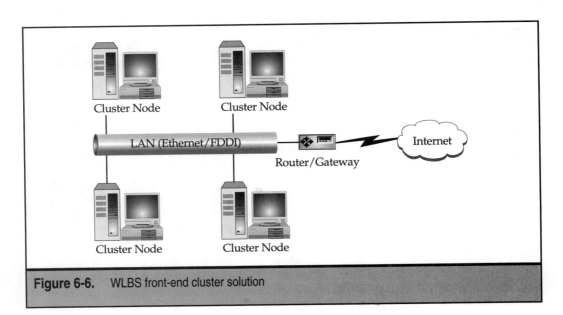

Figure 6-6.   WLBS front-end cluster solution

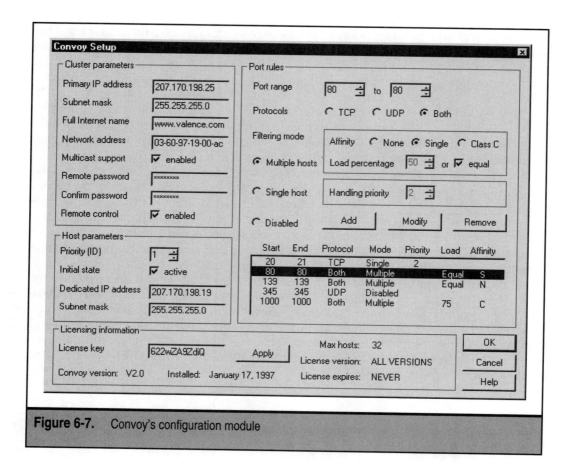

Figure 6-7.   Convoy's configuration module

Convoy supports all forms of Ethernet and FDDI, including switched connections such as those utilizing routing switches from vendors like Packet Engines (which provides level 2 switching).

Valence Research is a wholly owned subsidiary of Microsoft Corporation. Convoy Cluster Software has been renamed Windows NT Load Balancing Service (WLBS). WLBS is now a component of Windows NT 4.0 Enterprise Edition (effective January 1999). All registered users of NTS/E may obtain a copy of WLBS free of charge by downloading it from the NTS/E Web site located at **www.microsoft.com/ntserverenterprise**. In order to correctly install WLBS there must be at least one license of NTS/E present. WLBS has more extensive documentation provided with it than that provided by Convoy Cluster Server. This documentation is a very good addition because it is not easy to configure without this information. In addition, WLBS will be a standard component of Windows 2000 Advanced Server and Datacenter versions.

Refer to Table 6-4 for a product comparison.

Solution	Maximum Nodes	Front/Back End	Load Balancing Type
Cubix - BCS	8+	Back	RDP Clients
Convoy (MS-WLBS)	32	Front	IP Traffic

Table 6-4. Comparison of Load Balancing-Type Clusters for Windows NT

Storage Area Network (SAN) Clusters

Storage Area Networks (SANs) are a relatively new name for a fairly mature concept (and for the most part, a fairly mature technology). This concept is based on the idea of "anything to everything connectivity" among storage devices. SANs feature the use of a dedicated, high-speed, low-latency network for interconnecting storage devices (which sounds much like the description of a system area network used to interconnect cluster nodes). The default interconnection technology being utilized for SANs is Fibre Channel (although ESCON and SSA have been used for many years in earlier implementations).

The concepts behind these SAN clusters are still being formulated, but Veritas has stepped up to the plate in advance of others and has announced their Cluster Server, a SAN-based, scalability cluster for Windows NT and UNIX (currently only for Solaris). Advertised as an "architecturally-neutral availability management solution," this cluster architecture promises to tie together the concepts of storage area networks, system area networks, and aware applications to create the most flexible and extensible cluster architectures found to date.

Veritas Cluster Server

Based on the emerging SAN model, Veritas's Cluster Server is targeted at large cluster environments (2–32 nodes currently, up to 128 in the future) where availability and performance are not driven by managing the behavior of individual nodes, but by managing application services. In the types of SAN clusters envisioned by Veritas, the availability and scalability of individual applications and services is under the control of the cluster regardless of conditions and configuration. These so-called application services are managed as service groups in the SAN cluster model. Figure 6-8 provides block diagrams of these components of a SAN cluster.

Service groups consist of all the resources associated with a particular application or service, and they move together around the cluster as required. They are managed and monitored independently. In the event of a failure, the service group is restarted on a local basis or on any other designated node in the cluster. Cascading and multidirectional failover of service groups are supported, and application services can be manually migrated to other nodes for maintenance purposes.

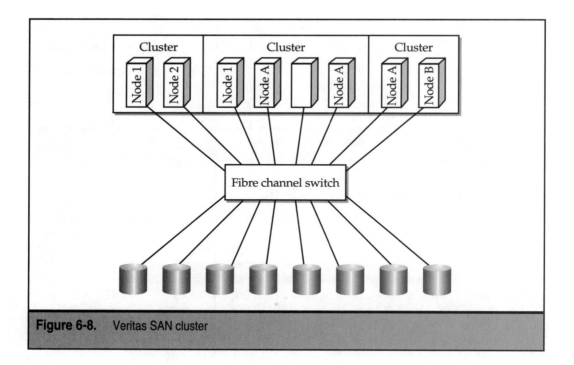

Figure 6-8. Veritas SAN cluster

The key features of the Veritas Cluster Server are:

▼ Scalability to 32 or more nodes

■ Architectural and platform independence

■ Multidirectional and cascading failover

▲ Multithreaded recovery

The lines of demarcation between what MSCS Phase 2 is intended to be, and the availability, scalability, and manageability that SAN clusters will be able to support are going to become nearly unintelligible in the near future. In December of 1998, Compaq and Microsoft signed yet another technology-sharing agreement. This one is intended to create a new extension to the Winsock 2 API for use in SAN environments. This collaborative effort will help to position Windows 2000 as the platform of choice for deploying SANs and SAN clusters. It will integrate much of what has been developed for MSCS (and the Wolfpack API) with the specifics of the empowering applications that storage/system area networks will require.

Switched SCSI Clusters

New to Windows NT, but not to the world of high-availability solutions, switched SCSI clusters have started to become generally available. Based upon the concept of switching a failed server's entire storage device complement over to a standby server and then rebooting it, these clusters are some of the lowest in cost and easiest to implement. Switched SCSI clusters support all types of NT environments and can provide rudimentary availability and fault-resilience enhancements for a reasonable price, with virtually no required changes to hardware or software.

Apcon PowerSwitch/NT

PowerSwitch is a switched SCSI clustering solution that monitors a system for failures and outages, and when they are found, it quickly switches over services, applications, and peripherals to a standby server. The standby server is then rebooted to restart these applications and services. It is a low-cost solution that can support up to 16 nodes and requires only one copy of each application, rather than one for both the primary and standby server. PowerSwitch detects outages based on administratively determined parameters. It attempts retries according to well-defined rules and then can failover automatically to one or several secondary servers if no other recourse is available. None of the servers in the cluster must be identical other than running Windows NT 4.0. See Figure 6-9 for a view of the Apcon PowerSwitch Administrator.

After failover, the standby nodes perform a clean reboot to gain access to the devices from the failed server. This allows the SCSI storage devices to be switched to the standby server after a failure, along with bringing down the failed server manually to prevent any corruption to its Registry. The failed server can then be serviced in place without creating any interruptions to traffic on the network or to the applications and services running on its SCSI storage devices.

PowerSwitch supports all software applications, utilities, and tools available for Windows NT and allows all peripherals previously attached to the failed server to be utilized by the standby node after failover. It requires the use of SCSI boot and application/data drives in each server, along with other storage peripherals (if needed) (for example, CD-ROM/DVD drives, optical disk drives, or tape drives).

Summary

As you have no doubt gathered by now, a growing number of various types of clustering/high-availability solutions are available for Windows NT. In spite of their differences in implementation methodology, they all meet the loose definition of a cluster and provide significant improvements in availability and scalability for Windows NT applications and services. Many of these can co-exist with MSCS to improve its overall performance, along with a number of the solutions supporting the Wolfpack API for use with off-the-shelf cluster-aware applications.

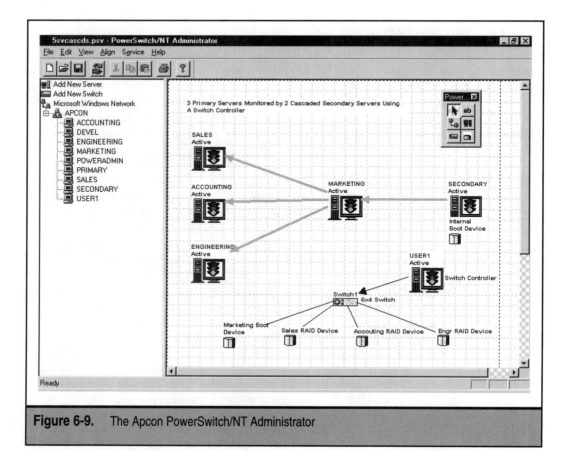

Figure 6-9.   The Apcon PowerSwitch/NT Administrator

In evaluating whether to use one of these other solutions in lieu of MSCS or in conjunction with it, you should make your decision using the following criteria:

▼ Performance

■ Cost

■ Complexity

■ Support

■ Extensibility

■ Computability

▲ Features and benefits relative to your particular requirements

After completing this "apples and apples" comparison, you can objectively determine if one (or more) of these other solutions better meets your overall requirements in respect to MSCS.

CHAPTER 7

Creating Cluster-Aware Software Applications and Services

MSCS, NTS/E, and their companion hardware systems constitute only half-a-loaf in terms of what clustering can provide as an end-to-end solution. To complete this solution, you need a suite of cluster-aware applications and services that take full (or at least partial) advantage of the Wolfpack API. Because non-cluster-aware applications cannot effectively communicate with the Cluster Service and its Resource DLLs, the options for improving their availability are limited. This chapter will provide details on the Wolfpack API as well as on how to make legacy applications and services partially cluster-aware via custom Resource DLLs.

The Wolfpack API specification (which runs over 100 pages in length) was first released in 1995 and was later incorporated into the MSCS SDK that was subsequently distributed to developers at the 1996 Microsoft Professional Developers Conference. It is now a standard component of the Platform SDK for Windows Base Services Developers. The following is a list of the SDK components:

▼ Win32 Build Environment
- Minimum build tools
- Microsoft Transaction Server Headers and Libs
- Active Directory Services Interface Headers and Libs
- Microsoft Message Queue Headers and Libs
- Internet Explorer Build Environment
- Internet Information Server Build Environment
- NetMeeting Build Environment
- Routing and Remote Access Service Headers and Libs
- TAPI Headers and Libs
- Platform SDK DirectX 5 foundation Headers and Libs
- DirectX Media Build Environment
- Image Color Management 2.0 Headers and Libs
- OpenGL Headers and Libs
- OLE DB Headers and Libs
- ODBC 3.0 Headers and Libs
- Microsoft Management Console Headers and Libs
- Microsoft Cluster Server Build Environment
- Certificate Server Headers and Libs
- SmartCard Headers and Libs
- Database Access Object Build Environment (DAO)
- Platform SDK Core Components

- ■ Microsoft Agent Build Environment
- ▲ Microsoft Platform SDK Icons and Environment Variables

THE WOLFPACK API

A cluster-aware application is one that utilizes the Wolfpack APIs to access the Cluster Service, the core software component of MSCS. The Cluster Service controls all cluster operations on a system managed by MSCS and is implemented as an NT service. Cluster Service comprises six closely coupled subcomponents—the Communication Manager, Database Manager, Event Processor, Resource and Failover Managers, Global Update Manager, and Node Manager. Chapter 2 contains a detailed description of the Cluster Service and its components.

The Wolfpack API comprises four basic components:

- ▼ Cluster API Set
- ■ Cluster Control Code Set
- ■ Resource API Set
- ▲ Cluster Administrator Extensions API Set

The use of all four are is required in order for an application to be fully cluster-aware. Standard and legacy-type applications and services can use the Resource API Set to become partially cluster-aware. In this mode the application supports a subset of the overall cluster aware capabilities supported by the Wolfpack API set, and has higher availability than a stand-alone, non-cluster-aware application.

The Cluster API

The Cluster API allows an application or service to do the following:

- ▼ Access information about cluster objects (resource, resource type, node, or group)
- ■ Initiate operations (online, offline, failover, failback)
- ▲ Update the cluster database

The Cluster API consists of seven sets of APIs, all under one umbrella. Refer back to Figure 2-7 for a diagram of the Cluster Service. This API provides access to the cluster as a whole, not just a particular, node. Access to the cluster through the API is unaffected by node failures as long as one node remains online. However, an individual function call may return an error response if one of the nodes failed while performing a task on behalf of that node's outstanding function call.

The seven Cluster APIs are as follows:

1. *Cluster Management*   This API provides access to event notification, cluster objects, and overall cluster state information, which are used by cluster-aware

applications to perform a wide range of management and maintenance tasks on a cluster. The following functions are supported by the Cluster Management API:

Function	Description
CloseCluster	Closes a cluster by invalidating its handle.
CloseClusterNotifyPort	Closes a notification port established by CreateClusterNotifyPort by invalidating its handle.
ClusterCloseEnum	Closes a cluster enumeration object, and returns a handle to it.
ClusterEnum	Enumerates the objects in a cluster, returning the name of one object with each call.
ClusterOpenEnum	Opens a cluster enumeration object, and returns a handle to it.
CreateClusterNotifyPort	Creates a notification port to handle cluster event notification.
GetClusterInformation	Returns a cluster's name and version.
GetClusterNotify	Returns the next notification event from a notification port.
GetClusterQuorumResource	Returns the state of the quorum resource for the cluster.
OpenCluster	Opens a cluster, and returns a handle to it.
RegisterClusterNotify	Adds an event type to the list of events stored for a notification port.
SetClusterName	Establishes a name for the cluster.
SetClusterQuorumResource	Establishes the quorum resource for the cluster.
SetClusterTime	Establishes the time for the cluster.

These function calls are responsible for the creation of a cluster, the opening and closing of connections to it, and the creation of the cluster's quorum resource, time service, and its unique name.

2. *Cluster Configuration Database Management*   Allows a cluster-aware application or Resource DLL to access and update the cluster database. Chapter 10 has sample listings of these Registry-type entries. These entries are replicated across all nodes in the cluster. This API is used to access and update this database via similar functionality found in Regedit and other Registy editing

tools. This API includes additional functionality to allow multiple updates to be committed atomically. The following functions are supported by the Cluster Configuration Database Management API:

Function	Description
ClusterRegCloseKey	Releases the handle of a cluster Registry key.
ClusterRegCreateKey	Creates a specified key in the cluster Registry. It the key already exists, then it is opened without change.
ClusterRegDeleteKey	Deletes a cluster Registry key.
ClusterRegDeleteValue	Removes a named value from a cluster Registry key.
ClusterRegEnumKey	Enumerates the subkeys of an open cluster Registry key.
ClusterRegEnumValue	Enumerates the values of an open cluster Registry key.
ClusterRegOpenKey	Opens a cluster Registry key.
ClusterRegQueryValue	Retrieves the name, type, and data components associated with a value for an open cluster Registry key.
GetClusterGroupKey	Opens the root of the Registry subtree for a group.
GetClusterKey	Opens the root of the Registry subtree for a cluster.
GetClusterNodeKey	Opens the root of the Registry subtree for a node.
GetClusterResourceTypeKey	Opens the root of the Registry subtree for a resource type.

Like all Win32-type registries, the MSCS Configuration Database is critical to not only the proper operation of the cluster, but is also critical to the changing/updating all of its settings. All cluster-aware applications and services need to be able to access and change this information as required.

3. *Group Management*   Provides access to each of the failover groups in a cluster. It allows callers to change a group's membership or state and to retrieve information. Group Management functions also allow an application to manage a cluster's group states, with all of these under the control of the Resource Manager and Failover Manager in the Cluster Service. These operations can be executed on either the node that owns the group or resource, or on the node that is currently hosting them.

The following functions are supported by the Group Management API:

Function	Description
CloseClusterGroup	Closes a cluster group by invalidating its handle.
ClusterGroupCloseEnum	Closes a group enumeration by invalidating its handle.
ClusterGroupEnumResource	Enumerates the resources in a group, and returns the name of one particular resource with each call.
ClusterGroupOpenEnum	Opens a group enumeration, and returns a handle to it.
CreateClusterGroup	Adds a group to a cluster, and returns a handle to the new group.
DeleteClusterGroup	Removes a group from a cluster.
GetClusterGroupState	Returns the current state of a group.
MoveClusterGroup	Moves a group and all of its resources from one node to another.
OfflineClusterGroup	Brings an online group offline.
OnlineClusterGroup	Brings an offline group online.
OpenClusterGroup	Opens a group, and returns a handle to it.
SetClusterGroupName	Establishes a name for a group.
SetClusterGroupNodeList	Establishes the preferred node list for a group.

4. *Node Management*   Allows callers to change a node's state, perform operations, and to retrieve information. The majority of the functions of this API affect the Node Manager, with the exception of the Evict Cluster.

The following functions are supported by the Node Management API:

Function	Description
CloseClusterNode	Closes a node by invalidating its handle.
EvictClusterNode	Deletes a node from the configuration database.
GetClusterNodeId	Returns the identifier for a cluster node.
GetClusterNodeState	Returns the current state of a cluster node.
GetCurrentClusterNodeId	Returns the identifier of the cluster node that the application is currently running on.
OpenClusterNode	Opens a node, and returns a handle to it.

| PauseClusterNode | Requests that a node temporarily suspend its cluster activity. |
| ResumeClusterNode | Requests that a node resume its cluster activity following a suspension. |

5. *Resource Management* Allows callers to perform a range of operations on one or more resources. These operations include retrieval of dependency information, creation and deletion of resources, and initiation of operations defined by resource control codes.

The following functions are supported by the Resource Management API:

Function	Description
AddClusterResourceDependency	Creates a dependency relationship between two resources.
AddClusterResourceNode	Adds a node to the list of possible nodes that a resource can run on.
CanResourceBeDependent	Determines if one resource can be dependent upon another resource.
ChangeClusterResourceGroup	Moves a resource from one group to another.
CloseClusterResource	Closes a cluster resource by invalidating its handle.
ClusterResourceCloseEnum	Closes a cluster enumeration object by invalidating its handle.
ClusterResourceControl	Provides for communication and control between an application and a resource.
ClusterResourceEnum	Enumerates objects relating to a resource in a cluster.
ClusterResourceOpenEnum	Opens an enumeration object, and returns a handle to it.
ClusterResourceTypeControl	Provides for communication and control between an application and a resource type.
CreateClusterResource	Creates a resource in a cluster.
CreateClusterResourceType	Creates a new resource type in a cluster.
DeleteClusterResource	Removes an offline resource from a cluster.
DeleteClusterResourceType	Removes a resource type from a cluster.
FailClusterResource	Initiates a resource failure.

GetClusterResourceState	Returns the current state of a resource.
OfflineClusterResource	Brings and online resource offline.
OnlineClusterResource	Brings and offline resource online.
RemoveClusterResourceDependency	Removes a node form a resource's list of possible hosts.
RemoveClusterResourceNode	Removes a dependency relationship between two resources.
SetClusterResourceName	Establishes a name for a cluster resource.

6. *Network Interface Management*   Opens and closes the network interface, performs selected operations, and retrieves information.

7. Network Management   Provides access to information about networks (private and public) that are monitored by the Cluster Service.

The specific syntax and variables for all of these functions can be found in the Wolfpack API specification contained in the "Microsoft Wolfpack Clustering for Windows NT Server Programmer's Reference."

Code Samples for the Wolfpack API

The following code samples are provided to give you examples of how each API call is formatted during normal usage. When writing your own specific API code, you will insert variables that are specific to your applications needs. These samples are excerpted from the overall list of API calls.

Open Cluster

HCLUSTER WINAPI *OpenCluster(*
LPCWSTR *lpszClusterName*
);

Set Cluster Name

DWORD WINAPI *SetClusterName(*
HCLUSTER *hCluster,*
LPCWSTR *lpszNewClusterName*
);

Set Cluster Quorum Resource

DWORD WINAPI *SetClusterQuorumResource(*
HRESOURCE *hResource*
);

Open Cluster Node

HNODE WINAPI *OpenClusterNode(*
HCLUSTER *hCluster,*
LPCWSTR *lpszNodeName*
);

Create Cluster Group

HGROUP WINAPI *CreateClusterGroup(*
HCLUSTER *hCluster,*
LPCWSTR *lpszGroupName*
);

Create Cluster Resource

HRESOURCE WINAPI *CreateClusterResource(*
HGROUP *hGroup,*
LPCWSTR *lpszResourceName,*
LPCWSTR *lpszResourceType,*
DWORD *dwFlags*
);

Get Cluster Key

KHKEY *GetClusterKey(*
HCLUSTER *hCluster,*
REGSAM *samDesired*
);

The variables in the Wolfpack API are as follows:

Variable	Description
lpszClusterName	Pointer to the name of an existing cluster
hCluster	Handle to an existing cluster
hResource	Handle to an existing resource
lpszNodeName	Pointer to the name of an existing node
lpszGroupName	Pointer to the name of the group to be added to the cluster
lpszResourceName	Pointer to the name of the new resource
lpszResourceType	Pointer to the type of the new resource
dwFlags	Bitmask describing how the resource should be added to the cluster
samDesired	Access mask that describes the desired security access for the new key

Cluster Control Codes

Cluster control codes (32-bit values) are used to describe operations being performed on cluster objects and are categorized as either internal or external.

Internal codes are used by the Cluster Service only and are not available to application and Resource DLLs. They are sent by the Cluster Service to resources to notify them of events.

External codes are those operations that can be performed by applications, with a small subset of these codes used to manage cluster properties. These properties are used to describe the attributes that a cluster object has and are divided into *common* and *private* groupings. Common and private properties may be read-only or read-write. Common properties are static and apply to all objects of a particular type (that is, a resource). They are stored in the cluster database. Private properties are either static or dynamic in nature and are also used to describe a particular type of resource. The values for these properties can be stored in either the cluster database or in an alternate location.

The Resource API

The Resource API is used to define functions, structures, and macros that allow the Cluster Service to communicate with all of the resources available to it. This communication is facilitated by the Resource Monitor, which acts as an agent of the Cluster Server (CS) to pass messages and event notifications back and forth between the CS and the resources. Figure 7-1 depicts how this process works.

The Resource Monitor imports a Resource DLL for each type of resource used and is responsible for monitoring the state of the online resource (or resources) assigned to it. The Resource Monitor runs as a separate process from the Cluster Service to prevent Resource DLLs from being able to "hang" the Cluster Service or to interfere with the cluster's operation in general. It makes no decisions and determines no policies, but acts as an agent of the Cluster Service. By default, the Cluster Service starts up with only one Resource Monitor to serve all the Resource DLLs on the system. This can be modified by enabling a separate Resource Monitor for each resource under its property settings.

The Resource API comprises the following:

▼ *Entry Point Functions*   Allow the particular Resource Monitor to manage its resources.

■ *Callback Functions*   Allow a Resource DLL to report status, log events, and respond to Cluster Service requests to perform particular tasks.

▲ *Structures and Macros*   Describe a function table that has been returned by the Startup entry point, and then describe the current status of a particular resource.

The Resource API contains eight basic functions. Only one of these functions, Startup, is exported; all others are accessed through the function table returned by Startup. Each

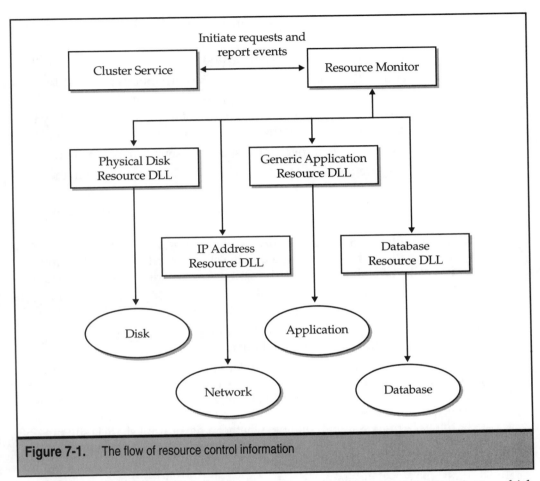

Figure 7-1.   The flow of resource control information

function can be called only once for each resource instance, except for Terminate, which can occur at any time even if other threads in a Resource DLL are blocked while waiting for an Online or Offline call to complete.

The functions are as follows:

1. *Startup*   The Startup routine is invoked after the Resource DLL is loaded. At that time the Startup entry point is exported. All other entry points that are implemented in the Resource DLL are accessed through the function table that the Startup routine returns.

   There are several entries in the Startup routine. They are as follows:

   ■ ResourceType (the type of resource to be started)

   ■ MinVersion Supported (version matching minimum value)

   ■ MaxVersion Supported (version matching maximum value)

- SetResourceStatus (used if the resource command will take more than 300 ms to complete)

- LogEvent (for reporting events and errors)

- FunctionTable (the function addresses of the entry points in the DLL)

2. *Open*   After the Startup routine is successfully exported, the Resource Monitors call the Open entry point function for each resource managed by the Resource DLL. There are three entries in the Open routine. They are as follows:

   - ResourceName (an identifier for the specific resource being opened)

   - ResourceKey (refers to resource-specific information contained in the cluster database)

   - ResourceHandle (used in calls to the SetResource Status and LogEvent callback functions)

3. *Online*   After the resource opens successfully (that is, it is not being used by another node or it is not corrupted in the cluster database), the Resource Monitor calls the Online routine to bring it online. There are two entries in the Online routine. They are the following:

   - ResourceId (a unique identifier for each resource)

   - EventHandle (a parameter that the Resource DLL uses to signal the Resource Monitor regarding its status)

4. *Looks Alive*   LooksAlive is a cursory check used by the Resource Monitor to periodically check the status of each resource once it is online. There is one entry in the LooksAlive routine: ResourceId (a unique identifier for each resource as it is being polled by the Resource Monitor). The LooksAlive routine is used to determine if a process is still running, whether a file or print share is still present, and other so-called "cursory" checks. LooksAlive polling occurs frequently.

5. *Is Alive*   IsAlive is a more detailed check used by the Resource Monitor to periodically check the status of each resource once its is brought online. It has one entry in its routine: ResourceId (a unique identifier for each resource as it is being polled by the Resource Monitor). The IsAlive routine does a complete check of the resource to determine that it is functioning correctly and polls each resource at a specific frequency.

6. *Offline*   Offline is used to unload resources that are no longer required. It has one basic entry: ResourceId (a unique identifier for each resource as it is being polled by the Resource Monitor). Once the resource is taken offline it can be used by other nodes in the cluster.

7. *Close*   Close is used to close out a resource and to deallocate any structures that were allocated to the particular resource by Open, Offline, ResourceControl, and ResourceTypeControl entry point functions. Its one basic entry is ResourceId (a unique identifier for each resource as it is being polled by the Resource Monitor).

8. *Terminate*   The Terminate function is used to immediately end a process that is not responding correctly to the Offline function call. It has one basic entry: ResourceId (a unique identifier for each resource as it is being polled by the Resource Monitor).

9. *Resource Control*   The Resource Control function is used by cluster management tools and cluster-aware applications to communicate information to the resource for use in setting common and private properties and to request operations. The ResourceControl routine has several entries:

   - ResourceId (a unique identifier for each resource as it is being polled by the Resource Monitor)
   - ControlCode (the unique 32-bit code used to determine which operation is to be performed)
   - InBuffer (a pointer to a buffer for use in the operation)
   - InBufferSize (the size of the buffer in bytes)
   - OutBuffer (a pointer to the buffer containing the results of the operation)
   - OutBufferSize (the available space for these results)
   - BytesReturned (the number of bytes in the OutBuffer that contain actual data)

10. *Resource Type Control*   The Resource Type Control is another type of function for use by the cluster management tools, along with cluster-aware applications, in communicating information to the resource pertaining to common and private properties and operations to be performed. The Resource Type Control routine has the following entries:

    - ResourceTypeName (identifies the type of resource being affected by operation)
    - ControlCode (the unique 32-bit code used to determine which operation is to be performed)
    - InBuffer (a pointer to a buffer for use in the operation)
    - InBufferSize (the size of the buffer in bytes)
    - OutBuffer (a pointer to the buffer containing the results of the operation)
    - OutBufferSize (the available space for these results)
    - BytesReturned (the number of bytes in the OutBuffer that contain actual data)

11. *Arbitrate* and *Release*   These two functions are specifically used in Resource DLLs for the quorum resource.

Code Samples for the Resource API

The following code samples are provided to give you examples of how each API call is formatted during normal usage. When writing your own specific API code you will insert variables that are specific to your applications needs. These samples are excerpted from the overall list of API calls.

Startup

```
DWORD WINAPI Startup(
LPCWSTR ResourceType,
DWORD MinVersionSupported,
DWORD MaxVersionSupported,
PSET_RESOURCE_STATUS_ROUTINE SetResourceStatus,
PLOG_EVENT_ROUTINE LogEvent,
PCLRES_FUNCTION_TABLE * FunctionTable
);
```

Open

```
RESID WINAPI Open(
LPCWSTR ResourceName,
HKEY Resource Key,
RESOURCE_HANDLE ResourceHandle
);
```

Online

```
DWORD WINAPI Online(
RESID ResourceId,
PHANDLE EventHandle
);
```

Looks Alive

```
BOOL WINAPI LooksAlive(
RESID ResourceId
);
```

Is Alive

```
BOOL WINAPI IsAlive(
RESID ResourceId
);
```

Offline

DWORD WINAPI *Offline(*
RESID *ResourceId*
);

Resource Control

DWORD WINAPI *ResourceControl(*
RESID *ResourceId,*
DWORD *ControlCode,*
LPVOID *InBuffer,*
DWORD *InBufferSize,*
LPVOID *OutBuffer,*
DWORD *OutBufferSize,*
LPDWORD *BytesReturned*
);

Resource Type Control

DWORD WINAPI *ResourceTypeControl(*
LPCWSTR *ResourceTypeName,*
DWORD *ControlCode,*
LPVOID *InBuffer,*
DWORD *InBufferSize,*
LPVOID *OutBuffer,*
DWORD *OutBufferSize,*
LPDWORD *BytesReturned*
);

The following variables are in the Resource API:

Variable	Description
ResourceType	The type of resource to be started
SetResourceStatus, LogEvent	Pointers to callback functions in the resource monitor
Function Table	Structure containing the function addresses of the rest of the entry points in the Resource DLL

Variable	Description
ResourceName	The specific resource to be opened
ResourceKey	Resource-specific information, private properties, and other information contained in the cluster database
ResourceHandle	Used to call the SetResource Status and LogEvent functions
ResourceId	Parameter passed to the entry point that uniquely identifies the resource
EventHandle	Parameter passed to the Resource Monitor by the Resource DLL
ControlCode	The 32-bit control code for the operation to be performed
InBuffer/InBufferSize	Pointer and size information for the buffer that contains the data used in the operation
OutBuffer/OutBufferSize	Pointer and size information for the buffer that contains the data resulting from the operation
ResourceTypeName	Parameter to identify the type of resource to be affected by the operation.
BytesReturned	The number of bytes in the buffer that actually contain data

Cluster Administrator Extension API

The Cluster Administrator (CA) program included with MSCS presents a series of property sheets, wizards, and context menus for manipulating the individual properties of each cluster component. The CA is equipped to support standard resources that are included with MSCS, along with additional types developed using the Resource API.

CA Extension DLLs are implemented as Component Object Model (COM) "in-process" servers. These servers provide services, such as property sheets that display resource properties to clients through COM interfaces. These interfaces are created through objects that are represented as unique class identifiers (CLSIDs). These CLSIDs are replicated in the registries of the nodes as well.

These DLLs can be created manually or via the use of the CA Extension AppWizard contained in the Wolfpack SDK.

The interfaces used by the CA program are the following:

Interface	Description
IGetClusterDataInfo	Returns information about a cluster component.
IGetClusterGroupInfo	Returns information specific to group cluster components.
IGetClusterNodeInfo	Returns information specific to node cluster components.
IGetClusterObjectInfo	Returns information about a specific cluster component.
IGetClusterResourceInfo	Returns information specific to resource cluster components.
IGetClusterUIInfo	Returns information about displaying extension property sheets or wizard pages.
IWCContexMenuCallback	Adds items to a Cluster Admin context menu.
IWCPropertySheetCallback	Adds property sheet pages to a CA property sheet.
IWCWizardCallback	Adds property sheet pages to a CA wizard.
IWEExtendContextMenu	Extends a CA context menu.
IWEExtendPropertySheet	Extends a CA property sheet.
IWEExtendWizard	Extends a CA wizard.
IWEInvokeCommand	Performs commands associated with items added to context menus.

Cluster Administrator Extension Functions and Tools

To facilitate proper interface between the Cluster Administrator (CA), the Cluster Server, and the Resource DLLs, there are three functions that every CA extension DLL must export:

▼ *DllGetCluAdminExtensionCaps*   This function returns the CS extension class identifier, the cluster components that it extends, and a list of resource types that it supports.

■ *DllRegisterServer*   This function adds entries associated with the CA extension DLL to the system Registry. Client-side registration must be done on each machine that the CA is used on.

▲ *DllUnregisterServer*   This function removes entries associated with a CA extension DLL from the system Registry.

The Wolfpack SDK also has a utility called REGCLADM that is used to register CA extensions. This must be used for all machines running the Cluster Administrator. To run this program, perform the following steps:

1. Enter the name of the cluster.
2. Enter the path to where the CA extension DLL is located.
3. Choose Install or Uninstall as the mode you are using this utility for.

Code Samples for the CA Extensions API

The following code samples are provided to give you examples of how each API call is formatted during normal usage. When writing your own specific API code you will insert variables that are specific to your applications needs. These samples are excerpted from the overall list of API calls.

IGetClusterName

HRESULT *GetClusterName(*
BSTR *lpszName,*
LONG * *pcchName*
);

DIIGetCluAdminExtensionCaps

STDAPI *DIIGetCluAdminExtensionCaps(*
DWORD * *pdwCaps,*
CLSID * *pclsid,*
LPWSTR *pwszResTypenames,*
DWORD * *pcchResTypeNames,*
);

The variables in the Cluster Administrator Extension API are as follows:

Variable	Definition
LpszName	Pointer to the name of the cluster
PcchName	The number of characters in the buffer
PdwCaps	Pointer to a bitmask describing the capabilities of the extension
Pclsid	Pointer to the class identifier of the CA extension
PwszResTypeNames	Pointer to the names of the resource types supported by the CA extension
PcchResTypeNames	The count of characters in the buffer

USE OF ENTERPRISE EDITION, STANDARD EDITION, AND LEGACY-TYPE APPLICATIONS WITH MSCS

As of this writing, only a small subset of the more than 700 BackOffice-certified applications are vendor certified to be fully conforming to the Wolfpack API and are able to take advantage of its functionality in a MSCS cluster.

An additional number of these applications have been made cluster-aware by creating specific Resource and Cluster Administrator DLLs that are used to help maximize the availability benefits of MSCS, while not having to completely rewrite application code. Figure 7-2 is a diagram depicting how these Resource DLLs interface with applications and the Cluster executive (Cluster.exe).

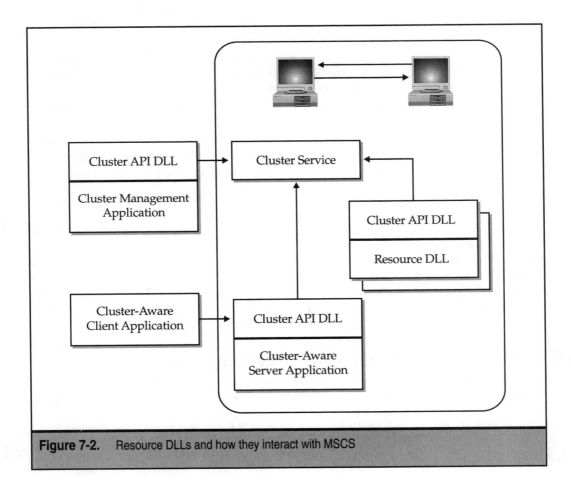

Figure 7-2.   Resource DLLs and how they interact with MSCS

Using the APIs and control codes outlined in this chapter to create partially cluster-aware applications when using MSCS (and other clustering solutions that utilize the Wolfpack API) is a primary focus of many of the Independent Software Vendors (ISVs) who make products that feature the "Designed for BackOffice" logo. The types and usages of the products run the gamut.

MSCS can also support the use of standard and legacy applications that utilize its "generic application and services" resources, but these implementations lack the following basic capabilities:

▼ When a generic application fails over to a standby node, many files may be left open that are not cleaned up in the process. This is due to the generic application not being shut down cleanly prior to failover.

■ A generic service cannot take advantage of resource polling, which is key to determining whether the application, service, or node itself has failed or is unavailable (via LooksAlive and IsAlive routines).

■ Many resources require specific sets of parameters (common and private) to be transferred during failover. These parameters are normally transferred in a cluster-aware application by a Cluster Administrator extension that is integrated with the Resource DLL. The generic resources do not support this functionality except in a limited regard.

▲ Generic applications and services cannot support Active/Active deployment methods, which are especially critical when using symmetric modes of clustering and shared/partitioned databases and database applications.

Figure 7-3 shows how generic applications and services are configured for use with MSCS.

Because this support for generic applications and services is limited, it is advantageous to write custom Resource DLLs to make major applications and services as cluster-aware as possible without having to rewrite them altogether. To make an application fully cluster-aware, you must use the Cluster and Resource APIs, the Cluster control codes, and the CA Extension APIs that were described earlier to create application and Resource DLLs. These APIs, in turn, are used by the cluster management tools, the Resource Monitors, and DLLs included in MSCS.

Making Existing Applications Wolfpack Compliant

Writing a Resource DLL is just one step in making an application or service partially cluster-aware. To make an application partially cluster-aware, you must use the Cluster API and other cluster-related functions, along with providing a CA extension DLL to manage and configure the application or service. This section will focus on making standard and legacy applications more cluster-aware by writing Resource and CA extension DLLs, two important steps in the right direction.

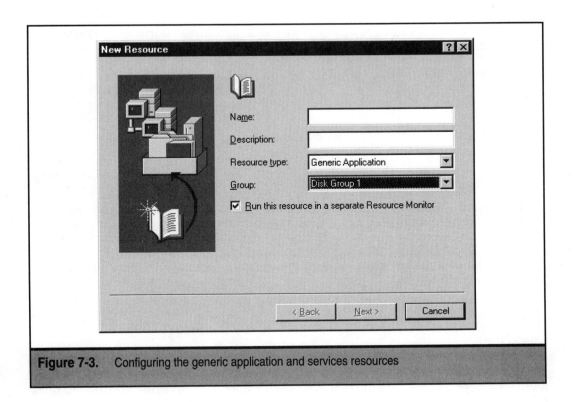

Figure 7-3.   Configuring the generic application and services resources

The Microsoft Cluster Server SDK development environment is part of the Windows Platform SDK, which can be found at the Microsoft Web site at **www.microsoft.com/ msdn**. To develop resource DLLs, you must use Visual C++ version 4.2b or later as a language platform. You will also need to extract the following items from the Platform SDK for use during the DLL development process:

▼   MIDL Compiler version 3.00.44 or later

▲   Active Template Library version 2.0 or later

Creating and Customizing Resource DLLs and CA Extension DLLs

The easiest way to create a new resource type (consisting of a Resource DLL and a CA extension DLL) is to use the Resource Type AppWizard located in the Active Template Library. Doing so builds the framework of these two types of DLLs with their entry points defined, declared, and exported. These frameworks provide only the most basic of functionality (failover and failback) but give you a working set of code to modify to meet the specific requirements of your application or service. This code is marked with comments such as TODO and ADDPARAM to indicate where you need to enter resource-specific information.

Most, if not all, of these code entry points must be addressed in order to make your resource DLL function correctly. These entry points include the following:

▼ *Startup*   Loads your Resource DLL and returns a function table.

■ *Open*   Opens a specific resource.

■ *Online*   Makes a specific resource available for use.

■ *LooksAlive*   Performs a quick check to make sure a resource is still available for use.

■ *IsAlive*   Performs a comprehensive check to make sure a resource is available for use.

■ *Offline*   In a controlled manner, it makes a resource unavailable for use and waits for the cleanup process to end (closing files and connections).

■ *Close*   Closes a specific resource.

■ *Terminate*   Immediately makes a specific resource unavailable without waiting for cleanup to end.

■ *ResourceControl*

▲ *ResourceTypeControl*

API Development Tips and Traps

As with all APIs, the MSCS Wolfpack has its own quirks and issues that must be addressed in order to deliver the required functionality. The following are tips and traps to be conscious of when developing your own Resource DLLs:

▼ Some resources require both cluster-wide configuration as well as per-node configuration. This configuration information should be stored in both the cluster configuration database as well as in the nodes' cluster Registry subkeys.

■ When developing Resource DLLs, you will be linking against the MSCS Cluster API library file clusapi.lib. When developing CA extension DLLs, you will be linking against the MSCS Cluster Administrator Extensions library file cluadmex.lib.

■ In terms of maximum call times, the following is a list of maximums based on the type of routine:

Routine Name	Maximum Time
Startup	300 ms
Open	300 ms
Online	300 ms

Routine Name	Maximum Time
Looks Alive	150 ms
Is Alive	300 ms
Offline	300 ms
Close	300 ms
Terminate	N/A
Resource Control	N/A
Resource Type Control	N/A

■ When using the Open routine, if the resource called is already online, the DLL should attempt to take it offline.

■ If any resource fails to come online, your DLL should use the LogEvent function to log the event and then call the SetResourceStatus function to indicate the state of the resource. If any resource fails to come online within three minutes, the Resource Monitor calls the Terminate function to abort the operation.

■ If any resource fails to shut down within the timeout period or returns a Win32 error value, the Resource Monitor calls the Terminate function to terminate the resource.

■ To increase the efficiency of the Cluster Service, it is recommended that when writing Resource DLLs that you use separate threads to perform long operations. These include:

   ■ Opening resources

   ■ Bringing resources online

   ■ Taking resources offline

   ■ Closing resources

▲ Properties should be read in the Open or Online functions.

DEBUGGING YOUR RESOURCE DLLS   Debugging Resource DLLs is a bit more challenging than debugging other NT-based DLLs, but you can use many of the same tools. The following debuggers can be used to debug your Resource DLLs:

▼ WinDbg

■ Microsoft Developer Studio

▲ DebugEx Cluster Administrator extension DLL

Each of these debuggers works fine, although DebuxEx is the preferred tool due to its tight integration with MSCS and lack of logon requirements.

These tools can be used to debug either the resource type or DLL. During the process, you can monitor the output of the Cluster Service, as well as debug on a resource-by-resource basis. To use any of these debuggers, follow the instructions provided by their vendors.

INSTALLATION OF RESOURCE DLLS   Once you have completed the design, test, and debug of your Resource and CA extension DLLs, it is time to install them on the cluster along with the application and/or service. This task is facilitated in most cases by writing a setup routine that does the following:

1. Installs the application or service:
   - A copy is required on each node.
   - The Cluster Service needs to be up and running.
   - Data files should be on a storage device on the shared-storage bus.
   - Application files should be on a non-shared-storage bus device.
2. Configures the cluster component of the application or service:
   - Use the CreateClusterResourceType function to install the new resource type on each node.
   - Copy the DLL to the application installation directory on each node, and register it with its full path.
3. Installs and registers the CA extensions (including client-side):
   - Register the CA extension DLL with the cluster via the DIIRegisterCluAdminExtension function.
   - Register the CA extension in the system Registry via the DIIRegisterServer function.
   - Copy the client-side CA extension to the machine that will run CA and which is registered as the Inproc Server.

PART III

Maximizing the Capabilities of Your MSCS Cluster

CHAPTER 8

Windows 2000 and Microsoft Cluster Service Phase 2

ometime in 1999 (or 2000), Microsoft will release the Windows 2000 Server family (along with a workstation version called "Windows 2000 Professional"). Windows 2000 will ultimately be available in at least three versions:

▼ Windows 2000 Server (which does not include Cluster Service and is primarily intended to replace NT Server Standard Edition for use in small and mid-sized networks)

■ Windows 2000 Advanced Server (a more powerful system designed to replace NT Server Enterprise Edition)

▲ Windows 2000 Datacenter Server (a totally new version targeted at large-scale applications such as ERP and Decision Support, along with supporting scientific and engineering computing environments)

All versions are intended to be more in line with true "application server platforms," rather than network operating systems, which Windows NT was previously categorized as (networking services are just one component of a true enterprise computing OS). This reflects Microsoft's strategy of providing mission-critical applications as much as operating systems.

Windows 2000 Advanced Server and Datacenter Server will support MS Cluster Service (replacing MSCS), with the Datacenter version supporting Microsoft Cluster Service Phase 2 environments. This stratification of clustering capabilities, along with other capabilities found in the world of Windows 2000 at large (memory capacity, CPU licenses, and so on), will have significant implications for both today's users of MSCS, as well as those who want to use MS Cluster Service bundled with the varying versions of Windows 2000 in the future. This chapter discusses Windows 2000, MS Cluster Service in general, and MS Cluster Service Phase 2. We'll also cover what the future holds for existing users of Windows NT and MSCS, as well for new users who will embrace MS Cluster Service for the first time in the form of Windows 2000 Advanced or Datacenter Server.

WINDOWS 2000 SERVER—PRODUCT OVERVIEW

Windows 2000 will have many new features and capabilities that are common to all versions. These core features are:

▼ *Active Directory Service (ADS)*   A completely new directory service that is fully scalable and is designed around Internet-standard technologies fully integrated with the OS. ADS is intended to simplify administration and to make it easier for clients to find resources on enterprise-wide networks. Clients will be able to find information on users, files, printers, and other shared resources from the Active Directory. Objects in the directory are assigned to logical workgroups and units rather than through hard connections to specific servers. This eliminates the need to reconfigure access settings when a resource is moved or changed in some way. ADS uses the LDAP protocol for directory access. See Figure 8-1 for a view of the Active Directory structure. ADS is a direct replacement for the current NT 4.0 domain model and provides for the establishment of automatic trusts between servers, with all servers being equal in terms of domain control. The concepts of PDC and BDC are not used in ADS.

■ *Microsoft Management Console (MMC)*   A centralized management tool used to configure and monitor resources and applications that operate over ADS. Applications and services "expose" information and operations to the MMC framework as objects. Special-purpose (vendor-supplied, for the most part) management tools integrate with the MMC user interface via extensions or "snap-ins." These are a direct replacement for the numerous applets and standalone application screens that dominate the world of Windows NT today. In addition, the MMC serves as the host for scripts that can be written to control specific functions. A block diagram of the MMC and its structure is shown in Figure 8-2.

Note that the initial release of Windows 2000 Advanced Server will not use an MMC snap-in for Cluster Server management. The existing CA will continue to be used.

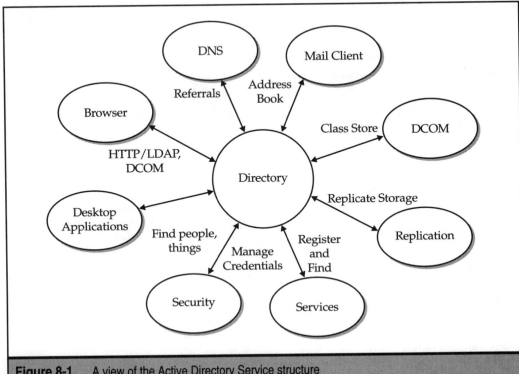

Figure 8-1.   A view of the Active Directory Service structure

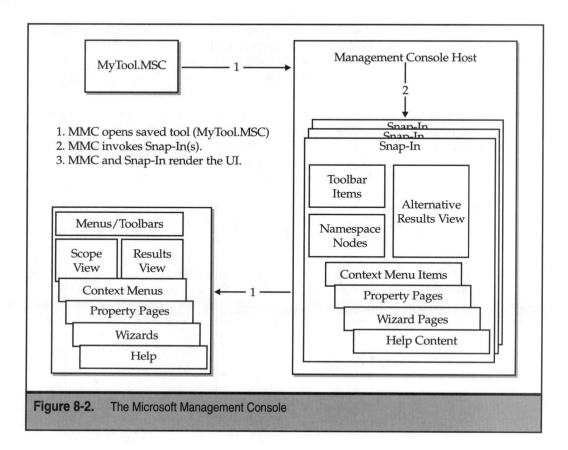

Figure 8-2. The Microsoft Management Console

- *NTFS Enhancements* The Windows NT file system has been enhanced and upgraded significantly. In conjunction with other new security functionality built into Windows 2000, which is based on the use of the Kerberos Public Key architecture, the NTFS can now operate in an encrypted mode. It can be enabled on either a per-file or per-directory basis. In addition, NTFS itself has been upgraded to be more robust. These new capabilities include the ability to add space to an NTFS volume without the need to reboot, to establish disk quotas, and to support distributed link-tracking, and major increases in overall performance.

- *Distributed File System (Dfs)* Used in conjunction with NTFS and the enhanced network security provided by the Kerberos Public Key architecture, Dfs can be used to create single directory trees that include multiple file servers and shares within a group, division, or enterprise.

■ *Enterprise Storage Management (ESM)*   A integrated set of tools, applications, and utilities that address the growing requirements for "built-in" ESM tightly coupled with the OS. These capabilities include:

   ■ *Enhanced backup*   NTBACKUP and Advanced System Recovery (increased target choices and options)

   ■ *Disk defragmentation*   FAT, FAT32, and NTFS support

   ■ *Volume management*   Logical Disk Manager (enhanced manageability and recoverability)

   ■ *RAID disk*   FT Disk Manager with cluster support

   ■ *Remote storage manager*   Tape library and optical jukebox control and media management

   ■ *Remote storage services Hierarchical Storage Management (HSM)*   Management of files based on age and capacity, with movement of files to and from primary storage media (disk) to secondary storage media (tape, optical, and so on).

▲ *Support for the Zero Administration Initiative*   A server-based tool that allows the centralized management of all desktop systems across the enterprise. A key component of this initiative is the use of "IntelliMirror," a new technology within Windows 2000.

IntelliMirror centralizes all configuration and state information for each user, application, and machine so that administrators can more readily access it. This information then allows administrators to create specific profiles for individuals and groups, so they can move around the enterprise and log into any machine under the control of IntelliMirror and have their core services and applications made available to them on any machine. These capabilities can be established on policies or via a hierarchy of user access and capabilities.

▼ A number of second-order features and performance enhancements are contained in the base code for all versions of Windows 2000. The features include the following significant enhancements (with many more not listed here):

   ■ *Scatter/gather I/O*   Read and write functionality to compensate for data located in discontiguous memory that needs to be written to a contiguous file location.

   ■ *High-performance sorting*   A presorting process for use with large data sets that will be ultimately loaded into decision support applications, along with other large data set–type applications (print or batch).

Scalability and Availability Enhancements

In addition to all of the other new platform-wide features and capabilities, Windows 2000 provides major enhancements to scalability and availability. Many of these enhancements are version specific; the Standard Edition does not fully support clustering, large SMPs, or the Enterprise Memory Architecture. These enhancements are

▼ *Enterprise Memory Architecture (EMA)*   Use of a 64-bit memory address architecture to provide up to 64 GB of (processor dependent) physical memory for use in supporting business-critical applications. These applications include those that can utilize outboard memory schemes such as Compaq/Digital's Memory Channel (see Figure 8-3). The systems supported are based upon those that utilize the Intel Page Size Extension 36 processors (Xeon, Katmai [IA-32], and future IA-64 types), along with the Alpha Very Large Memory extension (via special Win32 APIs) for use with Alpha 64-bit processors.

■ *Higher SMP CPU counts*   Support for 8 to 16 CPUs (Alpha or IA-32/64) on standard servers, as well as up to 32 for select OEMs, (dependent upon OS version and server configuration [32-bit or 64-bit CPUs]).

■ *Enhanced clustering services*   Support for dial-in network connections, enhanced services offerings (DHCP, WINS, Dfs), rolling upgrades, (rules-based) dynamic load balancing, Virtual Interface Architecture (VIA), cluster interconnects, Fibre Channel, and ATM networks. These features are independent of those found in the IP clustering functionality called WLBS, which supports up to 32 nodes.

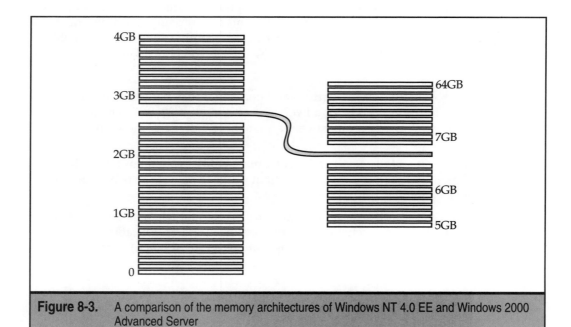

Figure 8-3.   A comparison of the memory architectures of Windows NT 4.0 EE and Windows 2000 Advanced Server

Note that Windows 2000 Advanced Server will feature three levels of cluster support: NCBS (32 node); Component Load Balancinig (0 node); and Cluster Service (2 nodeHA).

- *I2O architectures*   Support for outboard I2O I/O processors to off-load interrupt-intensive I/O tasks from the CPU. This creates extended performance for all types of servers and their applications. These architectures are very effective when supporting I/O-intensive environments like video, groupware (mail and messaging), and large client/server distributed applications.

- *System area networks*   WinSock/SAN and its API are used to create wide bandwidth, low-latency system area networks for communications within clusters (heartbeat, systems data, application data, housekeeping info, and so on), as well as creating a new architecture for all components (storage, servers, and communications) to be used in emerging enterprise computing environments. Figure 8-4 illustrates this new protocol standard.

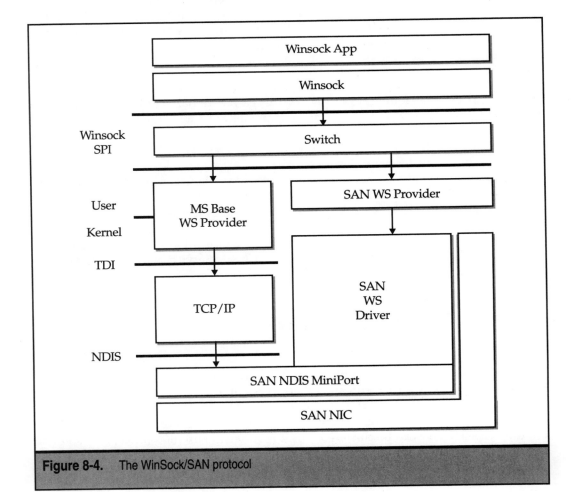

Figure 8-4.   The WinSock/SAN protocol

▲ *Multiple node clustering (Datacenter Server version only)*   Upon release of Cluster Service Phase 2, the ability to have more than two (four in some OEM configurations) nodes in a server-based cluster under Windows 2000 (as opposed to the existing 32-node capacity of WLBS IP cluster) will become a reality. A minimum of 16 nodes in total will be supported, with larger numbers expected to be available from key OEMs. This will allow systems architects to create true "scalability clusters." Scalability clustering will allow additional computation capabilities to be added on the fly, with dynamic redistribution of workloads so that they can be scaled over the total number of nodes in the cluster. These clusters will utilize advanced shared storage bus configurations using Fibre Channel and other high-speed storage buses, along with the Winsock/SAN and VIA specifications for advanced intra-cluster communication networking schemes. These SAN schemes will allow internode communications to pass at rates of up to 125 GB/s, eliminating I/O and CPU bottlenecks in high transaction rate—oriented environments. Additional functionality enabled by Phase 2 will include low-level utilities like Distributed Message Passing (DMP), input/output shipping, full transaction monitoring with recovery services, remote mirroring, a clustered file system, remote system management, and health monitoring.

In addition to scalability enhancements, these Phase 2 clusters will feature substantial improvements in availability as well. The enhanced functionality of Phase 2, along with the use of advanced interconnect schemes and architectures will allow true fault-tolerant schemes to be designed and utilized. Nodes will be able to be distributed over wide geographical distances, while maintaining total data integrity and synchronization with other nodes in the cluster regardless of location.

In total, the overall enhancements and improvements found in Windows 2000 in respect to scalability, availability, and manageability are significant. They address all of the often-derided deficiencies of NT 4.0 (and MSCS) and collectively push this OS into the forefront of enterprise computing.

In subsequent sections of this chapter we will explore the capabilities and deployment issues surrounding Windows 2000's Cluster Service as it applies to both the Advanced Server and Datacenter Server editions.

WINDOWS 2000 CLUSTER SERVICE— GENERAL OVERVIEW

Previously referred to in product plans and advanced marketing activities as "NT 5.0" and "MSCS Phase 2" by Microsoft and others, these products are now called "Windows 2000 and its Cluster Service" (Phase 1 and Phase 2), respectively. Cluster Service is available only on the Advanced Server and Datacenter versions of Windows 2000. Windows 2000 Server can be clustered, but it requires the use of a third party solution from providers such as Vinca, Legato/Full Time, and Veritas. Table 8-1 compares the features and benefits of the clustered versions of Windows 2000.

From Table 8-1 you can clearly see that there are major differences between the Advanced Server and Datacenter Server versions of Windows 2000 in respect to clustering and the levels of scalability/availability that can be supported. This two-tier offering has been developed to allow end-users to choose the level of clustering horsepower that they want, while not paying for more than they need. The Standard and Advanced Server versions of Windows 2000 will be upgradeable to more full-featured versions with costs being calculated depending upon the version being upgraded from and to. These cost structures will become more visible once the entire Windows 2000 Server family is rolled out to the public. (Datacenter Server is not expected to be available until 120 days or more after the general availability of the other products in the Windows 2000 family.)

Regardless of the version of Windows 2000 Cluster Service that you immediately deploy, you will achieve the following basic benefits and functionality:

▼　Support for rolling upgrades" on all nodes. These upgrades can include OS versions, service packs, engineering hot fixes, cluster-aware applications, and drivers and applets for storage, networking, and other peripherals used in the cluster. This rolling upgrade mode will eliminate most server reboots and the need to interrupt user connections or to take applications offline during

OS Version/Name	Replaces	CPU Licenses (SMP) Standard/OEM	Maximum Physical Memory (GB)	Clustering Solution	Maximum Nodes
Windows NT 4.0 Enterprise Edition	"Baseline"	4/8	4	MSCS Phase 1	2
Windows 2000 Advanced Server	NTS/E 4.0	8/16	32	Cluster Service Phase 1 NLBS	2^+ and 32 WLBS and COM clustering
Windows 2000 Datacenter	New	16/32	64	Cluster Service Phase 2	16^+ and 32 NLBS and COM clustering

Table 8-1.　A Comparison of Windows NT and Clustering Versions

upgrades. In addition there is no need to recreate the clusters' configuration during the upgrade as it remains entirely intact.

■ Use of the MMC for control and administration of the Cluster Service. Via a snap-in module, the Cluster Administrator is now tightly integrated into the MMC, along with all other administration required to operate the server (node) itself (disk admin., networking, and so on). This snap-in will also allow administrators to develop "rules-based" dynamic load balancing schemes for use with applications and services provided to users of the cluster.

■ The Active Directory Service is fully integrated with Cluster Service and its MMC snap-in, allowing information about clusters to be published in its directories, as well allowing administrators to better monitor the status of all resources used by the cluster. This functionality is fully integrated with the COM+ and Transaction Services found in Windows 2000 for exploitation by component-based services.

■ Network failure immunity enhancements have been incorporated into the Cluster Service. The new monitoring algorithm can better detect and isolate network failures, allowing for improved recovery from outages and failures. It detects and rates the type of networking outage and based on rules-defined criteria, it sets the appropriate response. These enhancements now support multiple NIC card scenarios where either a redundant NIC connection can be enabled or a standby network can be enabled for those types of applications that cannot tolerate network outages (for example, IP-based connections).

■ Cluster Service now supports plug-and-play NIC cards, physical disks (on the shared storage bus), and network stacks.

■ Cluster Service now supports Windows Internet Naming Service (WINS), Dynamic Host Configuration Protocol (DCHP), and Distributed file system (Dfs) environments. All three of these are now available as cluster-aware resources for use with applications and services that require them. For example, a SMB file share can now act as a Dfs root or share its subdirectories.

■ Cluster Service utilizes the same Wolfpack API found in earlier versions of Windows NT but now supports the use of COM. COM-based applications can be accessed by the Windows Scripting Host to control cluster behavior and to automate administrative tasks, including dynamic load balancing.

■ A full-function transaction monitor is built into Cluster Service to allow for worry-free OLTP environments. This eliminates the need to roll-back and restart transactional databases that experience outages while transactions are on the fly.

▲ Remote mirroring of data among cluster nodes is now built in, allowing for even higher levels of data integrity and data availability under all types of operating conditions.

These capabilities, in total, can support the following types of enterprise computing environments:

▼ OLTP, OLAP, Data Warehouse, and Data Mart systems with databases in excess of 100 TB

■ Fault-tolerant/self-healing systems featuring directed application failover (takeover), transparent automatic load balancing, and dynamic data partitioning

■ Multi-thousand seat mail and messaging systems

■ E-commerce and other mission-critical Web-based systems (intranet, extranet, and so on)

▲ Widely distributed corporate and government enterprises with centralized file shares and data repositories

Microsoft Cluster Service Phase 2

Besides the broad enhancements to the basic Cluster Service provided in the Advanced Server version of Windows 2000, one of the major benefits for enterprise computing users will be found in the Datacenter version and its N-node clustering capabilities. N-node clustering is touted to be the nirvana of clustering regardless of platform. Previously only available on proprietary (for example, IBM S/390, Tandem Himalaya, Digital VMS) and high-end UNIX platforms (IBM AIX SP/2, Digital TruClusters), N-node scalability and availability solutions will now be deployed on SHV, commodity type, low-cost (relatively speaking) servers. This opens the door to the wider overall adoption of clustering as a means to abate industry-wide shortcomings in scalability, availability, and manageability in all types of application and end-user scenarios.

N-node clusters solve many of the problems found in computing today. On an overall basis, they support the following types of computing capabilities:

▼ True scalability via "horsepower on demand"—the ability to add more nodes as user and application demand warrants. In these scenarios the administrator simply configures additional nodes in the cluster for use with an application or service that has become underpowered or slow in response. The additional nodes pick up some portion (either dynamically or manually) of an application's data and process it in parallel with other existing nodes, or alternatively it can take on certain groups of users who are not receiving adequate response times from overly busy applications or services.

■ Parallel application support via the use of either multiple nodes running separate segments of a particular partitioned database (IBM DB2 Universal Database Extended Edition) or a true parallel database where multiple nodes may be able to access the same portion of a large database that is located in some type of an outboard Very Large Memory environment for maximum performance (Oracle OPS). (These applications require a DLM for control of access to the same file, along with the external memory scheme such as Memory Channel.)

■ Full fault-tolerance via wide physical dispersion of nodes, along with the use of remote mirroring to insure that no single points of data access failure exist. In these scenarios an instance of the core application (or applications) is located on multiple nodes, along with distribution of the database among these same nodes, which is then being distributed to other nodes at these geographically disbursed sites on a real-time basis. These deployments require the use of multiple nodes as well as high-speed, low-latency cluster interconnects (VIA and WinSock/SAN), and wide-bandwidth shared storage buses (Fibre Channel).

▲ Application takeover during system faults or network outages using sophisticated transaction monitoring (TM) schemes to insure that each and every transaction in an OLTP or OLAP environment is fully processes regardless of the state of any individual node at the time. In combination with parallel application support schemes, the transaction monitor is a critical watchdog of the health of the entire transaction environment. In the event that any node (and its application instance) fails to complete a transaction, the TM enables another node (and its application instance) to take over this transaction and those subsequent to it until such time as the original node is revived. Takeover mode prevents any on-the-fly transactions from being lost or corrupted.

All of these scenarios rely on the use of multiple nodes running individual instances of key applications, along with a high-speed, low-latency cluster interconnect such as VIA (and WinSock/SAN) and a wide-bandwidth shared storage bus architecture such as Fibre Channel (or storage area network). Many high-performance databases use outboard VLM schemes such as Compaq's Memory Channel (MC) to provide a high-speed computational cache where an entire database can be located and accessed in nanoseconds to meet the requirements of very high transaction rate–driven environments. None of these capabilities or scenarios can be supported by simple two-node (or even four, for the most part) failover architectures found in MSCS today or in the Advanced Server version of Windows 2000. All are clearly enterprise architectures in terms of orientation and represent the types of computing environments that Windows 2000 Datacenter version was targeted to support.

System Area Networks, Virtual Interface Architecture, and the WinSock/SAN API

System Area Networks (SANs) are a class of high-performance communication interconnect that have started to be used in clusters based on SHV servers. SANs deliver very high bandwidth (1GB/s and more) with very low latency, especially in respect to conventional LAN and WAN technologies. Most SANs are switched implementations with hubs typically supporting 4–8$^+$ nodes. Larger networks can be fabricated by cascading these hubs. Interconnect lengths range from several meters all the way up to several kilometers. SANs are much different than conventional networking schemes because they implement a transport service (like TCP/IP and IPX) in hardware via a dedicated network interface card (NIC). These data transport endpoints (via the NIC) handle data packets over the network and can map this data directly into the address space of the user-mode process. SANs support both small and large data transfer modes and handle these either as messages or DMA-mapping schemes. SANs allow system architects to reorganize servers, storage, and communications into a scalable, expandable network. These new networks are quickly becoming the backbone for emerging distributed computing and clustering solutions in the enterprise computing space of the market. SANs provide benefits in the following areas of mission-critical computing:

▼   *Clustering*   Internode communications and data transfer are greatly improved.

■   *Distributed computing*   Communications and data transfer between distributed clusters or high-powered standalone servers are greatly improved and facilitated.

▲   *Network I/O*   Movement of system data off corporate networks greatly improves overall systems performance and reliability.

These capabilities are critical to achieving the promised payback of the SHV-cluster business model where IT managers are constantly pushing the envelope to "do more with less." All SANs feature the following basic performance attributes:

▼   *High bandwidth*   High-performance, point-to-point interconnects carrying massive amounts of data and system messages.

■   *Low latency*   A minimum overhead architecture for moving data at the highest speeds with the shortest delays and with the least amount of CPU/system overhead per message/transfer.

■   *Scalable architecture*   SAN topologies are designed to support millions of connection points, each with the same level of performance.

▲   *Fully fault-tolerant*   Transferred data packets are fully redundant both in regard to the packets themselves as well as the paths they take. High bandwidth and low latency are useless without equal levels of data integrity.

A critical component of Windows 2000 Cluster Service Phase 2 is found in the use of the recently standardized Virtual Interface Architecture (VIA) for creating SANs, along with the use of the emerging WinSock/SAN API specification to create applications that can take full advantage of this hardware/software interconnect link to move massive amounts of application data among cluster nodes at rates in excess of 125 GB/s.

VIA Overview

Developed in 1997 by Compaq, Intel, and Microsoft, the Virtual Interface Architecture (VIA) specification defines a standard architecture for communication within clusters of servers and workstations. VIA standardizes the interface for SANs. See Figure 8-5 for a typical VIA-based SAN. The VIA specification is intended to help transform collections of SHV-type servers into highly scalable clusters for use in enterprise computing environments. VIA networks have the ability to enhance application scalability by running a single application across multiple nodes or speeding up the interchange of distributed data among nodes.

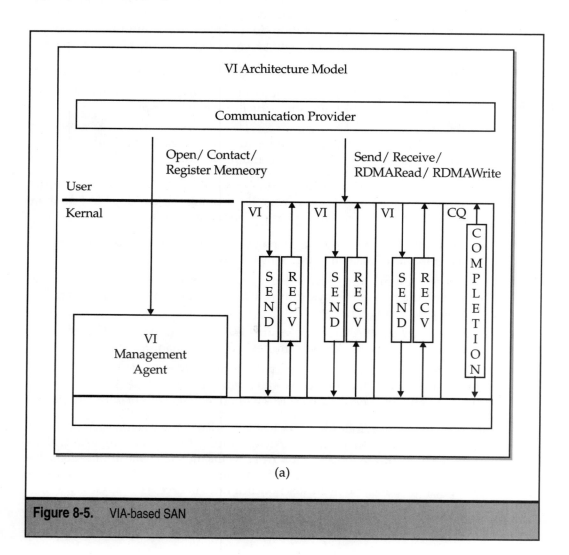

(a)

Figure 8-5. VIA-based SAN

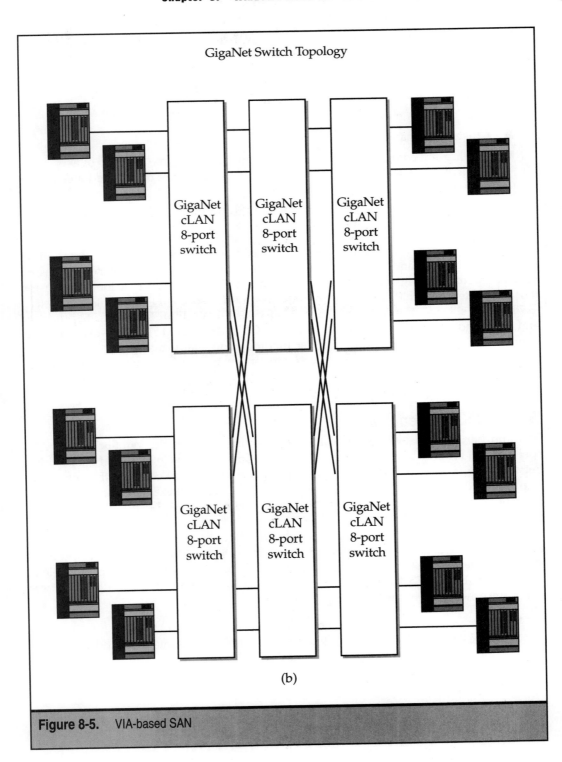

GigaNet Switch Topology

(b)

Figure 8-5.   VIA-based SAN

VIA is important in Phase 2 of Cluster Service because more than just simple heartbeat information will be carried between nodes. This data includes the following data types:

▼ Heartbeats of all cluster nodes

■ Replicated state information containing group and resource data

■ Cluster commands used to trigger events among cluster nodes

■ Application commands common to all nodes running one instance of a particular application (for example, function shipping or distributed message passing)

▲ Application data being shared among nodes running separate instances of an application (for example, I/O shipping)

All of these inter-node data types can cause simple cluster interconnects to fail in respect to both the bandwidth available as well as overall systems latency in terms of response to commands given. What was acceptable for Phase 1 clusters is no longer viable for those being deployed in Phase 2—for example, Ethernet (all speeds), Token Ring, FDDI, etc.

The VIA specification is supported by more than 100 vendors of networking products and is intended to be media, processor, and OS independent. Its software interface supports a wide range of programming methods and platforms, while its hardware interface is compatible with both standard networking protocols, as well as SAN-specific products (such as Tandem ServerNet and GigaNet ClusterLAN) from numerous vendors.

WinSock/SAN Specification

Part and parcel of the VIA specification for creating SANs is the WinSock/SAN API specification for use with Windows 2000-based applications. WinSock/SAN is a bridge between the worlds of Windows 2000 applications and services and that of SANs implemented around the VIA specification. It links the WinSock API specification to SAN interconnect technology, allowing the vast arsenal of NT-type (Win32-based) applications to take full advantage of VIA SANs. This technology will greatly improve overall application performance because it moves data directly between the application and other hardware, such as clusters and storage, bypassing both the TCP/IP protocol stack and the LAN, along with much of the OS in process. See Figure 8-6 for a block diagram of the WinSock/SAN environment. This "shortening of the path" produces major improvements in the following critical areas:

▼ *Processor usage* Host processor cycles are not required to transfer information across a SAN. This produces higher transaction-processing rates and more query processing.

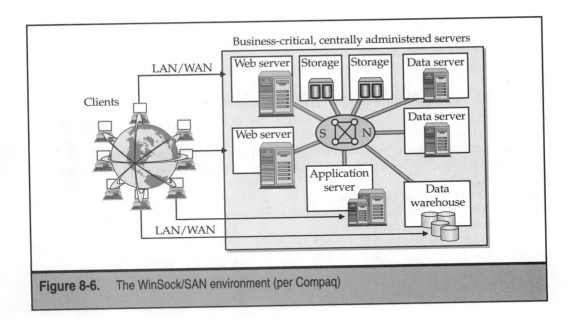

Figure 8-6.   The WinSock/SAN environment (per Compaq)

- ■ *Scalability improvements*   Nodes can be added to meet increased concurrent user requirements.
- ▲ *Fault tolerance and data integrity enhancements*   Redundancy and multiple data paths are used throughout the SAN with no server loading, thereby greatly decreasing the potential for lost or corrupted data.

WinSock/SAN uses an innovative architecture to bypass the TCP/IP protocol stack and transport (and all of its associated overhead) to move data directly to VIA-based SAN interconnect drivers, while appearing to applications as the standard WinSock 2 API environment. This provides an environment where SANs and standard applications can coexist, a major boon to the wider deployment of Windows 2000 clusters.

PLANNING FOR THE DEPLOYMENT OF WINDOWS 2000 CLUSTER SERVICE

With all the new features and capabilities to be delivered in Cluster Service in the future, it is important to plan for them by deploying new cluster solutions, as well as upgrading existing MSCS-based ones when you move from NT 4.0 to Windows 2000. To accomplish this with the minimum of hassle, this chapter contains a checklist of items to be addressed, along with methodologies for accomplishing these tasks.

Deployment Checklist

The following areas should be addressed prior to deploying Microsoft Cluster Service from scratch or as an upgrade from existing Windows NT 4.0 MSCS installations.

Establish Your Active Directory Domain Model

This model is quite different and more robust than that used in NT 4.0. Active Directory can support some $10MB^+$ objects per domain. The domain itself is a security boundary in spite of its ability to span locations. When choosing your domain name, be aware that the root name cannot be changed once established, so you must use so-called "stable names." The domain model that you establish will be part of your organization's overall domain hierarchy and will establish "transitive trusts" between itself and other domains in your organization's domain tree. You no longer have to worry about PDCs and BDCs because all servers are treated equally.

Once you have established your AD domain model, you can then migrate over existing domains from NT 4.0 (or 3.51) using Windows 2000's built-in migration tools, or you can leave the existing domains as they are and set up one-way trust relationships with your new AD model. You make this decision based upon how your existing pre-Windows 2000 environment is structured.

Install and/or Upgrade Windows 2000 on all Cluster Nodes

Use the appropriate version of Windows 2000 (Advanced Server or Datacenter Server), depending upon your clustering requirements. Advanced Server will have migration routines for converting your MSCS-based cluster to one based on the Windows 2000 Cluster Service. Failover groups and resources will be established and/or moved over to the new cluster, along with the Quorum Resource database. It will be critical to back up all NT 4.0 data prior to any and all upgrades and/or migrations. A full backup is the best policy just in case you have to rebuild your MSCS-based solution from scratch.

Note that you can also use the built-in "Rolling Upgrade" functions to avoid taking offline any mission-critical application and to upgrade your 2-node cluster to Windows 2000.

Test and/or Reconfigure Your Cluster Using the MMC CA Snap-In

At this time you can test the behavior of existing failover groups and their resources, along with making any modifications you find necessary (such as adding new resources or changing existing ones). You can also set up new applications and services for failover, based on the parameters suggested by the vendor. If you are using Windows 2000 Datacenter Server, you can add additional nodes and set up failover/failback scenarios for these new nodes (primary and secondary failover paths, along with takeover scenarios where supported). You will also be able to set up expanded symmetric virtual servers to take advantage of partitioned databases for scalability enhancements. Many of the actual setup details for Advanced Server and Datacenter Server are still being developed, but when the products are finally released for general availability, you will be able to take full advantage of all the functionality and performance attributes built into Cluster Service as found in each particular version.

Install and/or Upgrade Applications and Services

Once you have reconfigured and tested your cluster after the upgrade/install, you can then either install new cluster-aware applications or upgrade existing ones that have been enhanced to take full advantage of the Windows 2000 Cluster Service. Follow the directions provided by the vendor for each of these applications. Note that under Windows 2000, you will probably not have to reboot your nodes after installation, which is a major improvement.

Perform Cluster Fire-Drill Tests

Once the installations are complete, you can perform system-level testing to monitor and fine-tune failover/failback behavior, as well as set up takeover behavior for those applications (and clustering solutions) that can support this mode of enhanced availability. These basic level tests can then be augmented with more formal fire-drill tests where random failures can be introduced and system and application performance can be monitored for conformance to policies established by administrators during setup.

Having completed all of these basic steps and performed these tests, you should now be on your way to using Cluster Service in much of the same way that you used MSCS. Once a cluster is properly configured and tested for validation, it can be left alone for the most part, other than running the necessary fire-drills and reviewing logs to determine what actions have taken place or are currently being triggered. As with all new installations, a full backup is recommended along with developing a schedule of unattended backups to be performed as frequently as required.

CAN'T WAIT FOR WINDOWS 2000 AND CLUSTER SERVICE PHASE 2?

Unfortunately, for many enterprise users of Windows NT and MSCS there are numerous immediate requirements for both increases in scalability and manageability. In these instances there are a number of "interim" offerings from individual vendors to help meet these challenges today. Many of these are MSCS compatible, while others are unique point-type solutions. I will focus in this section on those solutions that are compatible with MSCS and will remain compatible when Windows 2000 and Cluster Service Phase 2 become available.

Interim Scalability and Availability Solutions

Currently, there are two interim scalability and availability solutions for MSCS. Not surprisingly both are from IBM (and its Lotus subsidiary); IBM was named the leader in clustering technology by D.H. Brown and Associates—a leading market analyst firm that follows high-availability computing. Both of these solutions are unique in respect to the particular way that they are applied to hardware and software applications. These two solutions are as follows:

▼ IBM/Lotus Domino Server V4.6 (or later) using a combined MSCS and Domino Cluster solution

▲ IBM and Microsoft's "Cornhusker" software for combining four MSCS 2-way clusters into an 8-node MSCS scalability solution

IBM/Lotus Domino/MSCS Cluster Solution

In essence, the Domino Server 6-node clustering solution relies on database replication between nodes. This replication is event driven and is meant to insure the integrity of all data within the databases scattered about the cluster. On the other hand, MSCS is inherently based upon a shared-storage bus and is implemented at the OS level, making it essentially transparent to the application(s) running on it. These two methods of clustering are not mutually exclusive by any means; they can actually be combined together to deliver an ideal solution.

In these types of solutions, Domino is responsible for the integrity of the database that it relies upon to operate. If a node fails, all client requests to access the failed server's database are automatically redirected to another node(s) that contains a replicated copy of the database experiencing the outage. Domino server also does dynamic load balancing both during normal operations as well as during failovers.

MSCS is then responsible for all OS related high-availability functions (e.g., networking, storage, etc.).

This combination of forces is very advantageous in environments where Lotus Notes (the Domino client application) is widely dispersed geographically in respect to a Notes network, but also requires high-availability at each site. To create this type of solution, configure a 4-node Domino Cluster that is spread over several sites (up to four); these sites are components of two MSCS clusters. This type of solution is called a *nested cluster*.

While Domino is an application-level solution and MSCS is an OS-level solution, combining them in a Nested Configuration creates even higher levels of availability for business critical Lotus Notes networks.

IBM-Microsoft "Cornhusker" Switched MSCS Clusters

As part of their certification program, *Cluster Proven* (also referred to as Netfinity-X architecture), IBM, in partnership with Microsoft, has migrated some of its AIX HACMP clustering technology to MSCS to create an 8-node MSCS cluster solution. Code-named "Cornhusker," this software development has been focused in creating an environment where four, 2-node MSCS clusters can be combined to create an 8-way scalability solution. This solution will be used to support scalability-hungry applications such as SQL Server and Oracle for Windows NT. This solution is expected to be available in the summer of 1999 and will be followed up by the addition of a high-speed 8-node (SP family) switch for cluster interconnect between MSCS nodes and IBM's venerable RS/6000 SP HACMP clustering solution.

IBM, like other enterprise vendors is bridging the gap between the worlds of high-end clustering solutions (AIX and S/390) and SHV clusters based on Windows NT (and in the future, Windows 2000). This strategy is based on not only delivering the best value for the dollar, but to retain existing customers who are moving to lower TCO platforms.

SUMMARY

Windows 2000 and its Cluster Service are a powerful combination with major improvements and enhancements in availability, scalability, and manageability for enterprise computing environments previously supported by Windows NT. Whether you are deploying a cluster using the Advanced Server version or the Datacenter version, you will derive major benefits almost immediately. Advanced Server is a good match for those environments where high-availability, along with maximum flexibility and functionality, are of the highest priorities in your clustering solution. If you environment is based on performing transactions at the highest rates possible or one where data and facilities are widely distributed, yet mission critical, then the Datacenter Server version and its N-node clustering capabilities are the way to go. If your need is also for an IP-type, front-end cluster, then you can choose either version because WLBS will be included with both.

If your needs cannot wait until Windows 2000 becomes generally available then there are several emerging "interim-type" solutions that take MSCS and add expanded availability and scalability options today, that will ultimately be core components of Cluster Service Phase 2 in the future.

As I stated early on in this book, clustering is the cornerstone of Microsoft's product strategy for meeting the needs of enterprise computing environments, and this strategy will not change with the introduction and wide deployment of Windows 2000. Clustering is still the most efficient means to deliver high availability, wide scalability, and reduced management workloads, while embracing low-cost, SHV, commodity-type hardware solutions.

CHAPTER 9

MSCS Cluster-Aware Applications Reference Guide

As discussed in Chapter 7, the key to achieving the highest level of benefits from Microsoft Cluster Server environments is to use cluster-aware applications and services that take advantage of the Wolfpack API. This chapter discusses and reviews the range of off-the-shelf applications available from the industry's leading providers, as well as the ISV community at large.

The cluster-aware applications for MSCS that are currently available fall into the following main categories:

▼ Internet collaboration mail and messaging, intranet, and extranet

■ OLTP (Online Transaction Processing), OLAP (Online Analytical Processing), DSS (Decision Support System), and data warehouse/datamart (relational database driven)

■ Enterprise Resource Planning (ERP) (relational database driven)

■ Enterprise Systems Management (ESM)

▲ Storage (backup/restore, HSM, archiving, DR/BCS)

These categories represent many of the same so-called "killer apps" that dominate the enterprise today. The fact that they are included in this early listing of cluster-aware applications is by no means an accident. As part of Microsoft's overall efforts to make NT the platform of choice for the enterprise they have enlisted the support of the majority of the developers of these killer apps to make their dream a reality. These vendors also realize that in order for their own companies to be successful, they must embrace all the major platforms, especially those that are gaining the most attention and market share. To this end, Microsoft has gathered a highly visible group of partners, and competitors, who do not want to be left behind or cut out of the NT enterprise opportunity.

CLUSTER-AWARE APPLICATIONS, UTILITIES, AND TOOLS

In almost all of the main categories listed in the previous section, the vendor has taken a core, noncluster-aware product and developed new DLLs that conform to the Wolfpack API. In a majority of these first-generation cluster-aware applications, the clustering capabilities provided are basic for most part (as is MSCS), but they do achieve the desired result of increased availability, providing limited scalability enhancements (limited), and creating general improvements in overall manageability. Typical of these first-generation applications are the following:

▼ MS Exchange 5.5 Enterprise Edition

■ Lotus Domino Server

■ MS SQL Server 6.5/7.0 Enterprise Edition

- IBM DB2 Universal DB Enterprise Extended Edition
- Oracle8.0 and 8i (with Fail Safe Option)
- Tandem SQL/MX
- Informix Dynamic Server
- Sybase Adaptive Server
- SAP R/3
- Baan IV
- CA UniCenter TNG
- NuView ClusterX
- Legato NetWorker Power Edition
- HP OpenView with OmniBack II and MSCS cluster management add-ons
- ▲ IBM ADSM V3.1

The rest of this chapter discusses these particular applications (as well as a few others) in detail, along with the appropriate main application area that they fit into. This discussion also focuses on how each application works with MSCS today, as well as how it will evolve as Cluster Service Phase 2, with its N-node scalability, becomes available.

Internet Collaboration Applications (Mail and Messaging)

This group includes the suites of applications and utilities that drive the enterprises of many organizations in respect to mail, messaging, and workgroup collaboration. High availability and scalability are critical requirements for these killer apps, and MSCS provides substantial improvements in these areas.

The two most dominant providers of these solutions and their products are

- ▼ Microsoft Exchange 5.x Enterprise Edition
- ▲ Lotus Domino Server 4.6 and 5.x

A comparison of these two products can be found in Table 9-1.

Microsoft Exchange 5.x Enterprise Edition

Microsoft Exchange is a full-featured mail, messaging, groupware, and Internet collaboration environment. It supports the following email-based functions:

- ▼ Group scheduling
- Discussions
- Task management
- Simple workflow

Product Name	Version	Vendor	Clustering Type(s)/Number of Nodes	Mode of Operation
Exchange EE	5.5	Microsoft	MSCS/2	Active/standby
Domino	4.6.2/5.0	Lotus/IBM	MSCS/2 and Domino Clustering/6	Active/active Active/standby

Table 9-1.   A Comparison of Messaging, Mail, and Internet Collaboration Products

- Document routing
- Electronic forms
- ▲ Real-time chat

As a messaging platform, Exchange has the following attributes:

▼ *Solid messaging foundation*   Exchange is scalable, reliable, and secure. It offers high performance and high availability.

- *Connectivity and coexistence*   Exchange allows customers to choose the protocols and clients that are best for them, rather than being locked into a single messaging protocol environment. The Internet protocols should be part of the core server architecture, maintaining high performance. It supports Internet and OSI standards and can integrate with other mail systems such as PROFS SNADS, Notes/Domino, MS Mail, and cc:Mail. It can also act as a switch between these differing solutions.

- *Common, familiar tools for collaboration*   Exchange has common and familiar tools for a common development environment between its mail and messaging/collaboration environment and services used to build line-of-business applications. Access to information via a Web browser creates a standard interface. Exchange also includes real-time chat services and support for server-side event-driven scripting.

- *Management and adsministration*   Exchange is easy to manage and administer and is tightly integrated with Windows NT. It shares the security context and is integrated with NT's management tool.

- *Exchange 5.5 EE*   Is fully integrated with MSCS and provides substantial improvements in reliability and/or availability over other solutions, one of the three cornerstones of any enterprise-type mail and messaging solution. (The others are security and scalability; the latter is addressed via larger memory found in NTS/E and its support for higher-way SMPs.) See Figure 5-7 for a block diagram of a typical Exchange 5.5/MSCS deployment. In terms of reliability and/or availability, Exchange supports the MSCS environments in active/standby mode. Exchange also enhances overall reliability and availability by the use of the Transacted message store function. Each transaction is written to a log file using a write-ahead model, meaning the log file is updated simultaneously with the occurrence of the transaction. In the event of a disaster, all server data can be recovered up to the point of failure by replaying the log.

- *Server Monitor*   An Exchange utility that monitors server health and takes predetermined action in the event of a problem.

- *Link Monitor*   An Exchange utility that monitors links between sites, the Internet, and X.400 clouds.

- *Dynamic rerouting*   If a link anywhere in the system, or from the system to the public network, is unavailable, then queued messages are automatically rerouted via the next available link, without administrative intervention.

- ▲ *Message Tracker*   An Exchange utility that allows an administrator to track messages anywhere in the LAN, WAN, Internet, or X.400 cloud, using the message ID, recipient name, data sent, or sender's name.

Microsoft Exchange is fully cluster-aware and utilizes MSCS in an active/standby configuration for maximum high-availability. It is the most dominant of all offerings in the NT part of the market and is available on NT only as a platform.

IBM/Lotus Domino 4.x/5.0

Domino is now the name most used to refer to the Lotus Notes environment. Domino is the server application environment that supports the Notes desktop client environment for mail, messaging, and collaboration. Domino and Notes together create a feature- and functionality-rich environment. This Lotus solution is directly competitive with MS Exchange, and very public and private battles occur between Microsoft and IBM/Lotus who are attempting to win the hearts and minds of mail and messaging users. Lotus started the whole idea of "workgroup collaboration" when they released Notes a number of years ago. Since then everyone has copied these capabilities, and it's now a war fought on a "per-seat cost basis."

Domino Server (release 4.5 or later) supports both MSCS as well as its own clustering solution for availability and scalability enhancements. The Domino clustering solution supports both cross-operating system deployments (on NT, AIX, and AS/400), as well as wide disbursement geographically. Figure 9-1 shows a diagram of Domino Cluster and Domino in a MSCS Cluster environment. In many environments, MSCS and Domino clustering can be used together to create a highly fault-tolerant, scalable Notes environment. In these instances, Domino is installed as an NT service. Domino allows

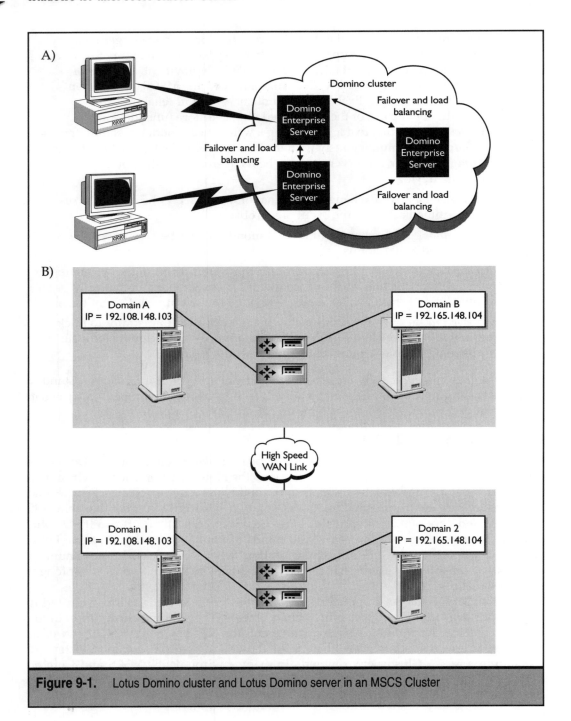

Figure 9-1. Lotus Domino cluster and Lotus Domino server in an MSCS Cluster

partitioned services to be defined as an NT service. A separate NT service is then defined for each of the two servers in the MSCS Cluster. Domino uses standard resource types provided with MSCS when being configured and does not require any special DLLs for use in Wolfpack clusters.

Relational Databases

Relational Databases are the "engines that drive the enterprise." They are responsible for all of an organization's sales, customer information, cost tracking, accounting, human resources operations, and all other key areas of day-to-day operations. Previously the sole bastion of "big iron," these systems are now commonplace in the world of Windows NT. Given their overall significance it is clear that high-availability is a critical requirement.

As you can see from Table 9-2, a large number of MSCS cluster-aware relational database offerings are available. These offerings come from the major vendors of database technology in the market today and include support for OLAP, ERP platforms, and other advanced database features not previously found in standalone database solutions. This category of application is critical to Windows NT's success in the enterprise. It is also one of the most competitive spaces of the software market for Windows NT. In that respect, Microsoft and Oracle are in a constant battle for the dominant share of this segment, with each winning the race from one quarter to the next, depending upon whether you believe that the market share leader is determined by higher license counts or revenues recognized.

Product Name	Version	Vendor	Clustering Type(s)/Number of Nodes	Mode of Operation
SQL Server	7.0 EE	Microsoft	MSCS/2	Active/active SVS
SQL Server	6.5 EE	Microsoft	MSCS/2	Active/active SVS
Universal DB EE	N/A	IBM	MSCS/2	Active/active SVS
Universal DB EE	N/A	IBM	IBM/8-72	Active/active
8 for NT	8.05	Oracle	MSCS/2	Active/standby
Dynamic Server	7.3	Informix	MSCS/2	Active/active
Adaptive Server	11.X	SyBase	MSCS/2	Active/active
SQL/MX	Beta	Tandem	MSCS/NSK-Lite	Active/active

Table 9-2.   A Feature Comparison of Cluster-Aware Databases

SQL Server (7.0 EE, 6.5 EE)

SQL Server 7.0 is a new release from Microsoft's database products group, building on the enterprise foundation established by SQL Server 6.5. Its many new features and capabilities have been driven by customer requirements, where they demanded significant enhancements in the areas of ease of use, scalability, and data warehousing.

Typical of these enhancements are:

▼ Scalability from the laptop to the enterprise, using the same code base with 100 percent code compatibility

■ Simplified management with many new wizards

■ Automated database configuration and performance tuning

■ Integrated OLAP services

■ Integrated data transformation services

■ Integrated text search

■ Wide array of replication options

■ Simplified multiserver management

■ Distributed and heterogeneous query capabilities

■ Integration with Microsoft Office, BackOffice, and Visual Studio

▲ Universal data access to enable high-performance access to a variety of information resources

Microsoft's strategy with version 7.0 was to make SQL Server the easiest database for building, managing, and deploying business applications. That meant automating configuration and tuning, including the addition of sophisticated tools to simplify complex operations and to provide a fast and simple programming model.

SQL Server 7.0 was also enhanced to support high-end OLTP and data warehousing systems, with scalability features like dynamic row-level locking, intra-query parallelism, distributed query, and very large database (VLDB) enhancements.

SQL Server 7.0 is one of the platforms of choice for NT in the enterprise for many vendors of applications that require a relational database engine. Typical of the vendors using it for this purpose are:

▼ SAP

■ Baan

■ PeopleSoft

■ J.D. Edwards

■ Applied Systems

▲ Policy Management Systems Corporation

SQL Server as a platform can take advantage of MSCS and Cluster Service as it evolves over time. See Figure 5-8 for a block diagram of SQL Server and MSCS in a Symmetric Virtual Server configuration. Version 7.0 currently supports Phase 1 MSCS clusters, with future "parallel" versions being able to take full advantage of Phase 2.

PHASE 1   *Hot-standby* enables a two-node cluster to support one SQL server that automatically fails over to the second server if the first server fails.

Symmetric Virtual Server enables a two-node cluster to support multiple SQL servers. When one node fails or is taken offline, all the SQL servers migrate to the surviving node.

PHASE 2   *Massive parallelism* enables more than two servers to be connected for higher performance. The first design preview of this architecture was completed in the summer of 1996. Phase 2 of Cluster Service will enable SQL Server 8.0 to achieve massive parallelism on N-node clusters. When the overall load exceeds the capabilities of a cluster, additional systems may be added to scale up or speed up the system. This will allow customers to add horsepower on demand. For client-server applications like online-transaction processing, file services, mail services, and Internet services, data can be spread among many nodes of the cluster, to form a workload consisting of many independent small jobs that can be executed in parallel. For batch workloads like data mining and decision support queries, parallel database technology can parse a single large query into many small independent queries that can be executed in parallel.

SQL Server 7.0 supports the pipeline parallelism architecture, while version 8.0 will support partition parallelism.

MSCS Deployment

SQL Server can be deployed on MSCS in several fashions, depending not only on the version that you are using. In the following section I discuss the features and benefits of each deployment methodology.

HOT STANDBY (SQL SERVER 6.5 MODE)   SQL Server 6.5 is the first generation of SQL Server to embrace the concept of a Virtual Server (VS). A 6.5 VS is one logical instance of SQL Server running on MSCS. One node of the cluster is designated as the primary node for the VS, and the other node is designated as the backup node. When a failure occurs on the primary node, the Wolfpack coordinates a failover to the secondary node. Control of the SQL Server database instance is transferred to the backup secondary node. The definition of a server includes

▼   Executables on the shared disks, which includes all executables and all server databases including the Master, Model, MSDB, and Temp DB

■   All user databases and log files on the clusters' shared disks

■   All server contexts stored in the Windows NT Registry

■   The named pipe that serves as the connection point to the database and the IP address corresponding to that named pipe

▲   The SQL Executive and the Distributed Transaction Coordinator of the VS

SQL Server 6.5 ensures that all databases and logs, and everything stored in the master database (configuration parameters, groups and users, replication information, and so on) stays consistent between the primary server and backup server. The databases and logs reside in the same place (the shared disks) regardless of whether the virtual server runs on the primary or backup node. Registry information is kept consistent between the primary and secondary nodes by using Registry replication.

Clients connect to the 6.5 Virtual Server using the VS name. Any client that uses WINS or directory services to locate servers automatically tracks the VS as it moves between nodes. This automatic tracking happens without client modification or reconfiguration. This includes SQL Enterprise Manager (included in SQL Server), and any third party OLE-DB, ODBC, or DB-Lib applications. When a VS fails over, the clients are disconnected and then reconnected to the same logical VS name. The database reconnect is implemented in the client application and should be transparent to the user. Transactions that were in process when the failover happened are rolled back and restarted as part of the SQL Server standard recovery process. The overall effect is as though the VS failed and was instantly restarted on the secondary node.

SQL Server 6.5 supports only one virtual SQL Server on a pair of nodes. SQL Server 7.0 relaxes that restriction.

TRUE SYMMETRIC VIRTUAL SERVERS (SQL SERVER 7.0)   SQL Server version 7.0 provides both scalability and availability using MSCS with the true Symmetric Virtual Servers (SVS). In this mode you run several virtual servers on a single node of the cluster. This allows each node to act as the primary server for the VS and to also act as the secondary server for the VS that is the primary server on the other node. Large databases are then partitioned logically between the VSs running on the cluster

The SVS cluster solution is symmetric in that both a primary and a backup server can be run on each node of the cluster. This offers full utilization of the cluster resources while still offering availability of server resources in the event of a hardware or software failure. Administration of multiple SQL servers is accomplished via a single administrative object from just one console. SVSs on the cluster can be administered as a single system by defining a "group" of servers for the cluster. Administrative jobs and policies can then be applied to the cluster group rather than individually to each SQL server.

SQL Server 7.0 also supports the placement of different tables on each VS to support distributed queries and updates coordinated automatically via the Distributed Transaction Coordinator. It also supports optimized distributed execution of queries between SQL instances (and between heterogeneous data sources using the OLE-DB rowset interface). Updates to data distributed between cluster nodes are automatically coordinated to ensure data integrity and consistency.

PHASE 2—MSCS N-NODE CLUSTERS AND SQL SERVER 8.0   SQL Server 8.0 also supports failover for high availability and scalability of SQL Server applications across clusters of Windows 2000 nodes. These SQL Server clusters will form a federated database in which each system can make requests to any of the others. An application running at one node can query and join tables residing at any cluster node and can invoke stored procedures at any node. All these operations are orchestrated by Microsoft's Distributed Transaction Coordinator (DTC).

IBM DB2 Universal Database Enterprise Extended Edition

The newest generation of a time-proven database from IBM has been designed to bring to bear an "industrial-strength" database management environment for data warehousing, decision support, data mining, financial modeling, and line-of-business OLAP and OLTP application environments. For the world of Windows NT (and Windows 2000), DB2 UD has been designed specifically to take advantage of large SMPs and built-in clustering capabilities. The features in DB2 UD provide the following capabilities:

▼ DB2's built-in cost-based optimizer provides optimal query performance in complex environments by utilizing a detailed model of I/O, CPU, and communications costs. DB2 also automatically generates a parallel execution strategy for each SQL statement transparently of whatever the client application is expecting.

■ Its shared-nothing architecture allows it to take full advantage of any hardware and clustering architecture. This allows instances to be run on each node of a large cluster without the need to share server memory or disk access. Large databases are divided into partitions, each of which can be stored and managed on individual nodes. This then enables parallel queries over all the nodes of the cluster, dramatically increasing speed. During this process, the nodes communicate and share data over a VIA-based System Area Network (SAN). Communications over this node is via TCP/IP.

■ DB2's native support for the VIA allows for high-bandwidth, reliable data interchange within clusters for major performance improvements. VIA is used in a SAN to facilitate high-speed, low-latency movement of data and messages among cluster nodes.

▲ It has a built-in ability to define and automatically route queries to summary tables to enhance the overall performance of business intelligence queries, without using costly join processing.

This version of DB2 has quickly become one of the highest performance databases for use on Windows NT and has run the first 1 TB TPC-D benchmark on NT of any database platform in the market. This benchmark was based on a 32-way cluster containing 128 Xeon processors interconnected with a GigaNet VIA-based SAN.

Oracle8 for Windows NT

Oracle is the leading high-performance database in the enterprise computing space today. It is ported to all the leading platforms (S/390, VMS, NSK, all variants of UNIX, and NT). In the NT segment, Oracle is tied for the most part with Microsoft in regards to share. (This is always in dispute by both parties because Oracle claims a larger share based on revenue and Microsoft claims a larger share based on licenses shipped.)

Oracle8 is more than just a relational database—it is a family of products for use in decision support environments. This family consists of:

▼ Oracle Universal Server

■ Oracle Web Application Server

■ Oracle InterOffice

▲ Oracle Applications

All of these products are designed to meet the requirements of NT users in the enterprise. Oracle for NT is available in both a Standard version that can utilize MSCS and Oracle's own Fail Safe management add-on, or in a parallel server version called OPS (which is based on version 7). In addition, Oracle has a Parallel Query option where a database can be partitioned among the processors in each node of a cluster. This provides even higher levels of performance than either Oracle8 w/Fail Safe or OPS can provide. Figure 9-2 shows the performance enhancements that each of these configurations provide. All of these products feature the look and feel of an Oracle database as found on any platform, with OPS having the ability to scale itself over six or more nodes in an OPS-based cluster. (See Chapter 6 for more details on OPS.) OPS is expected to be replaced at some point in time by one of Oracle's "big-iron" implementations of their new Internet-based database system, 8i.

Oracle8 for NT touts higher performance than any of its competitors on many levels. Through the more efficient usage of Windows NT and networking resources, thousands of concurrent users can access their Oracle8 database via multiple network protocols. Oracle uses connection pooling to temporarily drop the physical connections of idle users and then transparently reestablishes them when needed, thereby increasing the effective number of users who can be supported.

Oracle8 can support the most demanding database applications with databases ranging in size from GB's to TB's in size. It achieves this through Enhanced Parallelism (as applied to insert, update and delete operations, along with running all queries in parallel i.e. index scans, single partition scans and full-table scans), and through the use of Partitioned Tables and Indexes to decrease the time required to perform administrative operations and to break storage units down to increase parallelism.

Sybase Adaptive Server Enterprise (ASE) for Windows NT

This is the latest release of SyBase's SQL Server, a well-established database solution that delivers scalability and high performance across a wide range of data sources and data types. It is designed to support mixed workload environments that have increasing numbers of users and application demands.

As part of Sybase's Adapter Component Architecture, ASE was designed not only to provide high performance for transaction processing and decision support, but to be adaptable to the unpredictable requirements of the Internet.

ASE for Windows NT includes an integrated suite of tools with capabilities that range from building dynamic, data-rich Web sites, to designing, administering, analyzing, and

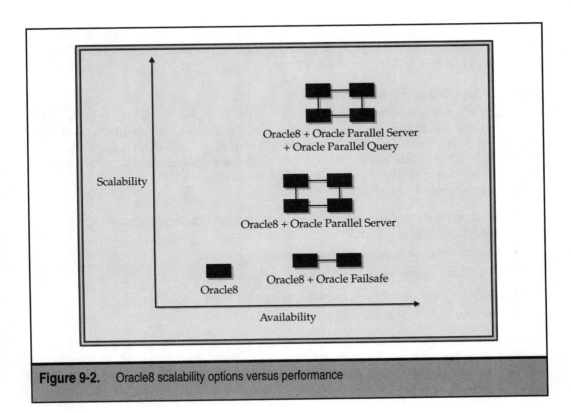

Figure 9-2.   Oracle8 scalability options versus performance

replicating enterprise databases. ASE was designed with high availability in mind and includes the following built-in HA features:

▼ Mirrored database devices with automatic fail-over for fault tolerance

■ MSCS support to eliminate local node failures

■ High-speed parallel backup and restore for up to 32 devices

■ Online unattended backup

▲ Point-in-time recovery

MSCS SUPPORT   Adaptive Server Enterprise can be deployed under MSCS in an active/active configuration, which can then be configured to failover either manually or automatically, depending upon the requirements of the particular application environment. In this mode of operation, two instances of ASE are required. Sybase recommends this mode for environments that during failover situations do not produce service degradations that are unacceptable to the user community connected to the ASE application.

ASE can also be deployed in an active/standby mode, which requires only one instance of ASE to operate. This mode provides the highest levels of availability, but at a higher cost in terms of hardware investments.

Informix Dynamic Server

Dynamic Server is a multithreaded database server designed to deliver high levels of scalability, manageability, and performance via the exploitation of SMPs, and SMP clusters. It is based upon Informix's core technology called "Dynamic Scalable Architecture (DSA)," an advanced parallel database architecture. Informix refers to Dynamic Server as a "parallel everywhere" database solution.

Key advantages of Dynamic Server include:

▼ A superior multithreaded parallel processing architecture for maximum performance and scalability

■ OS overhead reductions through bypass operations

■ Local table partitioning for high-performance parallel I/O

■ Dynamic and distributed database administration

▲ Built-in high-availability support

Dynamic Server's high-availability performance is driven by a number of built-in features, including:

▼ Database and log mirroring to enhance data fault-tolerance and recovery from failures

■ Fast recovery to bring the system up quickly in the event of a shut down, all with no data losses

■ Restartable restore to allow for error recovery from where the last process "left off" prior to the error

■ Table reorganization to allows DBAs to alter table schema "in place" without making data unavailable during the process.

■ Exception handling improvements to better identify and diagnose system problems

▲ MSCS support in both active/active and active/standby deployment modes

Dynamic Server fully supports MSCS Phase 1 today and is well poised to take advantage of Phase 2 when it becomes available, especially in light of its parallel architecture.

Compaq/Tandem SQL/MX for Windows NT

Although not a formally released product at this time, SQL/MX in its beta release has done a lot to foster the concepts regarding how well Windows NT can fit into the enterprise at some point in the near future. SQL/MX was the database used at the first Microsoft Scalability Day in 1997. It ran as a 2 TB database partitioned over a 16-node MSCS beta cluster. This event set many critics of Windows NT on their heads and opened the eyes of many in the enterprise community as to the viability of NT.

SQL/MX is a port of Tandem's well known SQL/MP database from their NonStop Himalaya system to Windows NT. It blurs the distinction between processors and nodes by creating a single system image across large clusters. Tables and indexes transparently span nodes, while operations such as backup, restore, audit, and table maintenance are performed on a systemwide basis as if they were running on a single node. In SQL/MX all queries are performed in parallel over the entire cluster.

SQL/MX is in essence a parallel relational database management system designed for critical decision support and OLTP applications. By taking advantage of large clustering environments SQL/MX provides

▼ High performance by employing parallelism throughout to dramatically improve response time and throughput

■ Incomparable reliability via 24x365 availability and zero data looses

▲ Scalability beyond conventional server limitations

Enterprise Resource Planning

Enterprise Resource Planning, more affectionately known as "ERP," applications have been killer apps of the '90s. They are the true ubiquitous application environment that enterprise computing environments have embraced on a wholesale basis to run all facets of their organizations. These applications are responsible for accounting, manufacturing, distribution, human resources, and so on and are all fully integrated and multinational in orientation. The two leading suppliers of these applications are SAP and Baan. Both are closely partnered with Microsoft on an application (SQL Server, Exchange, and the entire BackOffice family), along with embracing Windows NT as their development platform of choice. These two vendors also use Oracle8, IBM-DB2, Informix, and SyBase as database engines in many deployments, depending upon the customer's preferences. Table 9-3 is a comparison of these two ERP platforms.

Product Name	Version	Application	DB Baseline	MSCS Mode/# of Nodes
SAP	R/3	ERP	SQL Server	Active/active SVS/2
SAP	R/3	ERP	Oracle8X	Active/standby - FailSafe
Baan	IV	ERP	SQL Server	Active/active SVS/2

Table 9-3.   Basic Specifications of the Two Leading ERP Applications.

SAP R/3 for Windows NT

SAP's R/3 ERP solution is the world leader according to most analysts. It is deployed on many platforms, and in the past few years SAP has focused on Windows NT as their development platform of choice. To that end they have formed a high-level relationship with Microsoft and have achieved BackOffice Certification for their NT-based solution. Within their development efforts, SAP has embraced ActiveX and DCOM as core technologies to exploit on NT.

SAP has delivered more than 3,000 installations on Windows NT with approximately half of those being deployed with SQL Server as the companion database.

MSCS DEPLOYMENT The R/3 System is dependent upon the use of a high-availability architecture to ensure maximum uptime and to eliminate single points of failure due to server outages. For these reasons, along with the promise of N-node scalability for the future, SAP has worked very closely with Microsoft in making their core application cluster-aware.

SAP takes advantage of MSCS on two fronts:

▼ Overall performance is enhanced when the R/3 application resides on one node and the database (SQL Server, Oracle, IBM, SyBase, and Informix) resides on the other. This works well given MSCS's two-node capabilities today.

▲ Even if an outage of several minutes transpires from the time that MSCS fails over and all users are reconnected to the application, it is statistically unlikely that another failure will occur on the surviving node prior to the failed node being repaired and returned to online status. This effectively eliminates any hardware-based single points of failure, a must for an enterprise R/3 environment.

The goal of deploying R/3 on MSCS-based systems is to protect and eliminate two potential system failures:

▼ The loss or unavailability of the R/3 central instance

▲ The loss or failure of the database (and any transactions committed)

To support the deployment of R/3 on MSCS, SAP has developed a new resource type called the "SAP Resource." It contains a resource type and a CA extension, named saprc.dll and saprcex.dll, respectively.

The SAP Resource has three basic application specific properties:

SID	SA
PSID of the R/3 system	
Instance	R/3 system number
Maximum start time	Maximum wait time until R/3 is started

The SAP Resource DLL implements a number of specific functions from either the Cluster Service or the Resource Monitor. They include:

SaprcOnline	Start the R/3 service and work processes
SaprcOffline	Stop the R/3 service and work processes
SaprcTerminate	Stop the R/3 service immediately
SaprcIsAlive	IsAlive check by MSCS
SaprcLooksAlive	LooksAlive check by MSCS (follows IsAlive check)

This implementation of R/3 allows for the maximum levels of availability in an MSCS environment, while achieving some scalability via locating the R/3 application on one node and the database on the other (during normal operations). Figure 9-3 is a dependency tree diagram of SAP R/3 as deployed on MSCS.

Baan IV ERP for Windows NT

The Baan Company is another leading supplier of ERP solutions worldwide and has also embraced Windows NT as their development platform of choice. This focus on Windows NT goes hand in hand with a high-level strategic partnership Microsoft, including BackOffice Certification.

Baan has been delivering ERP systems to customers in 50 countries for more than 20 years now. Their ERP suite consists of applications for small, medium, and large enterprises and ranges from advanced business modeling to financial reporting.

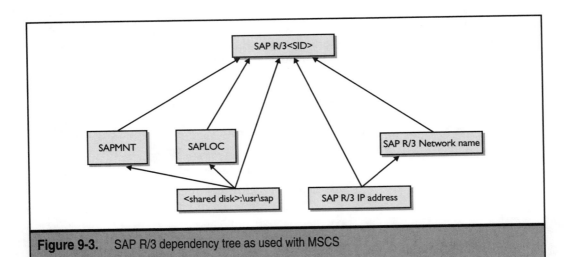

Figure 9-3.   SAP R/3 dependency tree as used with MSCS

MSCS DEPLOYMENT   Baan IV is the current version of this ERP family and utilizes SQL Server 7.0 as its database platform on Windows NT. It is deployed in a similar fashion to SAP R/3 in that the database resides on one cluster node and the Baan application on the other. This deployment provides high availability with some scalability in the process. A specific set of resource DLLs for Baan are available for use with MSCS.

Enterprise Systems and Storage Management Applications

This category of cluster-aware applications includes those enterprise-wide applications responsible for systems management, as well as those specifically focused on storage. Both categories consist of solutions from market leaders who are partnered with Microsoft in the pursuit of Windows NT for the enterprise and are BackOffice Certified for the most part.

Enterprise Systems Management Applications

These applications are targeted at managing computing assets across the enterprise or within a cluster environment. All are designed to increase management functionality, while reducing administrative costs. Table 9-4 provides a brief feature comparison of the two applications that are reviewed in this chapter.

UNICENTER TNG FOR WINDOWS NT ENTERPRISE EDITION   Unicenter is the leading ESM application in the marketplace today. It is installed in tens of thousands of sites across the world and supports all major platforms (hardware and software), with a specific focus on Windows NT for the enterprise. This focus is based upon a Strategic Enterprise Initiative formed in 1997, which is well in place today.

Unicenter TNG was the first open-systems solution to manage, monitor, and control global IT resources. In respect to Windows NT, this solution includes servers, clients, MSCS clusters, and the entire range of BackOffice applications. TNG is based upon a scalable and distributed management framework. TNG supports TCP/IP, SNA, IPX/SPX, and DECnet networking environments. Its management solution covers network discovery and topology, performance, events and status, security, storage

Product Name	Version	Vendor	EM App.	MSCS Support
Unicenter TNG	4.X	CAI	Enterprise management	Full
ClusterX	1.0	NuView	Cluster management	Full

Table 9-4.   Cluster-Aware Enterprise Systems Management Applications

management, and other functions used in distributed computing environments. Unicenter TNG uses intelligent manager/agents for monitoring and managing hardware and software.

In that regard TNG interfaces directly with MSCS's Cluster Service to monitor and manage the cluster and its resources. In addition, the Unicenter platform can take full advantage of MSCS through its cluster-aware API support, which allows users not only to deploy TNG in a highly-available fashion on Windows NT, but to manage all MSCS clusters on the network. This dual-mode usage allows for maximum return on investment for those organizations that deploy Unicenter on their NT systems in a clustered fashion. The dual-mode usage also makes it possible to   manage critical applications and services that are clustered using MSCS.

NUVIEW CLUSTERX MSCS MANAGEMENT SOFTWARE   NuView is a supplier of high-availability management solutions. They have developed a product called ClusterX for management of MSCS clusters and their high-availability applications and services. ClusterX helps administrators optimize their clustered systems to provide maximum availability. ClusterX configures, monitors, diagnoses, manages, and administers MSCS clusters and is an effective tool in reducing TCO further than what MSCS provides on a standalone basis.

ClusterX is optimized for applications such as SAP R/3, IIS, Exchange, SQL Server, Oracle, and others. It provides statistics on cluster uptime and allows administrators to monitor and measure actual resource usage. It uses a "one-to-many" model for monitoring and managing large clustered environments from one main console. ClusterX also gives a view of dependencies so that failovers can be managed either manually or automatically. It also provides a detailed cluster log and can send event alerts to ESMs like Unicenter TNG and HP OpenView.

ClusterX can easily manage more than 100 MSCS clusters and appears to administrators as an MMC snap-in. It uses COM as its communication standard between clusters and their nodes. ClusterX's GUI also uses an ActiveX container so it can be accessed from a browser. It is also bundled with the leading vendors' MSCS-based solutions.

ClusterX enhances MSCS environments in the following ways:

▼   It provides an automation engine for MSCS commands.

■   It extends MSCS commands.

■   It provides a load balancing infrastructure.

■   It provides backup and restore for the cluster database (not the QR).

■   It supports duplication of cluster groups across multiple clusters.

■   It enables moving resources from one group to another

■   It enables the modification of a forward and backward dependency in a graphical fashion

▲   It logs all problems and changes in the cluster.

Figure 9-4 is a view of ClusterX in action.

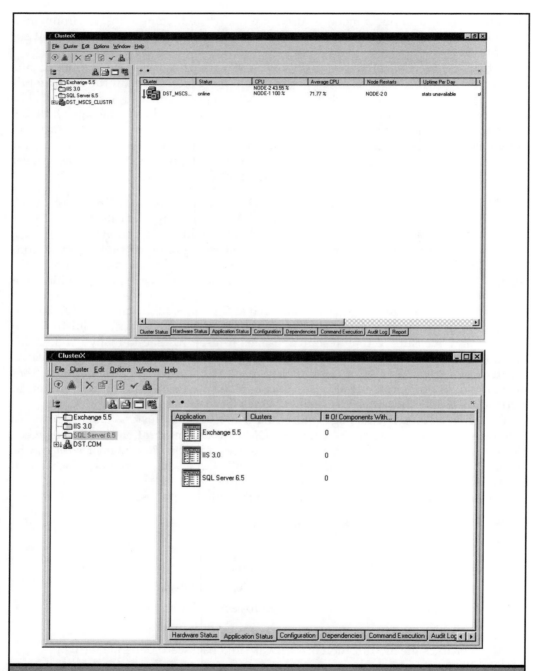

Figure 9-4. Views of ClusterX in an MSCS environment

Cluster-Aware Storage Management Applications

As we discussed in earlier chapters, MSCS clusters require a backup and restore application that is cluster-aware in order not only to be able to "reach out" and back up both the local boot drives, but the entire chain of shared storage bus drives. It also requires an application that can failover and failback in order to maintain consistency in backup and restore activities. It is simply not sufficient to just backup the nodes, the storage management application must be highly available itself in terms of moving from one node to another in the event of its own failure.

Table 9-5 lists the leading vendors of cluster-aware storage management applications.

IBM ADSM V3.1 ADSM is a well-seasoned storage management suite from IBM, now via its Tivoli subsidiary. It delivers an end-to-end solution for MSCS clustered environments.

ADSM provides the following functionality:

▼ Unattended network-based backup and restore

■ Storage management

▲ Disaster recovery support

ADSM, like all of the other storage management products listed in Table 9-5, provides all of the basic storage functions, while being able to take advantage of MSCS in respect to making itself more highly available. In addition, ADSM is able to control shared storage bus drives during backup and restore.

LEGATO NETWORKER POWER EDITION Networker Power Edition (PE) was the first MSCS-aware storage management product to come to market after its release with NTS/E in late 1997. Its current release is 5.5; like most other storage management software vendors, Legato is moving beyond the support of simple server-based clusters, to those based on SANs. They have acquired Full Time Software (Octopus) and Intelliguard Corporation in support of this strategy.

Legato has also restructured many of their product offerings to embrace their GEMS (Global Enterprise Management of Storage), which is a centralized storage administration scheme.

Product Name	Version	Vendor	Storage Applications	MSCS Support
ADSM	3.1	IBM	ESM	Yes
Networker PE	4.4	Legato	Backup/restore	Yes
ArcServe IT	6.6	CAI	Backup/restore	Limited
Backup Exec	7.2	Seagate	Backup/restore	Limited
OmniBack	II	HP	Backup/restore	Yes

Table 9-5.   Cluster-Aware Storage Management Applications

Networker PE is cluster-aware in respect to its own operation under MSCS. It can also restore information to any drive on the shared storage bus, regardless of its current owner.

COMPUTER ASSOCIATES ARCSERVE IT   ArcServe IT is the most recent version of the long-established ArcServe product family. It is now fully integrated into the Unicenter product family and is no longer positioned as a standalone storage management application suite. It is now part of a more global offering, taking advantage of the broad reach of Unicenter TNG in enterprise systems management. As part of TNG it is fully cluster-aware in respect to MSCS and can backup and restore all drives on the shared storage bus regardless of the current status of the node that normally owns any storage device.

ArcServe IT is currently is release 6.6 and is also being extended to support SANs and their shared tape resources.

SEAGATE SOFTWARE BACKUP EXEC   Backup Exec, now in release 7.2, is the baseline technology that Microsoft licenses from Seagate for use in Windows NT in the feature-disabled utility known as NT Backup. Promised to be available in a MSCS cluster-aware version at the time of the release of Windows NT Enterprise Edition, it has, to my knowledge, never materialized. In the meantime, Seagate (soon to be a part of Veritas) made their backup Exec product cluster-aware, as well as capable of embracing emerging SA paradigm by developing a "shared storage option" for this product family.

Backup Exec is a mature and feature-rich product offering for those folks who want to backup and restore files and data on their MSCS shared storage buses and add functionality modules.

HEWLETT-PACKARD OMNIBACK II   Well-recognized as a storage management software provider, HP has developed a cluster-aware, comprehensive backup and restore application for use with their OpenView enterprise management environment. It supports high-availability environments and systems to dramatically improve system uptime and reduce administrative burdens in the process.

Other MSCS Applications, Tools, and Utilities

This is a "catch-all" category for other products that have been announced as supporting MSCS and its nodes.

Compaq Enterprise Software for Windows NT

Compaq has three categories of software available for enterprise users of Windows NT. This portfolio of products is designed to enhance the BackOffice environment and to compliment existing investments in MSCS. The three categories are:

▼   Continuous computing

■   Application development

▲   Enterprise extensions for MS Exchange environments

Each category provides different benefits to enterprise users.

CONTINUOUS COMPUTING   Included in this category are four basic offerings:

▼ Storage and cluster software extensions

■ Batch job scheduler

■ Reliable transaction Router

▲ Compaq storage and cluster software extensions for Windows NT, which provide storage visualization and data replication for Windows NT systems via host-based software

These extensions provide advanced storage management capabilities for MSCS environments and allow administrators to deploy cluster-based storage solutions with more flexibility and cost affectivity.

Basic features include:

▼ *Virtual disk management*   From pools of storage, you can create virtual disks that are sized to suit the particular needs of users and their applications.

■ *Snapshots*   Use snapshots to create replicas of virtual disks in a very short time. This provides online backup and restore with little, if any, impact on applications.

■ *Network disks*   Use network disks to provide virtual disks (or physical ones) along with snapshots to applications or users from a centralized storage server.

■ *Batch job scheduler*   Brings a mainframe class, automated job scheduler to the world of Windows NT. The scheduler provides a GUI for job creation and scheduling and uses an object-oriented development tool. Jobs are created and launched using a visual drag-and-drop interface. The scheduler also has a notification option for alerting administrators that a job has completed or that an error has been reported.

▲ *Reliable Transaction Router (RTR)*   Compaq's router for use in transactional environments where continuous application availability is paramount. Developed by Digital for their VMS and UNIX environments, it has now been ported to Windows NT. RTR is used to enhance transaction integrity and real-time transaction completion.

APPLICATION DEVELOPMENT   Compaq has developed an application development environment for Windows NT that provides the ability to add the following attributes to applications:

▼ Fault-tolerance for 24x7x52 operations

■ Scalability to extend existing systems

■ Investment protection by migrating existing production systems to Web-based applications

▲ Flexibility to adapt rapidly to changing business requirements

This environment is based on the Alta Vista Process Flow for Windows NT. This software platform is based on business process management procedures used to automate work flow and work processes across existing production environments, as well as newer Web-based ones, while maintaining a fault-tolerant architecture and operational environment.

In addition to the Alta Vista Process Flow platform, there are substantial enhancements to MTS via the addition of a unique "Portable Transaction Processor (TP)" for making transaction processing applications more portable and flexible in multiplatform environments, as well as the "Application Optimizer" for improved performance optimization via thread management.

ENTERPRISE EXTENSIONS FOR MS EXCHANGE ENVIRONMENTS Compaq has developed a number of add-on applications and utilities for use with MS Exchange to make it a more robust and flexible mail and messaging environment for enterprise users. These products are used to help manage mail as an asset via expanded archive and retrieval capabilities, the use of distribution control profiles and management schemes, along with the life-cycle management of mail documents through a project's entire lifetime. Included in these add-on offerings are the following products:

▼ Enterprise Vault

■ Communiqué Program

■ Work Expediter

■ Netflow Workflow Administrator

▲ Commander for Mail and Messaging

All of these products are based on earlier products developed for non-Exchange environments that are now fully supported on Exchange and Windows NT. They bring major improvements in functionality for enterprise mail and messaging environments.

▼ *Enterprise Vault* An archival, storage, and retrieval service for exchanging mail and documents. It manages all exchange data in a central archive, and uses the AltaVista search engine for search and retrieval based on multiple attributes.

■ *Communiqué Program* An enterprise-wide information distribution system for use in disseminating "need-to-know" information to specific users, customers, and Internet-list subscribers.

■ *Work Expediter* A document storage and handling solution for use with project document sets. It automatically provides notification of key dates and project milestones to team members.

■ *Netflow Workflow Administrator* Business process software that allows the creation and automation of *ad hoc* business approval and information review over multiple mail systems. It can track processes, handle exceptions, and provide a history of all activities.

▲ *Commander for Mail and Messaging* A monitoring and management product for use in bridging numerous mail and messaging solutions used across an enterprise. It also acts as a sophisticated monitoring and troubleshooting platform to advise administrators of the health of their entire mail and messaging environment.

SUMMARY

Microsoft and its software partners have taken the lead in MSCS-based clustering by providing a wide, and growing, range of enterprise killer apps for use by end users in meeting their EC requirements. These applications, tools, and utilities represent the "best of breed" in the marketplace and will be leading the charge as Windows NT makes its push into the enterprise (either on NT 4.0 or Windows 2000–based platforms). This list of products will grow substantially as all BackOffice-Certified applications are written to be cluster-aware from their inception.

Appendix C lists Web site addresses for obtaining demonstration and evaluation copies of many of these cluster-aware applications and for gathering more information on their deployment and usage in your EC environment.

CHAPTER 10

Troubleshooting Procedures, Examples, and Tools

A s with any complex system such as an MSCS cluster, a good amount of every administrator's time is spent learning how to troubleshoot the large and small problems that can arise when one is least prepared to diagnose and dispatch them quickly. This chapter provides a comprehensive set of procedures, examples, and tools to support rapid diagnosis and repair and the development of workarounds. This information will be helpful to administrators, and the troubleshooting section of my Web site (**www.dst.com**) will be maintained and frequently updated in order to support readers of this book.

This chapter begins with a list of example-type problems and solutions for situations often encountered by individuals who administer MSCS. A list of resources is also provided to help you develop your own solutions.

The following sections are included:

▼ Registry entries (typical for MSCS nodes that it resides on). These registry hives have numerous entries affecting all aspects of the cluster (such as cluster service, disks, networks, and administration). Included are typical entries for HKEY_LOCAL_MACHINE (HKLM)—Hardware and Application Software configuration data and HKEY_CURRENT_USER (HKCU)—Current Setup configuration data.

■ A list of all files (including system and hidden) for MSCS and their locations

■ Test utilities

■ Typical log entries

■ Uninstall information

■ Service bulletins from Microsoft (as of June 1, 1998) for MSCS

▲ MSCS Frequently Asked Questions (FAQs)

TIPS, EXAMPLES, AND TOOLS FOR TROUBLESHOOTING MSCS

The first tip is to set up automated logs for gathering critical systems information as processes and interrupts are occurring. Under MSCS you can set up logging (called the Cluster Log) in a few simple steps (a more detailed explanation can be found in *MS Service Bulletin #Q168801*). The steps are as follows:

1. There are two variables that you must set up in the NT environment variable list: ClusterLog and ClusterLogLevel. You can access the set up of these from the System | Envronment | System Environment Variable control panel tab.

2. Type in **ClusterLog** and set the path for the folder that you already created. Next, enter ClusterLogLevel with a number value of 0-3 (0 indicates no logging, 3 indicates everything logged).

3. Close out the control panel and restart your system. This process needs to be done on both nodes.

This section lists (in no particular order) a number of recurring problems encountered while working with the production release of MSCS. I discuss the solutions and workarounds to these problems—this information should provide a strong foundation to aid you in developing your own resolution capabilities.

Problem: Both the public and private networks are unavailable

When the Cluster Administrator is run on the working node, it indicates that both networks (public and private) are unavailable. Power down re-boot does not solve the problem.

Solution

When either network experiences an outage during startup of MSCS, you will not be able to add that node to the cluster. To work around this problem and to troubleshoot which network is affecting the cluster, go into the Cluster Administrator (CA), and click Networks. You will then see both your public and private networks on the right side of the window. Choose the Public network first, and then select Properties. To verify the health of the network and to hopefully bring up the cluster temporarily (to troubleshoot further or to work around the problem at the present time), select this network for both cluster and client communications. This will set your cluster to use the Public network for both communicating with clients as well as inter-node communications. Exit out of this, select the Private network, and then choose Properties. Disable this network for cluster use by unchecking the Disable checkbox.

You can then use the CA to restart cluster service on the other node and see if it comes up without error. This process will enable you to at least determine which network is down (because both previously indicated errors on the CA display—the circle crossed with a line icon; an explanation of these symbols is provided in Chapter 5). If your private network is down, you can work around it temporarily by using the public network for all communications.

If this workaround fails to produce the desired end result, then it is most likely that your public network is out. The cause can be as simple as a cable being loose or disconnected or a bad NIC (and driver) in that particular node. MSCS will help you isolate which network is out while remaining up and running, but will show that both networks are out upon startup even if a problem exists with only one of them.

Problem: Node 2 cannot join the cluster due to a logon error

After making changes to NTS/E and attempting to restart the cluster on both nodes from power-up, you may get a message that node 2 cannot join the cluster due to a "logon error."

Solution

Because of some strangeness in either NTS/E or MSCS, the system can actually change the password associated with MSCS logon. To determine if this is the problem, you have to run the Services applet from the Control Panel, and double-click on Cluster Server. You can then scroll down to the bottom of the window to see the name and password of the administrator authorized on this node. Chances are that you will find the password is incorrect because it has somehow been mysteriously lengthened or shortened. You can then re-enter the password, close out the applet, and reboot your node. It should then be able to successfully join the cluster.

Problem: Physical disk resources unavailable

Sometimes when starting CA, after both nodes have come up without errors and formed a cluster, you may see physical disk resources shown as unavailable. Yet when you run Disk Administrator, everything appears to be okay.

Solution

This problem seems to be driven by power-down and power-up sequencing—specifically, having a particular drive (the physical disk) "owned" by the opposite node when that node was powered down first. A simple fix to the problem is to use the CA to "move the resource" to the other node and then move it back again. Doing so will usually return the resource to its original state and bring it back online right away. Through the use of SCSI hubs and switches, which keep all the drives powered regardless of the state of the servers, you can virtually eliminate the potential for this quirk becoming a problem.

Problem: Installation of cluster-aware application is successful, but it won't come online

When installing a cluster-aware application using its wizard, you may get a message that "installation was successful," but the application will not come online.

Solution

In many cases, you must prepare MSCS for a particular application before you use that application's own wizard to set it up, which is covered in Chapter 5. It is recommended that you always preconfigure your cluster for the type of cluster-aware application that you are setting up and then choose those settings when using the app's setup wizard, rather than just blindly accepting its defaults.

Problem: RPC server errors originating from second node

When a cluster first starts, you may intermittently get RPC server errors that appear to be originating from your second node. A cold reboot of both nodes seems to correct this problem.

Solution

MSCS uses RPC for communications between nodes and is very sensitive to the sequence you use to start up your cluster. It is recommended that you start your primary node first and take it all the way through logon. You can then start your second node and, assuming that no problems occur with your shared SCSI bus, it should load all the way to logon without any errors. Once both machines are up all the way, it is imperative that you check the system logs with Event Viewer (or some other log-viewing product). Check for any startup errors associated with CLUSVC or RPC. A service bulletin (Document ID# Q171450) on this problem is listed in the section "Service Bulletins from Microsoft Technical Support, later in this chapter.

Problem: NT Backup cannot access all shared SCSI storage devices

You may encounter a problem in which NT Backup does not have the ability to access all your shared SCSI storage devices for backing up.

Solution

NT Backup, along with most non-cluster-aware backup and restore applications, can only "see" and back up a limited number of devices on the shared storage bus. It can be used to back up NTS/E, the quorum resource (on the primary node that owns it), the physical disk, and other resources owned by the primary node, but it cannot typically "see" all the physical disks that are assigned to a cluster-aware application, especially those that are owned by the other node but reside on the common shared storage bus. This limitation creates special problems when one wants to use a single tape drive/library or wants to back up the entire cluster from one node. Microsoft promised a cluster-aware version of NT Backup with NTS/E but has yet to provide one. In the meantime, the only storage management products that are truly cluster-aware and can provide much of this needed functionality are IBM's ADSM V3.1 and Legato's NetWorker Power Edition. Appendix A has more information on these products and the issues associated with cluster storage management.

Problem: How do I increase paging file size on my nodes when I have one boot drive and my other storage is on the shared bus?

You cannot store page data on your shared bus storage devices.

Solution

You can add non-shared bus drives (local) with either another SCSI HBA if you are using EIDE for your boot drive or with additional EIDE devices (up to four can be supported by most built-in controllers). If you really want to increase performance, the best approach is to add another SCSI HBA. You can purchase several 2–4GB drives and spread your page file across them. This will give you some degree of parallelization, while not incurring the CPU penalty associated with EIDE drives.

Problem: How do I Implement availability and better management to my Oracle database using my MSCS cluster?

Set up and configure Fail-Safe, a high-availability option for single-instance Oracle database solutions on MSCS.

Solution

Fail-Safe provides high-availability to single-instance Oracle databases. It utilizes the Wolfpack API and is fully integrated with MSCS clusters. Fail-Safe uses MSCS in active/standby mode and provides a familiar "Oracle-oriented" interface for users and administrators familiar with Oracle databases.

To add Fail-Safe to your MSCS cluster, you must perform the following steps:

1. Once your MSCS cluster is fully functional, install a single instance of Oracle for Windows NT on one of the shared-bus drives.

2. After successfully completing the installation of the database and restarting the node that you installed from, install Fail-Safe for Oracle on both nodes, following the Installation Wizard's instructions.

3. Restart both nodes, and form a cluster. Fail-Safe is now available for final configuration. This can be accomplished by using both the Fail-Safe GUI and the Cluster Administrator.

Problem: I recently made changes to my cluster and want to verify its health and functionality

Testing your cluster using *fire drill* type techniques is necessary on a regular basis—even if you don't make any changes to it—to ensure that when a real failure or outage occurs, you will know that your cluster is operating properly.

Solution

Administrators use fire drills to make sure that they are prepared for the real thing. Fire drills should be run regularly and on all components of your cluster to ensure that some type of unknown fault has not crept into the system.

The simplest form of this test is to manually fail resource groups on both nodes and observe how they failover (if at all), restart, and then failback at the appropriate time (and under the appropriate manual or automatic conditions). You can also use a test application such as Notepad, which we configured in Chapter 5.

It is also a good idea to take each node offline occasionally to watch how the cluster behaves overall. Do this during slow periods so the entire cluster doesn't come to a grinding halt when a hidden error or fault is encountered.

FREQUENTLY ASKED QUESTIONS (FAQS)

A number of FAQs covering many aspects of MSCS are located at Microsoft's Web site (**www.microsoft.com/ntserverenterprise/support**). This section expands upon their scope and content.

Question

Why must both my server systems be identical?

Answer

For MSCS to operate properly, the configuration of both servers must be identical, down to the firmware level on the motherboards, HBAs, NICs, and so on. In addition, due to the way that NTFS log file page sizes are configured between the X86 and Alpha versions of NTS/E, you cannot mix architectures in your MSCS cluster. Digital (now Compaq) has promised the ability to support mixed CPU clusters at some point in the future.

Question

Do I really need a separate public and private network connection to make MSCS work?

Answer

No, you can share one network, but you run the risk of disrupting cluster communications if the single network should fail and of causing the cluster to failover when a fault is not present, or conversely, not failover at all due to quorum resource contention. Many cluster providers recommend that not only do you have both a public and private network for your cluster, but that you provide redundant paths for them. This can be facilitated using so-called multi-way NICs, available from a number of vendors.

Question

Am I limited in how far I can locate my nodes from each other?

Answer

No. With the use of either SCSI hubs or SCSI switches and bus extenders for conventional SCSI, or through the use of SSA or fiber channel storage interconnects, you can greatly lengthen the distance that your shared storage bus can operate over. Until now, this has been the limiting factor.

Question

Can I run other protocols on my MSCS cluster?

Answer

Currently, TCP/IP is both the default and only protocol that can be used with MSCS. You can have other protocol stacks loaded during your installation of NTS/E, but you cannot use them with MSCS.

Question

How will I move from MSCS Phase 1 to Phase 2 when it becomes available?

Answer

In Chapter 8 I discussed MSCS Phase 2 (now referred to as Cluster Service, a component of Windows 2000 Datacenter Server). In general, when migrating from Windows NT 4.0 to Windows 2000 there will be a number of changes required. Many of these changes will involve the use of the Active Directory Service, as well as the need to migrate from stand-alone management tools to snap-ins designed for the Microsoft Management Console. In terms of cluster service itself, there will be migration tools as well as opportunities to re-configure your cluster to take advantage of more memory, advanced interconnect schemes (VIA), and Storage Area Networks. Please refer to my Web site (**www.dst.com**) for more specific information as it becomes available.

With respect to moving to Phase 2, changes will be associated with the overall architecture, as well as the QR and other MSCS-specific resources. Most users will be able to migrate from one version to another with a minimum of effort and hassle. Others will be required to go back to square one. Much of the great unknown regarding MSCS Phase 2 is in the applications and middleware, not the cluster services.

In many cases, you may not need to reconfigure your cluster when Windows 2000 becomes available, especially if a two-node failover solution is what you needed to begin with. As indicated in Chapters 1 and 2, the majority (over 75 percent) of clusters in use today are the two-node failover type. Most organizations need to make specific applications or services highly available and choose clustering for these specific ones. However, the number of these so-called business-critical applications is on the rise, so it is anticipated that clustering requirements will grow.

Question

Will remote mirroring ever be a part of MSCS?

Answer

Remote mirroring provides even higher levels of availability and fault-tolerance than MSCS alone can deliver. It is therefore expected that several vendors will provide third-party products for MSCS, which support such functionality, especially when Phase 2 becomes available. System developers can then deliver true fault-tolerant (and disaster-proof) solutions based on NT.

Question

Is MSCS the best Windows NT clustering solution today?

Answer

A number of other solutions are available that use similar techniques as MSCS, and others that use mirroring to achieve the same results such as Vinca, Veritas, NCR, Legato/Full Time, Oracle, Apcon, etc. All perform similarly in many respects, and legacy and cost issues determine most decisions. MSCS' key strengths are its wide industry support by the leading hardware and software vendors, along with the general acceptance of the Wolfpack API as a defacto standard.

TROUBLESHOOTING METHODOLOGIES AND RESOURCES

The first order of business in diagnosing and repairing problems with your cluster is to determine whether the problem lies in NTS/E, MSCS, or the hardware itself. If you determine that the problem lies within NTS/E, stop your cluster via the Services applet (under the Control Panel). You should shut down Cluster.exe by selecting it in the listbox and disabling it from automatically restarting by switching it to manual mode or switching it off altogether. Doing so enables you to then troubleshoot NTS/E without the interaction of MSCS after you restart your computer.

If you have determined that the problem lies in MSCS or one of its cluster-aware applications (in terms of interface and behavior), then you should use this section, along with the materials contained in the MSCS Administrators' Manual Diagnostics Section to begin to diagnose the source of the problem.

If, ultimately, you determine that the problem lies in the hardware on either node, you should use the process described in the following section to properly shut down your cluster; this will eliminate other problems from entering the picture as a result of an incorrect shut-down or power-up sequence.

Shutting Down and Restarting Your Cluster under Varying Scenarios

When starting up or shutting down your cluster, all the components must be powered up in the correct sequence; otherwise, MSCS may not start properly. Failure to adhere to this sequencing process may result in the cluster not being able to access the Quorum Resource correctly, or the shared-storage bus drives and arrays may be marked as having faults due to all the drives and volumes not being accessed. To help eliminate these problems, each node in the cluster should be brought up one at a time to eliminate contention for the shared-storage bus. (See the section "NT Backup Cannot Access all Shared SCSI Storage Devices," earlier in this chapter.)

Cluster Shut-Down Sequence

Nodes should not be powered down until all applications and services (cluster-aware and non-cluster-aware) are in a stable state (that is, they are not in the middle of a transaction or transfer). After verifying that the cluster failover groups have stopped I/O operations, you can use the CA to take all failover groups offline to ensure that no further disk I/Os will take place. In addition, you should always power-down your computing nodes prior to the shared-storage bus devices. Doing so eliminates the potential for any type of data corruption or RAID-set degradation due to a drive being powered down during a write operation.

The proper shutdown sequence is as follows:

1. Advise all users connected to the cluster that a shutdown is imminent.

2. Use the CA to verify that all failover groups have stopped I/O operations. You can then take them all offline.

3. Using the Windows taskbar, shut down each cluster node. Power them down so that the primary node is shut down last. (Doing so establishes the relationship between the QR and the primary node during restart.)

4. If your cluster is using SCSI, SSA, or Fibre- Channel hubs or switches, power them down at this time.

5. Shut down the shared-storage bus devices and cabinets.

6. Power down all other cluster components (such as the monitor, keyboard, and mouse switches).

7. Your cluster has now powered down in the correct sequence and should restart properly (assuming that you use the suggested sequence that follows).

Cluster Restart (and Cold Start) Sequence

Earlier in this book I defined a normal start up sequence for MSCS. This should be used as your default procedure. However, when troubleshooting a systems-level problem in a cluster you need to do things a little differently. This is done to completely isolate some of the strange interactions that happen among components and software modules when they are simultaneously powered up. The following procedure, like the one outlined above for power-down, should not be construed as the norm due to the great amount of detail and time required to execute them.

1. Power up all ancillary cluster components (such as the monitor, keyboard, and mouse switches).

2. Power up the shared-storage bus devices and cabinets. Allow a minute or so for all drives to spin up to operating speed (simultaneously or sequentially).

3. Power up all other storage peripherals located on a non-shared storage bus (such as the tape drives, libraries, optical drives, and jukeboxes).

4. Power up the primary node of the cluster through the logon process. Use the CA to verify that the cluster has formed on startup and that the QR is intact. Verify that all failover groups and their resources are online (for this node).

5. Power up the other nodes through the logon process. Use the CA to verify that the other nodes have joined the cluster. Verify that all its failover groups and their resources are now online.

Single-Node Shutdown

In many troubleshooting and repair scenarios, it may be necessary to bring down just one node for service or replacement, while keeping the other node (and the cluster itself) operational. Doing so requires a specific sequence of actions to ensure that no disruptions to either client connections or cluster services occur. The following sequence is recommended:

1. Move all failover groups residing on the node to be shut down to the surviving nodes. If the node to be shut down is the primary node, you must use the CA to take it offline. Doing so moves both the QR and all of its failover groups to the surviving nodes.

2. Using the Windows taskbar, shutdown the node and then power it down.

3. Using the appropriate methods for the type of shared-storage bus connection that you are using (SCSI, SSA, or Fibre Channel), disconnect the shared-storage bus cabling from the node. Do so only at the nodes' connection point itself; otherwise, cluster data corruption may occur (especially to SCSI connections). Label all disconnected cables appropriately so you'll know how to connect them later.

4. Disconnect the public and private network connections from the node.

5. Disconnect all remaining power and peripheral connections from the node.

6. Perform the required maintenance on the powered-down node, or replace it with one that has been properly configured for substitution (including the transfer of the boot drive from the old node to the new one so that the cluster recognizes the NTFS signatures as being consistent).

7. Power up the repaired or new node in the sequence listed previously.

8. Use the CA to verify that the cluster is operating properly. If so, move the appropriate failover groups (and their resources) back to their original node, along with the QR (where appropriate).

Hot Swapping in an Active Cluster

MSCS supports a limited range of hot swap type repairs while the cluster and its nodes are up and running. The following types of components may be changed on the fly with proper care:

▼ Fans and power supplies in servers and shared-storage bus systems (where redundant ones have already come online)

■ Circuit boards and other components in servers and shared-storage systems where redundant ones have already come online (in servers, these components do not include HBAs but do include NICs, protected memory, cache, and so on)

■ Disk drives in RAID arrays (server and shared-storage system based) where hot-swapping and on-the-fly rebuilds are supported

▲ Standalone disk drives that are hot-swappable and located on the non-shared storage bus, with the exception of the NTS/E boot drive

To properly diagnose and service MSCS, you must develop many (if not numerous) methodologies, and pick the right tools to use along the way. These methodologies can be developed only if you have a good working knowledge of MSCS and know where to begin and end when troubleshooting a particular problem (or a series of them occurring simultaneously). To facilitate this process, this chapter contains a wealth of information regarding how MSCS is installed, which files and DLLs it depends on, and the typical settings for the several Registry entries that it uses.

When troubleshooting, it is critical that you isolate the problem to a particular area. You can spend hours chasing your tail if you do not isolate the area of the problem in the early stages. Earlier chapters covered a number of tools for use during the installation and startup of your cluster. All of those are applicable when troubleshooting—for example, Cluster Sanity Test, the ping utility, NetMon, and Performance Monitor.

Test Utilities

Augmenting the tools and procedures outlined earlier in this book (in Chapters 4 and 5) are two very useful tools for looking at the shared SCSI storage bus and the interaction of DLLs used in MSCS (and NTS/E as well). The following sections describe them in detail.

As more of these tools become available, information about them will be posted on my Web site (**www.dst.com**).

Cluster Verification Utility

Included with Supplement 3 of the *Windows NT Server 4.0 Resource Kit* is the utility in the Cluster Verification Utility (CVU) directory, which is used to test the shared storage bus for proper operation prior to installing MSCS.

The CVU test program is designed to test a shared SCSI bus for functionality that is required by MSCS.

To properly run this test, you must have your two servers configured as follows:

1. With a multi-initiator SCSI bus.

2. With at least one drive (each) configured for use on the shared storage bus.

3. Each drive on the bus must have a signature on the drive so the test can match up the same drive from both controllers. To get a signature, run windisk on one node, and respond Yes to the prompt.

4. You must not have cluster software installed on either node.

5. You must have NT 4.0 SP3 (Windows 2000 build 1426 or later can be used if you are a developer) on both nodes.

6. Both nodes must be able to talk to each other. You can ping to test this.

7. You must have the ntlog.dll file (see the CVU folder) in the path on both nodes.

8. You must have the clustsim.exe file (see the CVU folder) on both nodes.

CAUTION: This test is a destructive test. It will wipe out data on all disks on the shared bus that you select the test to run on. The default is to run on all shared drives.

After running this test, you will probably have to run windisk again to get partitions and signatures back on the drives.

The test should run for about two hours per drive.

▼ *Starting the test* To start the test, run **clustsim /s** on one node. This node then becomes the server node. After this node is finished looking for shared drives it will prompt you when to start the test on the other node. At that point, run **clustsim /n:*node_name*** where *node_name* is the name of the machine on which you ran **clustsim /s**.

■ *Logging of information* Both nodes of the test will log information into a standard NT log file. On the /s node, it will be called clustsim_server.log and clustsim_client.log on the client node.

■ *Testing Overview* This test will search the list of signatures found on both nodes for matches. It will also test the failover behavior of the drives on the shared-storage bus as their controlling HBA is moved from one node to another and then back again. The test will perform a loop type routing consisting of the following:

- Basic SCSI commands to get Drive layout, Inquiry data, and Addressing.
- Write/read verify commands
  - Using a random block address
  - Using a random write length
  - Generating a random string
  - Reading back that block from the other initiator and comparing bits
  - Issuing a verify command
  - Performing reserve/release testing
  - Issuing a reserve command from node 1
  - Trying to reserve on node 2
  - Verifying the write and read command failover from node 2
  - Verifying that the release command works on node 2
  - Issuing a bus reset
  - Verifying that node 2 can now reserve the disk drive being tested
  - Verifying that test unit ready fails on node 1
  - Verifying that node 2 can release its reservation

The first two steps are executed for a certain number of iterations, which can be controlled using the /i switch. The default value can be obtained by using /? from the command line.

The Cluster Verification utility is a useful troubleshooting tool when you are preparing to first install MSCS or are rebuilding an existing cluster that may have suffered an unrecoverable drive failure. In these scenarios, you can test the shared storage bus functionality, along with the drives themselves, without having to worry about their interaction with MSCS, which may obstruct a clear path to a shared bus or drive problem.

Dependency Walker

Another tool for helping in the diagnosis of problems with MSCS is Dependency Walker (V1.0 is included in Supplement 3 of the *Windows NT 4.0 Resource Kit*). It is used for viewing dependency and relationship information among DLLs and other modules. Figure 10-1 shows one of its displays.

As you can see from Figure 10-1, Dependency Walker (DW) shows all of the other DLLs that are used in conjunction with the Cluster Administrator DLL. By double-clicking any one of them, you can find out their status and their syntax for usage.

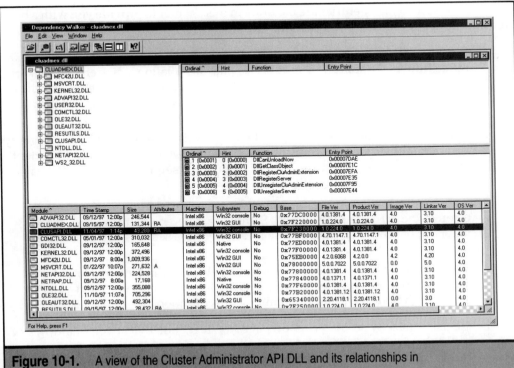

Figure 10-1.   A view of the Cluster Administrator API DLL and its relationships in
Dependency Walker

Dependency Walker is a useful troubleshooting tool for MSCS (as well as for NTS/E in general) for a number of reasons. Principally, it provides a means to verify and observe the interaction between the MSCS middleware, the OS, and all applications and services on a software DLL level. This is powerful for both the developer as well as the seasoned administrator or engineer who wants to dig down deep into the internals of MSCS and its applications when problem solving.

TYPICAL REGISTRY ENTRIES

The Windows NT Registry is key to everything that NT does (with or without MSCS in the picture). The Registry is a critical component from the time that the machine boots (in order for NT and MSCS to come up at all), throughout the entire operation of your servers and MSCS cluster. It contains entries for applications, drivers, and services. If a Registry entry is somehow changed or corrupted, it can cause Windows NT to fail spectacularly (the dreaded Blue Screen of Death is displayed), and in most cases, the system won't restart at all. It is for these reasons that this chapter includes a detailed review of the Registry as it applies to MSCS.

These sample Registry entries are included in this chapter to provide you with a bit of an insurance policy in case you encounter the following:

1. Registry entries can become corrupted by a variety of events. These events can range from bad application and service pack installations, disk errors, hacker intrusions, pilot error, and file restores run amuck. You won't know that they have happened in most cases until it is too late, i.e., an application crashes the node on start-up or the node will not boot up on restart.

2. Registry entries are easily changed. During routine examination of the Registry you might be drilling down through a particular section and then inadvertently change an entry's status to another of its possible settings, leaving you unable to determine what the default setting was.

3. Registry entries provide a roadmap to how a service or application flows through the NT operating system. Sample or Reference Settings provide a mapping of how specific applications and services settings will be reflected throughout NTS/E and MSCS.

4. Reference Registry Entries can be created in Word or in Notepad and then imported into the Registry for use. This applies in reverse such that you can export each node's entries for archiving or replication.

The Registry (size-wise in terms of pages of text, not bytes) for Windows NT Enterprise Edition is some 3,000 pages in length when viewed in Word (when working with RegEdit you can elect to export the contents of the registry by hive—or section—or in total to a text file). Of these thousands of pages some forty or more are specific to MSCS. The two main Registry hives that contain this information are:

▼   HKEY_LOCAL_MACHINE (HKLM)

▲   HKEY_CURRENT_USER (HKCU)

HKLM is the most populated because it contains all of the serverwide and clusterwide configuration data (including the QR on the primary node). This hive includes hardware configuration data that is necessary in order to boot NTS/E and start MSCS. It also contains settings for the public and private networks, HBAs, device drivers, security, and so forth.

HKCU contains all of the profile and environmental settings for MSCS and its administrators, and it contains the cluster-aware applications and services on the node.

Why Do I Need to Know these Registry Settings?

Microsoft Cluster Server stores cluster-specific information in the Windows NT Registry on each node. These Registry entries are comprised of the following types of information:

▼   Configuration information used to start cluster drivers and services at system startup. This information can be used to verify that the correct software components have been successfully installed and MSCS is ready to run.

- Configuration information for use in controlling the operation of MSCS. This information can be used to verify that MSCS is configured correctly.

▲ Dynamic state information describing the current state of the cluster and its software. This state information is a replica of the information contained in the clusters' configuration database, which is controlled by the database manager, a key component of the Cluster Service. This database is encrypted and is located in the clusters folder under NTS/E's default directory. It cannot normally be viewed, so it is logical to use the replicated settings in the Registry as a method to view the contents of this database.

HKLM

When Windows NT boots up (see Figure 10-2 for a diagram of this entire process), it starts NTDETECT, a program that determines which hardware is connected to the server and the cluster. It creates an inventory of all physical aspects of the connected hardware (CPU, memory, I/O, buses, and devices connected to buses).

This information is stored in memory and then mapped to the HKLM\Hardware entry in the Registry. After this, the NT kernel is loaded, and it finds the right drivers for the hardware components that were detected by NTDETECT. These drivers are loaded in a hierarchy starting with low level for basic services, middle level for drivers labeled "system," and then high level for those drives labeled "automatic." No matter where a

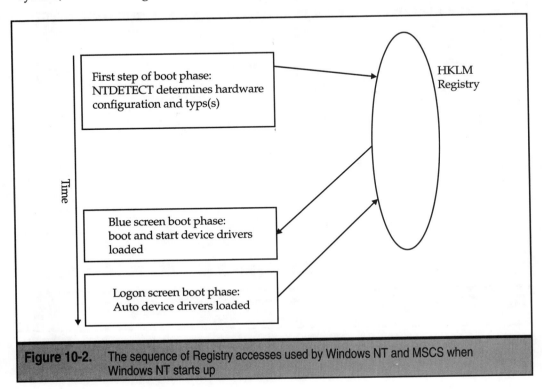

Figure 10-2. The sequence of Registry accesses used by Windows NT and MSCS when Windows NT starts up

driver fits in this hierarchy, it makes heavy use of the Registry during initialization. It uses the Registry to determine the inventory of hardware to be supported, the available drivers to support each component, and to reserve resources required by each driver. In addition, this Registry hive contains settings for all cluster-aware applications and services installed on your cluster.

HKCU

This section contains Registry entries for the MSCS Cluster Administrator, the critical control interface for your cluster. These settings are critical to allowing the CA to manage your cluster properly, especially in respect to specific settings for each Group and its Resources.

HKEY_LOCAL_MACHINE REGISTRY ENTRIES

This group of Registry entries supports the services and applications on the node itself and covers every aspect of the interaction of NTS/E, MSCS, and the hardware in the server. Included in this section are sample settings for cluster-aware applications MS Exchange 5.5 EE and SQL Server 6.5 EE.

Figure 10-3 shows all the Registry folders for this grouping of settings.

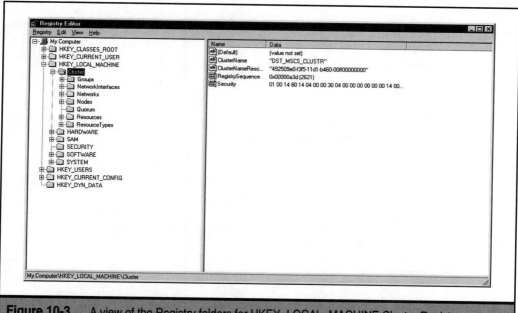

Figure 10-3. A view of the Registry folders for HKEY_LOCAL_MACHINE Cluster Registry

The following registry entry is the first entry under the main folder for all cluster information pertaining to the particular node that you are using Regedit to view. This particular entry pertains to the cluster name which the node is a member.

```
[HKEY_LOCAL_MACHINE\Cluster]
"ClusterName"="DST_MSCS_CLUSTR"
"Security"=hex:
"ClusterNameResource "
"RegistrySequence"=dword:
```

Cluster Group Registry Settings

This grouping of Registry settings pertains to the failover groups in your MSCS cluster and their general descriptions. This Registry Setting information can be used to determine that all of the necessary failover groups are listed and that their descriptions are accurate.

```
[HKEY_LOCAL_MACHINE\Cluster\Groups]
@=""

[HKEY_LOCAL_MACHINE\Cluster\Groups\ "Name"="Cluster Group"
"PersistentState"=dword:
"Contains"=hex(7):

[HKEY_LOCAL_MACHINE\Cluster\Groups\ "Name"="Disk Group 1"
"PersistentState"=dword:
"Contains"=hex(7):

[HKEY_LOCAL_MACHINE\Cluster\Groups\ "Name"="Exchange 5.5 Group"
"PersistentState"=dword:"Contains"=hex(7):

[HKEY_LOCAL_MACHINE\Cluster\Groups\ "Name"="Disk Group 3"
"PersistentState"=dword:"Contains"=hex(7):

[HKEY_LOCAL_MACHINE\Cluster\Groups\
  "Name"="Disk Group 4"
"PersistentState"=dword:"Contains"=hex(7):

[HKEY_LOCAL_MACHINE\Cluster\Groups\ "Name"="SQL Server 6.5 EE"
"Description"="Failover Group Server #1"
"PreferredOwners"=hex(7):"PersistentState"=dword:"Contains"=hex(7):
```

Cluster Network Registry Settings

This group of Registry entries pertains to both the public and private networks in your MSCS cluster. This information can be used to verify that IP address information and network protocol bindings are correctly set for both networks.

```
[HKEY_LOCAL_MACHINE\Cluster\NetworkInterfaces]
@=""


[HKEY_LOCAL_MACHINE\Cluster\NetworkInterfaces\ "Network"=" "
"Node"="2"
"Name"="SnNdis3 - NODE-2"
"Description"=""
"Adapter"="SnNdis3"
"Address"="10.0.0.2"
"ClusnetEndpoint"="3343"


[HKEY_LOCAL_MACHINE\Cluster\NetworkInterfaces\ "Name"="SnNdis3 - NODE-1"
"Description"=""
"Network"=" "
"Node"="1"
"Adapter"="SnNdis3"
"Address"="10.0.0.1"
"ClusnetEndpoint"="3343"


[HKEY_LOCAL_MACHINE\Cluster\NetworkInterfaces\ "Name"="El90x1 - NODE-1"
"Description"=""
"Network"="
"Node"="1"
"Adapter"="El90x1"
"Address"="172.16.48.240"
"ClusnetEndpoint"="3343"


[HKEY_LOCAL_MACHINE\Cluster\NetworkInterfaces\ "Network"=" "
"Node"="2"
"Name"="El90x1 - NODE-2"
"Description"=""
"Adapter"="El90x1"
"Address"="172.16.48.245"
"ClusnetEndpoint"="3343"


[HKEY_LOCAL_MACHINE\Cluster\Networks]
@=""
```

```
[HKEY_LOCAL_MACHINE\Cluster\Networks\ "Name"="ServerNet Private Network"
"Description"=""
"Role"=dword:
"Priority"=dword:
"Transport"="Tcpip"
"Address"="10.0.0.0"
"AddressMask"="255.255.255.0"


[HKEY_LOCAL_MACHINE\Cluster\Networks\ "Name"="DST_CORP_NET"
"Description"=""
"Role"=dword:"Priority"=dword:"Transport"="Tcpip"
"Address"="172.16.48.0"
"AddressMask"="255.255.240.0"
```

Cluster Node Registry Settings

This group of Registry settings determines the names of the cluster nodes, along with the location of the cluster's QR drive and/or volume. These settings must be correct in order for your cluster to form and operate correctly.

```
[HKEY_LOCAL_MACHINE\Cluster\Nodes]


[HKEY_LOCAL_MACHINE\Cluster\Nodes\1]
"NodeName"="NODE-1"


[HKEY_LOCAL_MACHINE\Cluster\Nodes\2]
"NodeName"="NODE-2"


[HKEY_LOCAL_MACHINE\Cluster\Quorum]
@=""
"Resource"=" "Path"="S:\\MSCS\\"
```

Cluster Resource Registry Settings

These Registry entries pertain to the overall list of resource types that your cluster supports in addition to binding of your chosen cluster name to the appropriate resources.

```
[HKEY_LOCAL_MACHINE\Cluster\Resources]
@=""


[HKEY_LOCAL_MACHINE\Cluster\Resources\ "Name"="Cluster IP Address"
"Type"="IP Address"
"Flags"=dword:"IsAlivePollInterval"=dword:
"LooksAlivePollInterval"=dword:
[HKEY_LOCAL_MACHINE\Cluster\Resources\ \Parameters]
```

```
"Address"="172.16.48.200"
"SubnetMask"="255.255.240.0"
"Network"="492509dc-f3f5-11d1-b460-00ff00000000"

[HKEY_LOCAL_MACHINE\Cluster\Resources\ \Parameters\1]
"InterfaceInstance"=dword:"NbtDeviceInstance"=dword:
"InterfaceContext"=dword: "NbtDeviceName"="\\Device\\NetBt_If2"

[HKEY_LOCAL_MACHINE\Cluster\Resources\ \Parameters\2]
"InterfaceInstance"=dword:
"NbtDeviceInstance"=dword:

[HKEY_LOCAL_MACHINE\Cluster\Resources\ ]
"Name"="Cluster Name"
"Type"="Network Name"
"Flags"=dword:00000001
"IsAlivePollInterval"=dword:
"LooksAlivePollInterval"=dword:
"DependsOn"=hex(7):

[HKEY_LOCAL_MACHINE\Cluster\Resources\ \Parameters]
"Name"="DST_MSCS_CLUSTR"

[HKEY_LOCAL_MACHINE\Cluster\Resources\ \Parameters\1]
"LastName"="DST_MSCS_CLUSTR"

[HKEY_LOCAL_MACHINE\Cluster\Resources\ \Parameters\2]
"LastName"="DST_MSCS_CLUSTR"

[HKEY_LOCAL_MACHINE\Cluster\Resources\ ]
"Name"="Time Service"
"Type"="Time Service"
"Flags"=dword:
"IsAlivePollInterval"=dword:
"LooksAlivePollInterval"=dword:

[HKEY_LOCAL_MACHINE\Cluster\Resources\ \Parameters]

[HKEY_LOCAL_MACHINE\Cluster\Resources\ ]
"Name"="Disk S:"
"Type"="Physical Disk"
"Flags"=dword:
"IsAlivePollInterval"=dword:
"LooksAlivePollInterval"=dword:
```

```
[HKEY_LOCAL_MACHINE\Cluster\Resources\ \Parameters]
"Signature"=dword:
"DiskInfo"=hex:

[HKEY_LOCAL_MACHINE\Cluster\Resources\ ]
"Name"="Disk T:"
"Type"="Physical Disk"
"Flags"=dword:"IsAlivePollInterval"=dword:"LooksAlivePollInterval"=dword:
"Description "PersistentState"=dword:

[HKEY_LOCAL_MACHINE\Cluster\Resources\\Parameters]
"Signature"=dword:
"DiskInfo"=hex:

[HKEY_LOCAL_MACHINE\Cluster\Resources\]
"Name"="Disk U:"
"Type"="Physical Disk"
"Flags"=dword:
"IsAlivePollInterval"=dword:"LooksAlivePollInterval"=dword:"PersistentState"
=dword:

[HKEY_LOCAL_MACHINE\Cluster\Resources\\Parameters]
"Signature"=dword:
"DiskInfo"=hex:

[HKEY_LOCAL_MACHINE\Cluster\Resources\]
"Name"="Disk V:"
"Type"="Physical Disk"
"Flags"=dword:"IsAlivePollInterval"=dword:
"LooksAlivePollInterval"=dword:
"PersistentState"=dword:

[HKEY_LOCAL_MACHINE\Cluster\Resources\\Parameters]
"Signature"=dword:
"DiskInfo"=hex:

[HKEY_LOCAL_MACHINE\Cluster\Resources\1]
"Name"="Exchange Address"
"Type"="IP Address"
"LooksAlivePollInterval"=dword:
"IsAlivePollInterval"=dword:
"DependsOn"=hex(7):
"PersistentState"=dword:
```

```
[HKEY_LOCAL_MACHINE\Cluster\Resources\\Parameters]
"Network"="
"Address"="172.16.48.205"
"SubnetMask"="255.255.240.0"

[HKEY_LOCAL_MACHINE\Cluster\Resources\\Parameters\1]
"InterfaceInstance"=dword:
"NbtDeviceInstance"=dword:

[HKEY_LOCAL_MACHINE\Cluster\\Parameters\2]
"InterfaceInstance"=dword:
"NbtDeviceInstance"=dword:

[HKEY_LOCAL_MACHINE\Cluster\Resources\"Name"=""Type"="Network Name"
"LooksAlivePollInterval"=dword:
"IsAlivePollInterval"=dword:
"DependsOn"=hex(7):
"PersistentState"=dword:

[HKEY_LOCAL_MACHINE\Cluster\\Parameters]
"Name"=""RemapPipeNames"=dword:
```

Microsoft Exchange 5.5 EE HKLM Settings

Microsoft Exchange 5.5 Enterprise Edition is one of the most widely used "cluster-aware" applications for use with MSCS. Its Registry entries are included to give the administrator a reference in respect to both what he/she will encounter when installing this application, as well as if there is a corrupted Registry entry subsequent to this installation.

```
[HKEY_LOCAL_MACHINE\Cluster\006097a1e291EXCHANGE_55EESystem
AttendantMicrosoft Exchange System Attendant
"PendingTimeout"=dword:
"PersistentState"=dword:

[HKEY_LOCAL_MACHINE\Cluster\Resources\ Parameters]
"ServiceName"="MSExchangeSA"
"UseNetworkName"=dword:

[HKEY_LOCAL_MACHINE\Cluster\Resources\ \RegSync]
 "="SYSTEM\\CurrentControlSet\\Services\\MSExchangeSA"

[HKEY_LOCAL_MACHINE\Cluster\Resources\ ]
"Name"="Microsoft Exchange Directory"
```

```
"Type"="Generic Service"
"LooksAlivePollInterval"=dword:
"IsAlivePollInterval"=dword:
"DependsOn"=hex(7):
"Description"="Microsoft Exchange Directory"
"PendingTimeout"=dword:
"PersistentState"=dword:

[HKEY_LOCAL_MACHINE\Cluster\Resources\ \Parameters]
"ServiceName"="MSExchangeDS"
"UseNetworkName"=dword:

[HKEY_LOCAL_MACHINE\Cluster\Resources\ \RegSync]
 "="SYSTEM\\CurrentControlSet\\Services\\MSExchangeDS"

[HKEY_LOCAL_MACHINE\Cluster\Resources\ ]
"Name"="Microsoft Exchange Message Transfer Agent"
"Type"="Generic Service"
"LooksAlivePollInterval"=dword:
"IsAlivePollInterval"=dword:
"DependsOn"=hex(7):
"Description"="Microsoft Exchange Message Transfer Agent"
"PendingTimeout"=dword:
"PersistentState"=dword:

[HKEY_LOCAL_MACHINE\Cluster\Resources\ade25822-f63b-11d1-b46e-00ff00000000\
Parameters]
"ServiceName"="MSExchangeMTA"
"UseNetworkName"=dword: [HKEY_LOCAL_MACHINE\Cluster\Resources\ \RegSync]
 "="SYSTEM\\CurrentControlSet\\Services\\MSExchangeMTA"

[HKEY_LOCAL_MACHINE\Cluster\Resources\
"Name"="Microsoft Exchange Information Store"
"Type"="Generic Service"
"LooksAlivePollInterval"=dword:
"IsAlivePollInterval"=dword:
"DependsOn"=hex(7):
"Description"="Microsoft Exchange Information Store"
"PendingTimeout"=dword:
"PersistentState"=dword:

[HKEY_LOCAL_MACHINE\Cluster\Resources\ \Parameters]
"ServiceName"="MSExchangeIS"
"UseNetworkName"=dword:
```

```
[HKEY_LOCAL_MACHINE\Cluster\Resources\ \RegSync]
 "="SYSTEM\\CurrentControlSet\\Services\\MSExchangeIS"

[HKEY_LOCAL_MACHINE\Cluster\ ]
"Name"="connect$"
"Type"="File Share"
"LooksAlivePollInterval"=dword:
"IsAlivePollInterval"=dword:
"DependsOn"=hex(7):
"Description"="\"Access to gateway connectors\""
"PersistentState"=dword:
[HKEY_LOCAL_MACHINE\Cluster\Resources\\Parameters]
"ShareName"="connect$"
"Path"="T:\\exchsrvr\\connect"
"Remark"="\"Access to gateway connectors\""
"MaxUsers"=dword:HKEY_LOCAL_MACHINE\Cluster\Resources\
"Name"="Address"
"Type"="File Share"
"LooksAlivePollInterval"=dword:
"IsAlivePollInterval"=dword:
"DependsOn"=hex(7):
"Description"="\"Access to address objects\""
"PersistentState"=dword:

HKEY_LOCAL_MACHINE\Cluster\Resources\\Parameters]
"ShareName"="Address"
"Path"="T:\\exchsrvr\\address"
"Remark"="\"Access to address objects\""
"MaxUsers"=dword:
"Security"=hex:
[HKEY_LOCAL_MACHINE\Cluster\Resources"Name"="Add-ins"
"Type"="File Share"
"LooksAlivePollInterval"=dword"IsAlivePollInterval"=dword"DependsOn"=hex(7):
"Description"="\"Access to EDK objects\""
"PersistentState"=dword
[HKEY_LOCAL_MACHINE\Cluster\ResourcesParameters]"ShareName"="Add-ins"
"Path"="T:\\exchsrvr\\add-ins"
"Remark"="\"Access to EDK objects\""
"MaxUsers"=dword:
"Security"=hex[HKEY_LOCAL_MACHINE\Cluster\Resources"Name"="tracking.log"
"Type"="File Share"
"LooksAlivePollInterval"=dword"IsAlivePollInterval"=dword:
"DependsOn"=hex(7):
"Description"="\"Exchange message tracking logs\""
"PersistentState"=dword:
```

```
[HKEY_LOCAL_MACHINE\Cluster\Resources\ \Parameters]
"ShareName"="tracking.log"
"Path"="T:\\exchsrvr\\tracking.log"
"Remark"="\"Exchange message tracking logs\""
"MaxUsers"=dword:
"Security"=hex:

[HKEY_LOCAL_MACHINE\Cluster\Resources\ ]
"Name"="Resources"
"Type"="File Share"
"LooksAlivePollInterval"=dword:
"IsAlivePollInterval"=dword:
"DependsOn"=hex(7):
"Description"="\"Event logging files\""
"PersistentState"=dword:

[HKEY_LOCAL_MACHINE\Cluster\Resources\Parameters]
"ShareName"="Resources"
"Path"="T:\\exchsrvr\\res"
"Remark"="\"Event logging files\""
"MaxUsers"=dword:
"Security"=hex:

[HKEY_LOCAL_MACHINE\Cluster\Resources\ ]
"Name"="MS Mail Connector Interchange"
"Type"="Generic Service"
"LooksAlivePollInterval"=dword:
"IsAlivePollInterval"=dword:
"DependsOn"=hex(7):
"Description"="MS Mail Connector Interchange"
"PendingTimeout"=dword:
"RestartAction"=dword:
"PersistentState"=dword:

[HKEY_LOCAL_MACHINE\Cluster\Resources\ \Parameters]
"ServiceName"="MSExchangeMSMI"
"UseNetworkName"=dword:

[HKEY_LOCAL_MACHINE\Cluster\Resources\ \RegSync]
"00000001"="SYSTEM\\CurrentControlSet\\Services\\MSExchangeMSMI"

[HKEY_LOCAL_MACHINE\Cluster\Resources\ ]
"Name"="MS Schedule+ Free/Busy Connector"
```

```
"Type"="Generic Service"
"LooksAlivePollInterval"=dword:
"IsAlivePollInterval"=dword:
"DependsOn"=hex(7): "Description"="MS Schedule+ Free/Busy Connector"
"PendingTimeout"=dword:
"RestartAction"=dword:
"PersistentState"=dword:
"SeparateMonitor"=dword:

[HKEY_LOCAL_MACHINE\Cluster\Resources\ \Parameters]
"ServiceName"="MSExchangeFB"
"UseNetworkName"=dword:

[HKEY_LOCAL_MACHINE\Cluster\Resources\ \RegSync]
"00000001"="SYSTEM\\CurrentControlSet\\Services\\MSExchangeFB"

[HKEY_LOCAL_MACHINE\Cluster\Resources\ ]
"Name"="maildat$"
"Type"="File Share"
"LooksAlivePollInterval"=dword:
"IsAlivePollInterval"=dword:
"DependsOn"=hex(7):
"Description"="\"Access for MSMI postoffice\""
"PersistentState"=dword:

 [HKEY_LOCAL_MACHINE\Cluster\Resources\ \Parameters]
"ShareName"="maildat$"
"Path"="T:\\exchsrvr\\connect\\msmcon\\maildata"
"Remark"="\"Access for MSMI postoffice\""
"MaxUsers"=dword:
"Security"=hex:

[HKEY_LOCAL_MACHINE\Cluster\Resources\ ]
"Name"="Microsoft Exchange Directory Synchronization"
"Type"="Generic Service"
"LooksAlivePollInterval"=dword:
"IsAlivePollInterval"=dword:
"DependsOn"=hex(7):
"Description"="Microsoft Exchange Directory Synchronization"
"PendingTimeout"=dword:
"RestartAction"=dword:
"PersistentState"=dword:
```

```
[HKEY_LOCAL_MACHINE\Cluster\Resources Parameters]
"ServiceName"="MSExchangeDX"
"UseNetworkName"=dword:

[HKEY_LOCAL_MACHINE\Cluster\Resources\ \RegSync]
"00000001"="SYSTEM\\CurrentControlSet\\Services\\MSExchangeDX"

[HKEY_LOCAL_MACHINE\Cluster\Resources\ ]
"Name"="Microsoft Exchange Connector for Lotus cc:Mail"
"Type"="Generic Service"
"LooksAlivePollInterval"=dword:
"IsAlivePollInterval"=dword:
"DependsOn"=hex(7):
"Description"="Microsoft Exchange Connector for Lotus cc:Mail"
"PendingTimeout"=dword:
"RestartAction"=dword:
"PersistentState"=dword:
"SeparateMonitor"=dword:

[HKEY_LOCAL_MACHINE\Cluster\Resources\ \Parameters]
"ServiceName"="MSExchangeCCMC"
"UseNetworkName"=dword:

[HKEY_LOCAL_MACHINE\Cluster\Resources\ \RegSync]
" "="SYSTEM\\CurrentControlSet\\Services\\MSExchangeCCMC "

[HKEY_LOCAL_MACHINE\Cluster\ ]
"Name"="Microsoft Exchange Event Service"
"Type"="Generic Service"
"LooksAlivePollInterval"=dword:
"IsAlivePollInterval"=dword:
"DependsOn"=hex(7):
"Description"="Microsoft Exchange Event Service"
"PendingTimeout"=dword:
"PersistentState"=dword:

[HKEY_LOCAL_MACHINE\Cluster\Resources\ \Parameters]
"ServiceName"="MSExchangeES"
"UseNetworkName"=dword:

[HKEY_LOCAL_MACHINE\Cluster\Resources\ \RegSync]
"00000001"="SYSTEM\\CurrentControlSet\\Services\\MSExchangeES"
```

SQL Server 6.5 EE Typical Registry Entries

SQL Server 6.5 (and now 7.0) Enterprise Edition is another one of the widely used cluster-aware applications for MSCS environments. Its Registry entries are included to provide a roadmap for administrators who will be deploying this application, as well as subsequently troubleshooting it.

```
[HKEY_LOCAL_MACHINE\Cluster\Resources\ ]
"Name"="SQL Service IP "
"Type"="IP Address"
"LooksAlivePollInterval"=dword:
"IsAlivePollInterval"=dword:
"DependsOn"=hex(7):
"PersistentState"=dword:

[HKEY_LOCAL_MACHINE\Cluster\Resources \Parameters]
"Network "
"Address"="172.16.48.210"
"SubnetMask"="255.255.240.0"

[HKEY_LOCAL_MACHINE\Cluster\Resources\ \1]
"InterfaceInstance"=dword:
"NbtDeviceInstance"=dword:

[HKEY_LOCAL_MACHINE\Cluster\Resources\ \Parameters\2]
"InterfaceInstance"=dword:
"NbtDeviceInstance"=dword:

[HKEY_LOCAL_MACHINE\Cluster\Resources\ ]
"Name"="SQL Server Name"
"Type"="Network Name"
"LooksAlivePollInterval"=dword:
"IsAlivePollInterval"=dword:
"DependsOn"=hex(7):
"PersistentState"=dword:

[HKEY_LOCAL_MACHINE\Cluster\Resources\ \Parameters]
"Name"="SQL_SERVER65"
"RemapPipeNames"=dword:

[HKEY_LOCAL_MACHINE\Cluster\Resources\ \Parameters\1]
"LastName"="SQL_SERVER65"

[HKEY_LOCAL_MACHINE\Cluster\Resources\ \Parameters\2]
"LastName"="SQL_SERVER65"
```

MSCS Cluster Resources Registry Entries

There are many types of resources available for use by failover groups. These resources are all based on the use of a dedicated resource DLL along with a Cluster Administrator extension for each. This Registry section contains information on all of these resources, both those provided with MSCS, as well as others that may have been developed specifically for legacy applications and services to make them cluster-aware.

```
[HKEY_LOCAL_MACHINE\Cluster\ResourceTypes]
@=""

[HKEY_LOCAL_MACHINE\Cluster\ResourceTypes\Distributed Transaction
Coordinator]
"DllName"="clusres.dll"
"Name"="Distributed Transaction Coordinator"
"IsAlivePollInterval"=dword:
"LooksAlivePollInterval"=dword:

[HKEY_LOCAL_MACHINE\Cluster\ResourceTypes\File Share]
"DllName"="clusres.dll"
"Name"="File Share"
"IsAlivePollInterval"=dword:
"LooksAlivePollInterval"=dword:
"AdminExtensions"=hex(7):

[HKEY_LOCAL_MACHINE\Cluster\ResourceTypes\Generic
Application]"DllName"="clusres.dll"
"Name"="Generic Application"
"IsAlivePollInterval"=dword:
"LooksAlivePollInterval"=dword:
"AdminExtensions"=hex(7):

[HKEY_LOCAL_MACHINE\Cluster\ResourceTypes\Generic Service]
"DllName"="clusres.dll"
"Name"="Generic Service"
"IsAlivePollInterval"=dword:
"LooksAlivePollInterval"=dword:
"AdminExtensions"=hex(7):

[HKEY_LOCAL_MACHINE\Cluster\ResourceTypes\IIS Virtual Root]
"DllName"="iisclus3.dll"
"Name"="IIS Virtual Root"
"IsAlivePollInterval"=dword:
"LooksAlivePollInterval"=dword:
"AdminExtensions"=hex(7):
```

```
[HKEY_LOCAL_MACHINE\Cluster\ResourceTypes\IP Address]
"DllName"="clusres.dll"
"Name"="IP Address"
"IsAlivePollInterval"=dword:
"LooksAlivePollInterval"=dword:
"AdminExtensions"=hex(7):

[HKEY_LOCAL_MACHINE\Cluster\ResourceTypes\Microsoft Message Queue Server]
"DllName"="clusres.dll"
"Name"="Microsoft Message Queue Server"
"IsAlivePollInterval"=dword:
"LooksAlivePollInterval"=dword:

[HKEY_LOCAL_MACHINE\Cluster\ResourceTypes\Network Name]
"DllName"="clusres.dll"
"Name"="Network Name"
"IsAlivePollInterval"=dword:
"LooksAlivePollInterval"=dword:
"AdminExtensions"=hex(7):

[HKEY_LOCAL_MACHINE\Cluster\ResourceTypes\Physical Disk]
"DllName"="clusres.dll"
"Name"="Physical Disk"
"IsAlivePollInterval"=dword:
"LooksAlivePollInterval"=dword:
"AdminExtensions"=hex(7):

[HKEY_LOCAL_MACHINE\Cluster\ResourceTypes\Print Spooler]
"DllName"="clusres.dll"
"Name"="Print Spooler"
"IsAlivePollInterval"=dword:
"LooksAlivePollInterval"=dword:
"AdminExtensions"=hex(7):

[HKEY_LOCAL_MACHINE\Cluster\ResourceTypes\Time Service]
"DllName"="clusres.dll"
"Name"="Time Service"
"IsAlivePollInterval"=dword:
"LooksAlivePollInterval"=dword:
```

This grouping of entries changes dynamically as you add and remove cluster-aware applications and services. You should always verify that the settings are listed in the correct order and contain the correct resource types for each application and service used.

Cluster Software Classes Registry Settings

This group of Registry entries pertains to all of the specific software executables and DLLs contained within MSCS. All of these are critical to the operation of MSCS and this listing can be cross-referenced to what is actually in use through the capabilities of the Dependency Walker utility that was discussed earlier.

```
HKEY_LOCAL_MACHINE\SOFTWARE\Classes\CLSID\{ @="Cluster Administrator
Standard Extension"

[HKEY_LOCAL_MACHINE\SOFTWARE\Classes\CLSID\{
@="c:\\ntsvr4ee\\cluster\\cluadmex.dll"
"ThreadingModel"="Apartment"

[HKEY_LOCAL_MACHINE\SOFTWARE\Classes\CLSID }\ProgId]
@="CLUADMEX.Standard"

[HKEY_LOCAL_MACHINE\SOFTWARE\Classes\CLSID }\VersionIndependentProgId]
@="CLUADMEX.Standard"

[HKEY_LOCAL_MACHINE\SOFTWARE\Classes\CLSID\{ ]
@="Cluster Administrator IIS 3.0 Extension"

[HKEY_LOCAL_MACHINE\SOFTWARE\Classes\CLSID\{ \InProcServer32]
@="c:\\ntsvr4ee\\cluster\\iisclex3.dll"
"ThreadingModel"="Apartment"

[HKEY_LOCAL_MACHINE\SOFTWARE\Classes\CLSID ProgId]
@="CLUADMEX.IIS"

[HKEY_LOCAL_MACHINE\SOFTWARE\Classes\CLSID \VersionIndependentProgId]
@="CLUADMEX.IIS"


[HKEY_LOCAL_MACHINE\SOFTWARE\Classes\CLUADMEX.IIS]
@="Cluster Administrator IIS 3.0 Extension"

[HKEY_LOCAL_MACHINE\SOFTWARE\Classes\CLUADMEX.IIS\CLSID]
@="{ }"
```

```
[HKEY_LOCAL_MACHINE\SOFTWARE\Classes\CLUADMEX.Standard]
@="Cluster Administrator Standard Extension"

[HKEY_LOCAL_MACHINE\SOFTWARE\Classes\Interface\{ }]
@="IClusterControl"
```

Cluster RPC Registry Settings

These Registry entries pertain to the RPC (Remote Procedure Call) services that enable the nodes of the cluster to communicate. All of these are critical to the operation of MSCS.

```
HKEY_LOCAL_MACHINE\SOFTWARE\Microsoft\Rpc\ClientProtocols]
"ncacn_np"="rpcltc1.dll"
"ncalrpc"="ncalrpc"
"ncacn_ip_tcp"="RpcLtCcm.Dll"
"ncadg_ip_udp"="RpcLtCcm.Dll"
"ncacn_nb_tcp"="rpcltccm.dll"
"ncadg_cluster"="rpcltccl.dll"
```

Current Version Registry Settings

As MSCS goes through its release phases, it is critical that the most recent version of this application is used on each node. This information can be confirmed here in advance of any compatibility problems.

```
[HKEY_LOCAL_MACHINE\SOFTWARE\Microsoft\Windows\CurrentVersion\App Paths\
CluAdmin.exe]
@="c:\\ntsvr4ee\\cluster\\CluAdmin.exe"

[HKEY_LOCAL_MACHINE\SOFTWARE\Microsoft\Windows\CurrentVersion\App Paths\
clustsrv.exe]
"Path"="C:\\RECYCLER\\ \\DC1\\mscs"
@="[data]\\clustsrv.exe"
```

Uninstall Registry Settings

In debugging a problem with MSCS or its node, it may be necessary to uninstall the software completely. This Registry entry must be correct for this to occur.

```
[HKEY_LOCAL_MACHINE\SOFTWARE\Microsoft\Windows\CurrentVersion\Uninstall\
Microsoft Cluster Server]
"DisplayName"="Microsoft Cluster Server"
"UninstallString"="c:\\ntsvr4ee\\cluster\\setup -uninstall"
```

HotFix Registry Settings

Many cluster-aware applications won't run under MSCS unless the right version of Hotfixes has been applied. You can verify this information here.

```
HKEY_LOCAL_MACHINE\SOFTWARE\Microsoft\Windows
NT\CurrentVersion\Hotfix\Q147222]
"Installed"=dword:
"Comments"="Fixes required for Microsoft Enterprise Edition Clustering"
"Backup Dir"=""
"Fix Description"="Fixes required for Microsoft Enterprise Edition
Clustering"
"Installed By"=""
"Installed On"=""
"Valid"=dword:
```

Cluster Control Set Registry Settings (1–3 and Current)

Having the appropriate settings in all three control sets is critical to keeping your MSCS cluster up and running. All three are identical, and only the current control set is listed here for your reference.

CURRENT CONTROL SET This is the control set that is actually being used to control NTS/E and MSCS at the time that these Registry entries were listed.

```
[HKEY_LOCAL_MACHINE\SYSTEM\CurrentControlSet\Enum\Root\LEGACY_CLUSDISK]
"NextInstance"=dword:

[HKEY_LOCAL_MACHINE\SYSTEM\CurrentControlSet\Enum\Root\LEGACY_CLUSDISK\0000]
"Service"="ClusDisk"
"FoundAtEnum"=dword:
"Class"="Unknown"
"ClassGUID"="{ }"
"Problem"=dword:
"StatusFlags"=dword:
"BaseDevicePath"="HTREE\\ROOT\\0"
"DeviceDesc"="Cluster Disk"

[HKEY_LOCAL_MACHINE\SYSTEM\CurrentControlSet\Enum\Root\LEGACY_CLUSDISK\
\Control]
"ActiveService"="ClusDisk"
```

```
[HKEY_LOCAL_MACHINE\SYSTEM\CurrentControlSet\Enum\Root\LEGACY_CLUSNET]
"NextInstance"=dword:

[HKEY_LOCAL_MACHINE\SYSTEM\CurrentControlSet\Enum\Root\LEGACY_CLUSNET\ ]
"Service"="ClusNet"
"FoundAtEnum"=dword:
"Class"="Unknown"
"ClassGUID"="{ }"
"Problem"=dword:
"StatusFlags"=dword:
"BaseDevicePath"="HTREE\\ROOT\\0"
"DeviceDesc"="Cluster Network"

[HKEY_LOCAL_MACHINE\SYSTEM\CurrentControlSet\Enum\Root\LEGACY_CLUSNET\
\Control]
"ActiveService"="ClusNet"

[HKEY_LOCAL_MACHINE\SYSTEM\CurrentControlSet\Enum\Root\LEGACY_CLUSSVC]
"NextInstance"=dword:

[HKEY_LOCAL_MACHINE\SYSTEM\CurrentControlSet\Enum\Root\LEGACY_CLUSSVC\ ]
"Service"="ClusSvc"
"FoundAtEnum"=dword:
"Class"="Unknown"
"ClassGUID"="{ }"
"Problem"=dword:
"StatusFlags"=dword:
"BaseDevicePath"="HTREE\\ROOT\\0"
"DeviceDesc"="Cluster Server"

[HKEY_LOCAL_MACHINE\SYSTEM\CurrentControlSet\Enum\Root\LEGACY_CLUSSVC\
\Control]
"ActiveService"="ClusSvc"

[HKEY_LOCAL_MACHINE\SYSTEM\CurrentControlSet\Enum\Root\LEGACY_
CLUSTERNAMESERVER]
"NextInstance"=dword:

 [HKEY_LOCAL_MACHINE\SYSTEM\CurrentControlSet\Enum\Root\LEGACY_CLUSDISK]
"NextInstance"=dword:

[HKEY_LOCAL_MACHINE\SYSTEM\CurrentControlSet\Enum\Root\LEGACY_CLUSDISK\ ]
"Service"="ClusDisk"
"FoundAtEnum"=dword:
```

```
"Class"="Unknown"
"ClassGUID"="{ }"
"Problem"=dword:
"StatusFlags"=dword:
"BaseDevicePath"="HTREE\\ROOT\\0"
"DeviceDesc"="Cluster Disk"

[HKEY_LOCAL_MACHINE\SYSTEM\CurrentControlSet\Enum\Root\LEGACY_CLUSDISK\
\Control]
"ActiveService"="ClusDisk"

[HKEY_LOCAL_MACHINE\SYSTEM\CurrentControlSet\Enum\Root\LEGACY_CLUSNET]
"NextInstance"=dword:

[HKEY_LOCAL_MACHINE\SYSTEM\CurrentControlSet\Enum\Root\LEGACY_CLUSNET\0000]
"Service"="ClusNet"
"FoundAtEnum"=dword:
"Class"="Unknown"
"ClassGUID"="{ }"
"Problem"=dword:
"StatusFlags"=dword:
"BaseDevicePath"="HTREE\\ROOT\\0"
"DeviceDesc"="Cluster Network"

[HKEY_LOCAL_MACHINE\SYSTEM\CurrentControlSet\Enum\Root\LEGACY_CLUSNET\
\Control]
"ActiveService"="ClusNet"

[HKEY_LOCAL_MACHINE\SYSTEM\CurrentControlSet\Enum\Root\LEGACY_CLUSSVC]
"NextInstance"=dword:

[HKEY_LOCAL_MACHINE\SYSTEM\CurrentControlSet\Enum\Root\LEGACY_CLUSSVC\ ]
"Service"="ClusSvc"
"FoundAtEnum"=dword:
"Class"="Unknown"
"ClassGUID"="{ }"
"Problem"=dword:
"StatusFlags"=dword:
"BaseDevicePath"="HTREE\\ROOT\\0"
"DeviceDesc"="Cluster Server"

[HKEY_LOCAL_MACHINE\SYSTEM\CurrentControlSet\Enum\Root\LEGACY_CLUSSVC\
\Control]
"ActiveService"="ClusSvc"
```

```
[HKEY_LOCAL_MACHINE\SYSTEM\CurrentControlSet\Enum\Root\LEGACY_
CLUSTERNAMESERVER]
"NextInstance"=dword:

[HKEY_LOCAL_MACHINE\SYSTEM\CurrentControlSet\Services\ClusDisk]
"Type"=dword:
"Start"=dword:
"ErrorControl"=dword:
"Tag"=dword:
"ImagePath"=hex(2):
"DisplayName"="Cluster Disk"
"Group"="Filter"

[HKEY_LOCAL_MACHINE\SYSTEM\CurrentControlSet\Services\ClusDisk\Parameters]
@=""

[HKEY_LOCAL_MACHINE\SYSTEM\CurrentControlSet\Services\ClusDisk\Parameters\
Scsi]
@=""

[HKEY_LOCAL_MACHINE\SYSTEM\CurrentControlSet\Services\ClusDisk\Parameters\
Signatures]

[HKEY_LOCAL_MACHINE\SYSTEM\CurrentControlSet\Services\ClusDisk\Parameters\
Signatures\ ]

[HKEY_LOCAL_MACHINE\SYSTEM\CurrentControlSet\Services\ClusDisk\Parameters\
Signatures\ ]
"DiskName"="\\Device\\Harddisk1"

[HKEY_LOCAL_MACHINE\SYSTEM\CurrentControlSet\Services\ClusDisk\Parameters\
Signatures\ ]

[HKEY_LOCAL_MACHINE\SYSTEM\CurrentControlSet\Services\ClusDisk\Parameters\
Signatures\ ]

[HKEY_LOCAL_MACHINE\SYSTEM\CurrentControlSet\Services\ClusDisk\Security]
"Security"=hex:

[HKEY_LOCAL_MACHINE\SYSTEM\CurrentControlSet\Services\ClusDisk\Enum]
"0"="Root\\LEGACY_CLUSDISK\\ "
"Count"=dword:
"NextInstance"=dword:
```

```
[HKEY_LOCAL_MACHINE\SYSTEM\CurrentControlSet\Services\ClusNet]
"Type"=dword:
"Start"=dword:
"ErrorControl"=dword:
"Tag"=dword:
"ImagePath"=hex(2):
"DisplayName"="Cluster Network"
"Group"="Tdi"
"DependOnService"=hex(7):
"DependOnGroup"=hex(7):

[HKEY_LOCAL_MACHINE\SYSTEM\CurrentControlSet\Services\ClusNet\Parameters]

[HKEY_LOCAL_MACHINE\SYSTEM\CurrentControlSet\Services\ClusNet\Parameters\
Winsock]
@=""
"Mapping"=hex:
"HelperDllName"=hex(2):
"MinSockaddrLength"=dword:
"MaxSockaddrLength"=dword:

[HKEY_LOCAL_MACHINE\SYSTEM\CurrentControlSet\Services\ClusNet\Security]
"Security"=hex:

[HKEY_LOCAL_MACHINE\SYSTEM\CurrentControlSet\Services\ClusNet\Enum]
"0"="Root\\LEGACY_CLUSNET\\ "
"Count"=dword:
"NextInstance"=dword:

[HKEY_LOCAL_MACHINE\SYSTEM\CurrentControlSet\Services\ClusSvc]
"Type"=dword:
"Start"=dword:
"ErrorControl"=dword:
"ImagePath"=hex(2):
"DisplayName"="Cluster Server"

"DependOnService"=hex(7):
"DependOnGroup"=hex(7):
"ObjectName"="DST.COM\\Administrator"

[HKEY_LOCAL_MACHINE\SYSTEM\CurrentControlSet\Services\ClusSvc\Parameters]
@=""
"NodeId"="1"
```

```
[HKEY_LOCAL_MACHINE\SYSTEM\CurrentControlSet\Services\ClusSvc\Security]
"Security"=hex:

[HKEY_LOCAL_MACHINE\SYSTEM\CurrentControlSet\Services\ClusSvc\Enum]
"0"="Root\\LEGACY_CLUSSVC\\ "
"Count"=dword:
"NextInstance"=dword:

HKEY_LOCAL_MACHINE\SYSTEM\CurrentControlSet\Services\EventLog\Application\
CluCis]
"EventMessageFile"="C:\\NTSVR4EE\\System32\\clucis.dll"
"TypesSupported"=dword:

[HKEY_LOCAL_MACHINE\SYSTEM\CurrentControlSet\Services\EventLog\Application\
ClusterNameService]
"EventMessageFile"=hex(2):
"CategoryCount"=dword:
"TypesSupported"=dword:

[HKEY_LOCAL_MACHINE\SYSTEM\CurrentControlSet\Services\EventLog\System\
ClusSvc]
"EventMessageFile"="c:\\ntsvr4ee\\cluster\\clussvc.exe"
"TypesSupported"=dword:
```

Cluster Network Registry Settings

These Registry entries pertain to the actual devices that NTS/E is using for the public and private network interfaces found in an earlier networking hardware driver Registry section in the HKLM (see HKLM Current Control Set) hive.

```
[HKEY_LOCAL_MACHINE\SOFTWARE\Microsoft\Windows
NT\CurrentVersion\NetworkCards]

[HKEY_LOCAL_MACHINE\SOFTWARE\Microsoft\Windows
NT\CurrentVersion\NetworkCards\1]
"ServiceName"="El90x1"
"Manufacturer"="3Com"
"Title"="[1] 3Com Fast EtherLink XL Adapter (3C905)"
"Description"="3Com Fast EtherLink XL PCI 10/100Mb Adapter (3C905)"
"ProductName"="El90x"
"InstallDate"=dword:

[HKEY_LOCAL_MACHINE\SOFTWARE\Microsoft\Windows NT\CurrentVersion\
NetworkCards\1\NetRules]
"InfName"="oemnad4.inf"
```

```
"type"="E190x E190xAdapter"
"bindform"="\"E190x1\" yes yes container"
"class"=hex(7): "InfOption"="3C905"


[HKEY_LOCAL_MACHINE\SOFTWARE\Microsoft\Windows NT\CurrentVersion\
NetworkCards\2]
"ServiceName"="Snet2"
"Manufacturer"="Tandem"
"Title"="[2] ServerNet PCI Adapter"
"Description"="Tandem ServerNet PCI Adapter"
"ProductName"="Snet"
"InstallDate"=dword:


[HKEY_LOCAL_MACHINE\SOFTWARE\Microsoft\Windows NT\CurrentVersion\
NetworkCards\2\NetRules]
"InfName"="oemnad0.inf"
"type"="snet snetAdapter"
"bindform"="\"Snet2\" yes yes container"
"class"=hex(7): "InfOption"="ServerNet"


[HKEY_LOCAL_MACHINE\SOFTWARE\Microsoft\Windows NT\CurrentVersion\
NetworkCards\3]
"ServiceName"="SnNdis3"
"Manufacturer"="Insight"
"Title"="[3]ServerNet Adapter Driver (Upper Layer)"
"Description"="ServerNet Adapter Driver (Upper Layer)"
"ProductName"="SnNdis"


[HKEY_LOCAL_MACHINE\SOFTWARE\Microsoft\Windows NT\CurrentVersion\
NetworkCards\3\NetRules]
"InfName"="oemnad1.inf"
"type"="snetndis snetndisAdapter"
"bindform"="\"SnNdis3\"yes yes container"
"class"=hex(7): "InfOption"="SnNdis"
```

TANDEMSERVERNET REGISTRY SETTINGS   These settings are specific to the ServerNet Private Network NIC's.

```
[HKEY_LOCAL_MACHINE\SOFTWARE\Tandem]


[HKEY_LOCAL_MACHINE\SOFTWARE\Tandem\Snet]


[HKEY_LOCAL_MACHINE\SOFTWARE\Tandem\Snet\CurrentVersion]
"ServiceName"="Snet"
"RefCount"=dword:
```

```
"SoftwareType"="driver"
"MajorVersion"="2"
"MinorVersion"="00"
"Title"="ServerNet PCI Adapter Driver"
"Description"="ServerNet PCI Adapter Driver"
"InstallDate"=dword:

[HKEY_LOCAL_MACHINE\SOFTWARE\Tandem\Snet\CurrentVersion\NetRules]
"InfName"="oemnad0.inf"
"InfOption"="ServerNet"
```

HKEY_CURRENT_USERS REGISTRY ENTRIES (HKCU)

These Registry settings relate to the applications running under NTS/E and MSCS. Maintaining these settings is critical to ensure that your applications operate correctly under MSCS. These settings should be reviewed when a new problem develops with an application that has previously operated correctly. These settings pertain to the specifics of the node itself and are independent of the overall clusters operation.

Figure 10-4 lists this Registry group and its folders.

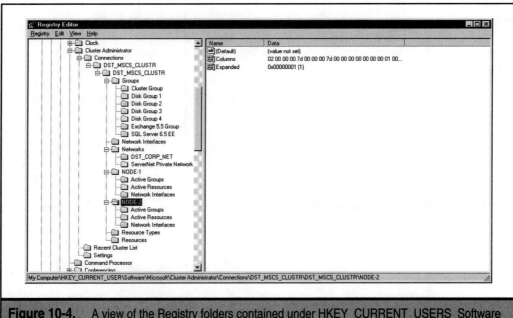

Figure 10-4. A view of the Registry folders contained under HKEY_CURRENT_USERS_Software_ Microsoft_Cluster Administrator

Cluster Administrator Registry Settings

The CA is the most important tool for use with your MSCS cluster. It must be properly configured to operate your cluster correctly.

```
[HKEY_USERS\ - \Software\Microsoft\Cluster Administrator]
@=""


[HKEY_USERS\ - \Software\Microsoft\Cluster Administrator\Connections]
"Connections"="DST_MSCS_CLUSTR"


[HKEY_USERS\S - \Software\Microsoft\Cluster
Administrator\Connections\DST_MSCS_CLUSTR]
"WindowCount"=dword:
"WindowPos"="
"SplitterBarPos"=" "View"=dword:
"Selection"="Connections\\DST_MSCS_CLUSTR\\DST_MSCS_CLUSTR\\NODE-1"


[HKEY_USERS\ - \Software\Microsoft\Cluster
Administrator\Connections\DST_MSCS_CLUSTR\DST_MSCS_CLUSTR]
"Expanded"=dword:
"Columns"=hex:


[HKEY_USERS\  \Software\Microsoft\Cluster
Administrator\Connections\DST_MSCS_CLUSTR\DST_MSCS_CLUSTR\Groups]
"Expanded"=dword:
"Columns"=hex:


[HKEY_USERS\  \Software\Microsoft\Cluster
Administrator\Connections\DST_MSCS_CLUSTR\DST_MSCS_CLUSTR\Groups\Cluster Group]
"Expanded"=dword:
"Columns"=hex:


[HKEY_USERS\ - \Software\Microsoft\Cluster
Administrator\Connections\DST_MSCS_CLUSTR\DST_MSCS_CLUSTR\Groups\Disk Group 1]
"Expanded"=dword:
"Columns"=hex:


[HKEY_USERS\  \Software\Microsoft\Cluster
Administrator\Connections\DST_MSCS_CLUSTR\DST_MSCS_CLUSTR\Groups\Disk Group 2]
"Expanded"=dword:
"Columns"=hex:
```

```
[HKEY_USERS\ - \Software\Microsoft\Cluster
Administrator\Connections\DST_MSCS_CLUSTR\DST_MSCS_CLUSTR\Groups\Disk Group 3]
"Expanded"=dword:
"Columns"=hex:


[HKEY_USERS\ - \Software\Microsoft\Cluster
Administrator\Connections\DST_MSCS_CLUSTR\DST_MSCS_CLUSTR\Groups\Disk Group 4]
"Expanded"=dword:
"Columns"=hex:


[HKEY_USERS\  \Software\Microsoft\Cluster
Administrator\Connections\DST_MSCS_CLUSTR\DST_MSCS_CLUSTR\Groups\Exchange 5.5
Group]
"Expanded"=dword:
"Columns"=hex:


[HKEY_USERS\ - \Software\Microsoft\Cluster
Administrator\Connections\DST_MSCS_CLUSTR\DST_MSCS_CLUSTR\Groups\SQL Server 6.5
EE]
"Expanded"=dword:
"Columns"=hex:


[HKEY_USERS\ - \Software\Microsoft\Cluster
Administrator\Connections\DST_MSCS_CLUSTR\DST_MSCS_CLUSTR\Network Interfaces]
"Expanded"=dword:


[HKEY_USERS\ - \Software\Microsoft\Cluster
Administrator\Connections\DST_MSCS_CLUSTR\DST_MSCS_CLUSTR\Networks]
"Expanded"=dword:
"Columns"=hex:


[HKEY_USERS\ - \Software\Microsoft\Cluster
Administrator\Connections\DST_MSCS_CLUSTR\DST_MSCS_CLUSTR\Networks\DST_CORP_NET]
"Expanded"=dword:
"Columns"=hex:


[HKEY_USERS\  \Software\Microsoft\Cluster Administrator\Connections\
DST_MSCS_CLUSTR\DST_MSCS_CLUSTR\Networks\ServerNet Private Network]
"Expanded"=dword:
"Columns"=hex:


[HKEY_USERS\  \Software\Microsoft\Cluster Administrator\Connections\
DST_MSCS_CLUSTR\DST_MSCS_CLUSTR\NODE-1]
"Expanded"=dword:
"Columns"=hex:
```

```
[HKEY_USERS\  \Software\Microsoft\Cluster Administrator\Connections\
DST_MSCS_CLUSTR\DST_MSCS_CLUSTR\NODE-1\Active Groups]
"Expanded"=dword:
"Columns"=hex:

[HKEY_USERS\  \Software\Microsoft\Cluster Administrator\Connections\
DST_MSCS_CLUSTR\DST_MSCS_CLUSTR\NODE-1\Active Resources]
"Expanded"=dword:
"Columns"=hex:

[HKEY_USERS\  \Software\Microsoft\Cluster Administrator\Connections\
DST_MSCS_CLUSTR\DST_MSCS_CLUSTR\NODE-1\Network Interfaces]
"Expanded"=dword:
"Columns"=hex:

[HKEY_USERS\  \Software\Microsoft\Cluster Administrator\Connections\
DST_MSCS_CLUSTR\DST_MSCS_CLUSTR\NODE-2]
"Expanded"=dword:
"Columns"=hex:

[HKEY_USERS\  \Software\Microsoft\Cluster Administrator\Connections\
DST_MSCS_CLUSTR\DST_MSCS_CLUSTR\NODE-2\Active Groups]
"Expanded"=dword:
"Columns"=hex:

[HKEY_USERS\  \Software\Microsoft\Cluster Administrator\Connections\
DST_MSCS_CLUSTR\DST_MSCS_CLUSTR\NODE-2\Active Resources]
"Expanded"=dword:
"Columns"=hex:

[HKEY_USERS\  \Software\Microsoft\Cluster Administrator\Connections\
DST_MSCS_CLUSTR\DST_MSCS_CLUSTR\NODE-2\Network Interfaces]
"Expanded"=dword:
"Columns"=hex:

[HKEY_USERS\  \Software\Microsoft\Cluster Administrator\Connections\
DST_MSCS_CLUSTR\DST_MSCS_CLUSTR\Resource Types]
"Expanded"=dword:

[HKEY_USERS\S  \Software\Microsoft\Cluster Administrator\Connections\
DST_MSCS_CLUSTR\DST_MSCS_CLUSTR\Resources]
"Expanded"=dword:
"Columns"=hex:
```

```
[HKEY_USERS\  \Software\Microsoft\Cluster Administrator\Recent Cluster List]
"Cluster1"="DST_MSCS_CLUSTR"

[HKEY_USERS\  \Software\Microsoft\Cluster Administrator\Settings]
"WindowPos"="0,1,-32000,-32000,-1,-1,44,44,812,551"
"ShowToolBar"=dword:
"ShowStatusBar"=dword:

[HKEY_CURRENT_USER\Software\Microsoft\Cluster Administrator]
@=""

[HKEY_CURRENT_USER\Software\Microsoft\Cluster Administrator\Connections]
"Connections"="DST_MSCS_CLUSTR"

[HKEY_CURRENT_USER\Software\Microsoft\Cluster Administrator\Connections\
DST_MSCS_CLUSTR]
"WindowCount"=dword:
"WindowPos"="0,1,-1,-1,-1,-1,0,0,747,389"
"SplitterBarPos"="200,0"
"View"=dword:
"Selection"="Connections\\DST_MSCS_CLUSTR\\DST_MSCS_CLUSTR\\NODE-1"

[HKEY_CURRENT_USER\Software\Microsoft\Cluster Administrator\Connections\
DST_MSCS_CLUSTR\DST_MSCS_CLUSTR]
"Expanded"=dword:
"Columns"=hex:

[HKEY_CURRENT_USER\Software\Microsoft\Cluster Administrator\Connections\
DST_MSCS_CLUSTR\DST_MSCS_CLUSTR\Groups]
"Expanded"=dword:
"Columns"=hex:

[HKEY_CURRENT_USER\Software\Microsoft\Cluster Administrator\Connections\
DST_MSCS_CLUSTR\DST_MSCS_CLUSTR\Groups\Cluster Group]
"Expanded"=dword:
"Columns"=hex:

[HKEY_CURRENT_USER\Software\Microsoft\Cluster Administrator\Connections\
DST_MSCS_CLUSTR\DST_MSCS_CLUSTR\Groups\Disk Group 1]
"Expanded"=dword:
"Columns"=hex:
```

```
[HKEY_CURRENT_USER\Software\Microsoft\Cluster Administrator\Connections\
DST_MSCS_CLUSTR\DST_MSCS_CLUSTR\Groups\Disk Group 2]
"Expanded"=dword:
"Columns"=hex:

[HKEY_CURRENT_USER\Software\Microsoft\Cluster Administrator\Connections\
DST_MSCS_CLUSTR\DST_MSCS_CLUSTR\Groups\Disk Group 3]
"Expanded"=dword:
"Columns"=hex:

[HKEY_CURRENT_USER\Software\Microsoft\Cluster Administrator\Connections\
DST_MSCS_CLUSTR\DST_MSCS_CLUSTR\Groups\Disk Group 4]
"Expanded"=dword:
"Columns"=hex:

[HKEY_CURRENT_USER\Software\Microsoft\Cluster Administrator\Connections\
DST_MSCS_CLUSTR\DST_MSCS_CLUSTR\Groups\Exchange 5.5 Group]
"Expanded"=dword:
"Columns"=hex:

[HKEY_CURRENT_USER\Software\Microsoft\Cluster Administrator\Connections\
DST_MSCS_CLUSTR\DST_MSCS_CLUSTR\Groups\SQL Server 6.5 EE]
"Expanded"=dword:
"Columns"=hex:

[HKEY_CURRENT_USER\Software\Microsoft\Cluster Administrator\Connections\
DST_MSCS_CLUSTR\DST_MSCS_CLUSTR\Network Interfaces]
"Expanded"=dword:

[HKEY_CURRENT_USER\Software\Microsoft\Cluster Administrator\Connections\
DST_MSCS_CLUSTR\DST_MSCS_CLUSTR\Networks]
"Expanded"=dword:
"Columns"=hex:

[HKEY_CURRENT_USER\Software\Microsoft\Cluster Administrator\Connections\
DST_MSCS_CLUSTR\DST_MSCS_CLUSTR\Networks\DST_CORP_NET]
"Expanded"=dword:
"Columns"=hex:

[HKEY_CURRENT_USER\Software\Microsoft\Cluster Administrator\Connections\
DST_MSCS_CLUSTR\DST_MSCS_CLUSTR\Networks\ServerNet Private Network]
"Expanded"=dword:
```

```
"Columns"=hex:

[HKEY_CURRENT_USER\Software\Microsoft\Cluster Administrator\Connections\
DST_MSCS_CLUSTR\DST_MSCS_CLUSTR\NODE-1]
"Expanded"=dword:
"Columns"=hex:

[HKEY_CURRENT_USER\Software\Microsoft\Cluster Administrator\Connections\
DST_MSCS_CLUSTR\DST_MSCS_CLUSTR\NODE-1\Active Groups]
"Expanded"=dword:
"Columns"=hex:

[HKEY_CURRENT_USER\Software\Microsoft\Cluster Administrator\Connections\
DST_MSCS_CLUSTR\DST_MSCS_CLUSTR\NODE-1\Active Resources]
"Expanded"=dword:
"Columns"=hex:

[HKEY_CURRENT_USER\Software\Microsoft\Cluster Administrator\Connections\
DST_MSCS_CLUSTR\DST_MSCS_CLUSTR\NODE-1\Network Interfaces]
"Expanded"=dword:
"Columns"=hex:

[HKEY_CURRENT_USER\Software\Microsoft\Cluster Administrator\Connections\
DST_MSCS_CLUSTR\DST_MSCS_CLUSTR\NODE-2]
"Expanded"=dword:
"Columns"=hex:

[HKEY_CURRENT_USER\Software\Microsoft\Cluster Administrator\Connections\
DST_MSCS_CLUSTR\DST_MSCS_CLUSTR\NODE-2\Active Groups]
"Expanded"=dword:
"Columns"=hex:

[HKEY_CURRENT_USER\Software\Microsoft\Cluster Administrator\Connections\
DST_MSCS_CLUSTR\DST_MSCS_CLUSTR\NODE-2\Active Resources]
"Expanded"=dword:
"Columns"=hex:
```

```
[HKEY_CURRENT_USER\Software\Microsoft\Cluster Administrator\Connections\
DST_MSCS_CLUSTR\DST_MSCS_CLUSTR\NODE-2\Network Interfaces]
"Expanded"=dword:
"Columns"=hex:

[HKEY_CURRENT_USER\Software\Microsoft\Cluster Administrator\Connections\
DST_MSCS_CLUSTR\DST_MSCS_CLUSTR\Resource Types]
"Expanded"=dword:

[HKEY_CURRENT_USER\Software\Microsoft\Cluster Administrator\Connections\
DST_MSCS_CLUSTR\DST_MSCS_CLUSTR\Resources]
"Expanded"=dword:
"Columns"=hex:

[HKEY_CURRENT_USER\Software\Microsoft\Cluster Administrator\Recent
Cluster List]
"Cluster1"="DST_MSCS_CLUSTR"

[HKEY_CURRENT_USER\Software\Microsoft\Cluster Administrator\Settings]
"WindowPos"=" "
"ShowToolBar"=dword:
"ShowStatusBar"=dword:
```

MSCS FILES, FILE TYPES, AND INSTALLATION LOCATIONS

This section provides a comprehensive inventory of the files installed by MSCS, their locations, their groupings, and their abbreviations. Also included is a comprehensive list of the files, registry entries, and other items that are removed when MSCS is uninstalled by using the Add/Remove Software Control Panel function.

Knowing where all the files for MSCS reside is critical in the event that a disk becomes corrupted or some type of catastrophic failure takes place and you must either manually or automatically restore your MSCS files from a backup tape or cartridge. In addition, should you ever have to completely uninstall MSCS or its applications, you need to know which files and Registry entries should be deleted to manually complete this process and which should be verified so as not to interfere with the reinstallation of MSCS at a later time.

These code listings can be used to determine where a restored file should properly reside or to make sure that all previous versions of MSCS have been removed in their entirety prior to a reinstallation or upgrade.

MSCS Identification

This section of the file code identifies the version of MSCS to which it pertains. Each version will have a different version or build number along with a code-name signature. It is good practice to verify that the particular version you are looking for is identical to your reference material.

```
MSCS Version 1.0, Build 224, Signature="$CHICAGO$"
```

Destination Directories for Installation and Operational Files

The following table contains entries regarding the type, number, and location for key MSCS files that are installed during setup and used during normal MSCS operation.

File Group Name	Typical Number of Files Installed	Default Location
Cluster System Files	11	\Windows\System32
Cluster Administration System Files	11	\Windows\System32
Cluster Driver Files	12	\Windows\System32\drivers
Cluster Files	0 (Operational Storage)	CLUSTERTARGETDIR
ClusterAdmin Files	0 (Operational Storage)	CLUSTERTARGETDIR
Cluster Security Files	0 (Operational Storage)	CLUSTERTARGETDIR\private
Cluster Uninstall Files	0 (Operational Storage)	CLUSTERTARGETDIR

Files and Services to be Uninstalled

The following list of files and services are deleted or removed in the normal course of uninstalling MSCS.

▼ *Delete Files*   Cluster Administrator Files, Cluster Driver Files, Cluster Files, Cluster Security Files, Cluster System Files, Cluster Uninstall Files

■ *Delete Service*   ClusDisk, ClusNet TimeServ, ClusSvc

▲ *Delete Registers*   Administrator Registry Entries, ClusSvc_EventLog_DelReg, ClusSvc_Services_DelReg, General

Files and Services to be Installed

The following files and services are added and/or enabled during the course of a normal installation of MSCS. "Copy" refers to copying an expanded version of the file from the source CD-ROM and "add" refers to listing those services in the Registry for use after the system reboots.

- ▼ *Copy Files*   Cluster Administrator Files, Cluster Administraor System Files, Cluster Driver Files, Cluster Files, Cluster Security Files, Cluster System Files

- ■ *Add Service*   ClusDisk,ClusDisk.Service, ClusNet ,ClusNet.Service, Cluster.Service, ClusSvc, ClusSvc_EventLog_Inst, TimeServ, Time.Service

- ▲ *Add Registry*   Administrator Registry Entries

Source Disk Files

The following files are expanded and copied from Disk 2 of NTS/E to the appropriate directories during the installation of MSCS on each node.

cluadmex.dll	clusnet.sys	resrcmon.exe
cluadmin.cnt	clusprxy.exe	resutils.dll
cluadmin.exe	clusres.dll	rpcltccl.dll
cluadmin.hlp	clussvc.exe	rpcltscl.dll
clusapi.dll	cluster.exe	security.dll
clusdb	cluster.inf	setup.exe
clusdb.log	debugex.dll	setup.hlp
clusdisk.sys	iisclex3.dll	timeserv.exe
clussprt.dll	iisclus3.dll	wshclus.dll

Cluster Driver Files

The clusdisk.sys and clusnet.sys driver files are expanded during copying from Disk 2 of NTS/E during the installation of MSCS.

Cluster Files

The following executables and DLLs are expanded during copying from Disk 2 for NTS/E during installation of MSCS. All of the DLL files in this group can be monitored by Dependency Walker when troubleshooting your system.

clusprxy.exe	resrcmon.exe	setup.hlp
clusres.dll	rpcltccl.dll	timeserv.exe
clussvc.exe	rpcltscl.dll	wshclus.dll
iisclus3.dll	setup.exe	

Cluster Administrator Files

These executables and DLLs are used to support the Cluster Administrator.

cluadmin.cnt	cluadmin.exe	debugex.dll
cluadmex.dll	cluadmin.hlp	iisclex3.dll

Other Cluster Files

The following table lists files are associated with various operations of the CA.

File(s)	Description
clussprt.dll	Dedicated system file used by MSCS
clusapi.dll, cluster.exe, and resutils.dll	Associated with the operation of the CA system files
security.dll	The main security file for MSCS
clusdb, clusdb.log, and cluster.inf	Special files uninstalled by MSCS when using Uninstall

Resource Type Names

The following list contains both the abbreviated and full names for all the resource types that are installed and utilized by MSCS during normal operations:

Abreviated Name	Full Name
GenApp.TypeName	Generic Application
GenSvc.TypeName	Generic Service
NetName.TypeName	Network Name
PhysDisk.TypeName	Physical Disk
PrtSplSvc.TypeName	Print Spooler
FileShr.TypeName	File Share
TpAddr.TypeName	IP Address
TimeSvc.TypeName	Time Service
TIS.TypeName	IIS Virtual Root
LocalQuorum.TypeName	Local Quorum
DhcpSvc.TypeName	DHCP Server
MSMQ.TypeName	Microsoft Message Queue Server
MSDTC.TypeName	Distributed Transaction Coordinator

Abreviated Name	Full Name
GenApp.LTypeName	Generic Application
GenSvc.LTypeName	Generic Service
NetName.LTypeName	Network Name
PhysDisk.LTypeName	Physical Disk
PrtSplSvc.LTypeName	Print Spooler
FileShr.LTypeName	File Share
TpAddr.LTypeName	IP Address
TimeSvc.LTypeName	Time Service
TIS.LTypeName	IIS Virtual Root
LocalQuorum.LTypeName	Local Quorum
DhcpSvc.LTypeName	DHCP Server
MSMQ.LTypeName	Microsoft Message Queue Server
MSDTC.LTypeName	Distributed Transaction Coordinator

Service Names (Descriptions)

The following are both the abbreviated and full names of all the services that MSCS installs and uses on each node during operation:

Abbreviate Name	Full Name
Time.SvcDesc	Time Service
Cluster.SvcDesc	Cluster Server
ClusDisk.SvcDesc	Cluster Disk
ClusNet.SvcDesc	Cluster Network

SERVICE PACK 4 FOR WINDOWS NT 4.0 (ALL EDITIONS)

As described in Chapter 2, you must have Service Pack 3 (SP3) available in order to properly install MSCS. As of October 1998 a new Service Pack became available (by either downloading from Microsoft or purchasing from their Web site at **www.microsoft.com/ntserver/nts/downloads/**). This service pack will be bundled with future copies of NTS/E as well (along with Windows Load Balancing Server—WLBS).

Service Pack 4 provides approximately 600 new fixes to Windows NT 4.0 (above and beyond the hotfixes being provided separately) and makes several changes to MSCS as well. In the following section on Service Bulletins you will note that a number of these problems have been abated by SP4.

SP4 contains an updated File Share Resource. This new Resource extends the capabilities of the original resource (for example, more than 900 shares) to allow multiple shares from a single resource (see *Microsoft Support Bulletin #Q194831*, entitled "File Share Resource Enhancements and Dynamic Updates," dated 11/5/98 for more information). It also simplifies manageability by reducing the system overhead created by large numbers of shares. The new Resource does not dynamically observe updates to the subdirectory structure, so to make changes you must take the Share Resource offline, make your modifications to the subdirectory structures, and then bring it back online. All changes will be reflected then.

As with all previous Service Packs, SP4 has brought with it a number of problems on its own. There are hotfixes posted on the MS Hotfix Web site to counter these (for example, new Named Pipes over RPC for SQL Server problems). The Hotfix Web site can be found at **ftp://ftp.microsoft.com/bussys/winnt/winnt-public/fixes/usa/NT40/hotfixes-postSP3/roll-up/cluster/**. I strongly suggest that everyone become very familiar with this site.

In addition, the CD-ROM version of SP4 comes with a number of NT Resource Kit tools and utilities. These include some good ones for use with MSCS.

SERVICE BULLETINS FROM MICROSOFT TECHNICAL SUPPORT

As mentioned in Chapter 2, Microsoft maintains a technical support Web site for their products (**www.microsoft.com**). Located within this site's database are a number of service bulletins (more than 70 at the time of this writing) pertaining to MSCS. You can find them by selecting the platform you wish information on (for example, Windows NT Server) and then entering a keyword for a search (in this case enter either"MSCS" or "cluster"). To help you find the bulletin you are looking for, the available bulletins are indexed here by the major areas of interest. The index categories are as follows:

▼ *Installation and Upgrade*   Deals with issues and problems regarding MSCS when it is first installed or when a demo or beta version is upgraded.

■ *MSCS General Errors*   This group of service bulletins covers generalized areas of concern. It includes documentation errors and basic overall problems and their workarounds (if any). These problems are endemic to MSCS v1.0 and may be eliminated by the installation of the MSCS hotfixes or SP 4. Most of these problems will be eliminated completely when NTS/E v5.0 is released.

■ *Group and Resources*   This group of bulletins pertains to generalized problems found in the groups and resources setup and operation. Most bulletins are focused on workarounds to known bugs.

■ *Quorum Resource*   This group of service bulletins is specific to the QR and its protection. Regardless of whether or not you have any problems with your

QR, you should print all of these bulletins and keep them on hand for emergency situations.

■ *Cluster Storage* This group pertains to the shared-storage bus and its devices. Many of these problems affect the QR device or volume as well.

■ *Cluster Network(s)* This group deals with both the public and private networks interfaced to MSCS, along with the NIC cards, protocol stacks, and drivers.

▲ *Cluster-aware Applications and Services* This final grouping of service bulletins deals with problems, workarounds, and "bomb outs" of the cluster-aware applications and services set up and running under MSCS. If you have a problem with a particular application, you should also consult the vendor of that product to determine if further information or suggestions are available.

Once you find that a description in the appropriate subcategory matches your particular problem (see the following table), you can then go to the Microsoft support Web site (**www.microsoft.com/support**) and enter the ID number of the bulletin in the search box. When you press the search button, the service bulletin requested is displayed, and you can then read information about the fix or workaround suggested by Microsoft. It may also be prudent to visit your vendor's Web site as well and look under their support section for NTS/E and MSCS to see if they have fixes and workarounds listed for their hardware and peripherals.

If you locate a particular problem that you are experiencing among those listed here, there are two paths to pursue to correct it.

▼ Those items that are marked with an asterisk * after the ID number have been addressed/corrected in Windows NT Service Pack 4 (October 1998).

▲ Visit the Microsoft Support Web site (**www.microsoft.com/support**) and after logging in, enter the ID number in the search engine to retrieve the most recent version of the service bulletin and its recommended fix or workaround.

Bulletin Number	Description	Date Issued/Updated
Installations and Upgrades		
Q185752	MSCS fails to start after installation	6/9/98
Q179776	Availability of hotfixes for MSCS	3/20/98
Q178924	How to upgrade an evaluation version of MSCS	3/20/98
Q175779	MSCS requires SP3 or later	3/20/98
Q10075	How to install Service Packs in a cluster	3/20/98
Q174617	CHKDSK runs while running MSCS setup	3/20/98

Bulletin Number	Description	Date Issued/Updated
Q174332	How to add additional Cluster Administrators	3/20/98
Q171883	Runtime error when installing MSCS	11/11/97
Q171265	Unable to uninstall Cluster Administrator tool	3/19/98
Q174944	How to use the –debug option for Cluster Service	3/20/98
Q168801	How to enable Cluster logging in MSCS	9/1/98
Q185051*	Restarting Cluster Service causes services.exe to crash	11/17/98
Q185212*	Cluster Server does not support more than 900 shares	10/20/98
Q193654*	Services continue to run after shutdown initiated	10/19/98
Q188652*	Error replicating registry keys	11/17/98
Q190354*	Unattended setup of MSCS with –JOIN parameter requires input	10/19/98

General Areas

Q178273	Error in MSCS Administration Guide	3/20/98
Q174944	How to use the –debug option for MSCS	3/20/98
Q174331	Error message received adding second time service to MSCS	3/20/98
Q174398	How to force time synchronization between cluster nodes	3/20/98
Q171450	Possible RPC errors on cluster startup	3/19/98
Q171451	Cluster node may fail to join cluster	3/20/98
Q171390	Cluster service may not start if domain controller is unavailable	3/19/98
Q170762	Cluster shares appear in browse list under other names	6/12/98
Q169414	Cluster service may stop after failover	3/19/98
Q143160	Enterprise server stops during print spooling	10/27/97

Bulletin Number	Description	Date Issued/Updated
Q185051*	Restarting cluster service causes services.exe to crash	5/4/98
Q174070	Registry replication in MSCS	3/20/98
Q168567	Clustering information on IP address failover	3/19/98
Q185788*	Windows NT hangs on boot on DEC alpha clustered servers	3/1/98
Q170771	Cluster may fail if IP address used from DCHP server	3/19/98
Q183832	GetHostName( ) must support alternate computer names	4/13/98
Q189469	Cluster Administrator can connect to all NetBIOS names	7/16/98

Groups, Resources, and Dependencies

Q181491	PRB: MFC generic app resources cannot interact with desktop	3/20/98
Q178276	Dependencies are unavailable when first modifying properties	3/20/98
Q174928	Dependencies page empty when running resource wizard	3/20/98
Q174940	Clients may receive access denied error	3/20/98
Q174956	WINS not supported as failover resource in MSCS	3/20/98
Q174956	Effects of using autodetect setting on cluster NIC	3/20/98
Q174641	Resource parameters tab is missing	3/20/98
Q174070	Registry replication in MSCS	3/20/98
Q172507	Resources go offline and online repeatedly in Cluster Administrator	3/20/98
Q171791	Creating dependencies in MSCS	3/20/98
Q171277	MSCS cluster resource failover time	3/19/98
Q169017	Information on groups and resources using MSCS	3/19/98
Q168948	Information about the cluster group	3/19/98

Bulletin Number	Description	Date Issued/Updated
Q195462*	WINS registration and ip address behavior for MSCS 1.0	11/9/98
Q168567	Clustering information on IP address failover	3/19/98

Quorum Resource

Q175664	Error creating dependencies for Quorum Resource	3/20/98
Q172944	How to change Quorum disk designation	3/20/98
Q172951	How to recover from a corrupted Quorum log	3/20/98

Cluster Storage

Q189149	Disk counters on clustered disk record zero values	7/9/98
Q176970	CHKDSK /f does not run on the shared cluster disk	7/7/98
Q175649	Adding new scsi controller on alpha may prevent startup	3/20/98
Q175275	How to replace shared SCSI controller when using MSCS	3/20/98
Q175278	How to install additional drives on the shared SCSI bus	3/20/98
Q174795	Cluster configuration for BusLogic controllers	3/20/98
Q174797	How to run CHKDSK on a shared drive	3/20/98
Q174397	HP NetRAID card may require updated firmware	3/20/98
Q171052	Software FT sets are not supported by MSCS	3/19/98
Q172968	Disk subsystem recovery documentation error	3/20/98
Q195636*	Fibre system loses SCSI reservation after multiple restarts	11/16/98

Bulletin Number	Description	Date Issued/Updated
Q193779*	Cluster server drive letters do not update using disk administrator	11/16/98
Q195635	Install/S100 series Compaq switched SCSI cluster	11/11/98
Q195630	Unable to fail-back the disk resource after a fail-over	11/11/98
Q189149	Disk counters on clustered disk record zero values	7/9/98

Cluster Networks

Q175767	Expected behavior of multiple adapters on same network	3/20/98
Q175141	Cluster service ignores network card	3/20/98
Q174945	How to prevent MSCS from using specific networks	3/20/98
Q174794	How to change network priority in a cluster	3/20/98
Q170771	Cluster may fail IP address used from DHCP server	3/19/98
Q176320	Impact of network adapter failure in a cluster	3/20/98
Q193890	Recommended WINS configuration for MSCS	10/8/98

Cluster-Aware Application and Services

Q187708*	Cannot connect to SQL virtual server via sockets	7/15/98
Q1752	Licensing policy implementation with MSCS	3/20/98
Q174837	MS BackOffice applications supported by MSCS	7/29/98
Q171452	Using MSCS to create a virtual server	3/20/98
Q147222*	Group of hotfixes for Exchange 5.5 and IIS 4.0	6/29/98

Bulletin Number	Description	Date Issued/Updated
Q188984	Office 97 is not supported in a clustered environment	7/7/98
Q189330	Heavy file I/O causes Windows NT server to hang	7/20/98
Q192773*	Cluster Server memory leak when transaction server (MTS) explorer is running	11/16/98
Q143160*	Enterprise Server stops during print spooling	10/27/98

All of these service bulletins may be obtained via the Microsoft Support Web site (**www.microsoft/com/support**) and are constantly being updated and their number increased. An interesting sidenote to those who have had some experience in using and supporting V1.0 releases of Microsoft products in the past is the fact that for such a sophisticated product as MSCS, the number of service bulletins is relatively small.

SUMMARY

Troubleshooting a complex system such as a cluster is an art that requires the right tools and approach in order to be mastered. This chapter has given you a lot of information for use in the troubleshooting process and some direction of how to best apply these tools. Additional information can be found in the *MSCS Systems Administrator* manual in the "Troubleshooting" section as well as at Microsoft's Web site (**w.microsoft.com/support**). Updates to this chapter will be posted on my Web site (**www.dst.com**) for readers of this book.

APPENDIX A

Storage Options for MSCS Systems

Some of us in the computer industry today feel that clustering was developed solely to provide higher levels of unencumbered access to storage devices and subsystems. Given this belief, it is obvious that storage and storage management are major focal points of any cluster design and deployment strategy. Within this appendix we will discuss storage devices and systems, along with storage management solutions, to support the unique requirements of MSCS clusters.

STORAGE INTERCONNECTS, DEVICES, AND SUBSYSTEM OPTIONS

Storage for clusters involves much more than just disk drives. It is, in essence, a series of solutions that provide at minimum greater cluster data integrity. More importantly, these solutions play a substantial role in enhancing the performance of the mission- and business-critical applications that reside on the cluster. In this regard, it is important to make storage solution decisions based upon the specific types of applications that each device or solution must support, along with the types of data that will reside on it. As we discuss the varying options and approaches, we will put all of these items into proper perspective.

Storage Interconnection Standards

Three dominant interconnects are in use today in the storage community. They are SCSI (multiconductor cables), fibre channel (SCSI protocols over high-speed copper and optical cabling), and SSA (Serial Storage Architecture—high-speed, relatively low-cost copper cabling). Table A-1 lists the basic specifications of all three of these standards.

Storage Interconnect Type	Bandwidth	Maximum Number of Devices on Bus	Hosts-per-Bus
SCSI-2 F/W/D	20MB/s	15	1-2
Ultra SCSI W/D	40-80MB/s	15	1-2
SSA	20-80MB/s	127	1-126
Fibre channel arbitrated loop (FC-AL)	100MB/s	127	1-126
FC Storage Area Network (SAN)	1GB/s+	Millions	Millions

Table A-1.   A Comparison of the Most Common Storage Interconnect Standards

SCSI

SCSI is used in two formats for the most part today. They are SCSI-2 (and its variants of Fast, Wide, and Differential) and Ultra-SCSI. Both are based on a low-cost/high-volume market model, while featuring reasonably high bandwidths (20-40MB/s) and wide industry support. Their most serious shortcoming is the overall length that their interconnect buses can support (which is 25 meters maximum). Measured in tens of meters at best, these bus lengths are practical for most computing environments but require careful attention to detail to keep them from "flying apart" on you.

Fibre Channel

FC comes in two flavors: optical and copper. Most systems today utilize the copper version to keep costs manageable. However, if extended distances (1,000 meters or more) are your driving requirement, you will probably find a mix of both copper and optical (with interface devices/bridges in between) works best. Optical fibre cable uses unique connectors and requires special tools when you need to attach a connector or make a splice in a cable. Most IT Departments will end up utilizing pre-made cables with connectors already attached for use on either copper or optical implementations of FC. These are available in standard lengths and colors very much like those cables for Ethernet.

When dealing with SCSI protocols over FC, it is critical to make sure that you have bridges between these two worlds where required. Many of the fibre channel storage products today use FC from the HBA to the controller (and over the storage network fabric of switches, hubs, and routers) but revert back to conventional Ultra-SCSI outside of the controller to where it connects to the drives/devices. This again requires you to choose a SCSI standard up front and have the appropriate drives/devices, cables, and terminators (the de facto standard used here is Ultra-SCSI Wide/Differential). FC buses can also support a large number of devices over a network.

SSA

Serial Storage Architecture (SSA) is a storage bus standard developed by IBM. It features reasonably high bandwidths over low-cost copper cabling and is supported from the drive to the controller and from the controller to the HBA. SSA is very straightforward to design and deploy. You usually do not have to contend with any of the interoperability issues that plague other standards. You design your storage solutions to be either just a bunch of disks or multiple disks in array configurations. All configurations share common interconnects and plug-and-play. A large number of devices can be supported on an SSA bus as well.

Storage Area Networks (SAN)

Storage Area Networks (SANs) are, essentially, a derivative of the Network Attached Storage (NAS) paradigm that was prototyped in the late 80s and early 90s by the high-performance computing community. This was done in an effort to get away from server-centric architectures that created tremendous storage bottlenecks in high-performance computing environments (HPCE). SANs feature the use of high-speed interconnects, wide bandwidth storage peripherals, and specialized data management software to support speedy transfers and large overall capacities. SANs are expected to be integral components for many MSCS clustering solutions, especially in environments where OLTP- and OLAP-type applications are of primary interest.

In this respect, many leading providers of RAID solutions, along with being FC advocates, are leading the charge in terms of providing SANs for clustered (and non-clustered) environments. SANs promise to be a major component of N-node clusters in Phase 2 of MSCS as they can take on the role of a node and support even higher levels of availability and fault tolerance for storage devices.

GENERAL STORAGE CONSIDERATIONS

In respect to overall cluster performance and data integrity, it is critical to make sure that the interface parameters, speed, and capacity of all shared drives are matched. Cluster performance will degrade substantially, if not fail outright, if disk interfaces, bandwidths, and capacity points are all mixed up. In addition, all drives other than the server's internal EIDE (or SCSI where found) boot drive must be formatted as NTFS. Currently, Windows NT 4.0 supports the use of FAT-16 or NTFS for the boot drive, with FAT-32 read available (FAT-32 read and write will be supported in NT 5.0). Housekeeping in this area is critical. The best approach is to choose a particular interface standard (SCSI-2, Ultra-SCSI, Fibre channel, or SSA) for both your shared and non-shared storage buses. (If you choose FC you should then pick either copper or optical as your interconnect means as well.) The standards chosen for the shared and non-shared storage do not have to be the same, but for the sake of troubleshooting and as a source of spares, it is convenient for them to be identical in all respects wherever possible.

To illustrate the importance of matching HBAs, buses, and drives, suppose the HBA (or RAID controller) for the shared storage bus is SCSI-2 Fast/Wide/Differential, then you should not have single-ended or narrow drives on this bus. You can do such things as use Ultra drives with these SCSI-2 HBAs (and vice-versa). However, you will not achieve the bandwidth performance that the HBA (using its native format) can support, but the system will behave just fine (as long as you don't mix and match drives). This works in reverse as well. Ultra drives will work with SCSI-2 HBAs but only at SCSI-2 bandwidths. You do need, however, to make sure that terminations and cable/bus lengths comply with the type of HBA that you are using. (The faster the performance of the standard, the shorter the overall bus lengths, along with increased sensitivity to proper terminations.) This example can be applied to the non-shared storage bus as well. As discussed earlier, it is possible to have different standards for the shared versus non-shared storage devices as long as they never require interoperability. Remember that most SCSI bus implementations can practically support a maximum of 18 devices.

Storage Device Options

Storage device options include disk drives (SCSI, fibre channel, and SSA), tape drives (SCSI and SSA), and optical disks (SCSI). These are very much the same options available for Windows NT servers and workstations, but we are now considering them in regard to how they can be used to improve cluster performance and data integrity, enhance the performance of cluster-aware applications, and provide backup for all data on the cluster. As you might expect, disk drives are the most relevant to the discussion in this chapter.

These three basic classes of devices—disk, tape, and optical—can all be used as either standalone drives or building blocks of larger systems such as RAID, automated tape libraries (ATLs), or optical jukeboxes (OJBs). These larger systems have more capacity on an aggregate basis along with supporting other features, such as RAID for fault tolerance and increased bandwidth and ATLs and OJBs for data archiving.

Disk Drives

The most prevalent capacities for disk drives (SCSI, FC, and SSA) today are 4, 9, and 18GB. Drives of 1 and 2GB have started to wane in the market, with 25GB and higher capacity drives becoming readily available. Essentially, the life of a particular disk drive capacity is about 18 months from introduction to maturity. It is important to be aware of this trend; when you purchase drives for your shared and non-shared storage requirements, you should get those with the longest market viability. This allows you to choose one vendor's product with a set configuration and then utilize it for the longest period of time before both user demands and economic pressures force you to move up to the next capacity point (usually two times larger from your present device). This tactic will also allow good access to additional drives if required during this time period. If you choose a drive capacity that is "obsolete" just because of its low price, there is a strong chance you will not only run out of capacity prematurely, but that you will not be able to purchase additional drives for expansion or replacement. Figure A-1 shows a 9GB Ultra-SCSI disk drive.

TAPE DRIVES   In the market, tape drives behave differently than disks. There are also different criteria for choosing a particular tape drive format. Tape drives are important to clusters because they provide a local backup/restore capability for that particular cluster.

NOTE: The use of distributed backups for clustering environments is recommended because backing up a large cluster over the network is just plain impractical. It is better to back up each cluster to its own backup drive or tape library/loader, unless you are using a SAN.

Tape format choices for MSCS begin with 4mm DDS and run all the way to half-an-inch-square cartridges and cassettes (e.g., IBM types 3490 and 3590). Overall

Figure A-1. A 9GB Ultra-SCSI disk drive
Photo reprinted permission of Western Digital Corporation

format choices include 8mm (e.g., Exabyte Mammoth, which is shown in Figure A-2, and Sony AIT) and Quantum DLT. A few more obscure choices from others are Sony DTF and Ampex DST. Each of these formats has its own particular attributes in terms of capacity, bandwidth, and cost (of the drive and the media). When choosing, you should be strongly influenced by the specifics of which one is native to the servers in the cluster.

OPTICAL DISK DRIVES   CD-ROM drives are read-only systems used primarily for data distribution and are included in every server and desktop unit regardless of application. They operate off the built-in EIDE controller on every motherboard, and for those reasons will not be discussed further, other than to say you cannot install either NTS/E or MSCS without one.

The optical disk drives that will be discussed are for archiving or long-term storage purposes. In an MSCS clustered environment they would typically be used on the non-shared SCSI bus, but that does not preclude them from being used on the shared bus in certain applications. Due to long-latency and low-bandwidth issues, they are not typically used for online storage purposes. With the adoption of Digital Video Disk (DVD) for data storage, this may change in the near future. In using all of these types of drives with Windows NT, you typically need a third-party optical file system product to make them behave well. In terms of supporting MSCS, it is envisioned that these drives

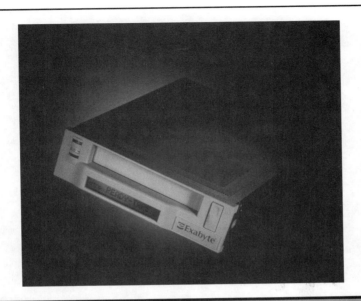

Figure A-2.   An 8mm Exabyte Mammoth tape drive
Photo reprinted with permission of Exabyte Corporation

will be installed in an optical jukebox. Figure A-3 shows a Compaq StorageWorks optical disk drive.

Storage Solution Options

Storage solutions are end-to-end storage subsytems that encompass the drives, an enclosure, control software, and any type of robotics required (for media movement).

The most prevalent storage solutions are RAID/JBOD (just a bunch of disks), automated tape libraries, and optical jukeboxes. Each of these utilizes a number of the drives that we discussed earlier, enclosed in some type of cabinet, with an internal scheme of interconnects for the drives and controllers (if required). In the case of both the automated tape library and the optical jukebox, they also utilize a robotic arm or "picker" to move the storage media from its storage area in the enclosure to and from the drives within it. Each of these solutions has a particular application in a clustered environment.

RAID

The most prevalent of the solution options is RAID. RAID is used is used in almost all cases to provide either higher levels of fault tolerance (via the addition of parity information to the data stream) or to increase overall I/O performance (via parallel

Figure A-3. A Compaq StorageWorks optical disk drive
Photo reprinted with permission of Compaq StorageWorks

striping of data across drives/volumes). There are also mixed classes of RAID, such as 0+1, which provide a mixture of both fault tolerance and wider bandwidth (or higher I/Os). All RAID solutions utilize different levels of redundancy (or parity, to use the vernacular) depending upon which level is used to support your fault-tolerance requirements. Most of these systems (i.e., RAID 0, 1, 5) will support the complete loss of a drive or volume without losing any data and are the mainstream storage solution for supporting all of the mission- and business-critical applications used across the enterprise. The majority of these RAID implementations are based on the assumption that users require a much higher number of read accesses versus write (high I/O counts, as opposed to raw bandwidth, for transaction-driven applications).

Other RAID configurations allow for increased I/O performance. These RAID levels (0, 1, and 3) allow you to split up the data stream into a RAID set and then parallelize it over multiple drives for higher I/O rates. These configurations provide support for large files and high write versus read environments and are used for such applications as video servers and data acquisition.

RAID sets can be created and managed either by software (included in NT Server is support for RAID 0 and 1) or by dedicated hardware controllers (RAID levels are configured via RAID management software or firmware residing on board the controller). In MSCS Phase 1, only hardware RAID can be used on the shared storage bus, while software RAID can be used for the EIDE boot and non-shared storage buses. In mixed, shared, and non-shared storage environments, you should use only hardware RAID, preferably a system that allows you to configure multiple RAID sets across all disks connected. You can then create an optimized RAID configuration for your shared data drives (and the applications that reside on them) as well as separate (but not necessarily different) RAID sets for your non-shared drives. This will also allow you to create a very robust and specific RAID set for the shared Quorum Resource drive, MSCS' only single point of failure. Figure A-4 provides two RAID options for MSCS.

Because MSCS is very specific about which storage solutions it supports, it is important to consult the Cluster HCL lists before choosing a particular HBA, controller, or RAID storage solution. The most up-to-date information can be found at **www.microsoft.com/hwtest/hcl**. This list grows each week as most of the early adopter partners are now self-certifying MSCS solutions and peripherals and are expanding the number of offerings overall.

Table A-2 provides a range of solution options that have all been approved by Microsoft for MSCS as of this writing. These options are limited to RAID and are a fraction of the overall HCL for Windows NT Server storage devices and solutions.

Figure A-4.   Some RAID Options for MSCS
Photos reprinted with permission of Compaq StorageWorks

Vendor	Model Number	Configuration	Interconnect
Amdahl	LVS4500	RAID	SCSI
AMI	MegaRaid	RAID	SCSI
Clariion	100	RAID	SCSI
Clariion	1000/2000	RAID	SCSI/FC
Clariion	3000	RAID	SCSI/FC
CMD	Viper II	RAID	SCSI
Compaq	ProLiant Storage	RAID	SCSI
Compaq	SMART Array	RAID	SCSI
Compaq	FC Array	RAID	FC
Dell	PowerRaid	RAID	SCSI
Digital	SW450	RAID	SCSI
Digital	SW 310	RAID	SCSI
Digital	SW 3000	RAID	SCSI
Digital	SW 7000	RAID	FC
Digital	SW 10000	RAID	FC
ECCS	Synchronix	RAID	SCSI
EMC	Symmetrix ICDA 3xxx	RAID	SCSI/FC
EMC	Symmetrix ICDA 5xxx	RAID	SCSI/FC
HP	Auto RAID	RAID	SCSI
HP	Model 30	RAID	FC
IBM	7133	RAID/JBOD	SSA
Siemens Nixdorf	PRIMERGY	RAID	SCSI
Symbios Logic	MetaStor 10E	RAID	SCSI
Symbios Logic	MetaStor 20	RAID	SCSI
Unisys	OSM3000-SC	RAID	SCSI

Table A-2. Storage Solution Options for MSCS

AUTOMATED TAPE LIBRARIES

Because MSCS will be used by many end-users for high-availability file and print services (with the emphasis on file servers), it is logical to assume the need to support archival storage. The most prevalent technology for data archiving continues to be magnetic tape.

While standalone tape drives or those with autoloaders are sufficient to support backup and restore, ATLs are the workhorses of data archiving. For a photo of a typical ATL, see Figure A-5.

These ATLs range in capacity from about 100GBs all the way up to tens of terabytes and support any type of drive format that you can imagine. All utilize SCSI as their interconnect of choice, with a few options available for those who prefer either fibre channel or SSA.

In most, if not all, cases when operating a tape archive system with MSCS, some number of tape drives in the ATL (one or two, typically) should be on a separate HBA for each node. (Each node essentially owns certain drives in the ATL, while sharing a common robotics mechanism.) Each node would then use another HBA (a shared bus) solely for robotics control purposes (raising the number of HBAs to three for each node).

When data from an ATL's tape drives is cached via a disk drive on the same bus as the tape drives, this creates a buffer to serve file requests coming from applications or users on the shared-storage bus in the cluster. Use of this architectural arrangement with MSCS creates a very highly available file server with essentially infinite capacity. For many Internet, intranet, or extranet sites, along with data warehouses, this type of data repository is highly desirable and is the primary requirement for using an ATL with MSCS.

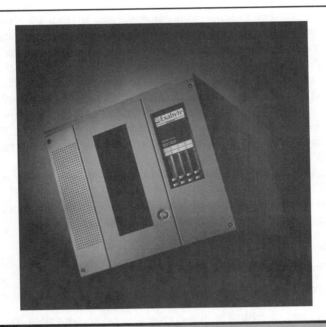

Figure A-5.   An automated tape library
Photo reprinted with permission of Exabyte Corporation

Optical Jukeboxes

Optical jukeboxes, or "jukes" as they are commonly referred to, fill a similar role to that of the ATL. They typically provide archiving of data on a long-term basis. The key differences between optical- and tape-based systems is that optical systems are random access in nature and they typically have substantially longer media life (with longer data protection). Tape systems, on the other hand, are sequential access and can last up to ten years if properly maintained, while optical disks can last up to 100 years under the same conditions. Most systems within MSCS environments are used for supporting data warehouses where large repositories of legacy and "filtered" data are required and access time is critical. A photo of an optical jukebox is shown in Figure A-6.

Again, it is anticipated that these jukes will be configured like their cousin the ATL, on a separate HBA and bus with hard-disk caching. Like the ATL, robotics control can be shared with another node over a shared SCSI bus so that both nodes on the cluster can utilize this device.

Storage Management (SM) Options

Storage systems for use in clustered environments require comprehensive cluster-aware storage management solutions to support them. If you use conventional, non-cluster-aware versions of popular SM applications they cannot access data properly on the shared-data bus and must be independently installed on all nodes with some accessibility to their databases by other nodes in the event of a failure. These solutions need to support the shared and non-shared storage devices on both nodes of the clusters. They need to be well behaved under all modes of operation (such as failover, failback, and node loss) without losing access to or control of data across the entire cluster. These requirements present special challenges for most solutions currently available, so only a few vendors have announced "enterprise editions" of their own in respect to Windows NT.

These enterprise editions include support for larger sized applications and SMPs, fibre-channel storage, and other non-cluster capabilities, as well as providing specific support for MSCS.

In terms of MSCS support, Cheyenne's ArcServe product is tightly integrated into its parent company CA's UniCenter TNG, which is cluster-aware, while Legato's NetWorker is a standalone cluster-aware storage management solution.

Storage management solutions provide the following functionality:

▼ Unattended and manual backup and restore

■ Hierarchical storage management (HSM)

▲ Data archiving and management

These functions are all critical to managing and protecting data, no matter where it resides in the cluster.

Figure A-6.   An optical disk jukebox
Photo reprinted with permission of Plasmon Corporation

The Windows NT Backup utility (a feature-disabled version of Seagate's Backup Exec) included in NTS/E is not currently cluster-aware despite Microsoft's promising to include a utility with MSCS. It is strongly recommended that you use this built-in capability only as a last resort. Be conscious of the fact that it must be used on each node independent of the other and will only provide backup to its "owned" disk resources. Restores will be difficult, if not impossible, if the node that created them is down or corrupted.

A comparison of the current leaders in storage management for NT Server is shown in Table A-3.

Choosing a storage management solution has far-reaching consequences. Contact the vendor who provided the balance of your enterprise and discuss the vendor's strategy and timetable for supporting MSCS. If you are not satisfied with the response, then you should consider an overall change, because piecemeal solutions for storage management can eventually be disastrous.

Vendor	Product Name	Current Version	Cluster-aware Yes/No
Cheyenne	ArcServe	6.5	Yes
IBM	ADSM	3.1	Yes
Legato	NetWorker	PE 4.4	Yes
Microsoft	NT Backup	NTS/E 4.0	No
Seagate	Backup Exec	7.2	Yes

Table A-3. Major Providers of Storage Management Solutions for Windows NT

SUMMARY

Storage requirements and options for MSCS need to be carefully considered well in advance of making a final decision. Even if these options are native to your vendor's overall MSCS solution, you should still give careful thought as to what overall capabilities and capacities they have to meet your particular requirements. Do not make a storage solution choice based solely on convenience, but rather based on how well it fits your actual needs.

Storage for MSCS requires careful attention to detail. You need to plan your requirements for storage while you are planning for the deployment of your cluster. Storage management should never be an afterthought and is equally as important in how well your cluster performs as the choice of CPU or applications that reside on it.

When in doubt refer to the Microsoft MSCS HCL for an up-to-date listing of the devices and solutions that have been tested extensively (either by Microsoft itself or through the self-certification process by the vendors) and blessed as being fully compatible with MSCS.

When considering a storage management solution, review each prospective vendor's offering to determine if it's "cluster-aware" in terms of conforming to the Wolfpack API. You can then compare it on an "apples and apples" basis with other offerings. In terms of functionality, it is important to choose a solution that meets your needs today as well as being expandable/upgradable in the future. Choosing a solution based on today's requirements alone leads you down a path to certain future disaster.

APPENDIX B

Cluster-Aware Applications, Tools, and Utilities Resource Guide

There are a growing number of cluster-aware software applications, tools, and utilities available today for MSCS users. This list is growing daily and, with the release of Windows 2000 in the not too distant future, it is sure to grow even faster. In this appendix, I provide a list of where to find these software resources on the Web in a demonstration or evaluation version. These demonstration/evaluation downloads provide good hands-on experience with these software applications, tools, and utilities prior to making your formal investment in them.

CLUSTER-AWARE APPLICATIONS

This group includes all of the major applications discussed in Chapter 9. For the most part, all are available in some form for evaluation or demonstration purposes. These typically are full-featured versions with 30 day expiration periods. Most are downloadable, but some are so large that you need to request an evaluation version on CD-ROM from the vendor.

Product Suites

In the Microsoft BackOffice Family, refer to these sites:

▼ *BackOffice Solutions Guide* **www.microsoft.com/backoffice**

▲ *Download Center* **www.backoffice.microsoft.com/downtrial/**

Mail and Messaging Solutions

For Microsoft Exchange, go to:

▼ **www.microsoft.com/exchange**

Relational Databases

For Microsoft SQL Server, see these sites:

▼ *Information* **www.microsoft.com/sql**

▲ *Evaluation CD Ordering Information* **www.microsoft.com/sql/70/trial.htm**

For IBM/Lotus Domino (Server) and Notes (Client), see:

▲ **www.lotus.com**

For information on IBM Universal Database EEE, go to:

▲ **www.software.ibm.com/data/db2/udb/udb-eeed.html**

For information on the Oracle8 family:

▼   *Information*   **www.ntsolutions/Oracle.com/products**

▲   **www.Oracle.com/download**

For Informix Dynamic Server, refer to the following site:

▲   **www.informix.com/informix/solutions/nt/**

For SyBase's Universal Database, got to this Web site:

▲   **www.sybase.com/products/databaseservers/ase/**

To learn about Compaq/Tandem SQL/MX, go to:

▲   **www.tandem.com**

Enterprise Resource Planning

For information on SAP R/3, go to:

▲   **www.sap.com/products**

To learn about Baan Version IV, see this site:

▲   **www.baan.com**

For PeopleSoft 6.5, go to:

▲   **www.peoplesoft.com/en/products_solutions/**

Enterprise Systems Management

For information about Computer Associates Unicenter TNG, go to this Web site:

▲   **www.cai.com/products/uctr.htm**

MSCS Management

Go to the following Web site for more information about NuView ClusterX:

▲   **www.nuview.com**

Storage Management

For more information on Legato Networker, go to the following sites:

▼   *Product Information*   **www.legato.com**

▲   **www.legato.com/Products/html/request_trial.html**

To learn more about IBM/Tivoli ADSM V3.X, go to:

▲ **www.storage.ibm.com/software/adsm/adsmhome.htm**

For more information on Seagate Software Backup Exec, see:

▲ **www.seagatesoftware.com/bewinnt/**

Go to this site for more information on Computer Associates ArcServeIT:

▲ **www.CAI.com/arcserveit/**

For the Hewlett Packard Omni back II resource, see the following Web site:

▲ **www.openview.hp.com/omniback/**

Microsoft Windows Load balancing Server

To learn more about Microsoft/Valence WLBS a.k.a. Convoy Cluster Solution, go here:

▲ **Www.microsoft.com/ntserverenterprise**

OTHER APPLICATIONS, TOOLS, AND UTILITIES

These "add-ons" adds functionality and performance enhancements to existing off-the-shelf products such as Microsoft Exchange. They also provide unique "vendor-specific" capabilities to particular hardware solutions. These too are available in demonstration or evaluation form for your review prior to purchase.

▼ *Compaq Storage and Cluster Software Extensions for Windows NT*
   www.compaq.com/products/software/ntenterprise/

■ *Application Development demonstration and evaluation versions*
   www.compaq.com/products/software/ntenterprise

■ *Batch Job Scheduler*   **www.windowsNT.digital.com/products/software/entsw/**

▲ *Reliable Transaction Router*   **www.software.digital.com/RTR/**

SUMMARY

As discussed earlier in this book there is no formal "certification" or "logo-ing" for MSCS cluster-aware applications, tools, and utilities. It is the responsibility of individual vendors to note this feature in their product descriptions so you know just what you are buying. It is anticipated at some point in the future that Microsoft will modify their BackOffice logo program to include "cluster-awareness" and that any BackOffice application after that point in time will be fully MSCS aware.

APPENDIX C

MSCS Resource Guide

ecause Microsoft Cluster Server is a relatively new product and a new type of technology for Microsoft and the Independent Software Vendors (ISV) partners, it can be difficult to find comprehensive information about MSCS, clustering, and MSCS's companion products (such as cluster-aware applications, utilities, and tools). This Resource Guide provides a detailed listing (by subject) of those resources that are of value. You will find the resources listed by both vendor and subject area. You will also find guides to where this information can be obtained online, as well as where to download white papers on a variety of subjects pertaining to MSCS. We also provide a listing of books, magazine articles, and collateral material that the reader might find beneficial.

RESOURCES FOR YOUR CLUSTER

Most organizations have embraced the Web as a means of information dissemination, so this appendix provides the addresses of the Web sites that contain the most pertinent information resources. Most of these Web sites do not provide pathways to other sites with related information. In that respect, the sites listed here represent a good starting point, and many point you to finding the information you want. In some cases, it is up to you to muster the patience necessary to "drill down" to the actual location where the desired information can be found.

Overview

Microsoft provides MSCS to the marketplace by two methods: Direct to OEMs who install NTS/E and MSCS on their cluster solutions for sale through a variety of sales and distribution methods. These solutions are certified by Microsoft (or by the vendor with Microsoft's blessing) as being fully compliant with the MSCS hardware standard (and as having passed certain tests).

The second method is direct to end users or other upgraders who purchase NTS/E from either their local Microsoft reseller (which is usually the route taken by end users) or one of Microsoft's distribution partners (which is the resellers' route) and are planning to use existing and new assets to build clusters from.

In both cases, the product comes with a minimum of documentation. The manuals and installation CD-ROMs are pretty thin so the buyer doesn't get much for his or her money. (NTS/E is currently priced at $4000 per node.)

Those OEMs who are Microsoft Alliance partners (and some lower visibility types as well) have the benefit of a close working relationship between their engineering and test personnel and those of Microsoft's. These relationships foster better information exchange, and in most cases, the OEM has a considerable volume of information that can be provided in their product manuals and training curricula.

However, in the early stages of the development of a product like MSCS, this type of information is often closely held and is not readily available to early adopters who want to understand this new technology and who want to develop plans for its orderly introduction into their computing environments. Hence, one of the reasons for writing this book is to readily provide the early adopters, as well as the information-starved end users and administrators, with a comprehensive knowledge base on the subject of MSCS and NT clusters.

Microsoft Resources

Microsoft has a wealth of information on MSCS—if you can just find it. The majority if it can be found on their Web site, but it also exists in other forms such as the Microsoft Developer Network (MSDN) and *Tech Net* (a CD-ROM subscription available from Microsoft).

Online

The main Web site for Microsoft is **www.microsoft.com**. This is the front door to a vast warehouse of information resources and marketing information. It is difficult, however, to navigate through this maze without establishing specific starting points by subject. These starting points are key to maximizing your efficiency in gathering specific information from Microsoft before you run out of patience or are refused by the server due to too many connections at one time.

- ▼ *MSCS*   **www.microsoft.com/ntserverenterprise** (general information on NTS/E and MSCS)
- *NT Server (4.0 and 5.0)*   **www.microsoft.com/ntserver** (NT server family)
- *MSCS Strategy and Deployment* **www.microsoft.com/ntserver/guide/whitepapers**
- *MSCS Training and Certification*   **www.microsoft.com/training** (keywords for course searches are "NT server" and "MSCS")
- *MSCS Support Information*   **www.microsoft.com/support** (keywords for searches are "cluster" and "MSCS")
- *Windows NT Hardware Compatibility List*   **www.microsoft.com/hwtest/hcl** (choose category "NT Server")
- *MSCS Certified Hardware Compatibility List*   **www.microsoft.com/hwtest/hcl** (choose category "Cluster")
- *Windows NT Enterprise Edition/MSCS "Hot Fix" Site* **ftp://ftp.microsoft.com/bussys/winnt/winnt-public/fixes/usa/nt40/hotfixes-postSP3/postsp3.txt** contains information on all hot fixes for MSCS
- *Microsoft Exchange EE*   **www.microsoft.com/exchange** (Exchange 5.5 Enterprise Edition)
- *Microsoft SQL Server EE*   **www.microsoft.com/sql/** (SQL Server 4.0 and 7.0 Enterprise Edition)
- *MSCS SDK*   **www.microsoft.com/msdn/sdk** (a valid ID and password are required to get beyond the basics)

- *BackOffice Applications Information* **www.backoffice.microsoft.com**
- *Windows NT Direct Access (Reseller program)* **www.microsoft.com/directaccess**
- ▲ *Alliance News Page* **www.microsoft.com/corpinfo/**

CD-ROM Subscriptions

Microsoft has two CD-ROM products that provide monthly and quarterly mailings containing an accumulation of information (and software applications, utilities, tools, patches, etc.) on all products. Within either of these products you can find a wealth of information about MSCS:

- ▼ *Microsoft Tech Net* **www.microsoft.com/technet**
- ▲ *Microsoft Developer Program* **www.microsoft.com/msdn** (three levels available with various deliverables)

Both of these products are available through annual subscriptions. *Tech Net* costs about $300 for a single user, and MSDN offers a multitier subscription, starting at around $500 and going up to about $2000. All of these subscriptions are worth their weight in gold for staying abreast of what Microsoft is up to with MSCS. In addition, they provide a wealth of patches, bug fixes, technical bulletins, SDKs (software development kits), and more. Participating in these services should be factored into your overall MSCS acquisition and deployment plan.

Early Adopter Hardware Partners

There are seven early adopter hardware partners, and each has its own online resource that provides information on MSCS and how each supports it. We list them here in alphabetical order.

Compaq Computer Corporation

Compaq's participation in MSCS is huge. Compaq itself is the largest provider of NT servers in the market, and their two newly acquired subsidiaries, Tandem and Digital (assuming the acquisition of Digital goes through), also contribute to Compaq's participation in MSCS.

Compaq has both a Web site and a fax-back documentation service, both of which provide information on their MSCS products and services, as well as their recently announced E2000 architecture for Windows NT in enterprise computing environments.

- ▼ *Compaq* **www.compaq.com/business** (servers and clusters)
- ▲ *Compaq/Microsoft Alliance* **www.compaq.com/partners/Microsoft** (NT 4 and NT 5 solutions)

Data General Corporation

Data General Corporation, or DG as they are known, has a number of information resources available on their Web site. Their customer base is very transaction-oriented so a lot of materials on their site caters to the requirements of these customers. DG also offers a "cluster-in-a-box" product family that uses either MSCS or Veritas' First Watch.

▼   *Data General*   **www.dg.com/products**

▲   *DG/Microsoft Alliance*   **www.dg.com/nt/**

Digital Equipment Corporation

Now a subsidiary of Compaq Computers, Digital is recognized by most in the industry as the undisputed leader in clustering. They were first to market in the early 1980s, and they have more than 75,000 systems in the field today. Their Web site contains vast amounts of information, and their technical journal, which is published each month, and their NT Wizards Symposiums, which are held throughout the world each year, also provide cluster resources.

Windows NT and clustering are Digital's major focuses, and all of their sites have something to say in regards to technology, products, and strategy. We recommend you start at their main Web address and then move to the particular area of interest that you currently have.

▼   *Digital*   **www.digital.com/products**

■   *Microsoft/Digital Alliance*   **www.alliance.digital.com/alliance/Microsoft**

■   *Digital Technical Journal*   **www.digital.com/DTJL01/**

▲   *NT Wizards*   **www.nt-wizards.com**

Hewlett-Packard Corporation

HP's Web site has a wide variety of information on their Windows NT/MSCS endeavors as well as on clustering in general. Their focus is on leading the pack in terms of supporting the coexistence of Windows NT and UNIX for enterprise computing environments. A lot of the information at their site is slanted towards this coexistence, as well as on integration of Windows NT into their existing customer's UNIX environments.

▼   *HP*   **www.hp.com /computing**

■   *HP NT*   **www.hp.com/netserver/index.htm**

▲   *HP/Microsoft Alliance*   **www.hp.com/wcso-support/Microsoft/html**

IBM Corporation

IBM has a rich legacy in clustering for their proprietary platforms (e.g., S/390 and AIX) and has been a major contributor to MSCS. On the Web they have a vast amount of information on their MSCS endeavors, as well as those for other platforms:

▼   *IBM*   **www.ibm.com/netfinity** or **www.pc.ibm.com/us/netfinity**
(NetFinity servers and MSCS)

■   *Information Redbooks*   **www.redbooks.ibm.com**

▲   *Other Clustering Solutions (AIX, S/390)*   **www.ibm.com**

Intel Corporation

Intel is the odd man out in this collaboration (as we discussed in earlier section of the book) but they nonetheless have "a lot of skin in the game" in terms of MSCS. You can find information relating to MSCS, VIA, and the emerging server hardware standards for Windows 2000 at the following site, as well as through links to other sites:

▼ *Intel*   **www.developer.intel.com/design/tech.htm**

NCR Corporation

NCR is another pioneer in clustering, and they have solutions based on MSCS as well as their own product, LifeKeeper (non-MSCS compatible). You can find information on these efforts as well as on their alliance with Microsoft at the following sites:

▼ *NCR*   **www.ncr.com/products**

▲ *NCR/Microsoft Alliance*   **www3.ncr.com/products/msalliance**

Tandem Computer Corporation (A Compaq Company)

Tandem, like Digital, is an early innovator in the field of clustering and made major contributions to MSCS. They have a number of sites that contain information on their clustering solutions for NT (MSCS and CAS) as well as on their cluster interconnect (ServerNet) and their cluster-aware software solutions (such as Non-Stop Lite, SQL/MX, etc.) Start at their main site, and click on links until you find what you are looking for. They too, have a site for their alliance with Microsoft.

▼ *Tandem*   **www.tandem.com** (choose "Products," then "Windows NT & Clusters")

▲ *Tandem/Microsoft Alliance*   **www.bizcritical.com**

Other MSCS Solution Providers

A number of other hardware vendors signed on for MSCS after the early adopters started their joint development efforts. These other vendors have substantial product and technology information as well. A listing of their sites follows:

▼ *Dell Computer*   **www.dell.com**

■ *Micron Computer*   **www.micron.com**

■ *Siemens Nixdorf*   **www.sni.com**

■ *Fujitsu Computer*   **www.fujitsu.com**

▲ *NEC Computer*   **www.nec.com**

Vendors with MSCS Cluster-Aware Applications

As discussed in detail previously in the book, mission- and business-critical applications drive the enterprise and the need for clustering. These applications come from a number of key vendors and cut across many functional boundaries. The following sites, listed by vendor and product, are major sources of information on the particulars of each product, its integration with MSCS, and its day-to-day operation:

▼ *Oracle Corporation* **www.oracle.com/nt/products/uds/oracle8** (Fail-Safe, Oracle8 for Windows NT, and Parallel Server)

■ *Software AG (SAP)* **www.sap.com** (SAP for Windows NT)

■ *Baan Corporation* **www.baan.com** (Baan IV for Windows NT)

■ *PeopleSoft, Inc.* **www.peoplesoft.com** (PeopleSoft 7.5 for Windows NT)

■ *IBM/Lotus* **www.lotus.com** (Domino Server)

■ *IBM* **www.software.ibm.com/is/mp/nt** (DB2 Universal Server)

■ *Tandem Computer Corporation* **www.tandem.com** (SQL/MX for Windows NT)

■ *Computer Associates* **www.cai.com** (UniCenter TNG, ArcServe)

■ *BEA Corporation* **www.beasys.com** (Tuxedo MW for Windows NT)

▲ *Legato Corporation* **www.legato.com** (Networker Power Edition)

Other Clustering Solution Providers

As discussed previously, both collaborative and competitive solutions are available for MSCS. A list of vendors, their respective products, and their Web sites follows. These sites supply good information on not only products and technology, but the vendors' relationship with MSCS.

▼ *Digital Equipment Corporation* **www.digital.com** (Digital Clusters[+] for Windows NT)

■ *Tandem Computer Corporation* **www.tandem.com** (Cluster Availability Solution, Non-Stop Lite)

■ *Veritas* **www.veritas.com** (First Watch)

■ *Vinca* **www.vinca.com** (Standby-Server and Co-Standby Server)

■ *Legato* **www.legato.com** (Octopus HA[+])

■ *Oracle* **www.oracle.com** (Parallel Server)

■ *IBM/Lotus* **www.lotus.com** (Domino Server)

■ *IBM* **www.software.ibm** (DB2 HA)

▲ *Marathon* **www.marathontechnologies.com** (Endurance 4000)

Magazines Focused on Windows NT

The success of Windows NT has spawned the formation of a number of industry publications focused on NT for the enterprise customer. All of these publications feature articles and advice by industry insiders and vendor spokespeople. These magazines are a reliable source of information and provide tips on MSCS, its applications, and competing and collaborative solutions.

- ▼ *Windows NT Magazine*   **www.winntmag.com**
- ■ *BackOffice Magazine*   **www.backoffice.com**
- ■ *Windows NT Systems Magazine*   **www.ntsystems.com**
- ■ *ENT Magazine*   **www.entmag.com**
- ▲ *Selling NT Solutions*   **www.sellingnt.com**

The following are magazines focused on clusters and clustering for Windows NT:

- ▼ *ComputerWorld Magazine*   **www.computerworld.com**
- ▲ *Information Week Magazine*   **www.pubs.cmpnet.com/iw**

Information Technology Consulting Firms

The IT industry is dominated by a number of so-called "independent consulting firms" who sell advice to both end users and vendors. They are the self-appointed gurus of technology and market direction, in spite of most of them having no "hands-on" capabilities at all. Nonetheless, they do produce their weight in publications, many of which are posted on their Web sites in abbreviated form to whet your appetite. They are a source of specifics on market size and provide analyses of trends. In addition, they can be of assistance in helping you make your business case to management in terms of using MSCS.

- ▼ *Aberdeen Group*   **www.aberdeen.com**
- ■ *Find/SVP*   **www.find.com**
- ■ *Forrester Research*   **www.forrester.com**
- ■ *Dataquest*   **www.dataquest.com**
- ■ *Gartner Group*   **www.gartner.com**
- ■ *Giga Info. Group*   **www.gigaweb.com**
- ■ *Hurwitz Consulting Group*   **www.hurwitz.com**
- ■ *IDC Research*   **www.idcresearch.com**
- ■ *Jupiter Communications*   **www.jupiter.com**
- ■ *Meta Group*   **www.metagroup.com**
- ■ *Yankee Group*   **www.yankeegroup.com**
- ▲ *Zona Research*   **www.zonaresearch.com**

For More Information

As a value added service to readers of this book, please visit my company's Web site (**www.dst.com**) for information updates and links to other sites that contain pertinent topics regarding each phase of *Microsoft Cluster Server—MSCS*. My company, Data Storage Technologies, is a management and technology consultantcy. We are actively involved in supporting clients with issues and opportunities surrounding Windows NT in the Enterprise.

ADDITIONAL READING ON CLUSTERS

Books:

Pfister, Gregory K., *In Search of Clusters*. New Jersey: Prentice Hall, Inc., 1998.

Articles/Journals:

Lee, Richard R. "A Technology Brief: Tandem Clustering Technologies," *Windows NT Magazine*, June 1997.

Digital Equipment Corporation Technical Journal (online edition), **www.digital.com/DTJL01/**

"Clustering—A Market Opportunity Analysis," Strategic Research Corporation analyst report, **www.sresearch.com**

"Hardware Design Guide Version 1.0 for Microsoft Windows NT Server," Intel and Microsoft Corporations, 10/10/97, **www.microsoft.com/hwdev/xpapers/nt/welcome.htm**

"High Availability for Clusters: Functional Analysis," D.H. Brown Associates, Inc. analyst report, **www.dhbrown.com**

"Making Enterprise-Class Clusters Come Alive," Tandem Computer Corporation white paper, **www.tandem.com**

"Microsoft Windows NT Server Cluster Strategy: High Availability and Scalability with Industry-Standard Hardware," Microsoft Business Systems Division white paper, **www.microsoft.com/NTServer**

"Virtual Interface Architecture Specification Version 1.0." Intel, Compaq, and Microsoft Corporations, 12/16/97, **www.viarch.org/**

GLOSSARY

A
s with any popular technology today, cluster server has its own language and code words. Much of the vernacular associated with clustering has been around for some time now, but with the development of MSCS, Microsoft and its partners have invented some new terms of their own. This appendix includes as many of these terms and their definitions as possible.

A

American Power Systems (APS)   A provider of UPS and line conditioning equipment for computer applications.

Ampex DST   A 19mm helical scan tape recording systems for high-capacity, wide-bandwidth storage requirements.

Atomic Consistent Isolated Durable (ACID)   An acronym for rules to be used in database systems design.

Automated tape libraries (ATLs)   A robotics device and enclosure for use with tape drives to increase overall capacity (TBs+), while keeping data close to online and in a small physical enclosure.

Availability   The time that a system is capable of providing service to its users (that is, uptime). It is expressed as a percentage that represents the ratio of the time in which the system provides acceptable service versus the total time during which the system is expected to be operational. (As a point of reference, consider that some potential 525,500 minutes of uptime are in a year.) % availability is calculated in the following manner:

$$\% \text{ availability} = \frac{\text{(total time in interval (year)} - \text{total amount of downtime)}}{\text{total time in interval (year)}}$$

B

Backup Domain Controller (BDC)   The NT server that contains a copy of the domain user account information from the PDC. It is available to authenticate users when they log on to the domain and can be promoted to PDC if the usual primary controller becomes unavailable due to a failure or outage.

Bus   A collection of conductors (wires or circuit board traces) used to transmit data and status and control signals.

C

Central Processing Unit (CPU) The part of the computer where instructions are executed. It is typically a CISC or RISC microprocessor mounted on a motherboard with local memory and support chipsets, along with interfaces to all other major subsystems under the control of the CPU—subsystems such as disk memory, input/output devices, display devices, and so on.

Cluster A group of independent systems (nodes) working together as a single system; that is, they operate as a single processing system and appear that way to users connected to the cluster.

Cluster-aware application An application that can run on a cluster node and be managed as a cluster resource. Cluster-aware applications are required to conform to the Cluster (Wolfpack) API to insure proper interaction with the services supported by MSCS.

Cluster.exe The CLI alternative to the Cluster Administrator. It is used for manual and automated control (via scripts) of the MSCS cluster.

Cluster Administrator (CA) CluAdmin.exe—the graphical user interface tool for managing and controlling MSCS (cluster server).

Cluster Availability Solution (CAS) An early Windows NT clustering solution developed by Tandem and used as a testbed for many of the concepts used in MSCS Phase 1. CAS continues to be supported by Tandem today.

Cluster Interconnect (CI) Otherwise known as Computer Interconnect, CI was developed by Digital during the early days of VAX clusters. It is a multiple path type of controller interface for connecting storage peripherals to CPUs. It can operate in the range of 70-140Mb/s.

Cluster log Log data stored by MSCS on the Quorum Resource. This data is maintained by MSCS and is used to determine which node owns the QR as well as which nodes are in the cluster.

Cluster Types Clusters come in many types and forms. Each subscribes to the basic definition, but their implementations and tasks performed are very different. Types of clusters include Server clusters (middleware and mirroring type), IP Load Balancing clusters, SAN clusters, and Switched SCSI clusters.

Server clusters are back-end clustering solutions that utilize either middleware or mirroring (or both) to provide high-availability and scalability on servers using failover and data copying techniques.

IP Load Balancing clusters are front-end clustering solutions that utilize software (and IP routing hardware) to manage incoming IP requests for static-type Web pages and other services. This software examines IP load traffic and routes requests to those servers that have the most available capacity to respond in the shortest time.

SAN clustering solutions utilize availability management software to create a high-availability environment for servers and storage resources that are interconnected in a storage area network.

Switched SCSI clusters utilize software and SCSI switches to create a high-availability environment for servers and applications by switching over the storage assets from one server to another in the event of a failure. The failover server assumes the identity of the failed server and continues its work after re-starting applications and services.

D

Dependency   Refers to the relationship of reliance between two resources such that both must run in the same failover group on the same node. At a minimum, an application is dependent upon the physical disk that contains its data.

Dependency tree   A tool for visualizing the dependency relationships between resources in a failover group. It is created as a block diagram with lines showing the interdependencies among all resources and the order or hierarchy that they reside in.

Differential   A SCSI bus transmission format where each signal is carried by two wires. The resultant signal is derived by taking the difference in voltage between the two wires, virtually eliminating all noise and interference in the process.

Digital Data Storage (DDS)   A magnetic tape format for storing computer data based on the use of the DAT helical scan tape system. It is available in three versions—DDS, DDS-2, and DDS-3, each of which has varying levels of capacity and bandwidth.

Digital Video Disk (DVD)   A (relatively) small diameter, high-capacity optical disk format for consumer video and professional applications.

Distributed Lock Manager (DLM)   Used in shared-disk clusters to arbitrate and serialize requests for data.

E

Enhanced Integrated Drive Electronics (EIDE or ATA)   A disk drive electronics interface specification developed by Western Digital in 1993 and licensed to all disk drive manufacturers worldwide. It is the de facto standard today for all PC-type disk drives.

Enterprise computing   A term that is bandied about the marketplace, but few products have the actual experience and capabilities to step up to this level of reliability, scalability, and bandwidth. Simply put, enterprise computing is availability from every dimension. This equates to both a high level of serviceability and linear scalability.

F

Failback   The process of moving groups and resources to their preferred node after the failed node has come back online (i.e., the heartbeat is reestablished).

Failover   The process in a MSCS cluster where one node's Groups and Resources are taken offline (due to a fault or network outage that was detected or taken off manually via the Cluster Administrator) and then transferred to the surviving node, where they are brought back online. The surviving node on the cluster can then execute those applications previously running on the faulted node and continue processing from the point where the last valid process was executed. In database applications, for example, this would require examining the log file from the faulted node, rolling back the database to that point where a valid record was last processed, and then restarting the database from there. Whatever data was in process at the time of the fault is lost and must be re-entered.

Failover policies   Developed as plans of action for the cluster manager to use in the event of a failure. These policies directly affect the failover groups and their resources and are determined by the cluster system administrator. These policies include the following items:

▼ Which node will be primary for each failover group

■ Which groups will failover automatically, which failure manually, and which not at all

■ How failback will occur—that is, automatically or manually

▲ Which nodes will participate in failover/failback (MSCS Phase 2)

Fault-tolerance Refers to a class of computing architectures where a mechanism is in place to switch over to another processor when a hardware or other fault is encountered to achieve some level of continued operation without loss of data. Fault-tolerance also refers to system availability in the range of 99.9 percent and is achieved through the use of highly refined design and manufacturing techniques.

Fibre Channel (FC) A family of standards for interconnecting storage devices and subsystems based on the use of either copper or optical cable and connectors. Two forms of FC are dominant today: FC-Arbitrated Loop and FC-Switched. Both support long distances, high data rates, and a large number of devices on any bus.

File share resource A file share that is accessible by a network path and is a cluster resource. It is also called an *SMB share*.

G

Generic application resource A resource DLL in MSCS that supports undefined applications that are available for failover.

Generic service resource A resource DLL in MSCS that supports undefined services that are available for failover.

Group (or failover group) A collection of dependent and related resources that are managed as a single entity by MSCS. A Group usually contains all the resources necessary to run an application or provide a service.

H

Hardware Compatibility List (HCL) A list provided and maintained by Microsoft of all devices and systems that they have certified to be fully compliant with their software.

Heartbeat (or Cluster Heartbeat) A message (signal) that is sent once per second (typically) between nodes in the cluster by the Cluster Service (on the primary node) to detect failures.

Hierarchical Storage Management (HSM) A rules-based data migration utility that moves data from online to offline storage media (and back again) based on the last access date and system resource availability.

High availability Refers to a scenario in which an application may be distributed over more than one node achieving some degree of parallelism, along with failure recovery, and therefore more availability.

High Availability Cluster Multi-Processing (HACMP) IBM's RS/6000 RISC /AIX-based clustering solution for high-performance computing applications.

Host Bus Adapters (HBAs) Electronic interface cards for SCSI-based systems. HBAs bridge the gap between the CPU motherboard (PCI) and the SCSI devices.

I

IIS virtual root resource The virtual root designator used with Microsoft Internet Information Server to support WWW, Gopher, and FTP services. It is supported by MSCS as a resource DLL.

Interconnect or Cluster Interconnect (CI) The path (in a private or public network) that ties all the nodes together in terms of heartbeat and cluster data. These interconnects can be either dedicated (private, the preferred mode) or shared (public, with clients) and range in technology from Ethernet (all types and speed) to ATM, with technologies such as Tandem's ServerNet being the emerging standard (VIA).

Internet Information Server (IIS) An internet/intranet application suite provided by Microsoft and bundled with Windows NT Server.

IP address resource A 32-bit number in dotted decimal format that represents the IP address for a virtual server created under MSCS using its resource DLL for IP addressing.

J

Just a bunch of disks (JBOD) A group of disk drives housed in an internal or external chassis, where each drive is independent from each other (non-RAID).

L

Load balancing (either static or dynamic) Activities performed by cluster systems administrators to insure that all nodes in the cluster are properly sized and contain sufficient resources to operate efficiently under both normal and failover conditions.

M

Massively Parallel Processors (MPP) A computer with hundreds to thousands of individual CPUs operating in parallel who share the OS, main memory, and I/O devices. This class of machine is used to divide large computational workloads into hundreds and/or thousands of sections for independent and parallel processing.

Mean Time Between Failure (MTBF) A metric used by many organizations to indicate the average time between failures of a system or its components. MTBF is determined using the following formula: MTBF = (total operating time (uptime))/ total number of failures.

Memory Channel (MC) A CPU interconnect technology pioneered by Digital and introduced in 1996. It operates at approximately 100MB/s.

Microsoft Cluster Server (MSCS) A two-node clustering service developed by Microsoft and seven early adopter partners. It was released as Phase 1 in September 1997 as part of Windows NT 4.0 Enterprise Edition.

Microsoft Message Queue Server (MMQS) A message store and forwarding application bundled by Microsoft with Windows NT Server.

Microsoft Transaction Server (MTS) An electronic commerce application bundled by Microsoft with Windows NT Server.

Middleware The layer of software between the operating system and the applications that reside on it. Middleware allows OS and application developers to write their software with the understanding that it is transportable from one platform to another that uses the same APIs and middleware structures. MSCS is considered a type of middleware.

Mirroring type cluster A type of cluster that utilizes disk mirroring as the primary method of producing high availability. Data from each node is mirrored on other nodes in the cluster using high speed interconnects. In the event of a failure, the surviving node utilizes the mirrored data to continue work on applications and services unavailable from the primary node.

MSMQ resource Used to support the MSMQ application in a cluster-aware configuration via a resource DLL.

N

Network File System (NFS) Developed by Sun Microsystems for their SunOS/Solaris operating environment (UNIX). It is the de facto file system in use today in client/server computing environments.

Network name resource A DLL-supported resource for defining names in failover groups that operate as virtual servers.

Node A server entity, whether it is a SMP processor box, storage system, or some other device, that is interconnected to other server entities (nodes) within a cluster. In MSCS Phase 1 there is support for two nodes, so it is assumed that they are processors with like configurations to support failover-type high availability. In MSCS Phase 2 there will be multi-node support (N-nodes up to 16+), which can not only be multiple SMP boxes, but storage systems and high speed peripherals, all in a switched data mode for takeover-type fault tolerance.

N-node clustering Advanced, multinode clusters (MSCS Phase 2) that can have many nodes configured in a variety of manners to provide true fault tolerance, linear scalability, and so forth.

Non-Uniform Memory Access (NUMA) An alternative computer architecture to that of the SMP, NUMA eliminates many of the memory management problems and bus contention issues found in SMP systems by its local caching as well as its non-uniform access to main memory.

NTS/E Windows NT Server 4.0 Enterprise Edition A high-end version of Windows NT 4.0 that was released in September 1997 for use by enterprise computing customers. It features MSCS Phase 1 and a number of cluster-aware applications and services, along with supporting more memory for applications and higher number SMPs for scalability enhancements.

O

Offline   A state in MSCS where a component is marked as unavailable. Nodes that are offline may continue to operate but are not part of the cluster that is operating at the time.

Online   A state in MSCS where a component is made fully available. Online nodes are active members of the current cluster and can own and manipulate Groups and Resources, as well as honor cluster database updates, contribute votes to the quorum algorithm, and maintain heartbeats.

Optical Jukeboxes (OJBs)   Optical disk drives and robotics mechanisms housed together in an enclosure for quicker access times and higher storage capacities.

P

Paused   A state in MSCS where a node is a fully active member of the cluster but cannot own or run failover groups and their resources. It is a state provided for maintenance purposes.

Pending   A state in MSCS where a resource is either being brought online or taken offline.

Physical disk resource   A shared-bus disk or volume used for storing shares and application data. It is the most fundamental resource in all failover groups and is supported by a resource DLL in MSCS.

Preferred node   A node in MSCS that is the default location for a failover group. It is used for establishing static load balancing during the setup of applications on an MSCS cluster.

Primary Domain Controller (PDC)   The server (node) that primarily manages all of the domain user account information. There can be only one per domain, and it is recommended that there only be one domain for all of the MSCS clusters in order to reduce server overhead due to logons and trusts.

Print Spooler resource   A resource that provides access to print queues for network attached printers that are configured as virtual servers. It is supported by a resource DLL in MSCS.

Private network   Used only for node-to-node communications within a cluster.

Public network   Is primarily used for client-to-cluster communications within a cluster but can also support node-to-node communications if required.

Q

Quantum DLT   A magnetic tape drive format based on the use of multi-track longitudinal recording technology and high-capacity data cartridges. Originally developed by Digital and later sold to Quantum, DLT is one of the de facto tape formats for use as backup/restore and archiving of systems data.

Quorum   A mathematical formula that uses the number of votes that are expected from all the nodes in a particular cluster to form the cluster and to determine ownership of the Quorum Resource.

Quorum Resource (QR)   More than a DLL-defined resource in MSCS capable of supporting the cluster's quorum activities (polling, voting, and so on), it is the heart of the cluster itself. The QR is a physical disk or volume that contains all the data relating to changes in the cluster database and is central to the operation of the cluster. It uses a voting mechanism to guarantee that all data necessary for the cluster to operate is owned only by one node at a time, and should a failure occur, it transfers itself to the surviving node to insure that the cluster remains available.

R

Redundancy   The removal of single points of failure by the duplication of key and critical hardware and software components.

Redundant Array of Independent Disks (RAID)   Based on the use of parity drives or sectors to overcome single level failures in storage devices. It can be implemented in either hardware or software, with varying levels of performance based on the RAID configuration chosen (0 through 5 are the basic implementation levels). Only hardware RAID can be used to support fault-tolerance on MSCS Phase 1 systems.

Reliability   Very similar to *availability* in terms of expectations by computer users. It is usually referred to as the number of expected failures (statistically) within a certain time interval (for example, MTBF). Availability is expressed in regards to the absence of failures.

Resource A physical or logical entity managed by a cluster node. All MSCS resources used a DLL written specifically to meet their needs based on the Wolfpack API (which is a collection of entry points, callback functions, and related macros used to manage resources).

Resource Monitor (RM) A mechanism used by MSCS to monitor the status of all resources in a group and/or cluster. Resources with high levels of risk in terms of cluster/application availability may be monitored independently by the cluster server to insure maximum performance. The Resource Monitor is an interface between the Cluster Service and the cluster resources and runs as an independent process. It is used by the Cluster Service to communicate with the Resource DLLs.

S

Scalability The ability of a system to increase its computing power by adding either additional processors or nodes (clusters). The addition of these processors or computing nodes is typically not a linear function because extra system overhead is usually associated with this process. An SMP processor or cluster is considered linearly scalable when the execution time speeds up linearly by the addition of additional processors—for example, the addition of one processor = 1×, two processors = 2×, and so forth.

Scalable Coherent Interface (SCI) A cluster interconnect standard developed by IEEE/ANSI in 1992. It features a NUMA-type I/O model and is designed to be scalable in bandwidth depending upon implementation.

Serial Storage Architecture (SSA) A moderate speed, medium bus length, storage interconnect bus.

Server Message Block (SMB) A protocol used by Windows NT to allow computers to access a shared resource as if it were local (similar to NPS for UNIX).

ServerNet A server-area network architecture for cluster interconnection developed by Tandem and endorsed by Microsoft, Compaq, and Intel for use with the Virtual Interface Architecture standard for cluster interconnects. It features high speed and low latency for maximum speed in data integrity in communications and data sharing among cluster nodes.

Shared disk clusters Shares common storage devices for those applications where a concurrent update of a single file or database record is required. This capability is usually associated with a distributed lock manager scheme—for example, Oracle Fail Safe and Oracle Parallel Server.

Shared nothing clusters Shares no system resources until a node fails over. This provides for less bottlenecks and better scalability because only messaging is shared between nodes, and data is replicated across partitions to support concurrent updates.

Shared storage bus Shared nothing clusters have a shared storage bus but no shared storage devices. This bus must be able to move ownership of storage devices in the event of a failure by the primary node that owns these resources. MSCS Phase 1 supports a number of bus types and topologies. They are SCSI (all flavors, but not mixed), SSA, Fibre Channel-Arbitrated Loop (FC-AL), and Fibre Channel-Switched.

Single Point of Failure (SPF) Any component (hardware) or routine (software) that can fail and create a loss of service. Redundancy is used to eliminate SPFs.

Single-ended A SCSI bus transmission format where each signal is carried by a single wire. This type of bus structure is much more susceptible to noise and interference than differential buses.

Small Computer System Interconnect (SCSI) A widely used storage interconnect bus that comes in many flavors (for example, SCSI-1, SCSI-2, SCSI-3, and Ultra-SCSI W/D). It is the default shared storage bus for MSCS.

Software Developers Kit (SDK) A platform type software package used to develop applications and tools for a specific platform (OS, baseline application, and so on).

Sony AIT An 8mm helical scan recording format featuring high-capacity and medium bandwidth for use in backup/restore and archiving applications

Sony DTF A ½" helical scan recording format featuring very-high capacity and high bandwidth for use in backup/restore and archiving applications

Spare capacity   The level of additional processing power and memory required by each node to handle its failover workload. Depending upon the configuration of the cluster (two or more nodes), each node may have to have at least double the overall capacity of its normal workload to absorb the workload of a failed node during a failure or outage.

Standard High Volume (SHV)   Intel's product strategy for servers based on the use of standard components and assemblies (CPUs, memory, PCI chipsets, motherboards, and so on), sold in high volume at relatively low prices.

Subnet   A related group of IP addresses. Subnet is an abbreviated description of a subnetwork.

Symmetric Multi-Processors (SMP)   A computer architecture where a number of CPUs (two or more) share main memory, I/O, and the OS and are housed in the same enclosure or on the same motherboard.

Symmetric Virtual Server   A special case of the MSCS virtual server concept where two instances of an application, such as SQL Server 6.5, are set up on each node. On each node one instance is primary, with a secondary copy being installed on the failover node, and the other being a secondary instance for the other node in the cluster. When configured to use the same database (varying partitions thereof), this mode can actually produce varying levels of scalability, which dramatically improves availability.

System Area Network (SAN)   A cluster-oriented architecture where main memory is extended outside the CPU. Tandem's ServerNet and Digital's Memory Channel are early implementations of this concept, with its full embodiment being found in the Intel/Compaq/Microsoft Virtual Interface Architecture standard.

T

Takeover   In Wolfpack release 2 where multinode capabilities are supported and where a ServerNet SAN is employed, another CPU node can completely take over, seamlessly and without loss of any data, the processes that were previously being executed on the failed node.

Terminator   An electrical circuit attached to the end of a SCSI bus to minimize signal reflections and extraneous noise.

Time service resource   A special class of resource owned exclusively by the Cluster Group. It is used by MSCS to maintain consistent time within the cluster and is supported by a DLL.

Total-Cost-of-Ownership (TCO)   The total cost of owning and operating a computing system. It includes acquisition cost, training, and maintenance and is meant to represent the true cost of owning and operating a particular computing platform.

Transaction Performance Council (TPC)   An independent lab that performs tests on database systems using simulated workloads.

U

Ultra Enterprise Cluster   Clustering solutions based on the Solaris UNIX OS and clustering software from Sun Microsystems now referred to as their Full Moon clustering product line.

Uptime   The amount of time that a system can provide services to appllications and clients. Very similar to *availability* in usage.

Unplanned downtime   An unexpected systems outage whose duration (and cause) are both unknown and unpredictable.

V

VAX/VMS   The proprietary operating and virtual memory system developed by Digital for its VAX computer product line in the 1960s. Hundreds of thousands of these systems remain in use today worldwide in many mission-critical environments.

Very Large Memory (VLM)   64-bit memory addressing to support main memory in Windows NT of approximately 32GB. VLM will be implemented in NT 5.0 in stages beginning with 16GB upon its first release (far above the 32-bit/4GB limit found today in Windows NT 4.0).

Virtual Interface Architecture (VIA)   An architectural standard proposed by Intel/Compaq/Microsoft for use in cluster interconnection beginning with the release of Windows NT V5.0.

Virtual server   Through the proper configuration of resources and dependencies, a failover group can appear to clients on the public network as a standalone server, while in essence being a floating service created within the confines of a MSCS cluster. All virtual servers require a physical disk, network name, and IP address resource to be in their failover group.

W

Windows NT File System (NTFS)   A journaling/logging type file system developed by Microsoft for Windows NT. It is optimized to recover from errors in transaction-oriented computing environments.

Index

▼ A

Active cluster, hot swapping in, 266
Active Directory Domain Model (Windows 2000), 224
Active Directory Service (ADS), 208-209, 216
Active Directory Service structure diagram, 209
Active Template Library, 201
Active/Active cluster implementation, 58-59
Active/Standby cluster block diagram, 62
Active/Standby cluster implementation, 58-59, 62
Adaptive Server Enterprise (ASE), 240-242

Administrator. *See* CA (Cluster Administrator)
ADSM V3.1 (storage management), 249
Advanced Properties (resource configuration), 120
Apcon PowerSwitch/NT, 179
Apcon PowerSwitch/NT Administrator, 180
API development tips and traps, 202-204
API specification (Wolfpack), 182-198. *See also* Wolfpack API
Application failover, 45
Application failover groups. *See* Groups
Application failover manager, 53

Application failover properties, 115
Application failover/failback, testing on cluster, 144-146
Application server platforms, 208
Application takeover, n-node cluster, 218
Applications
bundled cluster-ready, 41-42
configuring generic, 143
creating, 181-204
group and resource configuration, 124-143
included with NTS/E, 42
installing, 203
making Wolfpack-compliant, 201-204
Microsoft service bulletins for, 313-314
scaling of, 45
Web sites for cluster-aware, 330-332
Arbitrate function (Resource API), 193
Architecturally-neutral availability management solution, 177
Architectures. *See* Clustering architectures
ArcServe (Cheyenne), 326
ArcServe IT (Computer Associates), 250
ASE (Adaptive Server Enterprise), 240-242
Automated logs, setting up, 256
Automated tape libraries (ATLs), 324-325
Availability enhancements/solutions, 225-226
MSCS Phase 1, 38-40
Windows 2000 Server, 212

Backup domain controller (BDC/BAC) configuration, 80
Backup Exec (Seagate Software), 250
Backup utility (Windows NT), 259, 327
Balanced Cluster Service (Cubix), 172-174
BCS horizontal/vertical scaling, 173
BDC-BDC configuration mode, 80
Big Iron (Oracle), 163
Boot drives, 84-85
Boot and shared drives (Node 1), configured, 85
Bundled cluster-ready applications, 41-42
Buses, and drives and HBAs, 318
Business-critical applications, 18

▼ C

CA (Cluster Administrator), 108-146, 225
administrative tasks, 110-111
default groups, 113
designating, 86
files, 306
installing and registering extensions, 204
layout of controls and menus, 110
mastering, 110-111
password, 91
program interfaces, 196-197
Registry settings, 297-303
view with one node, 102
view with two nodes up, 103
warnings and status messages, 109
Callback functions (Resource API), 190
CAS (Cluster Availability Solution), 165
Cascading failover, 162
ccNUMA architecture, 25
CD-ROM subscriptions (Microsoft), 336
Challenge/defense protocol example, 51
Cheyenne's ArcServe, 326
Class identifiers (CLSIDs), 196

▼ B

Baan IV ERP for Windows NT, 245-246
Back office applications, cluster-aware, 41

CLI cluster control, 146-152
CLI for cluster.exe from DOS shell, 146
Close function (Resource API), 192
Cluster Access Permissions dialog
  box, 87
Cluster Administrator Extension API,
  196-198
    code samples, 197-198
    functions and tools, 197
    variables in, 198
Cluster Administrator Extension DLLs,
  196, 201-202
Cluster API. *See* Wolfpack API
Cluster Availability Solution (CAS), 165
Cluster component of applications,
  configuring, 204
Cluster Configuration Database
  Management API, 184-185
Cluster control from CLI, 146-152
Cluster control codes, 190
Cluster control set Registry settings,
  289-294
Cluster deployment models, 60-64
Cluster driver files, 305
Cluster executables, Task Manager view
  of, 91
Cluster file system (CFS), 161
Cluster files, 305-306
Cluster fire-drill tests, 225
Cluster groups. *See* Groups
Cluster hardware deployment
  requirements, 65-72
Cluster heartbeat, 51-52
Cluster key, code for getting, 189
Cluster log, 52
Cluster Management API, 183-184
Cluster models, 58-65
Cluster name, Wolfpack API code for
  setting, 188
Cluster network Registry settings,
  274-275, 294-296
Cluster networks, Microsoft service
  bulletins for, 313

Cluster nodes. *See* Nodes
Cluster operations, testing, 104-105
Cluster Proven certification program,
  226
Cluster registry, 52
Cluster resources. *See* Resources
Cluster RPC Registry settings, 288
Cluster Sanity Test (NT 4.0), 94-95
Cluster Server (MSCS). *See* MSCS
Cluster Server (Veritas), 177-178
Cluster Service (MSCS), 183
Cluster Service (MSCS Phase 2), 207-227
Cluster Service (Windows 2000),
  214-223
Cluster software classes Registry
  settings, 287-288
Cluster storage, Micorsoft service
  bulletins for, 312-313
Cluster syntax, 147
Cluster verification utility (CVU),
  267-268
Cluster-aware applications for MSCS
    categories of, 230
    database feature comparison, 235
    databases, 235-243
    provider Web sites, 330-332
    reference guide, 229-253
    storage management applications,
      249-250
Cluster.exe abbreviations, 152
Cluster-farm diagram, 82
Clustering. *See also* Clusters (MSCS)
    benefits of, 4
    defined, 4
    early pioneers of, 5-11
    need for, 18-32
Clustering architectures, 26-32
    choosing among, 30-32
    high availability of, 19-22
    manageability of, 25-26
    scalability of, 22-25
Clustering middleware, 158-169
    collaborative solutions, 164-169

comparison table, 165
competitive solutions, 160-164
Clustering services, Windows 2000
Server, 212
Clustering systems/solutions for
Windows NT, 15-17, 155-180
competitive/collaborative, 156
mirroring/copying-type, 171
providers of, 15-18, 339
technical approaches, 157
Windows NT Terminal Server
Edition, 158
ClusterLog environment variable, 256
ClusterLogLevel environment variable,
256
Cluster-ready applications, 41-42
Clusters (MSCS). *See also* Clustering
additional reading on, 341
deploying, 75-204
explained, 4-5
hot swapping in active, 266
installing and configuring, 77-106
operating, 109-146
planning for deployment, 55-74
restart sequence, 264-265
shut down sequence, 264
shutting down and restarting,
263-264
starting up, 109, 263-264
verifying health and functionality
of, 260-261
Clusters Plus for Windows NT
(Compaq/Digital), 164-165
ClusterX (NuView), 246-248
Code entry points, 201-202
Cold start sequence, 264-265
Command line interface cluster control,
146-152
Common properties (Wolfpack API), 190
Communication Manager, 50
Compaq Computer Corporation, 13, 336
application development, 251-252

continuous computing, 251
Tandem merger, 9
Compaq products
Enterprise Software for Windows
NT, 250-253
Microsoft Exchange Enterprise
Extensions, 252-253
StorageWorks optical disk drive,
322
Compaq/Digital Clusters Plus for
Windows NT, 164-165
Compaq/Tandem Non-Stop Kernel
(NSK), 165-166
Compaq/Tandem SQL/MX for
Windows NT, 242-243
Component Object Model (COM), 196
Computer Associates' ArcServe IT, 250
Concurrent User Support (CUS), 24-25
Configured boot and shared drives
(Node 1), 85
Continuous computing (Compaq), 251
Convoy Cluster Software, 174-176
Co-Standby Server (Vinca), 166-169
CPU
configuration, 68
minimum requirements, 66
recommendations, 67-68
Crystal Reports, 42
Cubix Balanced Cluster Service (BCS),
172-174
Current computing solutions pyramid, 36
Current control set Registry settings,
289-294
Current version Registry settings, 288

 D

Data General Corporation, 12-13,
336-337
Data mirroring, 170-171
Data Storage Technologies, 341

Database Manager, 49

Databases, relational cluster-aware, 235-243

Datacenter Server, multiple node clustering, 214

DB2 UD capabilities, 239

DB2 Universal Database (UD) EEE, 239

Debugging Resource DLLs, 203

Definitions of terms in this book, 343-358

Dependencies
disk resources as, 128
Microsoft service bulletins for, 311-312

Dependencies Properties (resource configuration), 120

Dependency trees
creating for groups, 118-119
Internet Information Server, 112
SAP R/3, 245

Dependency Walker (DW), 268-269

Deployment models, 56-74

Deployment (MSCS cluster), 75-204
final considerations, 72-74
Phase 1, 53-54
planning, 55-74
requirements for cluster hardware, 65-72

Deployment of Windows 2000 Cluster Service, 223-225

"Designed for BackOffice" logo, 199

Destination directories
installation files, 304
operational files, 304

Devices (storage), classes of, 319

Digital cluster with memory channel and CI switch, 7

Digital Equipment Corporation, 337
clustering technology, 6
VAX/VMS clusters, 5-6

Digital Video Disk (DVD), 320

Direct dependencies, 119

Disk Administrator (NT 4.0), 91

view of local and shared disks, 92
window, 85

Disk drives, 319-322
configuring, 84-86
and HBAs and buses, 318
My Computer views of, 93

Disk encapsulation, 166

Disk groups, 113
modifying, 127-129
moving between nodes, 105

Disk mirroring, 168

Disk resource, adding as a dependency, 128

Disk signature number, 86

Disk storage requirements, 67

Distributed File System (Dfs), 210, 216

Distributed Lock Manager (DLM), 163

Distributed Transaction Coordinator (DTC), 239

DLL monitor/status reporting tool, 94

Dll-agator (NT 4.0), 94

DLLs provided by MSCS, 111

Domain controller configuration choices, 80

Domain controllers, 80

Domain planning, 73-74

Domains, 80

Domino cluster and server (IBM/Lotus), 226, 233-235

Domino Server 6-node clustering solution, 226

Double-take (NSI software), 171

Downtime
average per week, 20
sources of and methods to remedy, 19
per year/week/day, 22

Drive letters, assigning, 84-86

Drivers, heavy use of Registry, 272

Drives, 17-20
configuring, 84-86

and HBAs and buses, 318
    My Computer views of, 93
Dynamic Host Configuration Protocol
    (DHCP), 216
Dynamic load balancing clusters,
    171-177
Dynamic Scalable Architecture (DSA),
    242
Dynamic Server (Informix), 242
Dynamic state information, 271

 E

Early adopter hardware partners,
    336-338
Early adopter partners for Wolfpack,
    11-15
Early pioneers of clustering, 5-11
EIDE devices/drives, 259-260
Eight-processor SMP license, 40-41
Eight-way SMP servers, 40-41
Encapsulated disks, 166
Enterprise computing
        defined, 36-42
        market forces, 37-38
        Microsoft's proposed roadmap
            for, 37
        strategic alliances for, 11
Enterprise Memory Architecture (EMA),
    212
Enterprise Resource Planning (ERP),
    243-246
        application specifications, 243
        provider Web sites, 331
Enterprise Software for Windows NT
    (Compaq), 250-253
Enterprise Storage Management (ESM),
    211, 326
Enterprise systems management
    applications, 246-247, 331

Entry point functions (Resource API),
    190
Event Processor, 49
Event Viewer Log (Cluster Server
    Setup), 79
Event Viewer (NT 4.0), 89-90
Exabyte Mammoth tape drive (8mm),
    321
Exchange Enterprise Extensions
    (Compaq), 252-253
Exchange 5.5 Enterprise Edition
    (Microsoft), 134-138, 231-233
        HKLM settings, 278-283
        installing, 135-138

▼ **F**

Fail Safe (Oracle), 169, 260
Failback properties, 116
Failback of resources, 45
Failover of applications, 45
Failover groups, 73, 112-113, 124. *See also*
    Groups
Failover manager, 53
Failover properties, 115
Failover/failback, testing on cluster,
    144-146
Failure types and causes, 20
Fault-tolerance, n-node cluster, 218
Fibre channel (FC), 316-317
File server/share, adding resources to,
    125
File share, 124-127
File Share Group, creating, 124
Files
        installation locations, 303-307
        to be installed, 304-305
        to be uninstalled, 304
Filever (NT 4.0), 94
Fire-drill tests, 225, 260-261

First Watch (Veritas), 160-162
4GB RAM tuning, 40
Frequently Asked Questions (FAQs), 261-263
FrontPage 97, 42
FullTime Cluster (Qualix/Legato), 164
Functions, Resource API, 191-193

G

GEMS (Global Enterprise Management of Storage), 250
General Properties (resource configuration), 114-115, 119
Generic application and services resources, 199-200
GigaNet Switch Topology, 221
Global update, 52
Global Update Manager, 49
Glossary of terms in this book, 343-358
Group Management API, 185-186
Groups, 73, 112-113
 commands, 148-149
 Common Property names, 149
 configuration requirements, 114-116
 configuring, 124-143
 creating dependency trees for, 118-119
 creating/modifying, 117-118
 diagram, 108
 explained, 111
 Microsoft service bulletins for, 311-312
 Registry settings, 271
 syntax, 148
 and their resources, 111
 Wolfpack API code for, 189

H

HACMP AIX Server (IBM), 11
Hardware deployment requirements, 65-72
Hardware partners, early adopter, 336-338
Hardware RAID, 86, 323
Hardware RAID sets, 86
Hardware standard (MSCS), 334
HBAs, and buses and drives, 318
Hewlett-Packard Corporation, 12, 337
Hewlett-Packard OmniBack II, 250
High availability of clustering architecture, 19-22
High availability with static load balancing, 60-61
High-availability server architectures, 20
High-availability solutions for Windows NT, 155-180
High-performance computing environments (HPCE), 317
Himalaya server architecture (Tandem), 8
HKEY_CURRENT_USERS (HKCU), 270, 272
 Registry entries, 296-303
 Registry folders, 296
HKEY_LOCAL_MACHINE (HKLM), 270-272
 Registry entries, 272-296
 Registry folders, 272
Horizontal Scaling TSE, 173
Hot standby (SQL Server), 237
Hot swapping in an active cluster, 266
HotFix Registry settings, 289
Hot-spare with maximum availability, 61

HPCE (high-performance computing environment), 317
Hybrid architecture/model, 28-30, 64
Hybrid cluster block diagram, 64

I

IA-32 processor (Pentium Pro 200), 66
IBM Corporation/products, 337
    ADSM V3.1 (storage management), 249
    clustering legacy, 9-11
    DB2 Universal Database (UD) EEE, 239
    HACMP AIX Server, 11
    Parallel Sysplex Server, 10
    VSD architecture, 31
IBM/Lotus Domino cluster and server, 233-235
IBM/Lotus Domino/MSCS Cluster solution, 226
IBM-MS Cornhusker switched MSCS clusters, 226-227
IIS (Internet Information Server), 41-42
    dependency tree for, 112
    installing, 131-134
IIS virtual root
    online tests, 134
    setting up, 131-134
Implementation roadmap (MSCS), 47-50
Independent consulting firms, 340
Independent server/independent server configuration, 80
Independent Software Vendors (ISVs), 199, 334
Index Server 1.1, 42
Information resources, NTS/E and MSCS, 42-44

Information technology consulting firms, 340
Informix Dynamic Server, 242
Initial tests, 102-105
In-process servers, 196
Installing and configuring MSCS cluster, 77-106
    files and services to install, 302-303
    measures of success, 78
    Microsoft service bulletins for, 309-310
    preparing for, 80-88
    from scratch, 88-105
    starting, 95-96
    step-by-step, 96-102
Installing Microsoft Exchange 5.5 EE, 135-138
Installing and registering CA extensions, 204
Installing resource DLLs, 203-204
Intel Corporation, 14-15, 338
    IA-32 processor (Pentium Pro 200), 66
    Pentium Pro (P6) SMP scalability, 24
    timeline for Windows NT Server processors, 14
IntelliMirror, 211
Internet Assigned Numbers Authority (IANA), 84
Internet collaboration applications, 231-235
Internet Information Server. *See* IIS
Internetworking requirements, 67
Inter-process communication (IPC), 163
IP addresses for cluster nodes, 81-84
Ipconfig utility (NT 4.0), 94
IsAlive function (Resource API), 192, 194
I2O architectures, 213

▼ J

JBOD (just a bunch of disks), 321
Jukes (optical jukeboxes), 326-327

▼ L

Legacy-type applications, with MSCS, 198-204
Legato Networker Power Edition, 249-250
Legato/Qualix Octopus HA+, 170-171
LifeKeeper (NCR), 162
Load balancing clusters, 171-177
Load balancing server, 332
Local disks, Disk Administrator view of, 92
LooksAlive function (Resource API), 192, 194
Lotus Domino cluster and server, 233-235

▼ M

Macros (Resource API), 190
Magazines, about Windows NT, 340
Mail applications (Internet collaboration), 231-235
Manageability of clustering architecture, 25-26
Marathon Technologies, 57
Market forces, enterprise computing, 37-38
Massive parallelism (SQL Server), 237
Maximum call times, 202

Membership activities (MSCS), 52
Memory
    minimum requirements, 66
    tuning, 40
Memory architectures diagram, 212
Messaging applications (Internet collaboration), 231-235
Microsoft alliance partners (OEMs), 334
Microsoft Cluster Server. *See* MSCS
Microsoft Cluster Service, 207-227
Microsoft Cluster Service Phase 2, 207-227
Microsoft Developer Program, 336
Microsoft Distributed Transaction Coordinator (DTC), 239
Microsoft Exchange Enterprise Extensions (Compaq), 252-253
Microsoft Exchange 5.5 EE, 134-138, 231-233
    HKLM settings, 278-283
    installing, 135-138
Microsoft FrontPage 97, 42
Microsoft Index Server 1.1, 42
Microsoft Internet Information Server. *See* IIS
Microsoft Message Queue Server 1.0, 41
Microsoft proposed enterprise computing roadmap, 37
Microsoft resources, 335-336
Microsoft SQL Server 6.5 Enterprise Edition, 138-142
Microsoft Tech Net, 336
Microsoft technical support service bulletins, 308-314
Microsoft Transaction Server 1.1, 41
Microsoft Web site, 335
Microsoft/Valence Research Convoy Cluster Software, 174-176

Middleware server-base clustering,
158-169
Minimum hardware requirements, 65-72
Mirroring
  data, 170-171
  disk, 168
  remote, 216, 260-261
  resource, 168
Mirroring/copying-type clustering
  solutions, 171
MMC (Microsoft Management Console),
  209-210
  CA Snap-In, 224
  in Windows 2000, 216
MSCS clusters. *See* Clusters (MSCS)
MSCS Phase 1
  availability enhancements, 38-40
  benefits and shortcomings, 46-47
  deployment considerations, 53-54
  object elements, 47-50
  moving from to Phase 2, 262
  scalability enhancements, 38, 40-41
MSCS (Windows NT Microsoft Cluster
  Server). *See also* Clusters (MSCS);
  MSCS Phase 1
  basic block diagram, 39
  concepts and deployment models,
    56-74
  core software component, 183
  DLLs provided by, 111
  hardware standard, 334
  file installation locations, 303-307
  identification, 304
  implementation roadmap, 47-50
  improved manageability of, 46
  information resources, 42-44
  installing from scratch, 88-105
  introduction to, 44-54
  key competitors of, 160
  limitations of, 65

main activities of, 50-53
and NTS/E, 33-54
operation, 107-153
resource guide, 333-341
with SCSI hub configuration, 70
with SCSI switch, 69
SDK components, 182-183
SDK development environment,
  201
standard configuration, 59, 71
starting installation, 95-96
step-by-step installation, 96-102
system storage options, 315-328
troubleshooting, 256-261
what it can and can't do, 45-47
will not come online, 258
as the Windows NT clustering
  solution, 263
MSCS/WLBS front-end/back-end
  cluster, 157
Multi-directional failover, 162
Multiple node clustering, Datacenter
  Server, 214
My Computer view (NT 4.0), 92-93

▼ N

Name abstraction, 50
Names for cluster nodes, 81-84
NCR Corporation, 12, 338
NCR LifeKeeper, 162
Net View (NT 4.0), 92
Netcons (NT 4.0), 94
Network Attached Storage (NAS), 317
Network failure immunity (in Windows
  2000), 216
Network interface cards (NICs), 81
Network Interface Management API, 188
Networker Power Edition (PE), 249-250

Networking recommendations, 69-72
Networks
    setting up, 99-100
    testing configuration and running,
      103-104
N-node clusters, 238
    capabilities, 217
    common requirements, 60
    implementing, 58-60
Node clustering, Datacenter Server, 214
Node Management API, 186-187
Node Manager, 50
Nodes. *See also* N-node clusters
    cannot join cluster due to logon
      error, 257-258
    configured, 85
    disk groups moving between, 105
    locating far from each other,
      261-262
    names and addresses, 81-84
    performance optimization, 87-88
    Registry settings, 275
    syntax, 147-148
    Wolfpack API code for opening,
      189
Non-cluster-aware application set up,
    143
NSI software double-take (D-T), 171
NSK-Lite (Compaq/Tandem), 165-167
NT. *See* Windows NT 4.0
NT Server/E. *See* NTS/E
NTFS enhancements in Windows 2000,
    210
NTSE. *See* NTS/E
NTS/E (Windows NT Server Enterprise
    Edition). *See also* Windows NT 4.0
    cluster solution, 158
    cluster-aware back office
      applications, 41
    configuration considerations, 80-88

contents of disk 1, 34
contents of disk 2, 35
design and marketing impetus, 35
information resources, 42-44
and MSCS, 33-54
NuView ClusterX, 246-248
N-way failover, 162

 O

Object Element architecture (MSCS
    Phase 1), 47-48
Object elements (MSCS Phase 1), 49-50
OCI (Oracle Call Interface), 164
Octopus, 18, 164, 170-171
Octopus HA+ (Legato/Qualix), 170-171
OEMs, Microsoft Alliance partners, 334
Offline function (Resource API), 192,
    194-195
OmniBack II (H-P), 250
Online routine (Resource API), 192, 194
Open Connection to Cluster dialog box,
    101
Open function (Resource API), 192, 194
Opening a cluster, Wolfpack API code
    for, 188
Optical disk drives, 320-322
Optical disk jukebox (photo), 327
Optical jukeboxes, 326-327
Oracle Call Interface (OCI), 164
Oracle database management, 260
Oracle Database Server, 169
Oracle Enterprise Manager, 169
Oracle Fail Safe, 169
Oracle Fail Safe Manager, 169
Oracle Fail Safe Server, 169
Oracle Parallel Server (OPS), 162-164
Oracle8 scalability options vs.
    performance, 241

Oracle8 for Windows NT, 239-241
Outages, sources of, 20

▼ P

Paging file, setting up, 88
Paging file size, optimizing, 87, 259-260
Parallel application support, n-node
    cluster, 217
Parallel Sysplex Server (IBM), 10
Partial cluster block diagram, 63
Partial cluster solution, 61-63
Password, cluster administrator, 91
PDC-BDC configuration mode, 81
Pentium Pro (P6) SMP scalability, 24
Pentium Pro 200, 66
Performance Monitor (NT 4.0), 92
Physical disk resource, unavailable, 258
Ping Utility (NT 4.0), 94
Planning
    a cluster, 1-74
    domains, 73-74
    for MSCS cluster deployment,
      55-74
    for Windows 2000 Cluster Service,
      223-225
Platform SDK for Windows Base
    Services Developers, 182
PowerSwitch/NT Administrator, 180
PowerSwitch/NT (Apcon), 179
Preparing for installation, 80-88
Primary domain controller (PDC/BDC)
    configuration, 80
Print spooler, 127-131
    bringing online, 130
    configuring, 127-130
Private properties (Wolfpack API), 190
Private and public networks
    separate connection, 261
    unavailable, 257

Process pairs feature, 166
Properties (Wolfpack API), 190
Protocols, running, 262
Public networks
    separate connection, 261
    setting up, 99-100
    unavailable, 257

▼ Q

Qualix Octopus, 18, 164
Qualix/Legato FullTime Cluster, 164
Quorum resource (QR), 51, 79
    Microsoft service bulletins for, 312
    properties, 98
    Wolfpack API code for, 188

▼ R

RAID, 321-324
    configurations, 322
    options for MSCS (photos), 323
RAID/JBOD, 321
RAM
    memory architectures diagram,
      212
    minimum requirements, 66
    tuning, 40
REGCLADM utility, 197
Regedt32 utility (NT 4.0), 94
Registry accesses diagram, 271
Registry entries
    HKEY_CURRENT_USERS
      (HKCU), 296-303
    HKEY_LOCAL_MACHINE
      (HKLM), 272-296
    MSCS cluster resources, 285-287
    SQL Server 6.5 EE typical, 284
    Windows NT typical, 269-303

Registry hives, two main, 270
Registry settings
    Cluster Administrator, 297-303
    cluster control set, 289-294
    cluster network, 294-296
    cluster RPC, 288
    cluster software classes, 287-288
    current control set, 289-294
    current version, 288
    HotFix, 289
    need to know, 270-271
    Tandem ServerNet, 295-296
    uninstall, 288
Registry staging, 168
Regroup activities, 52
Relational databases, 235-243, 330-331
Release function (Resource API), 193
Remote copying clusters (server-based),
   170-171
Remote mirroring, 216, 262-263
Resource API (Wolfpack), 190-196
    code samples, 194-195
    functions, 191-193
    variables in, 195-196
Resource configuration settings, 119-120
Resource Control function (Resource
   API), 193, 195
Resource control information, flow of,
   191
Resource definition process, 121-143
Resource DLLs, 111
    creating and customizing, 200-202
    debugging, 203
    installing, 203-204
    interaction with MSCS, 199
Resource Management API, 187-188
Resource mirroring, 168
Resource monitor, 52-53, 190
Resource parameters, 120-121
Resource Property Names, 150
Resource Type AppWizard, 201

Resource Type Control function
   (Resource API), 193, 195
Resource type names, 306-307
Resource/Failover Manager, 49
Resources, 119-143
    adding, 121
    adding to file server/share, 125
    explained, 111-112
    by failover group type, 122-123
    Microsoft service bulletins for,
      311-312
    options and descriptions, 150
    possible owners of, 125
    Registry entries, 285-287
    Registry settings, 275-278
    syntax, 149, 151-152
    troubleshooting, 263-269
    Wolfpack API code for, 189
Resources (online)
    for apps and utilities, 329-332
    Microsoft, 335-336
    for MSCS, 333-341
Restart sequence, 262-263
Rolling upgrades, 215
RPC server errors from second node,
   256-257
R/3 System (SAP), 244-245
Run dialog box, 97

 S

SANs (Storage Area Networks), 161, 177,
   317-318
    benefits of, 219
    features of, 219
    VIA-based SAN diagram, 220
    WinSock/SAN protocol diagram,
      213
    WinSock/SAN specification,
      222-223

SAP Resource DLL functions, 245
SAP Resource properties, 244
SAP R/3 dependency tree, 245
SAP R/3 for Windows NT, 244-245
Scalability
    of applications, 45
    of clustering architecture, 22-25
    n-node cluster, 217
    of small SMP servers
      (shared-nothing), 30
    solutions, 225-226
Scalability enhancements
    MSCS (Phase 1), 38, 40-41
    Windows 2000 Server, 212
SCSI, 316-317
    hub configuration, 70
    SCSI-2, 317
SCSI Probe (NT 4.0), 94
SCSI switch, 69
SDK (MSCS software development kit)
    components, 182-183
    environment, 201
Seagate Crystal Reports, 42
Seagate Software Backup Exec, 250
Serial Storage Architecture (SSA),
  316-317
Server architecture cost vs. acquisition
  cost, 21
Server availability by type vs. price, 21
Server configurations, recommended, 68
Server consolidation, 41
Server performance, optimizing, 88
Server status, showing in Services
  window, 90
Server systems, identical, 261
ServerNet
    parameters, 83
    properties dialog box, 83
    Registry settings, 295-296
    technology, 8

Service bulletins, Microsoft technical
  support, 308-314
Service names (descriptions), 307
Service Pack 4 for Windows NT 4.0,
  307-308
Service Pack 3 for Windows NT 4.0
  (SP3), 42, 95
Services
    creating, 181-204
    to be installed, 304-305
    installing, 203
    Microsoft service bulletins for,
      313-314
    optimizing, 89
    to be uninstalled, 304
Services Applet in Control Panel, 90
Services window showing server
  status, 90
Setup parameters, 102-105
Share name (file share), 126
Shared disks, Disk Administrator view
  of, 92
Shared drives (Node 1), configured, 85
Shared storage bus, testing, 104
Shared storage bus drives,
  configuring, 84
Shared-disk architecture, 26-27
Shared-everything architecture, 28-29
Shared-nothing architecture, 27-28, 59
Shared-nothing small server
  scalability, 30
Shut down sequence, 264
Shutting down and restarting a cluster,
  263-264
Single domain MSCS cluster-farm
  diagram, 82
Single-node shutdown, 265-266
SMB file share, 124-127
SMP architecture
    block diagram, 23

vs. other architectures, 23-24
scalability limitations, 29
SMP CPU counts, Windows 2000 Server, 212
Software RAID, 86, 323
Source disk files, 305
Sources of (and methods to remedy) downtime, 19
Sources of outages, 20
SQL Server 8.0, 238
SQL Server 7.0 and 6.5, 236-239
    bringing online, 142
    installing, 140-142
    Phase 1 and Phase 2, 237
    vendors using, 236
SQL Server 6.5 Enterprise Edition, 138-142
    administering, 138-139
    typical Registry entries, 284
SQL Server SVS, 139
SQL/MX for Windows NT (Compaq/Tandem), 242-243
SSA (Serial Storage Architecture), 316-317
Startup routine (Resource API), 191, 194
Status and warning messages (CA), 109
Storage Area Networks. *See* SANs
Storage devices, 316-317, 319-321
Storage interconnections, 316-317
    and networking, 69-72
    requirements, 67
    standards, 316
Storage management (SM)
    cluster-aware applications, 249-250
    options, 326-328
    providers, 328, 331-332
Storage for MSCS systems
    configuring, 84-86
    considerations, 318-324
    list of, 324

options, 315-328
recommendations, 72
subsystem options, 316-317
testing, 104
StorageWorks optical disk drive, 322
Strategic alliances for enterprise computing, 11
Structures (Resource API), 190
Sun Microsystems, 17
Supporting Microsoft Cluster Server: Course 958, 43
Switched SCSI clusters, 179
Sybase Adaptive Server Enterprise (ASE), 240-242
Symmetric Virtual Server mode (SQL 6.5 EE), 138
Symmetric Virtual Servers (SVS), 138, 237-238

T

Tandem Computer Corporation, 338
    clustered systems, 7-9
    and Compaq, 9, 338
    Himalaya server architecture, 8
    ServerNet, 8, 83, 295-296
Tape drives, 319-320
Tape format choices, 319-320
Tape libraries (ATLs), 324-325
Task Manager view of cluster executables, 91
Task Manager (Windows NT), 91
Technical support service bulletins (Microsoft), 308-314
Terminal Server Edition (TSE), 172
Terminate function (Resource API), 193
Terms in this book, glossary of, 343-358
Test utilities, 266-269
Testing, 102-105, 266-269

Thin-client environments, 171-177
Time service, 53
Tools and utilities (NT 4.0), 90-95
Transaction monitoring and
    management, 166
Transaction Server 1.1, 41
Troubleshooting MSCS, 256-261, 263-269
Two-node high-availability clusters, 57
        common requirements, 60
        implementing, 58-60

 U

Ultra-SCSI disk drive (9GB), 320
Unicenter TNG, 246-247
Uninstall
        files and services, 304
        Registry settings, 288
Upgrades, Microsoft service bulletins
    for, 309-310
Utilities (NT 4.0), 90-95

 V

VAX/VMS clusters (Digital), 5-6
Vendors with MSCS cluster-aware
    applications, 339
Veritas Cluster Server, 161, 177-178
Veritas First Watch, 160-162
Veritas SAN cluster, 178
Vertical Scaling TSE, 173
Very large database (VLDB), 236
VIA, overview, 220-222
VIA-based SAN (diagram), 220
Vinca Corporation, 17-18
Vinca Co-Standby Server, 166-169
Virtual Interface Architecture (VIA), 219
Virtual Memory window, 88
Virtual server cluster block diagram, 63
Virtual server only (no failover), 62

Virtual Servers (VS), 51, 62-63, 237
VSD architecture (IBM), 31

 W

Warnings and status messages (CA), 109
Web-based application environments,
    171-177
Windows Internet Naming Service
    (WINS), 216
Windows NT 4.0. *See also* NTS/E
        Backup utility, 259, 327
        diagnostics (Winmsd.exe), 92
        environment variables, 256
        Explorer, 92
        Load Balancing Service (WLBS),
            176
        magazines about, 340
        Performance Monitor, 92
        Service Pack 4, 307-308
        Service Pack 3 (SP3), 42, 95
        Task Manager, 91
        tools and utilities, 90-95
        typical Registry entries, 269-303
Windows NT Server Enterprise Edition.
    See NTS/E
Windows NT Server processors, Intel's
    timeline for, 14
Windows NT Server Resource Kit tools
    and utilities, 94
Windows 2000, 207-227
        core features, 208
        product overview, 208-214
        scalability/availability, 212
Windows 2000 Advanced Server, 208
Windows 2000 Advanced Server
    memory architecture, 212
Windows 2000 Cluster Service, 214-223
        deployment checklist, 224-225
        deployment planning, 223-225
Windows 2000 Datacenter Server, 208

Windows 2000 Server, 208
Winsock/SAN API, 219
    environment diagram, 223
    protocol diagram, 213
    specification, 222-223
Wolfpack API, 182-198
    CA Extension API, 196-198
    Cluster API, 183-189

code samples, 188-189
compliance for existing apps,
  201-204
components, 183-198
conforming applications, 230-253
early adopter partners for, 11-15
Resource API, 190-196
variables in, 189